Dedicated to:

Patricia Rentsler McCulloch and Hugh McCulloch
    The memory of Edna Keeter Raper and Julian R. Raper
        Rita Counter Sbrega and the memory of John B. Sbrega

# The American Experience
## Documents and Notes

**Constance M. Jones**
**Derris L. Raper**
**John J. Sbrega**

Kendall/Hunt
Publishing Company
Dubuque, Iowa

973 A512j

Jones, Constance M.

The American experience

This edition has been printed directly from the authors' manuscript copy.

Copyright © 1985 by Kendall/Hunt Publishing Company

Library of Congress Catalog Card Number: 85-80951

ISBN 0-8403-3738-8

All rights reserved. No part of this publication may be reproduced, stored in a retrieval system, or transmitted, in any form or by any means, electronic, mechanical, photocopying, recording, or otherwise, without the prior written permission of the copyright owner.

Printed in the United States of America

# TABLE OF CONTENTS

| Document | Page |
|---|---|
| Preface | ix |
| 1. Richard Hakluyt on the English Colonization of the New World (1584) | 1 |
| 2. James I on the Divine Right of Kings (1609) | 3 |
| 3. John Winthrop on the Puritan Mission | 4 |
| 4. John Winthrop on Liberty and Authority (1645) | 6 |
| 5. Roger Williams on Religion and the State (1655) | 7 |
| 6. The Trial of Anne Hutchinson (1637) | 8 |
| 7. Massachusetts School Law (1647) | 9 |
| 8. The Bill of Rights and the Supremacy of the English Parliament (1689) | 10 |
| 9. Virginia Law on Lifetime Servitude (1640) | 11 |
| 10. The Rev. Peter Fontaine on Slavery (1757) | 11 |
| 11. John Woolman on Slavery (1762) | 12 |
| 12. Jonathan Edwards on "Sinners in the Hands of an Angry God" (1741) | 13 |
| 13. Charles Chauncy on Religious Enthusiasm (1742) | 16 |
| 14. Peter Kalm on the Loyalty of the British Colonies in North America (1749) | 18 |
| 15. The Stamp Act Congress: Resolutions (1765) | 19 |
| 16. Benjamin Franklin on the Stamp Act (1766) | 21 |
| 17. Lord Mansfield on the Nature of the British Empire (1766) | 23 |
| 18. Edmund Burke's Speech on Conciliation with America (March 22, 1775) | 24 |
| 19. The Tory Position: Daniel Leonard (1775) | 26 |
| 20. Thomas Paine, Common Sense (1776) | 27 |
| 21. King George III on the Olive Branch Petition (1775) | 29 |
| 22. American Participants in the Revolution (1776-1781) | 30 |
| 23. The Treaty of Paris (1783) | 34 |
| 24. George Washington on Shays' Rebellion (1786) | 35 |
| 25. Patrick Henry on the Constitution in the Virginia Ratifying Convention (1788) | 36 |
| 26. George Washington's Farewell Address (September 17, 1796) | 38 |
| 27. Thomas Jefferson | 40 |
| 28. Alexander Hamilton | 43 |
| 29. The Sedition Act (1798) | 47 |
| 30. Red Jacket on the White Man's Religion (1805) | 48 |
| 31. Henry Clay on War with Great Britain (1810) | 50 |
| 32. Resolutions of the Hartford Convention (1815) | 52 |
| 33. John C. Calhoun Endorses Federal Funding for Internal Improvements (1817) | 53 |
| 34. McCulloch v. Maryland (1819) | 54 |
| 35. Thomas Jefferson on the Missouri Question (1820) | 56 |
| 36. The Monroe Doctrine (1823) | 56 |
| 37. Prince Metternich on the Monroe Doctrine (1824) | 58 |
| 38. The Inauguration of Andrew Jackson (1829) | 59 |

39. The South Carolina Protest Against the Tariff of 1828 (1828) . . . . . . . . . . . . . . . . . . . . . 61
40. Andrew Jackson on Nullification (1831) . . . . . . . . . . . . . 63
41. Andrew Jackson on the National Bank (1832) . . . . . . . . . . 66
42. George Catlin on the North American Indian (1839) . . . . . . . 70
43. David Walker's Appeal (1829) . . . . . . . . . . . . . . . . . 72
44. The Reaction to the Nat Turner Insurrection (1831) . . . . . . 72
45. William Lloyd Garrison on the Abolition of Slavery (1831) . . . 74
46. Alexis de Tocqueville on the Negro Race in the United States (1835) . . . . . . . . . . . . . . . . . . . . . 75
47. John L. O'Sullivan on Manifest Destiny (1845) . . . . . . . . . 77
48. James K. Polk on the War with Mexico (1846) . . . . . . . . . . 79
49. Abraham Lincoln on the Mexican War (1847) . . . . . . . . . . . 81
50. James Russell Lowell on the Mexican War (1848) . . . . . . . . 82
51. John Tyler on the China Trade (1843) . . . . . . . . . . . . . 85
52. The United States on Opening Relations with Japan (1852) . . . 86
53. Ralph Waldo Emerson on Reform (1842) . . . . . . . . . . . . . 88
54. Henry David Thoreau on Civil Disobedience (1848) . . . . . . . 89
55. Declaration of Sentiments at Seneca Falls (1848) . . . . . . . 91
56. John C. Calhoun on the Compromise of 1850 (March 4, 1850) . . . 93
57. Daniel Webster on the Compromise of 1850 (March 7, 1850) . . . 95
58. The Fugitive Slave Act (1850) . . . . . . . . . . . . . . . . . 97
59. George Fitzhugh, Cannibals All! Or, Slaves Without Masters (1857) . . . . . . . . . . . . . . . . . . . 98
60. Charles Sumner on the Kansas Question (1856) . . . . . . . . . 99
61. Dred Scott v. Sanford (1857) . . . . . . . . . . . . . . . . . 101
62. John Brown's Last Words (1859) . . . . . . . . . . . . . . . . 102
63. South Carolina's Declaration of the Causes of Secession (1860) . . . . . . . . . . . . . . . . . . . . . . . 103
64. Alexander Stephens Comments on the Confederacy (1861) . . . . . 105
65. William H. Seward on the Trent Affair (1861) . . . . . . . . . 105
66. Abraham Lincoln . . . . . . . . . . . . . . . . . . . . . . . . 108
67. Abraham Lincoln, Second Inaugural Address (1865) . . . . . . . 112
68. General Robert E. Lee's Farewell to His Army (1865) . . . . . . 114
69. Jefferson Davis on Lincoln's Assassination (1881) . . . . . . . 114
70. Edmund G. Ross on the Impeachment of Andrew Johnson (1896) . . 115
71. Thaddeus Stevens and the New York Times on Reconstruction (1865) . . . . . . . . . . . . . . . . . . . . 118
72. Benjamin Tillman on the Negro (1907) . . . . . . . . . . . . . 120
73. The Violent Side of American Racism . . . . . . . . . . . . . . 121
74. Plessy v. Ferguson (1896) . . . . . . . . . . . . . . . . . . . 122
75. Booker T. Washington on the Future of Blacks in America (1895) . . . . . . . . . . . . . . . . . . . 125
76. W. E. B. Du Bois on Segregation (1903) . . . . . . . . . . . . 126
77. George A. Custer on the American Indian (1872) . . . . . . . . 128
78. Chief Joseph on Fighting No More (1877) . . . . . . . . . . . . 129
79. The Treaty of Washington (1871) . . . . . . . . . . . . . . . . 130
80. Andrew Carnegie on the Gospel of Wealth (1889) . . . . . . . . 131
81. William Graham Sumner on Social Welfare (1914) . . . . . . . . 132
82. Russell Conwell on "Acres of Diamonds" (1915) . . . . . . . . . 134

83. Walter Rauschenbusch on Reform Darwinism (1907). . . . . . . . . . . 136
84. Jacob Riis on Slums and the Urban Poor (1890). . . . . . . . . . . 137
85. Lester Frank Ward on a Planned Society (1897). . . . . . . . . . . 140
86. People's Party Platform (1892) . . . . . . . . . . . . . . . . . . 142
87. William Jennings Bryan, The "Cross of Gold" Speech (1896). . . . . 145
88. Richard Olney on the Venezuelan
     Boundary Dispute (July 20, 1895) . . . . . . . . . . . . . . . . 147
89. Josiah Strong on U. S. Expansionism (1885) . . . . . . . . . . . . 149
90. The De Lome Letter (1898). . . . . . . . . . . . . . . . . . . . . 151
91. Henry M. Teller on the Annexation of Cuba (1898) . . . . . . . . . 152
92. Albert J. Beveridge on the "Large Policy"
     of Expansionism (1900) . . . . . . . . . . . . . . . . . . . . . 153
93. William Graham Sumner on the Conquest of
     the United States By Spain (1899). . . . . . . . . . . . . . . . 156
94. American Anti-Imperialist League Platform (1899) . . . . . . . . . 159
95. William McKinley on the Annexation of the
     Philippine Islands (1898). . . . . . . . . . . . . . . . . . . . 161
96. The Platt Amendment (1901) . . . . . . . . . . . . . . . . . . . . 162
97. Theodore Roosevelt on the Panama Canal (1904). . . . . . . . . . . 163
98. The Roosevelt Corollary to the Monroe Doctrine (1904-1905) . . . . 165
99. *McClure's Magazine* on Patriotism (1905). . . . . . . . . . . . . 168
100. Upton Sinclair on the Meatpacking Industry (1905). . . . . . . . 169
101. The Progressive Party Platform (1912). . . . . . . . . . . . . . 170
102. Woodrow Wilson, First Inaugural Address (1913) . . . . . . . . . 173
103. Woodrow Wilson on the Sinking of the *Lusitania* (1915). . . . . 175
104. Germany on Submarine Warfare (1915). . . . . . . . . . . . . . . 177
105. The Adamson Act (1916) . . . . . . . . . . . . . . . . . . . . . 178
106. The Zimmermann Note (1917) . . . . . . . . . . . . . . . . . . . 179
107. The Senate on the Versailles Treaty (1919) . . . . . . . . . . . 180
108. The Versailles Treaty (1919) . . . . . . . . . . . . . . . . . . 183
109. John Maynard Keynes on the Economic Consequences of
     the Treaty of Versailles (1918). . . . . . . . . . . . . . . . . 185
110. Schenck v. United States (1919). . . . . . . . . . . . . . . . . 187
111. Warren G. Harding on his Presidency (1922) . . . . . . . . . . . 189
112. The Ku Klux Klan on its Beliefs (1924) . . . . . . . . . . . . . 189
113. William Allen White on the Philosophy of
     Calvin Coolidge (1925) . . . . . . . . . . . . . . . . . . . . . 192
114. H. L. Mencken Comments on Calvin Coolidge (1933) . . . . . . . . 194
115. The Scopes Trial (1925). . . . . . . . . . . . . . . . . . . . . 194
116. Bruce Barton on Jesus, the Founder of Modern Business (1925) . . 197
117. Kellogg-Briand Pact (1928) . . . . . . . . . . . . . . . . . . . 199
118. Herbert Hoover on Rugged Individualism (1928). . . . . . . . . . 200
119. Herbert Hoover on the G.O.P. Record and the Dangers of
     the Democratic Party (1932). . . . . . . . . . . . . . . . . . . 202
120. Testimony Before Congress on the Depression (1932) . . . . . . . 207
121. Franklin D. Roosevelt on Progressive Government (1932) . . . . . 208
122. Franklin D. Roosevelt's First Inaugural Address (1933) . . . . . 213
123. Eleanor Roosevelt on her Husband's Personality (1949) . . . . . 216
124. Franklin D. Roosevelt's "Four Freedoms" Speech (1941) . . . . . 217
125. The Lend-Lease Act (1941). . . . . . . . . . . . . . . . . . . . 220

126. Charles Lindbergh on America and World War II (1941) . . . . . . . 222
127. The Atlantic Charter (1941). . . . . . . . . . . . . . . . . . . 223
128. Franklin D. Roosevelt on Racial Mixing (1942). . . . . . . . . . 224
129. The Fulbright and Connally Resolutions (1943). . . . . . . . . . 225
130. General Patton on Malingerers (1943) . . . . . . . . . . . . . . 226
131. Korematsu v. United States (1944). . . . . . . . . . . . . . . . 227
132. The (Yalta) Crimea Conference (1945) . . . . . . . . . . . . . . 230
133. The Decision to Use the Atomic Bomb (1945) . . . . . . . . . . . 234
134. Winston Churchill on the Iron Curtain in Europe (1946) . . . . . 240
135. George Kennan on Containing the Soviet Union (1947). . . . . . . 244
136. The Truman Doctrine (1947) . . . . . . . . . . . . . . . . . . . 247
137. NSC 68 (1950). . . . . . . . . . . . . . . . . . . . . . . . . . 249
138. Truman Vetoes the McCarran Act (1950). . . . . . . . . . . . . . 251
139. Joseph McCarthy on Treason (1951). . . . . . . . . . . . . . . . 253
140. Margaret Chase Smith on McCarthyism (1950) . . . . . . . . . . . 255
141. Truman and MacArthur on the Korean War (1951). . . . . . . . . . 256
142. Brown v. Board of Education of Topeka (1954) . . . . . . . . . . 258
143. The "Southern Manifesto" (1956). . . . . . . . . . . . . . . . . 260
144. Dwight D. Eisenhower on the Military-Industrial
     Complex (1961) . . . . . . . . . . . . . . . . . . . . . . . . . 261
145. John F. Kennedy's Inaugural Address (1961) . . . . . . . . . . . 264
146. The Port Huron Statement (1962). . . . . . . . . . . . . . . . . 266
147. Martin Luther King, Jr., "I Have a Dream" Speech (1963). . . . . 270
148. Stokely Carmichael on Black Power (1966) . . . . . . . . . . . . 272
149. Lyndon B. Johnson's War on Poverty (1964). . . . . . . . . . . . 274
150. Lyndon B. Johnson on the Voting Rights Act (1965). . . . . . . . 276
151. The Kerner Commission Report on Civil Disturbances (1968). . . . 278
152. The Equal Rights Amendment (1972). . . . . . . . . . . . . . . . 281
153. Origins of American Involvement in Indochina (1950). . . . . . . 282
154. Gulf of Tonkin Resolution (1964) . . . . . . . . . . . . . . . . 282
155. Lyndon B. Johnson on U. S. Involvement in Vietnam (1965) . . . . 284
156. Senator Robert F. Kennedy on the Vietnam War (1968). . . . . . . 288
157. Senator George McGovern on the Vietnam War (1969). . . . . . . . 291
158. Washington on Communist Violations of the
     1973 Treaty (1975) . . . . . . . . . . . . . . . . . . . . . . . 292
159. Richard M. Nixon on U. S. Promises to Protect
     the Republic of South Vietnam (1972-1973). . . . . . . . . . . . 293
160. Richard M. Nixon on China (1971-1972). . . . . . . . . . . . . . 295
161. Watergate, Impeachment Proceedings, and the
     Resignation of a President (1972-1974) . . . . . . . . . . . . . 297
162. Jimmy Carter on Human Rights (1977). . . . . . . . . . . . . . . 300
163. Jimmy Carter on the Crisis of the American Spirit (1979) . . . . 303
164. Ronald Reagan on his Conservative Mandate (1981-1985). . . . . . 306

## PREFACE

By their first year in College, most students have ample experience with textbooks, including history texts. They have learned to expect a bland, confident, homogeneous style that seems to exclude the possibility of passion or controversy. The synthetic quality of history texts may be necessary in the teaching of U. S. history survey courses, for a certain body of factual information furnishes the necessary foundation for an understanding of the American past. But a text is not enough. The student, exposed only to "textbook learning," may emerge from the experience bored, or with a distorted view of the past, or worst of all, unable to learn from any other sort of written material.

Professors should respect their students enough to believe that they can read primary historical documents and enjoy the experience. Students find the "real" material of history difficult to comprehend sometimes, but far more exciting and challenging then what they have read before, especially with material carefully chosen, introduced, and excerpted. The present collection seeks to provide such material.

What about this collection? First of all, it is not a "great documents" book that endeavors to exclude no major document in American history. Several such collections exist. We have indeed excluded a number of obviously significant items--some readily available elsewhere, some better summarized than read in their entirety, and some not easily excerpted. The documents we chose instead illustrate American history in a way most useful to student and teacher. Each document offers a major point in the course of teaching and learning American history. John Winthrop's speech to Puritans migrating to New England, for example, explains the Puritan notion of vocation and the "city upon a hill." There are a great number of grouped documents, too, designed to present alternative views of an issue--on the morality of slavery in the 18th century, for instance, or on Social Darwinism and welfare legislation. The documents differ from one another in style, content, and voice. There are sermons, laws, speeches, private letters, newspaper articles, and more. The various authors address many different sorts of audiences in many different times and places. Some are angry or passionate, others are analytical or persuasive, others are merely narrative.

For all their variety, these documents have in common that they are relatively short, and that they vividly represent an idea that plays a major part in the understanding of American history. They may be used in a number of ways. First, all or some of them may be used explicatively in class, to show students the evidence for some generalization about the past and to show them how to read and analyze such a document. Second, the documents may be assigned as reading supplements, to be used in conjunction with a text. Third, they can be employed as the basis for writing assignments that might or might not require additional student research. Finally, the documents and the controversies that emerge from them can serve as the basis for classroom discussions. Professors may note that the headnotes to the documents, while fully explaining setting and context, do not state the author's thesis or distract the reader with patronizing questions. This deliberate omission allows students the chance to discover the thesis themselves, an ability which most teachers wish to encourage in their students.

Reading primary documents requires more effort than reading a text, but students can earn great benefits by meeting the challenge. They can stretch their minds to consider unfamiliar voices, styles of writing, and ideas. They begin to learn how to generalize from the raw material of history, rather than relying on "experts" to interpret (or sometimes misinterpret) for them. They gain a solid understanding of the American past, but this time with some depth and specificity. They are respected enough to be trusted to do a little of what historians really do, and what all citizens ought to be able to do--make sound judgments based on evidence. They get a chance to see that the past is not dry and flat, but was once a "present"--with all the color and passion and conflict of today.

    We hope that this volume will make a traditional American history survey course a more enlightening and exciting adventure for students, will inspire them to learn more about the American experience in future years, and will help to equip them to continue the process of learning throughout their lives.

Virginia Beach, Virginia

# RICHARD HAKLUYT ON THE ENGLISH COLONIZATION OF THE NEW WORLD (1584)

Sir Walter Raleigh and his close friends had been attempting for years to persuade Queen Elizabeth I of the importance of colonization. This group requested Richard Hakluyt to write a book explaining to the Queen the necessity of England bestirring herself to contest Spain's growing domination of the New World. What follows are simply the chapter headings from that persuasive work.

A particuler discourse concerning the greate necessitie and manifolde comodyties that are like to growe to this Realme of Englande by the Westerne discoveries lately attempted, written in the yere 1584 by Richarde Hackluyt of Oxforde, at the requeste and direction of the righte worshipfull Mr. Walter Rayhly, nowe Knight, before the comynge home of his twoo barkes, and is devided into xxi chapiters, the titles whereof followe in the nexte leafe.

I. That this westerne discoverie will be greately for thinlargemente of the gospell of Christe, whereunto the princes of the refourmed relligion are chefely bounde, amongest whome her Majestie ys principall.

II. That all other Englishe trades are growen beggerly or daungerous, especially in all the Kinge of Spayne his domynions, where our men are dryven to flinge their bibles and prayer bokes into the sea, and to forsweare and renounce their relligion and conscience and consequently theyr obedience to her Majestie.

III. That this westerne voyadge will yelde unto us all the commodities of Europe, Affrica, and Asia, as far as wee were wonte to travell, and supply the wantes of all our decayed trades.

IV. That this enterprise will be for the manifolde imploymente of nombers of idle men, and for bredinge of many sufficient, and for utterance of the greate quantitie of the commodities of our realme.

V. That this voyadge will be a greate bridle to the Indies of the Kinge of Spaine, and a meane that wee may arreste at our pleasure for the space of tenne weekes or three monethes every yere, one or twoo hundred saile of his subjectes shippes at the fysshinge in Newfounde lande.

VI. That the mischefe that the Indian threasure wroughte in time of Charles the late Emperor, father to the Spanishe kinge, is to be had in consideration of the Queens moste excellent Majestie, leaste the contynuall commynge of the like threasure from thence to his sonne, worke the unrecoverable annoye of this realme, whereof already wee have had very dangerous experience.

VII. What speciall meanes may bringe Kinge Phillippe from his highe throne, and make him equall to the princes his neighbours, wherewithall is shewed his weakenes in the West Indies.

VIII. That the lymites of the Kinge of Spaines domynions in the West Indies be nothinge so large as is generally ymagined and surmised, neither those partes which he holdeth be of any suche forces as ys falsly geven oute by the popishe clergye and others his fautors, to terrifie the princes of the relligion and to abuse and blynde them.

A Discourse Concerning Western Planting Written in the Year 1584 by Richard Hakluyt, Charles Deane, ed., (Cambridge, 1877), pp. 1-5.

IX. The names of the riche townes lienge alonge the sea coaste on the northe side from the equinoctiall of the mayne lande of America under the kinge of Spayne.

X. A brefe declaration of the chefe ilands in the bay of Mexico beinge under the Kinge of Spaine, with their havens and fortes, and what comodities they yelde.

XI. That the Spaniardes have executed moste outragious and more then Turkishe cruelties in all the West Indies, whereby they are everywhere there become moste odious unto them, whoe woulde joyne with us or any other moste willingly to shake of their moste intollerable yoke, and have begonne to doe it already in dyvers places where they were lordes heretofore.

XII. That the passage in this voyadge is easie and shorte, that it cutteth not nere the trade of any other mightie princes, nor nere their contries, that it is to be perfourmed at all tymes of the yere, and nedeth but one kinde of winde, that Ireland beinge full of goodd havens on the southe and west sides, is the nerest parte of Europe to yt, which by this trade shall be in more securitie, and the sooner drawen to more civilitie.

XIII. That hereby the revenewes and customes of her Majestie, bothe outwardes and inwardes, shall mightely be inlarged by the toll, excises and other dueties, which without oppression may be raised.

XIV. That this action will be greately for the increase, mayneteynaunce and safetie of our navye, and especially of greate shippinge, which is the strengthe of our realme, and for the supportation of all those occupations that depende upon the same.

XV. That spedie plantinge in divers fitt places in moste necessarie upon these luckye westerne discoveries, for feare of the daunger of being prevented by other nations which have the like intentions, with the order thereof, and other reasons therewithall alleaged.

XVI. Meanes to kepe this enterprise from overthrowe, and the enterprisers from shame and dishonour.

XVII. That by these colonies the Northwest Passage to Cathaia and China may easely quickly and perfectly be searched oute, as well by river and overlande as by sea, for proofe whereof here are quoted and alleaged divers rare testymonies oute of three volumes of voyadges gathered by Ramusius and other grave authors.

XVIII. That the Queene of Englands title to all the West Indies, or at the leaste to as moche as is from Florida to the circle articke, is more lawfull and righte then the Spaniardes, or any other Christian Princes.

XIX. An aunswer to the Bull of the Donation of all the West Indies graunted to the Kinges of Spaine by Pope Alexander the VIth, who was himselfe a Spainarde borne.

XX. A brefe collection of certaine reasons to induce her Majestie and the state to take in hande the westerne voyadge and the plantinge there.

XXI. A note of some thinges to be prepared for the voyadge, which is sett downe rather to drawe the takers of the voyadge in hande to the presente consideration then for any other reason, for that divers thinges require preparation longe before the voyadge, withoute which the voyadge ys maymed.

## JAMES I ON THE DIVINE RIGHTS OF KINGS (1609)

King James believed that his authority was being challenged not only from outside of England (where Catholics continued to claim that God acted through the Pope and the Church) but also from inside England (where Parliament sought to reassert its own authority after having chafed under the long rule of his predecessor, "Good Queen Bess"). Consequently, James, who sometimes wondered why he ever left Scotland, felt a pressing need to establish the validity of his authority.

But as ye are clothed with two callings, so must ye be alike careful for the discharge of them both: that as yee are a good Christian, so yee may be a good King, discharging your Office. . . in the points of Iustice and Equitie: which in two sundrie waies ye must doe: the one, in establishing and excuting, (which is the life of the Law) good Lawes among your people: the other, by your behauiour in your owne person, and with your seruants, to teach your people by your example: for people are naturally inclined to counterfaite (like apes) their Princes maners. . . .

For the part of making, and executing of Lawes, consider first the trew difference betwixt a lawfull good King, and an usurping Tyran, and yee shall the more easily vnderstand your duetie herein:. . . . The one acknowledgeth himselfe ordained for his people, hauing receiued from God a burthen of gouerment, whereof he must be countable: the other thinketh his people ordeined for him, a prey to his passons and inordinate appetites, as the fruites of his magnanimitie: And therefore, as their ends are directly contrarie, so are their whole actions, as meanes, whereby the preasse to attaine to their endes. . . .

The State of Monarchie is the supremest thing vpon earth: For Kings are not onely Gods Lietuenants vpon earth, and fit vpon Gods throne, but euen by God himselfe they are called Gods. . . . In the Scriptures Kings are called Gods, and so their power after a certaine relation compared to the Diuine power. . . .

Kings are iuftly called Gods, for that they exercise a manner or resemblance of Diuine power vpon earth: For if you wil consider the Attributes to God, you shall see how they agree in the person of a King. God hath power to create, or destroy, make, ov vnmake at his pleasure, to giue life, or send death, to iudge all, and to bee iudged nor acomptable to none: To raise low things, and to make high things low at his pleasure, and to God are both soule and body due. And the like power haue Kings: They make and vnmake their subiects: they haue power of raising, and casting downe: of life, and of death: Iudges ouer all their subiects, and in all causes, and yet acomptable to none but God onely. They haue power to exalt low things, and abase high things, and make of their subiects like men at the Chesse; A pawne to take bishop or a Knight, and to cry vp, or downe any of their subiects, as they do their money. And to the King is due both the affection of the soule, and the seruice of the body of his subiects. . . .

But now in these our times we are to distinguish beteene the state of Kings in their first originall, and beteene the state of setled Kings and Monarches, that doe at this time gouerene in ciuill Kingdomes: For euen as

---

James I, The Workes (London, 1616), pp. 155-56, 527-37.

God, during the time of the olde Testament, spake by Oracles, and wrought by Miracles; yet how soone it pleased him to setle a <u>Church</u> which was bought, and redeemed by the blood of his onely Sonne <u>Crift</u>, then was there a cessation of both; Hee euer after gouerning his people and Church within the limits of his reueiledwill. So in the first originall of Kings, whereof some had their beginning by Conquest, and some by election of the people, their wills at that time serued for Law; Yet how soone Kingdomes began to be setled in ciuilitie and policie, then did Kings set downe their minds by Lawes, which are properly made by the King onely; but at the rogation of the people, the Kings grant being obteined thereunto. And so the King became to be <u>Lex loquens</u>, after a sort, binding himselfe by a double oath to the obseuation of the fundamentall Lawes of his kingdome: Tacitly, as by being a King, and so bound to protect aswell the people, as the Lawes of his Kingdome; and <u>Expresly</u>, by his oath at his Coronation. . . . Therefore all Kings that are not tyrants, or periured, wil be glad to bound themselues within the limits of their Lawes: and they that perswade them the contrary, are vipers, and pests, both against them and the Commonwealth. For it is a great difference betweene a Kings gouernment in a setled State, and what Kings in their originall power might doe. . . . As for my part, I thanke God, I haue euer giuen good proofe, that I neuer had intention to the contrary: And I am sure to goe to my graue with that reputation and comfort, that neuer King was in all his time more carefull to haue his Lawes duely obserued, and himselfe to gouerne thereafter, then I.

I conclude then this point touching the power of Kings, with this Axiome of Diuinitie, That as to dispute what God may doe, is Blasphemie;. . . So is it sedition in Subiects, to dispute what a King may do in the height of his power: But iust Kings wil euer be willing to declare what they wil do, if they wil not incurre the curse of God. I wil not be content that my power be disputed vpon: but I shall euer be willing to make the reason appeare of all my doings, and rule my actions according to my Lawes.


JOHN WINTHROP ON THE PURITAN MISSION (1630)

This is John Winthrop's sermon to Puritans making their way across the Atlantic to Massachusetts Bay. Winthrop, first Governor of the colony, defines the goals of New England Puritans in terms of the covenant between God and his people, chosen and saved by his grace. There is a strong emphasis here on the collective, community response that God's calling requires, and the way in which God will elevate the colony to a "city upon a hill."

God Almighty in His most holy and wise providence hath so disposed of the condition of mankind as in all times some must be rich, some poor; some high and eminent in power and dignity, others mean and in subjection.
The reason hereof:

---

John Winthrop, "A Model of Christian Charity," in Perry Miller, ed., <u>The American Puritans: Their Prose and Poetry</u> (Garden City, NY, 1956), pp. 79-83.

First, to hold conformity with the rest of His works, being delighted to show forth the glory of His wisdom in the variety and difference of the creatures and the glory of His power, in ordering all these differences for the preservation and good of the whole, and the glory of His greatness: that as it is the glory of princes to have any officers, so this great King will have many stewards, counting Himself more honored in dispensing His gifts to man by man than if He did it by His own immediate hand.

Secondly, that He might have the more occasion to manifest the work of His Spirit: first, upon the wicked in moderating and restraining them, so that the rich and mighty should not eat up the poor, nor the poor and despised rise up against their superiors and shake off their yoke; secondly, in the regenerate, in exercising His graces in them--as in the great ones, their love, mercy gentleness, temperance, etc., in the poor and inferior sort, their faith, patience, obedience, etc.

Thirdly, that every man might have need of other, and from hence they might be all knit more nearly together in the bond of brotherly affection. From hence it appears plainly that no man is made more honorable than another or more wealthy, etc., out of any particular and singular respect to himself, but for the glory of his creator and the common good of the creature, man. . . .

Thus stands the cause between God and us: we are entered into covenant with Him for this work; we have taken out a commission, the Lord hath given us leave to draw our own articles. We have professed to enterprise these actions upon these and these ends; we have hereupon besought Him of favor and blessing. Now if the Lord shall please to hear us and bring us in peace to the place we desire, then hath He ratified this covenant and sealed our Commission, [and] will expect a strict performance of the articles contained in it. But if we shall neglect the observation of these articles which are the ends we have propounded, and dissembling with our God, shall fall to embrace this present world and prosecute our carnal intentions, seeking great things for ourselves and our posterity, the Lord will surely break out in wrath against us, be revenged of such a perjured people, and make us know the price of the breach of such a covenant.

Now the only way to avoid this shipwreck and to provide for our posterity is to follow the counsel of Micah: to do justly, to love mercy, to walk humbly with our God. For this end, we must be knit together in this work as one man. We must entertain each other in brotherly affection; we must be willing to abridge ourselves of our superfluities, for the supply of others' necessities; we must uphold a familiar commerce together in all meekness, gentleness, patience and liberality. We must delight in each other, make others' conditions our own, rejoice together, mourn together, labor and suffer together: always having before our eyes our commission and community in the work, our community as members of the same body. So shall we keep the unity of the spirit in the bond of peace, the Lord will be our God and delight to dwell among us, as His own people, and will command a blessing upon us in all our ways, so that we shall see much more of His wisdom, power, goodness, and truth than formerly we have been acquainted with. We shall find that the God of Israel is among us, when ten of us shall be able to resist a thousand of our enemies, when He shall make us a praise and glory, that men shall say of succeeding plantations: "The Lord make it like that of New England." For we must consider that we shall be as a city upon a hill, the eyes of all people are upon us. So that if we shall deal falsely with our God in this work we have undertaken, and so cause Him to withdraw His present help from us, we shall be made a story and a by-word through the world: we shall open the mouths of enemies to speak evil of the ways of God and all professors for God's sake; we shall shame the faces of many of God's worthy servants, and cause their prayers to be turned into curses upon us, till we be consumed out of the good land whither we are going.

### JOHN WINTHROP ON LIBERTY AND AUTHORITY (1645)

John Winthrop's notion of the sources and exercise of authority differed considerably from Anne Hutchinson's. As an orthodox Puritan and as Governor of Massachusetts in perilous times, he believed that God in his providence had called ministers and magistrates to exercise a portion of his authority. In this speech to the general court, Winthrop explains his concept of liberty and obedience--one which would leave little room for the antinomianism of Anne Hutchinson, or the dispute over magistrates in the town of Higham that occasioned this debate. Winthrop was deputy-governor at the time.

There is a twofold liberty, natural (I mean as our nature is now corrupt) and civil or federal. The first is common to man with beasts and other creatures. By this, man, as he stands in relation to man simply, hath liberty to do what he lists. It is a liberty to evil as well as to good. This liberty is incompatible and inconsistent with authority, and cannot endure the least restraint of the most just authority. The exercise and maintaining of this liberty makes men grow more evil, and in time to be worse than brute beasts: . . . The other kind of liberty I call civil or federal; it may also be termed moral, in reference to the covenant between God and man, in the moral law, and the politic covenants and constitutions, amongst men themselves . . . . This liberty is maintained and exercised in a way of subjection to authority; it is of the same kind of liberty wherewith Christ hath made us free. The woman's own choice makes such a man her husband; yet being so chosen, he is her lord, and she is to be subject to him, yet in a way of liberty, not of bondage; and a true wife accounts her subjection her honor and freedom, and would not think her condition safe and free, but in her subjection to her husband's authority. Such is the liberty of the church under the authority of Christ, her king and husband; his yoke is so easy and sweet to her as a bride's ornaments; and if through forwardness or wantonness, etc., she shake it off, at any time, she is at no rest in her spirit, until she take it up again; and whether her lord smiles upon her, and embraceth her in his arms, or whether he frowns, or rebukes, or smites her, she apprehends the sweetness of his love in all, and is refreshed, supported, and instructed by every such dispensation of his authority over her. On the other side, ye know who they are that complain of this yoke and say, let us break their bands, etc., we will not have this man to rule over us. Even so, brethren, it will be between you and your magistrates. If you stand for your natural corrupt liberties, and will do what is good in your own eyes, you will not

---

John Winthrop, <u>The History of New England from 1630 to 1649</u> (Boston, 1853), II, 280-282.

endure the least weight of authority, but will murmur, and oppose, and be always striving to shake off that yoke; but if you will be satisfied to enjoy such civil and lawful liberties, such as Christ allows you, then will you quietly and cheerfully submit unto that authority which is set over you, in all the administrations of it, for your good. Wherein, if we fail at any time, we hope we shall be willing (by God's assistance) to harken to good advice from any of you, or in any other way of God; so shall your liberties be preserved, in upholding the honor and power of authority amongst you.

## ROGER WILLIAMS ON RELIGION AND THE STATE (1655)

Roger Williams, Puritan Separatist, Free Thinker, and Baptist, founded Rhode Island in 1636. Rhode Island defied the common practice of the time, which was to establish religion and to compel religious observation. Williams, who argued for the total separation of Church and State so as to safeguard religion from secular control, was considered radical and eccentric for many reasons. In this open letter to the town of Providence he defends himself against a charge that because he opposes the establishment of religion he also favors total license and anarchy.

That ever I should speak or write a tittle, that tends to such an infinite liberty of conscience, is a mistake, and which I have ever disclaimed and abhorred. To prevent such mistakes, I shall at present only propose this case: There goes many a ship to sea, with many hundred souls in one ship, whose weal and woe is common, and is a true picture of a commonwealth, or a human combination or society. It hath fallen out sometimes, that both papists and protestants, Jews and Turks, may be embarked in one ship; upon which supposal I affirm, that all the liberty of conscience, that ever I pleaded for, turns upon these two hinges--that none of the papists, protestants, Jews, or Turks, be forced to come to the ship's prayers or worship, nor compelled from their own particular prayers or worship, if they practice any. I further add, that I never denied, that notwithstanding this liberty, the commander of this ship ought to command the ship's course, yea, and also command that justice, peace and sobriety, be kept and practiced, both among the seamen and all the passengers. If any of the seamen refuse to perform their services, or passengers to pay their freight; if any refuse to help, in person or purse, towards the common charges or defence; if any refuse to obey the common laws and orders of the ship, concerning their common peace or preservation; if any shall mutiny and rise up against their commanders and officers; if any should preach or write that there ought to be no commanders or officers, because all are equal in Christ, therefore no masters nor officers, no laws nor orders, nor corrections nor punishments;--I say, I never denied, but in such cases, whatever is pretended, the commander or commanders may judge, resist, compel and punish such transgressors, according to their deserts and merits. This if seriously and honestly minded, may, if it so please the Father of lights, let in some light to such as willingly shut not their eyes.
  I remain studious of your common peace and liberty.

John Russell Bartlett, ed., <u>Letters</u> <u>of</u> <u>Roger</u> <u>Williams</u> <u>1632-1682</u> (Providence, 1874), VI, 278-279.

## THE TRIAL OF ANNE HUTCHINSON (1637)

Anne Hutchinson, a devout Puritan and midwife who had migrated from England in 1634, held meetings in her home to discuss Sunday's sermon with other women. The meetings grew in popularity and soon included criticism of the ministers, whom she accused of straying too far from the "covenant of faith." Hutchinson argued that salvation was an inner, personal event that could not be validated by any external agent. That this notion (called antinomianism) could undermine the authority of the ministers and magistrates alike in Massachusetts was not overlooked by Governor Winthrop. After her banishment Hutchinson went first to Rhode Island, and then to New York, where she and her family were killed by Indians. Governor Winthrop, upon hearing the news, remarked that he saw the hand of God, not Indians, at work.

November, 1637,
The Examination of Mrs. Ann Hutchinson at the court at Newtown

    Mr. Winthrop governor. Mrs. Hutchinson, you are called here as one of those that have troubled the peace of the commonwealth and the churches here; . . . you have spoken divers things as we have been informed very prejudicial to the honour of the churches and ministers thereof, and you have maintained a meeting and an assembly in your house that hath been condemned by the general assembly as a thing not tolerable nor comely in the sight of God nor fitting for your sex, and notwithstanding that was cried down you have continued the same, . . . Mrs. H. . . . I bless the Lord, he hath let me see which was the clear ministry and which the wrong. . . . Now if you do condemn me for speaking what in my conscience I know to be truth I must commit myself unto the Lord.
    Mr. Nowell. How do you know that that was the spirit?
    Mrs. H. How did Abraham know that it was God that bid him to offer his son, being a breach of the sixth commandment?
    Dep. Gov. By an immediate voice.
    Mrs. H. So to me by an immediate revelation.
    Dep. Gov. How! an immediate revelation.
    Mrs. H. By the voice of his own spirit to my soul. . . . Ever since that time I have been confident of what he hath revealed unto me. . . . You have power over my body but the Lord Jesus hath power over my body and soul, and . . . if you go on in this course you begin you will bring a curse upon you and your posterity, and the mouth of the Lord hath spoken it. . . .
    But now having seen him which is invisible I fear not what man can do unto me.
    Gov. Daniel was delivered by miracle do you think to be delivered so too?
    Mrs. H. I do here speak it before the court. I look that the Lord should deliver me by his providence. . . .

---

Thomas Hutchinson, The History of the Province of Massachusets-Bay, from the Charter of King William and Queen Mary in 1691, until the Year 1750 (Boston, 1767), Appendix II, 482, 508-520.

Gover. . . . all this while there is no use of the ministry of the word nor of any clear call of God by his word, but the ground work of her revelations is the immediate revelation of the spirit and not by the ministry of the word, and that is the means by which she hath very much abused the country that they shall look for revelations and are not bound to the ministry of the word, but God will teach them by immediate revelations and this hath been the ground of all these tumults and troubles, and I would that those were all cut off from us that trouble us, for this is the thing that hath been the root of all the mischief. . . . It is the most desperate enthusiasm in the world, . . .

I am persuaded that the revelation she brings forth is delusion.

All the court but some two or three ministers cry out we all believe it--we all believe it. . . .

Gov. Mrs. Hutchinson, the sentence of the court you hear is that you are banished from out of our jurisdiction as being a woman not fit for our society, and are to be imprisoned till the court shall send you away.

## MASSACHUSETTS SCHOOL LAW (1647)

Soon after the colonization of Massachusetts Bay, a law was passed laying the foundation for public education in America. The purposes of such a publicly-funded system are made clear here, and they are very different from the ends of public education today.

It being one chief project of the old deluder, Satan, to keep men from the knowledge of the Scriptures, as in former times by keeping them in an unknown tongue, so in these latter times by persuading from the use of tongues, that so at least the true sense and meaning of the original might be clouded by false glosses of saint-seeming deceivers, that learning may not be buried in the grave of our fathers in the church and commonwealth, the Lord assisting our endeavors . . . .

It is therefore ordered, that every township in this jurisdiction, after the Lord hath increased them to the number of 50 householders, shall then forthwith appoint one within their town to teach all such children as shall resort to him to write and read, whose wages shall be paid either by the parents or masters of such children, or by the inhabitants in general, by way of supply, as the major part of those that ordered the prudentials of the town shall appoint; provided, those that send their children be not oppressed by paying much more than they can have them taught for in other towns; and it is further ordered, that where any town shall increase to the number of 100 families or householders, they shall set up a grammar school, the master thereof being able to instruct youth so far as they may be fitted for the university, provided, that if any town neglect the performance hereof above one year, that every such town shall pay ₤5 to the next school till they shall perform this order.

Nathaniel B. Shurtleff, ed., Records of the Governor and Company of Massachusetts Bay in New England (Boston, 1853), p. 203.

## THE BILL OF RIGHTS AND THE SUPREMACY OF THE ENGLISH PARLIAMENT (1689)

> The century long struggle between the English monarchy and people reached a climax with the Glorious Revolution and the passage of the Bill of Rights. Englishmen everywhere realized that an historic transfer of power had occurred with this act granting supremacy to the Parliament.

An Act for Declaring the Rights and Liberties of the Subject, and Settling the Succession of the Crown. 1689.

1. That the pretended power of suspending of laws, or the execution of laws, by regal authority, without consent of Parliament, is illegal.
2. That the pretended power of dispensing with laws, or the execution of laws by regal authority, as it hath been assumed and exercised of late, is illegal.
3. That the commission for erecting the late Court of Commissioners for Ecclesiastical Causes, and all other commissions and courts of like nature, are illegal and pernicious.
4. That levying money for or to the use of the Crown by pretence of prerogative, without grant of Parliament, for longer time or in other manner than the same is or shall be granted, is illegal.
5. That it is the right of the subjects to petition the King, and all commitments and prosecutions for such petitioning are illegal.
6. That the raising or keeping a standing army within the kingdom in time of peace, unless it be with consent of Parliament, is against law.
7. That the subjects which are Protestants may have arms for their defence suitable to their conditions, and as allowed by law.
8. That election of members of Parliament ought to be free.
9. That the freedom of speech, and debates or proceedings in Parliament, ought not to be impeached or questioned in any court or place out of Parliament.
10. That excessive bail ought not to be required, nor excessive fines imposed; nor cruel and unusual punishments inflicted.
11. That jurors ought to be duly impanelled and returned, and jurors which pass upon men in trials for high treason ought to be freeholders.
12. That all grants and promises of fines and forfeitures of particular persons before conviction are illegal and void.
13. And that for redress of all grievances, and for the amending, strengthening, and preserving of the laws, Parliaments ought to be held frequently.

And they do claim, demand, and insist upon all and singular the premises, as their undoubted rights and liberties; and that no declarations, judgments, doings or proceedings, to the prejudice of the people in any of the said premises, ought in any wise to be drawn hereafter into consequence or example.

The Bill of Rights of 1689, Old South Leaflets (Boston, n.d.), No. 19, pp. 3-4.

## VIRGINIA LAW ON LIFETIME SERVITUDE (1640)[1]

The terms of indentured servitude were carefully settled in advance by all parties. Everyone, however, could not possibly know the actual conditions of each specific arrangement--the hardships to be faced in the new world. Thus, it was not unusual for disenchanted indentured servants to try to escape. Such fugitives, when caught, had more time added to their indenture. Consequently, it is not difficult to imagine indentured servants frequently running away and piling up many years of penalty service until--in the quaint legal description of the day--a servant was "incapable of making satisfaction by the addition of time." Here is a court report on the John Punch case.

9th of July, 1640. Whereas Hugh Gwyn hath, by order from this board, Brought back from Maryland three servants formerly run away from the said Gwyn, the court doth therefore order that the said three servants shall reveive the punishment of whipping and to have thirty stripes apiece; one called Victor, a dutchman, the other a Scotchman called James Gregory, shall first serve out their times with their master according to their Indentures, and one whole year apiece after the time of their service is Expired By their said Indentures in recompence of his Loss sustained by their absence, and after that service to their said Master is Expired to serve the colony for three whole years apiece, and that the third being a negro named John Punch shall serve his said master of his assigns for the time of his natural life here or else where.

## THE REV. PETER FONTAINE ON SLAVERY (1757)[2]

The Rev. Peter Fontaine, of Westover plantation in Virginia, carried on a lively correspondence with his brother Moses. In this letter he deals with the morality of slavery rather evasively, choosing other grounds on which to defend his position. This fairly complex view of slavery was not unusual in the South in the 18th century.

As to your second query, if enslaving our fellow creatures be a practice agreeable to Christianity, it is answered in a great measure in many treatises at home, to which I refer you. I shall only mention something of our present state here.
Like Adam we are all apt to shift off the blame from ourselves and lay it upon others, how justly in our case you may judge. The negroes are

---

[1] The Robinson Manscript, "Decisions of the General Court," Virginia Magazine of History and Biography, V (January, 1898), 236.

[2] Ann Maury, ed., Memoirs of a Huguenot Family (New York, 1853), pp. 351-352.

enslaved by the negroes themselves before they are purchased by the masters of the ships who bring them here. It is to be sure at our choice whether we buy them or not, so this then is our crime, folly, or whatever you will please to call it. But, our Assembly, foreseeing the ill consequences of importing such numbers amongst us, hath when attempted to lay a duty upon them which would amount to a prohibition, such as ten or twenty pounds a head, but no Governor dare pass such a law, having instructions to the contrary from the Board of Trade at home. By this means they are forced upon us, whether we will or will not. This plainly shows the African Company hath the advantage of the colonies, and may do as it pleases with the Ministry.

Indeed, since we have been exhausted of our little stock of cash by the war, the importation has stopped; our poverty then is our best security. There is no more picking for their ravenous jaws upon bare bones, but should we begin to thrive they will be at the same again. All our taxes are now laid upon slaves and on shippers of tobacco, which they wink at while we are in danger of being torn from them, but we dare not do it in time of peace, it being looked upon as the highest presumption to lay any burden upon trade. This is our part of the grievance, but to live in Virginia without slaves is morally impossible. Before our troubles, you could not hire a servant or slave for love or money, so that unless robust enough to cut wood, to go to mill, to work at the hoe, etc., you must starve, or board in some family where they both fleece and half starve you. There is no set price upon corn, wheat and provisions, so they take advantage of the necessities of strangers, who are thus obliged to purchase some slaves and land. This of course draws us all into the original sin and curse of the country of purchasing slaves, and this is the reason we have no merchants, traders or artificers of any sort but what become planters in a short time.

A common laborer, white or black, if you can be so much favored as to hire one, is a shilling sterling or fifteen pence currency per day; a bungling carpenter two shillings or two shillings and sixpence per day; besides diet and lodging. That is, for a lazy fellow to get wood and water, ₤19.16.3 current per annum; add to this seven or eight pounds more and you have a slave for life.

## JOHN WOOLMAN ON SLAVERY (1762)

John Woolman, a New Jersey Quaker who preached throughout the colonies, was the principal author of the Quaker view of slavery. Yet this view proceeds logically from the tenets of this radical and much persecuted sect. Friends, as they called themselves, believed that God dwelled within the heart of every person, a conviction which led them to respect the fundamental humanity and dignity of all of God's children. John Woolman's ideas helped to shape the 18th-century anti-slavery movement in America and in England as well.

---

John Woolman, "Considerations on Keeping Negroes, Part Second," in Phillips P. Moulton, ed., The Journal and Major Essays of John Woolman (New York, 1971), pp. 236-237.

If we seriously consider that liberty is the right of innocent men; that the mighty God is a refuge for the oppressed, that in reality we are indebted to them, that they being set free, are still liable to the penalties of our laws and as likely to have punishment for their crimes as other people, this may answer all our objections. And to retain them in perpetual servitude, without just cause for it, will produce effects in the event more grievous than setting them free would do when a real love to truth and equity was the motive to it.

Our authority over them stands originally in a purchase made from those who, as to the general, obtained theirs by unrighteousness. Whenever we have recourse to such authority, it tends more or less to obstruct the channels through which the perfect plant in us receives nourishment . . . .

He that hath a servant made so wrongfully, and knows it to be so, when he treats him otherwise than a free man, when he reaps the benefit of his labor without paying him such wages as are reasonably due to free men for the like service (clothes excepted), these things, tho' done in calmness without any show of disorder, do yet deprave the mind in like manner and with as great certainty as prevailing cold congeals water. These steps taken by masters, and their conduct striking the minds of their children whilst young, leave less room for that which is good to work upon them. The customs of their parents, their neighbors, and the people with whom they converse, working upon their minds, and they from thence conceiving ideas of things and modes of conduct, the entrance into their hearts becomes, in a great measure, shut up against the gentle movings of uncreated purity.

Negroes are our fellow creatures and their present condition amongst us requires our serious consideration. We know not the time when those scales in which mountains are weighed may turn. The parent of mankind is gracious. His care is over His smallest creatures, and a multitude of men escape not His notice; and though many of them are trodden down, and despised, yet He remembers them. He seeth their affliction, and looketh upon the spreading, increasing exaltation of the oppressor. He turns the channels of power, humbles the most haughty people, and gives deliverance to the oppressed, at such periods as are consistent with His infinite justice and goodness. And wherever gain is preferred to equity, and wrong things publicly encouraged, to that degree that wickedness takes root and spreads wide amongst the inhabitants of a country, there is real cause for sorrow to all such whose love to mankind stands on a true principle and wisely consider the end and event of things.

## JONATHAN EDWARDS ON "SINNERS IN THE HANDS OF AN ANGRY GOD" (1741)

Local ministers and itinerate preachers labored in the 1730's and 1740's to restore the old time religion. Jonathan Edwards, in particular, earned a reputation for his oratorical skills, in which he urged his listeners to accept not only the absolute sovereignty of God but also the total depravity of man. He sought to revive flagging Calvinism in New England.

---

Jonathan Edwards Papers, Deut. 32:35 (3), Beinecke Rare Book and Manuscript Library, Yale University, New Haven, Connecticut.

Deut. xxxii. 35.---Their foot shall slide in due time.---

The observation from the words that I would now insist upon is this.--"There is nothing that keeps wicked men at any one moment out of hell, but the <u>mere</u> pleasure of God."--By the mere pleasure of God, I mean his <u>sovereign</u> pleasure, his arbitrary will, restrained by no obligation, hindered by no manner of difficulty, any more than if nothing else but God's mere will had in the least degree, or in any respect whatsoever, any hand in the preservation of wicked men one moment. . . .

So that thus it is that natural men are held in the hand of God over the pit of hell; they have deserved the fiery pit, and are already sentenced to it; and God is dreadfully provoked, his anger is as great towards them as to those that are actually suffering the executions of the fierceness of his wrath in hell, and they have done nothing in the least to appease or abate that anger, neither is God in the least bound by an promise to hold them up one moment:  the devil is waiting for them, hell is gaping for them, the flames gather and flash about them, and would fain lay hold on them, and swallow them up; the fire pent up in their own hearts is struggling to break out; and they have no interest in any Mediator, there are no means within reach that can be any security to them.  In short, they have no refuge, nothing to take hold of; all that preserves them every moment is the mere arbitrary will, and uncovenanted, unobliged forbearance, of an incensed God. . . .

You probably are not sensible of this; you find you are kept out of hell, but do not see the hand of God in it; but look at other things, as the good state of your bodily constitution, your care of your own life, and the means you use for your own preservation. But indeed these things are nothing; if God should withdraw his hand, they would avail no more to keep you from falling, than the thin air to hold up a person that is suspended in it.

Your wickedness makes you as it were heavy as lead, and to tend downwards with great weight and pressure towards hell; and if God should let you go, you would immediately sink and swiftly descend and plunge into the bottomless gulf; and your healthy constitution, and your own care and prudence, and best contrivance, and all your righteousness, would have no more influence to uphold you and keep you out of hell, than a spider's web would have to stop a falling rock. Were it not for the sovereign pleasure of God, the earth would not bear you one moment; for you are a burden to it:  the creation groans with you; the creature is made subject to the bondage of your corruption, not willingly; the sun does not willingly shine upon you to give you light to serve sin and Satan; the earth does not willingly yield her increase to satisfy your lusts; nor is it willingly a stage for your wickedness to be acted upon; the air does not willingly serve you for breath to maintain the flame of life in your vitals, while you spend your life in the service of God's enemies.  God's creatures are good, and were made for men to serve God with, and do not willingly subserve to any other purpose, and groan when they are abused to purposes so directly contrary to their nature and end. And the world would spew you out, were it not for the sovereign hand of him who hath subjected it in hope.  There are the black clouds of God's wrath now hanging directly over your heads, full of the dreadful storm, and big with thunder; and were it not for the restraining hand of God, it would immediately burst forth upon you.  The sovereign pleasure of God, for the present, stays his rough wind; otherwise it would come with fury, and your destruction would come like a whirlwind, and you would be like the chaff of the summer threshing-floor. . . .

The God that holds you over the pit of hell, much as one holds a spider, or some loathsome insect, over the fire, abhors you, and is dreadfully provoked: his wrath towards you burns like fire; he looks upon you as worthy of nothing else, but to be cast into the fire; he is of purer eyes than to bear to have you in his sight; you are ten thousand times more abominable in his eyes, than the most hateful venomous serpent is in ours. You have offended him infinitely more than ever a stubborn rebel did his prince: and yet, it is nothing but his hand that holds you from falling into the fire every moment. It is to be ascribed to nothing else, that you did not go to hell the last night; that you was suffered to awake again in this world, after you closed your eyes to sleep. And there is no other reason to be be given, why you have not dropped into hell since you arose in the morning, but that God's hand has held you up. There is no other reason to be given why you have not gone to hell, since you have sat here in the house of God, provoking his pure eyes by your sinful wicked manner of attending his solemn worship. Yea, there is nothing else that is to be given as a reason why you do not this very moment drop down into hell.

O sinner! consider the fearful danger you are in: it is a great furnace of wrath, a wide and bottomless pit, full of the fire of wrath, that you held over in the hand of that God, whose wrath is provoked and incensed as much against you, as against many of the damned in hell. You hang by a slender thread, with the flames of divine wrath flashing about it, and ready every moment to singe it, and burn it asunder; and you have no interest in any Mediator, and nothing to lay hold of to save yourself, nothing to keep off the flames of wrath, nothing of your own, nothing that you ever have done, nothing that you can do, to induce God to spare you one moment. . . .

If you cry to God to pity you, he will be so far from pitying you in your doleful case, or showing you the least regard or favour, that, instead of that, he will only tread you under foot. And though he will know that you cannot bear the weight of omnipotence treading upon you, yet he will not regard that, but he will crush you under his feet without mercy; he will crush out your blood, and make it fly, and it shall be sprinkled on his garments, so as to stain all his raiment. He will not only hate you, but he will have you in the utmost contempt; no place shall be thought fit for you, but under his feet, to be trodden down as the mire of the streets. . . .

It would be dreadful to suffer this fierceness and wrath of Almighty God one moment; but you must suffer it to all eternity. There will be no end to this exquisite horrible misery. When you look forward, you shall see a long forever, a boundless duration before you, which will swallow up your thoughts, and amaze your soul; and you will absolutely despair of ever having any deliverance, any end, any mitigation, any rest at all. You will know certainly that you must wear out long ages, millions of millions of ages, in wrestling and conflicting with this almigtly merciless vengeance; and then when you have so done, when so many ages have actually been spent by you in this manner, you will know that all is but a point to what remains. . . .

How dreadful is the state of those that are daily and hourly in danger of this great wrath and infinite misery! But this is the dismal case of every soul in this congregation that has not been born again, however moral and strict, sober and religious, they may otherwise be. Oh that you would consider it, whether you be young or old! There is reason to think, that there are many in this congregation now hearing this discourse, that will actually be the subjects of this very misery to all eternity. We know not who they are, or in what seats they sit, or what thoughts they now have. It may be they are now at ease, and hear all these things without much disturbance, and are now flattering themselves that they are not the persons, promising themselves that they shall escape. If we knew that there was one person, and but one, in the whole congregation, that was to be the subject of this misery, what an awful thing would it be to think of! If we knew who it was, what an awful sight would it be to see such a person! How might all the rest of the congregation lift up a lamentable and bitter cry over him! But, alas! instead of one, how many is it likely will remember this discourse in hell! And it would be a wonder, if some that are now present should be in hell in a very short time, even before this year is out. And it would be no wonder if some persons, that now sit here, in some seats of this meeting-house, in health, quiet and secure, should be there before to-morrow morning.

## CHARLES CHAUNCY ON RELIGIOUS ENTHUSIASM (1742)

Boston Congregational minister Charles Chauncy was a leader of the "Old Lights," theological liberals who opposed the Great Awakening and its exaltation of emotion and the "gifts of the spirit" over the spirit of reason. In this tract Chauncy, who later eagerly supported the American Revolution, quotes St. Paul's warning against the abuse of the gifts of the spirit, and then proceeds to describe the religious enthusiasts he has encountered.

[T]he Enthusiast is one who has a conceit of himself as a person favored with the extraordinary presence of the Deity. He mistakes the workings of his own passions for divine communications, and fancies himself immediately inspired by the Spirit of God, when all the while, he is under no other influence than that of an overheated imagination.

The cause of this enthusiasm is a bad temperament of the blood and spirits; 'tis properly a disease, a sort of madness: And there are few, perhaps none at all, but are subject to it; though none are so much in danger of it as those in whom melancholy is the prevailing ingredient in their constitution. In these it often reigns; and sometimes to so great a degree that they are really beside themselves, acting as truly by the blind impetus of a wild fancy, as though they had neither reason nor understanding.

And various are the ways in which their enthusiasm discovers itself.

Sometimes, it may be seen in their countenance. A certain wildness is discernable in their general look and air, especially when their imaginations are moved and fired.

Sometimes, it strangely loosens their tongues, and gives them such an energy . . . .

Sometimes, it affects their bodies, throws them into convulsions and distortions, into quakings and tremblings. . . violent agitations and foamings, . . .

Sometimes, it will unaccountably mix itself with their conduct and give it such a tincture of that which is freakish or furious as none can have an idea of, but those who have seen the behavior of a person in a frenzy.

---

Charles Chauncy, <u>A Caveat Against Enthusiasm</u> (Boston, 1742), pp. 3-7.

Sometimes, it appears in their imaginary peculiar intimacy with heaven. They are, in their own opinion, the special favorites of God, have more familiar converse with Him than other good men, and receive immediate, extraordinary communications from him. The thoughts which suddenly rise up in their minds, they take for suggestions of the Spirit; their very fancies are divine illuminations; nor are they strongly inclined to anything, but 'tis an impulse from God, a plain revelation of his will.

. . . . Many have fancied themselves acting by immediate warrant from heaven, while they have been committing the most undoubted wickedness. There is indeed scare anything so wild, either in speculation or practice, but they have given in to it. They have, in many instances, been blasphemers of God and open disturbers of the peace of the world.

But in nothing does the enthusiasm of these persons discover itself more than in the disregard they express to the dictates of reason. They are above the force of argument, beyond conviction from a calm and sober address to their understandings. As for them, they are distinguished persons; God himself speaks inwardly and immediately to their souls. . . . And in vain will you endeavor to convince such persons of any mistakes they are fallen into. They are certainly in the right, and know themselves to be so. They have the Spirit opening their understandings and revealing the truth to them. They believe only as he has taught them: and to suspect they are in the wrong is to do dishonor to the Spirit; 'tis to oppose his dictates, to set up their own wisdom in opposition to his, and shut their eyes against that light with which he has shined into their souls. They are not, therefore, capable of being argued with; you had as good reason with the wind.

And as the natural consequence of their being thus sure of everything, they are not only infinitely stiff and tenacious, but impatient of contradiction, censorious, and uncharitable: they encourage a good opinion of none but such as are in their way of thinking and speaking. Those, to be sure, who venture to debate with them about their errors and mistakes, their weaknesses and indiscretions, run the hazard of being stigmatized by them as poor unconverted wretches, without the Spirit, under the government of carnal reason, enemies to God and religion, and in the broad way to hell.

They are likewise positive and dogmatical, vainly found of their own imaginations, and invincibly set upon propagating them: . . . they sometimes exert themselves with a sort of ecstatic violence: and 'tis this that gives them the advantage, among the less knowing and judicious of those who are modest, suspicious of themselves, and not too assuming in matters of conscience and salvation. The extraordinary fervor of their minds, accompanied with uncommon bodily motions, and an excessive confidence and assurance, gains them great reputation among the populace, who speak of them as men of God in distinction from all others, and too commonly hearken to and revere their dictate, as though they really were, as they pretend, immediately communicated to them from the Divine Spirit.

This is the nature of Enthusiasm, . . .

And much to be pitied are the persons who are seized with it. Our compassion commonly works towards those who, while under distraction, fondly imagine themselves to be kings or emperors, and the like pity is really due to those who, under the power of enthusiasm, fancy themselves to be prophets, inspired of God and immediately called and commissioned by him to deliver his messages to the world . . . . We should think as favorably of them as may be, and be disposed to judge with mercy, as we would hope to obtain mercy.

# PETER KALM ON THE LOYALTY OF THE BRITISH COLONIES IN NORTH AMERICA (1749)

Peter Kalm was a Swedish observer who traveled in England's North American colonies during 1748-1749. He made some keen observations on the relationship between the colonies in America and their mother country, stating that it was his opinion that the French threat in Canada was what had kept the English colonies loyal to British imperial policies. The prophetic nature of this opinion would later be demonstrated when the French were removed from Canada by the Great War for the Empire.

Each English colony in North America is independent of the other, and that each has its proper laws and coin, and may be looked upon in several lights as a state by itself. From hence it happens, that in time of war, things go on very slowly and irregularly here: for not only the sense of one province is sometimes directly opposite to that of another; but frequently the views of the governor, and those of the assembly, of the same province are quite different: so that it is easy to see, that while the people are quarrelling about the best and cheapest manner of carrying on the war, an enemy has it in his power to take one place after another. It has commonly happened, that whilst some provinces have been suffering from their enemies, the neighbouring ones were quiet and inactive, and as if it did not in the least concern them. They have frequently taken up two or three years in considering whether they should give assistance to an oppressed sister colony, and sometimes they have expressly declared themselves against it. There are instances of provinces who were not only neuter in these circumstances, but who even carried on a great trade with the power which at that very time was attacking and laying waste some other provinces.

The French in Canada, who are but an inconsiderable body, in comparison with the English in America, have, by this position of affairs, been able to obtain great advantages in times of war; for if we judge from the number and power of the English, it would seem very easy for them to get the better of the French in America.

It is however of great advantage to the crown of England, that the North American colonies are near a country, under the government of the French, like Canada. There is reason to believe that the king never was earnest in his attempts to expel the French from their possessions there; though it might have been done with little difficulty. For the English colonies in this part of the world have increased so much in their number of inhabitants, and in their riches, that they almost vie with Old England. Now in order to keep up the authority and trade of their mother country, and to answer several other purposes, they are forbid to establish new manufactures, which would turn to the disadvantage of the British commerce: they are not allowed to dig for any gold or silver, unless they send them to England immediately: they have not the liberty of trading to any parts that do not belong to the British dominions, excepting some settled places; and foreign traders are not allowed to send their ships to them. These and some other restrictions occasion the inhabitants of the English colonies to grow less tender for their mother

---

Peter Kalm, <u>Travels</u> <u>into</u> <u>North</u> <u>America</u> (London, 1772), I, 205-207.

country. This coldness is kept up by the many foreigners, such as Germans, Dutch, and French, settled here, and living among the English, who commonly have no particular attachment to Old England; add to this likewise, that many people can never be contented with their possessions, though they be ever so great, and will always be desirous of getting more, and of enjoying the pleasure which arises from changing; and their over great liberty, and their luxury, often lead them to licentiousness.

I have been told by Englishmen, and not only by such as were born in America, but even by such as came from Europe, that the English colonies in North America, in the space of thirty or fifty years, would be able to form a state by themselves, entirely independent of Old England. But as the whole country which lies along the sea-shore is unguarded, and on the land side is harrassed by the French in times of war, these dangerous neighbours are sufficient to prevent the connection of the colonies with their mother country from being quite broken off. The English government has therefore sufficient reason to consider the French in North America as the best means of keeping the colonies in their due submission . . . .

## THE STAMP ACT CONGRESS: RESOLUTIONS (1765)

With the American colonists in an uproar over the passage of the Stamp Act by the British Parliament, delegates from nine colonies met in New York City in October at what came to be called the Stamp Act Congress. They discussed the issues and passed a set of resolutions to be sent to their King and the Houses of Parliament.

The members of this congress, sincerely devoted, with the warmest sentiments of affection and duty to his majesty's person and government, inviolably attached to the present happy establishment of the protestant succession, and with minds deeply impressed by a sense of the present and impending misfortunes of the British colonies on this continent; having considered as maturely as time would permit, the circumstances of the said colonies, esteem it our indispensable duty to make the following declarations, of our humble opinions, respecting the most essential rights and liberties of the colonists, and of the grievances under which they labor, by reason of several late acts of parliament.

1st. That his majesty's subjects in these colonies, owe the same allegiance to the crown of Great Britain, that is owing from his subjects born within the realm, and all due subordination to that august body, the parliament of Great Britain.

2d. That his majesty's liege subjects in these colonies are entitled to all the inherent rights and privileges of his natural born subjects within the kingdom of Great Britain.

---

Journal of the First Congress of the American Colonies, in Opposition to the Tyrannical Acts of the British Parliament (New York, 1845), pp. 27-29.

3d. That it is inseparably essential to the freedom of a people, and the undoubted right of Englishmen, that no taxes should be imposed on them, but with their own consent, given personally, or by their representatives.

4th. That the people of these colonies are not, and from their local circumstances, cannot be represented in the house of commons in Great Britain.

5th. That the only representatives of the people of these colonies, are persons chosen therein, by themselves; and that no taxes ever have been, or can be constitutionally imposed on them, but by their respective legislatures.

6th. That all supplies to the crown, being free gifts of the people, it is unreasonable and inconsistent with the principles and spirit of the British constitution, for the people of Great Britain to grant to his majesty the property of the colonies.

7th. That trial by jury is the inherent and invaluable right of every British subject in these colonies.

8th. That the late act of parliament entitled, an act for granting and applying certain stamp duties, and other duties in the British colonies and plantations in America, etc., by imposing taxes on the inhabitants of these colonies, and the said act, and several other acts, by extending the jurisdiction of the courts of admiralty beyond its ancient limits, have a manifest tendency to subvert the rights and liberties of the colonists.

9th. That the duties imposed by several late acts of parliament, from the peculiar circumstances of these colonies, will be extremely burthensome and grievous, and from the scarcity of specie, the payment of them absolutely impracticable.

10th. That as the profits of the trade of these colonies ultimately center in Great Britain, to pay for the manufactures which they are obliged to take from thence, they eventually contribute very largely to all supplies granted there to the crown.

11th. That the restrictions imposed by several late acts of parliament, on the trade of these colonies, will render them unable to purchase the manufactures of Great Britain.

12th. That the increase, prosperity, and happiness of these colonies, depend on the full and free enjoyment of their rights and liberties, and an intercourse, with Great Britain, mutually affectionate and advantageous.

13th. That it is the right of the British subjects in these colonies, to petition the king, or either house of parliament.

Lastly, That it is the indispensable duty of these colonies to the best of sovereigns, to the mother country, and to themselves, to endeavor, by a loyal and dutiful address to his majesty, and humble application to both houses of parliament, to procure the repeal of the act for granting and applying certain stamp duties, of all clauses of any other acts of parliament, whereby the jurisdiction of the admiralty is extended as aforesaid, and of the other late acts for the restriction of American commerce.

## BENJAMIN FRANKLIN ON THE STAMP ACT (1766)

Benjamin Franklin, highly regarded among English Whigs and elsewhere in Europe as well, testified in 1766 before a committee of the House of Commons, the lower house of England's Parliament. There was considerable sympathy in Parliament for the American protest against the Stamp Act, ably stated here by Franklin. Neither the sympathy nor the testimony was able to deter the policies of the Tories' "new imperialism," however.

Q. What is your name, and place of abode?--A. Franklin, of Philadelphia.

Do the Americans pay any considerable taxes among themselves?--Certainly many, and very heavy taxes.

What are the present taxes in Pennsylvania, laid by the laws of the colony?--There are taxes on all estates real and personal, a poll-tax, a tax on all offices, professions, trades, and businesses, according to their profits; an excise on all wine, rum, and other spirit; and a duty of ten pounds per head on all negroes imported, with some other duties.

For what purposes are those taxes laid?--For the support of the civil and military establishments of the country, and to discharge the heavy debt contracted in the last war. . . .

Are not all the people very able to pay those taxes?--No, the frontier countries all along the continent, having been frequently ravaged by the enemy, and greatly impoverished, are able to pay very little taxes. . . .

Are not the colonies, from their circumstances, very able to pay the stamp duty?--In my opinion, there is not gold and silver enough in the colonies to pay the stamp duty for one year. . . .

What may be the amount of the produce of your province exported to Britain?--It must be small" How then do you pay the balance?--The balance is paid by our produce carried to the West Indies, and sold in our own islands, or to the French, Spaniards, Danes, and Dutch; by the same carried to other colonies in North America, as to New England, Nova Scotia, Newfoundland, Carolina, and Georgia; by the same carried to different parts of Europe, as Spain, Portugal and Italy. In all which places we receive either money, bills of exchange, or commodities that suit for remittance to Britain; which, together with all the profits on the industry of our merchants and mariners, arising in those circuitous voyages, and the freights made by their ships, centre finally in Britain to discharge the balance, and pay for British manufactures continually used in the province, or sold to foreigners by our traders. . . .

Do you think it right, that America should be protected by this country, and pay no part of the expence?--That is not the case. The colonies raised, clothed and paid, during the last war, near 25,000 men, and spent many millions.

Were you not reimbursed by parliament?--We were only reimbursed what, in your opinion, we had advanced beyond our proportion, or beyond what might reasonably be expected from us; and it was a very small part of what we spent. . . .

Do not you think the people of America would submit to pay the stamp duty, if it was moderated?--No, never, unless compelled by force of arms. . . .

Parliamentary History of England (London, 1813), XVI, 137-160.

What was the temper of America towards Great Britain before the year 1763?--The best in the world. They submitted willingly to the government of the crown, and paid, in all their courts, obedience to acts of parliament. . . . Natives of Britain were always treated with particular regard; to be an Old England man was, of itself, a character of some respect, and gave a kind of rank among us.

And what is their temper now?--O, very much altered.

Did you ever hear the authority of parliament to make laws for America questioned till lately?--The authority of parliament was allowed to be valid in all laws, except such as should lay internal taxes. It was never disputed in laying duties to regulate commerce.

In what proportion hath population increased in America?--I think the inhabitants of all the provinces together, taken at a medium, double in about 25 years. But their demand for British manufactures increases much faster, as the consumption is not merely in proportion to their numbers, but grows with the growing abilities of the same numbers to pay for them. . . .

In what light did the people of America use to consider the parliament of Great Britain?--They considered the parliament as the great bulwark and security of their liberties and privileges, and always spoke of it with the utmost respect and veneration. . . .

What do you think is the reason that the people of America increase faster than in England?--Because they marry younger, and more generally.

Why so?--Because any young couple that are industrious, may easily obtain land of their own, on which they can raise a family. . . .

Have not you heard of the resolution of this House, and of the House of Lords, asserting the right of parliament relating to America, including a power to tax the people there?--Yes, I have heard of such resolutions.

What will be the opinion of the Americans on those resolutions?--They will think them unconstitutional and unjust.

Was it an opinion in America before 1763, that the parliament had no right to lay taxes and duties there?--I never heard any objection to the right of having duties to regulate commerce, but a right to lay internal taxes was never supposed to in parliament, as we are not represented there. . . .

I think the difference is very great. An external tax is a duty laid on commodities imported; that duty is added to the first cost, and other charges on the commodity, and when it is offered to sale, makes a part of the price. If the people do not like it at that price, they refuse it; they are not obliged to pay it. But an internal tax is forced from the people without their consent, if not laid by their own representatives. The Stamp Act says, we shall have no commerce, make no exchange of property with each other, neither purchase nor grant, nor recover debts; we shall neither marry nor make our wills, unless we pay such sums, and thus it is intended to extort our money from us, or ruin us by the consequences of refusing to pay it. . . .

Can any thing less than a military force carry the Stamp Act into execution?--I do not see how a military force can be applied to that purpose.

Why may it not?--Suppose a military force sent into America, they will find nobody in arms; what are they then to do? They cannot force a man to take stamps who choses to do without them. They will not find a rebellion; they may indeed make one.

If the act is not repealed, what do you think will be the consequences?--A total loss of the respect and affection the people of America bear to this country, and of all the commerce that depends on that respect and affection.

How can the commerce be affected?--You will find, that if the act is not repealed, they will take very little of your manufactures in a short time.

Is it in their power to do without them?--I think they may very well do without them. . . .

America has been greatly misrepresented and abused here, in papers, and pamphlets, and speeches, as ungrateful, and unreasonable, and unjust, in having put this nation to immense expence for the defence, and refusing to bear any part of that expence. The colonies raised, paid, and clothed, near 25,000 men during the last war, a number equal to those sent from Britain, and far beyond their proportion; they went deeply into debt in doing this, and all their taxes and estates are mortgaged, for many years to come, for discharging that debt. Government here was at that time very sensible of this. The colonies were recommended to parliament. . . .

What used to be the pride of the Americans?--To indulge in the fashions and manufactures of Great Britain.

What is now their pride?--To wear their old clothes over again, till they can make new ones.

## LORD MANSFIELD ON THE NATURE OF THE BRITISH EMPIRE (1766)

> Tories in England were unsympathetic to American claims to direct representation, whether in the case of internal taxation or anything else. For them, nothing less than the unity and sovereignty of the British Empire were at stake. Speaking here for this conservative stance is Lord Mansfield, Chief Justice of the Court of King's Bench. He is addressing his peers in the House of Lords. His sentiments may be compared with the action of Parliament in the Declaratory Act.

I deny the proposition that parliament takes no man's property without his consent: it frequently takes private property without making what the owner thinks a compensation. . . .

The proposition before your lordships has unhappily been attended with a difference of opinion in England. I shall therefore use my endeavours, in what I have to offer your lordships on this occasion, to quiet men's minds upon this subject.

In order to do this, I shall first lay down two propositions:

1st, That the British legislature, as to the power of making laws, represents the whole British empire, and has authority to bind every part and every subject without the least distinction, whether such subjects have a right to vote or not, or whether the law binds places within the realm or without.

---

Parliamentary History of England (London, 1813), XVI, 172-176.

2nd, That the colonists, by the condition on which they migrated, settled, and now exist, are more emphatically subjects of Great Britain than those within the realm; and that the British legislature have in every instance exercised their right of legislation over them without any dispute or question till the 14th of January last.

As to the 1st proposition:

In every government the legislative power must be lodged somewhere, and the executive must likewise be lodged somewhere.

In Great Britain the legislative is in parliament, the executive in the crown. . . .

No distinction ought to be taken between the authority of parliament, over parts within or without the realm; but it is an established rule of construction, that no parts without the realm are bound unless named in the act. . . .

As to the second proposition I laid out,

It must be granted they migrated with leave as colonies, and therefore from the very meaning of the word were, are, and must be subjects, and owe allegiance and subjection to their mother country.

## EDMUND BURKE'S SPEECH ON CONCILIATION WITH AMERICA (MARCH 22, 1775)

Edmund Burke had been elected to the House of Commons in England for the city of Bristol, informing his constituents that "to reconcile British superiority with American liberty shall be my great object." Burke believed that although Parliament had a right to tax the colonies, it was impracticable and inexpedient to do so. He was convinced that any effort made to crush American resistance would be disastrous to the liberties of both Britons and Americans, and it was not worth risking such disaster by taking a stubborn stand on the powers of Parliament.

My hold of the Colonies is in the close affection which grows from common names, from kindred blood, from similar privileges, and equal protection. These are ties, which, though light as air, are as strong as links of iron. Let the Colonies always keep the idea of their civil rights associated with your government--they will cling and grapple to you, and no force under heaven will be of power to tear them from their allegiance. But let it be once understood that your government may be one thing, and their privileges another; that these two things may exist without any mutual relation--the cement is gone, the cohesion is loosened, and everything hastens to decay and dissolution. As long as you have the wisdom to keep the sovereign authority of this country as the sanctuary of liberty, the sacred temple consecrated to our common faith, whatever the chosen race and sons of

---

Albert S. Cook, ed., Edmund Burke's Speech on Conciliation with America (New York, 1905), pp. 76-78.

England worship freedom, they will turn their faces towards you. The more they multiply, the more friends you will have; the more ardently they love liberty, the more perfect will be their obedience. Slavery they can have anywhere. It is a weed that grows in every soil. They may have it from Spain, they may have it from Prussia. But, until you become lost to all feeling of your true interest and your natural dignity, freedom they can have from none but you. This is the commodity of price, of which you have the monopoly. This is the true Act of Navigation, which binds to you the commerce of the Colonies, and through them secures to you the wealth of the world. Deny them this participation of freedom, and you break that sole bond, which originally made, and must still preserve, the unity of the empire. Do not entertain so weak an imagination as that your registers and your bonds, your affidavits and your sufferances, your cockets and your clearances, are what form the great securities of your commerce. Do not dream that your letters of office, and your instructions, and your suspending clauses are the things that hold together the great contexture of this mysterious whole. These things do not make your government. Dead instruments, passive tools as they are, it is the spirit of the English communion that gives all their life and efficacy to them. It is the spirit of the English Constitution, which, infused through the mighty mass, pervades, feeds, unites, invigorates, vivifies every part of the empire, even down to the minutest member.

Is it not the same virtue which does everything for us here in England? Do you imagine then, that it is the Land Tax Act which raises your revenue? that it is annual vote in the Committee of Supply, which gives you your army? or that it is the Mutiny Bill which inspires it with bravery and discipline? No! surely, no! It is the love of the people; it is their attachment to their government, from the sense of the deep stake they have in such a glorious institution, which gives you your army and your navy, and infuses into both that liberal obedience, without which your army would be a base rabble, and your navy nothing but rotten timber.

All this, I know well enough, will sound wild and chimerical to the profane herd of those vulgar and mechanical politicans, who have no place among us: a sort of people who think that nothing exists but what is gross and material, and who therefore, far from being qualified to be directors of the great movement of empire, are not fit to turn a wheel in the machine. But to men truly initiated and rightly taught, these ruling and master principles, which in the opinion of such men as I have mentioned, have no substantial existence, are in truth everything, and all in all. Magnanimity in politics is not seldom the truest wisdom; and a great empire and little minds go ill together. If we are conscious of our situation, and glow with zeal to fill our places as becomes our station and ourselves, we ought to auspicate all our public proceedings on America with the old warning of the Church, <u>Sursum corda</u>! We ought to elevate our minds to the greatness of that trust to which the order of Providence has called us. By adverting to the dignity of this high calling, our ancestors have turned a savage wilderness into a glorious empire, and have made the most extensive, and the only honorable conquests, not by destroying, but by promoting, the wealth, the number, the happiness of the human race. Let us get an American revenue as we have got an American empire. English privileges have made it all that it is; English privileges alone will make it all it can be.

## THE TORY POSITION: DANIEL LEONARD (1775)

Over the signature "Massachusettensis," Daniel Leonard had published in the <u>Massachusetts Gazette</u> a series of letters supporting the Tory point of view in the controversy between Great Britain and her colonies. Subsequently John Adams, over the signature "Novanglus," would attempt to answer Leonard in the <u>Boston Gazette</u>.

MY DEAR COUNTRYMEN,

The security of the people from internal rapacity and violence, and from foreign invasion, is the end and design of government. The simple forms of government are monarchy, aristocracy, and democracy; that is, where the authority of the state is vested in one, a few, or the many. Each of these species of government has advantages peculiar to itself, and would answer the ends of government, were the persons intrusted with the authority of the state, always guided, themselves, by unerring wisdom and public virtue; but rulers are not always exempt from the weakness and depravity which make government necessary to society. Thus monarchy is apt to rush headlong into tyranny, aristocracy to beget faction, and multiplied usurpation, and democracy, to degenerate into tumult, violence, and anarchy. A government formed upon these three principles, in due proportion, is the best calculated to answer the ends of government, and to endure. Such a government is the British constitution, consisting of king, lords and commons. . . .It is allowed, both by Englishmen and foreigners, to be the most perfect system that the wisdom of ages has produced. . . . An Englishman glories in being subject to, and protected by such a government. The colonies are a part of the British empire. . . .

This doctrine is not new, but the denial of it is. It is beyond a doubt, that it was the sense both of the parent country, and our ancestors, that they were to remain subject to parliament. It is evident from the charter itself; and this authority has been exercised by parliament, from time to time, almost ever since the first settlement of the country, and has been expressly acknowledged by our provincial legislatures. It is not less our interest, than our duty, to continue subject to the authority of parliament. . . .

If there be any grievance, it does not consist in our being subject to the authority of parliament, but in our not having an actual representation in it. Were it possible for the colonies to have an equal representation in parliament, and were refused it upon proper application, I confess I should think it a grievance; but at present it seems to be allowed, by all parties, to be impracticable, considering the colonies are distant from Great Britain a thousand transmarine leagues. If that be the case, the right or privilege, that we complain of being deprived of, is not withheld by Britain, but the first principles of government, and the immutable laws of nature, render it impossible for us to enjoy it . . . .

---

Daniel Leonard, "To the Inhabitants of the Province of Massachusetts Bay, January 9, 1775," in <u>Novanglus, and Massachusettensis</u> (Boston, 1819), pp. 168-173.

## THOMAS PAINE, COMMON SENSE (1776)

> The war between England and her North American colonies that commenced in the spring of 1775 was not clearly a war for independence. Although it was such a war for some, the bold idea of seceding from the British Empire had to be sold to most Americans, or independence might never have been declared. Thomas Paine, a radical whose revolutionary soul knew no national or philosophical boundaries, wrote this persuasive and widely circulated tract after an invitation from Benjamin Franklin to journey from England to America.

In the following pages I offer nothing more than simple facts, plain arguments, and common sense; . . .

I have heard it asserted by some, that as America hath flourished under her former connection with Great Britain, that the same connection is necessary toward her future happiness, and will always have the same effect. Nothing can be more fallacious than this kind of argument. We may as well assert that because a child has thriven upon milk, that it is never to have meat, or that the first twenty years of our lives is to become a precedent for the next twenty. But even this is admitting more than is true, for I answer roundly, that America would have flourished as much, and probably much more, had no European power had anything to do with her. The commerce, by which she hath enriched herself, are the necessaries of life, and will always have a market while eating is the custom of Europe.

But she has protected us, say some. That she hath engrossed us is true, and defended the continent at our expense as well as her own, is admitted, and she would have defended Turkey from the same motives, viz. . for the sake of trade and dominion. . . .

But Britain is the parent country, say some. Then the more shame upon her conduct. Even brutes do not devour their young, nor savages make war upon their families; wherefore, the assertion, if true, turns to her reproach;. . .

Europe, and not England, is the parent country of America. This new world hath been the asylum for the persecuted lovers of civil and religious liberty from every part of Europe. Hither have they fled, not from the tender embraces of a mother, but from the cruelty of the monster; and it is so far true of England, that the same tyranny which drove the first emigrants from home, pursues their descendants still.

Much hath been said of the united strength of Britain and the colonies: that in conjunction they might bid defiance to the world. But . . . our plan is commerce, and that, well attended to, will secure us the peace and friendship of all Europe; because it is the interest of Europe to have America a free port. Her trade will always be a protection, and her barrenness of gold and silver secure her from invaders.

I challenge the warmest advocate for reconciliation, to show a single advantage that his continent can reap by being connected with Great Britain. . . .

But the injuries and disadvantages we sustain by that connection are without number, and our duty to mankind at large, as well as to ourselves, instructs us to renounce the alliance, because any submission to or dependence

---

Daniel Edwin Wheeler, ed., Life and Writings of Thomas Paine (New York, 1908), II, 29-58.

on Great Britain tends directly to involve this continent in European wars and quarrels; and set us at variance with nations who would otherwise seek our friendship, and against whom we have neither anger nor complaint.

As Europe is our market for trade, we ought to form no partial connection with any part of it. It is the true interest of America to steer clear of European contentions, which she never can do while, by her dependence on Britain, she is made the make-weight in the scale of British politics. . . .

Everything that is right or natural pleads for separation. The blood of the slain, the weeping voice of nature cries, 'tis time to part.

Even the distance at which the Almighty hath placed England and America is a strong and natural proof that the authority of the one over the other was never the design of heaven. . . The Reformation was preceded by the discovery of America, as if the Almighty graciously meant to open a sanctuary to the persecuted in future years, when home should afford neither friendship nor safety. . .

It is not in the power of Britain or of Europe to conquer America, if she does not conquer herself by delay and timidity . . . .

It is repugnant to reason, to the universal order of things, to all examples from former ages, to suppose that this continent can longer remain subject to any external power. The most sanguine in Britain does not think so. . . . Reconciliation is now a fallacious dream. . . .

Every quiet method for peace hath been ineffectual. Our prayers have been rejected with disdain; and only tended to convince us that nothing flatters vanity, or confirms obstinacy in kings more than repeated petitioning--. . .

Small islands, not capable of protecting themselves, are the proper objects for kingdoms to take under their care; but there is something very absurd in supposing a continent to be perpetually governed by an island. In no instance hath nature made the satellite larger than its primary planet; and as England and America, with respect to each other, reverse the common order of nature, it is evident that they belong to different systems: England to Europe--America to itself. . . .

No man was warmer wisher for reconciliation than myself before the fatal nineteenth of April, 1775, but the moment the event of that day was made known, I rejected the hardened, sullen-tempered Pharaoh of England forever; and disdain the wretch, that with the pretended title of Father of his people, can unfeelingly hear of their slaughter, and composedly sleep with their blood upon his soul. . . .

Ye that oppose independence now, ye know not what ye do; ye are opening a door to eternal tyranny, . . .

Yet that tell us of harmony and reconciliation, can ye restore to us the time that is passed? Can ye give to prostitution its former innocence? Neither can ye reconcile Britain and America. The last cord now is broken; the people of England are presenting addresses against us. There are injuries which nature cannot forgive; she would cease to be nature if she did. As well can the lover forgive the ravisher of his mistress, as the continent forgive the murders of Britain. The Almighty hath implanted in us these unextinguishable feelings for good and wise purposes. They are the guardians of His image in our hearts. They distinguish us from the herd of common animals. The social compact would dissolve and justice be extirpated from the earth, or have only a casual existence, were we callous to the touches of affection. The robber and the murderer would often escape unpunished, did not the injuries which our tempers sustain, provoke us into justice.

O ye that love mankind! Ye that dare oppose, not only the tyranny, but the tyrant, stand forth! Every spot of the old world is overrun with oppression. Freedom hath been hunted round the globe. Asia and Africa have long expelled her, Europe regards her like a stranger, and England hath given her warning to depart. O! receive the fugitive, and prepare in time an asylum for mankind.

## KING GEORGE III ON THE OLIVE BRANCH PETITION (1775)

King George III and his advisers were either incapable or unwilling to give serious consideration to colonial grievances, which they interpreted as treasonous attempts to undermine the unity of the British Empire and the sovereignty of Crown and Parliament. In the summer of 1775 the Continental Congress, still maintaining its allegiance to the King and its position that American patriots fought merely to redress grievances arising from the new imperial administration, sent an "Olive Branch Petition" to George III, in a final attempt to achieve conciliation and a moderation of colonial policies. The King was unsympathetic, and it seems ironic that angry colonists heaped blame on Parliament (which contained many warm supporters of the American position) while affirming their loyalty to the Crown. Irony or no, there remained strong resistance in the North American colonies to forswearing allegiance to the King and declaring independence. This is part of George III's speech to Parliament on October 26, 1775.

The authors and promoters of this desperate conspiracy have, in the conduct of it, derived great advantage from the difference of our intention and theirs. They meant only to amuse, by vague expressions of attachment to the parent state, and the strongest protestations of loyalty to me, whilst they were preparing for a general revolt. On our part, though it was declared in your last session that a rebellion existed within the province of the Massachuset's Bay, yet even that province we wished rather to reclaim than to subdue. The resolutions of parliament breathed a spirit of moderation and forbearance; conciliatory propositions accompanied the measures taken to enforce authority, and the coercive acts were adapted to cases of criminal combinations amongst subjects not then in arms. I have acted with the same temper, anxious to prevent, if it had been possible, the effusion of the blood of my subjects, and the calamities which are inseparable from a state of war; still hoping that my people in America would have discerned the traitorous views of their leaders, and have been convinced, that to be a subject of Great Britain, with all its consequences, is to be the freest member of any civil society in the known world.

Parliamentary History of England (London, 1813), XVIII, 695-697.

The rebellious war now levied is become more general, and is manifestly carried on for the purpose of establishing an independent empire. I need not dwell upon the fatal effects of the success of such a plan. The object is too important, the spirit of the British nation too high, the resources with which God hath blessed her too numerous, to give up so many colonies which many she has planted with great industry, nursed with great tenderness, encouraged with many commercial advantages, and protected and defended at much expence of blood and treasure. . . .

When the unhappy and deluded multitude, against whom this force will be directed, shall become sensible of their error, I shall be ready to receive the misled with tenderness and mercy[.]

## AMERICAN PARTICIPANTS IN THE REVOLUTION (1776-1781)

In 1818, Congress offered pensions to all participants in the Revoluntary War--provided that candidates could document their claims. These applications provide a rich source of historical information about the American Revolution. Among the many thousands of applicants are these three accounts.

(a) Statement of Edward Ellery

[A]nother requisition of men was called as a relief, which included me, and having just hired a substitute and not feeling myself able to hire if I could have obtained another substitute, I determined to fill my own place and took my horse and joined Lafayette's army. . . .and then marched down to Yorktown in Virginia. And we had several little engagements with the enemy before they were hemmed in at said town. A council of war was held by our officers, and some were in favor of storming the enemy's fort there under General Wallace [Cornwallis], but General Washington was opposed to that course and recommended a siege, as I was told. The enemy frequently fired upon us whilst engaged in making preparations for the siege and killed a few of our men. The militia officers were at this time employed with the soldiers getting brush, etc., to make wattling required in the fortifications. . . .

The works of the battery were thrown up by the militia soldiers, and whilst they were cutting brush a cannonball came bounding along on the ground, and a youngster put his heel against it and was thrown into lockjaw and expired a short time. And I recollect another circumstance which occurred near me. A ball came from the enemy, struck a man, and cut off his leg at the thigh, and then struck a stack of arms and rendered them unfit for service. . . . I frequently saw General Washington riding around and directing the operations, and after the siege began my place was at the guns in the battery called Washington's Grand Battery. There were in this battery four twenty-four-pounders, four eighteen pounders, four twelve pounders, and twelve mortar pieces, and these were fired in platoons, four at a time, and the

---

Record Group 15, "Records of the Veterans Administration," National Archives, Washington, D.C.

mortars three at a time, making four rounds of mortars, in order to keep up a constant fire. And, whilst firing, the elevator of the guns got in a violent passion because the men in assistance dodged when fired upon by the enemy from their portholes and produced a considerable confusion. And General Clinton, coming up just at that moment, put things to rights, and I remarked to the men in his hearing, "Come, my brave fellows, stick to your posts and the day will soon be ours," and for this remark I was very soon rewarded with a good breakfast from the general, which was very acceptable as I had not had a meal for twenty-four hours. And I never saw men more mystified than were these serving with me at the guns when I received the reward. Shortly after the siege began, thirty-three of the enemy deserted and came around in a boat about midnight and joined us, and General Clinton gave them a pass to General Washington. And whilst engaged in firing the guns, it appeared to me as if the earth would sink beneath us.

I continued in this service until within a few days of Wallace's surrender. . . .Before I left the service, I saw a number of dead horses on the beach which the enemy had drowned. I served myself in this turn two months, besides my substitute who served three months and paid him to his satisfaction. . . . I paid him a suit of good new clothes, a blanket, a knapsack, a cheese, and a thousand dollars in Continental paper, and thirty silver dollars, the price previously agreed upon by my wife.

(b)  Statement of Jehu Grant

In April 1834 I received a writing from Your Honor, informing me that my "services while a fugitive from my master's service was not embraced in said Act," and that my "papers were placed on file." In my said declaration, I just mentioned the cause of leaving my master, as may be seen by a reference thereunto, and I now pray that I may be permitted to express my feelings more fully on that part of my said declaration.

I was then grown to manhood, in the full vigor and strength of life, and heard much about the cruel and arbitrary things done by the British. Their ships lay within a few miles of my master house, which stood near the shore, and I was confident that my master traded wtih them, and I suffered much from fear that I should be sent aboard a ship of war. This I disliked. But when I saw liberty poles and the people all engaged for the support of freedom, I could not but like and be pleased with such thing (God forgive me if I sinned in so feeling). And living on the borders of Rhode Island, where whole companies of colored people enlisted, it added to my fears and dread of being sold to the British. These considerations induced me to enlist into the American army, where I served faithful about ten months, when my master found and took me home. Had I been taught to read or understand the percepts of the Gospel, "Servants obey your masters," I might have done otherwise, notwithstanding the songs of liberty that saluted my ear, thrilled through my heart. But feeling conscious that I have since compensated my master for the injury he sustained by my enlisting, and that God has forgiven me for so doing, and that I served my country faithfully, and that they having enjoyed the benefits of my service to an equal degree for the length [of] time I served with those generally who are receiving the liberalities of the government, I cannot but feel it becoming me to pray Your Honor to review my declaration on file and the papers herewith amended.

A few years after the war, Joshua Swan, Esq., of Stonington purchased me of my master and agreed that after I had served him a length of time named faithfully, I should be free. I served to his satisfaction and so obtained my freedom. He moved into the town of Milton, where I now reside, about forty-eight years ago. After my time expired with Esq. Swan, I married a wife. We have raised six children. Five are still living. I must be upward of eighty years of age and have been blind for many years, and, notwithstanding the aid I received from the honest industry of my children, we are still very needy and in part are supported from the benevolence of our friends.

(c) Statement of Sarah Benjamin

That after deponent had married said Osborn, he informed her that he was returned during the war, and that he desired deponent to go with him. Deponent declined until she was informed by Captain Gregg that her husband should be put on the comissary guard, and that she should have the means of conveyance either in a wagon or on horseback. That deponent then in the same winter season in sleighs accompanied her husband and the forces under command of Captain Gregg on the east side of the Hudson river to Fishkill, then crossed the river and went down to West Point. There remained till the river opened in the spring, when they returned to Albany. . . .

Deponent further says that she and her husband remained at West Point till the departure of the army for the South, a term of perhaps one year and a half, but she cannot be positive as to the length of time. While at West Point, deponent lived at Lieutenant Foot's, who kept a boardinghouse. Deponent was employed in washing and sewing for the soldiers. . . . On the return of the bargemen who assisted [Benedict] Arnold to escape, deponent recollects seeing two of them, one by the name of Montecu, the other by the name of Clark. That they said Arnold told them to hang up their dinners, for he had to be at Stony Point in so many minutes, and when he got there he hoisted his pocket handkerchief and his sword and said, "Row on boys," and that they soon arrived in Haverstraw Bay and found the British ship. That Arnold jumped on board, and they were all invited, and they went aboard and had their choice to go or stay. And some chose to stay and some to go and did accordingly. . . .

They, however, marched immediately for a place called Williamsburg, as she thinks, deponent alternately on horseback and on foot. There arrived, they remained two days till the army all came in by land and then marched for Yorktown, or Little York as it was then called. The York troops were posted at the right, the Connecticut troops next, and the French to the left. In about one day or less than a day, they reached the place of encampment about one mile from Yorktown. Deponent was on foot and the other females above named and her said husband still on the commissary's guard. Deponent's attention was arrested by the appearance of a large plain between them and Yorktown and an entrenchment thrown up. She also saw a number of dead Negroes lying round their encampment, whom she understood the British had driven out of the town and left to starve, or were first starved and then thrown out. Deponent took her stand just back of the American tents, say about a mile from the town, and busied herself washing, mending, and cooking for the soldiers, in which she was assisted by the other females; some men washed their own clothing. She heard the roar of the artillery for a number of days, and the last night the Americans threw up entrenchments, it was a misty, foggy night, rather wet but not rainy. Every soldier threw up for himself, as she understood, and she afterwards saw and went into the entrenchments. Deponent's said husband was there throwing up entrenchments, and deponent cooked and carried in beef, and bread, and coffee (in a gallon pot) to the soldiers in the entrenchment.

On one occasion when deponent was thus employed carrying in provisions, she met General Washington, who asked her if she "was not afraid of the cannonballs?" She replied, "No, the bullets would not cheat the gallows," that "It would not do for the men to fight and starve too."

They dug entrenchments nearer and nearer to Yorktown every night or two till the last. While digging that, the enemy fired very heavy till about nine o'clock next morning, then stopped, and the drums from the enemy beat excessively. . . .

The drums continued beating, and all at once the officers hurrahed and swung their hats, and deponent asked them, "What is the matter now?"

One of them replied, "Are not you soldier enough to know what it means?" Deponent replied, "No."

They then replied, "The British have surrendered". . . .

Deponent stood on one side of the road and the American officers upon the other side when the British officers. . . rode right on before the army, who marched out beating and playing a melancholy tune, their drums covered with black handkerchiefs and their fifes with black ribbands tied around them, into an old field and there grounded their arms and then returned into town again to await their destiny. Deponent recollects seeing a great many American officers, some on horseback and some on foot, but cannot call them all by name. Washington, Lafayette, and Clinton were among the number. The British general at the head of the army was a large, portly man, full face, and the tears rolled down his cheeks as he passed along. She does not recollect his name, but it was not Cornwallis. She saw the latter afterwards and noticed his being a man of diminutive appearance and having cross eyes. . . .

About three months after the birth of her last child, Aaron Osborn, Jr., she last saw her said husband, who then left her at New Windsor and never returned. He had been absent at intervals before this from deponent, and at one time deponent understood he was married again to a girl by the name of Polly Sloat above Newburgh about fifteen or sixteen miles. Deponent got a horse and rode up to inquire into the truth of the story. She arrived at the girl's father's and there found her said husband, and Polly Sloat, and her parents. Deponent was kindly treated by the inmates of the house but ascertained for a truth that her husband was married to said girl. After remaining overnight, deponent determined to return home and abandon her said husband forever, as she found he had conducted in such a way as to leave no hope of reclaiming him. About two weeks afterwards, her said husband came to see deponent in New Windsor and offered to take deponent and her children to the northward, but deponent declined going, under a firm belief that he would conduct no better, and her said husband the same night absconded with two others, crossed the river at Newburgh, and she never saw him afterwards. This was about a year and a half after his discharge. Deponent heard of him afterwards up the Mohawk River and that he had married again. Deponent, after hearing of this second unlawful marriage of her said husband, married herself to John Benjamin of Blooming Grove, Orange County, New York, whose name she now bears.

About twenty years ago, deponent heard that her said husband Osborn died up the Mohawk, and she has no reason to believe to the contrary to this day. . . .Deponent was informed more than forty years ago and believes that said Polly Sloat, Osborn's second wife above mentioned, died dead drunk, the liquor running out of her mouth after she was dead. Osborn's third wife she knows nothing about.

# THE TREATY OF PARIS (1783)

The American victory at Yorktown, while ending the military contest, marked only the beginning of a protracted diplomatic struggle. Under the leadership of the venerable Benjamin Franklin, the American negotiators, after considerable effort, fashioned the political rewards of the military victory.

Concluded September 3, 1783; Ratified by the Continental Congress January 14, 1784; Proclaimed January 14, 1784 . . . .

[ARTICLE I] His Britannic Majesty acknowledges the said United States, viz. New Hampshire, Massachusetts Bay, Rhode Island, and Providence Plantations, Connecticut, New York, New Jersey, Pennsylvania, Delaware, Maryland, Virginia, North Carolina, South Carolina, and Georgia, to be free, sovereign and independent States; that he treats with them as such, and for himself, his heirs and successors, relinquishes all claims to the Government, propriety and territorial rights of the same, and every part thereof. . . .

[ARTICLE III] It is agreed that the people of the United States shall continue to enjoy unmolested the right to take fish of every kind on the Grand Bank, and on all the other banks of Newfoundland; also in the Gulph of Saint Lawrence, and at all other places in the sea where the inhabitants of both countries used at any time heretofore to fish. And also that the inhabitants of the United States shall have liberty to take fish of every kind on such part of the coast of Newfoundland as British fishermen shall use (but not to dry or cure the same on that island) and also on the coasts, bays and creeks of all other of His Britannic Majesty's dominions in America; and that the American fishermen shall have liberty to dry and cure fish in any of the unsettled bays, harbours and creeks of Nova Scotia, Magdalen Islands, and Labrador, so long as the same shall remain unsettled; but so soon as the same or either of them shall be settled, it shall not be lawful for the said fishermen to dry or cure fish at such settlements, without a previous agreement for that purpose with the inhabitants, proprietors or possessors of the ground.

[ARTICLE IV] It is agreed that creditors on either side shall meet with no lawful impediment to the recovery of the full value in sterling money, of all bona fide debts heretofore contracted.

[ARTICLE V] It is agreed that the Congress shall earnestly recommend it to the legislatures of the respective States, to provide for the restitution of all estates, rights and properties which have been confiscated, belonging to real British subjects. . . .

[ARTICLE VI] That there shall be no future confiscations made, nor any prosecutions commenc'd against any person or persons for, or by reason of the part which he or they may have taken in the present war; and that no person shall, on that account, suffer any future loss or damage, either in his person, liberty or property; and that those who may be in confinement on such charges, at the time of the ratification of the treaty in America, shall be immediately set at liberty, and the prosecutions so commenced be discontinued.

---

U.S. Department of State, Treaties and Conventions Between the United States of America and Other Powers Since July 4, 1776 (Washington, D.C., 1889), pp. 375-79.

[ARTICLE VI] There shall be a firm and perpetual peace between His Britannic Majesty and the said States, and between the subjects of the one and the citizens of the other, wherefore all hostilities, both by sea and land, shall from henceforth cease: All prisoners on both sides shall be set at liberty, and His Britannic Majesty shall, with all convenient speed, and without causing any destruction, or carrying away any negroes or other property of the American inhabitants, withdraw all his armies, garrisons and fleets from the said United States, and from every post, place and harbour within the same; leaving in all fortifications the American artillery that may be therein: And shall also order and cause all archives, records, deeds and papers, belonging to any of the said States, or their citizens, which, in the course of the war, may have fallen into the hands of his officers, to be forthwith restored and deliver'd to the proper States and persons to whom they belong.

[ARTICLE VIII] The navigation of the river Mississippi, from its source to the ocean, shall for ever remain free and open to the subjects of Great Britain, and the citizens of the United States.

[ARTICLE IX] In case it should so happen that any place or territory belonging to Great Britain or to the United States, should have been conquer'd by the arms of either from the other, before the arrival of the said provisional articles in America, it is agreed, that the same shall be restored without difficulty, and without requiring any compensation. . . .

Done at Paris, this third day of September, in the year of our Lord one thousand seven hundred and eighty-three.

| | |
|---|---|
| [Seal.] | D. Hartley |
| [Seal.] | John Adams |
| [Seal.] | B. Franklin |
| [Seal.] | John Jay |


## GEORGE WASHINGTON ON SHAYS' REBELLION (1786)

Captain Daniel Shays led a mob of angry farmers from western Massachusetts in rebellion in 1786. Faced with taxes and debts they could not afford, they had suffered considerably during the depression that followed the Revolutionary War, and now they demanded relief. Shays' rebellion reflected the economic weakness of the United States under the Articles of Confederation.

Your sentiments, that our affairs are drawing rapidly to a crisis, accord with my own. What the event will be is also beyond the reach of my foresight. We have errors to correct; we have probably had too good an opinion of human nature in forming our Confederation. Experience has taught us that men will not adopt, and carry into execution, measures the best calculated for their own good, without the intervention of coercive power. I do not conceive we can exist long as a nation without lodging, somewhere, a power which will pervade the whole Union in as energetic a manner as the authority of the state governments extends over the several states.

---

Letter to John Jay, August 1, 1786.

To be fearful of investing Congress, constituted as that body is, with ample authorities for national purposes, appears to me the very climax of popular absurdity and madness. Could Congress exert them for the detriment of the people without injuring themselves in an equal or greater proportion? Are not their interests inseparably connected with those of their constituents? By the rotation of appointments, must they not mingle frequently with the mass of citizens?. . .

What then is to be done? Things cannot go on in the same train forever. It is much to be feared, as you observe, that the better kind of people, being disgusted with these circumstances, will have their minds prepared for any revolution whatever. We are apt to run from one extreme to another. To anticipate and prevent disastrous contingencies would be the part of wisdom and patriotism.

What astonishing changes a few years are capable of producing! I am told that even respectable characters speak of a monarchical form of government without horror. From thinking proceeds speaking; thence to acting is often but a single step. But how irrevocable and tremendous! What a triumph for our enemies to verify their predictions! What a triumph for the advocates of depotism to find that we are incapable of governing ourselves, and that systems founded on the basis of equal liberty are merely ideal and fallacious. Would to God that wise measures may be taken in time to avert the consequences we have but too much reason to apprehend.


## PATRICK HENRY ON THE CONSTITUTION
## IN THE VIRGINIA RATIFYING CONVENTION (1788)

Patrick Henry had emerged as one of the most formidable foes of the adoption of the new Constitution. Since it was considered essential that the large states ratify the document, his opposition in Virginia, the largest state, was a potential danger to the success of the new experiment ever getting off the ground. The following excerpt shows that Henry had not lost his touch at stirring men's passions on an issue.

I am not free from suspicion: I am apt to entertain doubts: I rose yesterday to ask a question, which arose in my own mind. When I asked that question, I thought the meaning of my interrogation was obvious: the fate of this question and of America may depend on this. Have they said, we the states? Have they made a proposal of a compact between states? If they had, this would be a confederation: It is otherwise most clearly a consolidated government. The question turns, sir, on that poor little thing--the expression, We, the People, instead of the states of America. I need not take much pains to show, that the principles of this system, are extremely pernicious, impolitic, and dangerous. Is this a monarchy, like England--a

---

William Wirt Henry, Patrick Henry: Life, Correspondence and Speeches (New York, 1891), III, 434-435, 437, 451.

compact between prince and people: with checks on the former to secure the liberty of the latter? Is this a confederacy, like Holland--an association of a number of independent states, each of which retains its individual sovereignty? It is not a democracy, wherein the people retain all their rights securely. Had these principles been adhered to, we should not have been brought to this alarming transition, from a confederacy to a consolidated government. We have no detail of those great considerations which, in my opinion, ought to have abounded before we should recur to a government of this kind. Here is a revolution as radical as that which separated us from Great Britain. It is radical, if in this transition, our rights and privileges are endangered, and the sovereignty of the states will be relinquished: and cannot we plainly see, that this is actually the case? The rights of conscience, trial by jury, liberty of the press, all your immunities and franchises, all pretensions to human rights and privileges, are rendered insecure, if not lost, by this change so loudly talked of by some, and inconsiderately by others. Is this tame relinquishment of rights worthy of freemen? Is it worthy of that manly fortitude that ought to characterize republicans? . . . You are not to enquire how your trade may be increased nor how you are to become a great and powerful people, but how your liberties can be secured; for liberty ought to be the direct end of your government. . . .

We are come hither to preserve the poor commonwealth of Virginia, if it can be possibly done: something must be done to preserve your liberty and mine. The confederation; this same despised government, merits, in my opinion, the highest encomium: it carried us through a long and dangerous war: it rendered us victorious in that bloody conflict with a powerful nation: it has secured us a territory greater than any European monarch possesses: and shall a government which has been thus strong and vigorous, be accused of imbecility and abandoned for want of energy? Consider what you are about to do before you part with this government. Take longer time in reckoning things: revolutions like this have happened in almost every country in Europe: similar examples are to be found in ancient Greece and ancient Rome: instances of the people losing their liberty by their own carelessness and the ambition of a few. We are cautioned by the honorable gentleman who presides, against faction and turbulence: I acknowledge that licentiousness is dangerous, and that it ought to be provided against: I acknowledge also the new form of government may effectually prevent it: yet, there is another thing it will as effectually do: it will oppress and ruin the people.

There are sufficient guards placed against sedition and licentiousness: for when power is given to this government to suppress these, or, for any other purpose, the language it assumes is clear, express, and unequivocal; but when this constitution speaks of privileges, there is an ambiguity, sir, a fatal ambiguity--an ambiguity which is very astonishing. In the clause under consideration, there is the strangest language that I can conceive. . . .

This constitution is said to have beautiful features; but when I come to examine these features, sir, they appear to me horribly frightful: among other deformities it has an awful squinting; it squints towards monarchy; and does not this raise indignation in the breast of every true American. Your president may easily become king: your senate is so imperfectly constructed that your dearest rights may be sacrificed by what may be a small minority; and a very small minority may continue forever unchangeably this government although horridly defective: where are your checks in this government? Your strongholds will be in the hands of your enemies; it is on a supposition that your American governors shall be honest, that all the good qualities of this government are founded: but its defective, and imperfect construction, puts it in their power to perpetrate the worst of mischiefs, should they be bad men: and, sir, would not all the world, from the eastern to the western hemisphere, blame our distracted folly in resting our rights upon the contingency of our rulers being good or bad? Show me that age and country where the rights and liberties of the people were placed on the sole chance of their rulers being good men, without a consequent loss of liberty? I say that the loss of that dearest privilege has ever followed with absolute certainty, every such mad attempt.

### GEORGE WASHINGTON'S FAREWELL ADDRESS (September 17, 1796)

The valedictory address of the new nation's first chief executive contains a wealth of paternal advice that reflects the concerns of Washington and his contemporaries. They were preoccupied with the problem of creating and sustaining national unity and sovereignty in an age when transportation and communication were poor, the western territories were remote, sectionalism already existed, and foreign influence in internal politics was constantly feared. Washington's advice to posterity concerns military establishments, political parties, and foreign policy. Some of his suggestions were heeded; some were not.

While, then, every part of our country thus feels an immediate and particular interest in union, all the parts combined can not fail to find in the united mass of means and efforts greater strength, greater resource, proportionably greater security from external danger, a less frequent interruption of their peace by foreign nations, and what is of inestimable value, they must derive from union an exemption from those broils and wars between themselves which so frequently afflict neighboring countries not tied together by the same governments, which their own rivalships alone would be sufficient to produce, but which opposite foreign alliances, attachments, and intrigues would stimulate and imbitter. Hence, likewise, they will avoid the necessity of those overgrown military establishments which, under any form of government, are inauspicious to liberty, and which are to be regarded as particulary hostile to republican liberty. In this sense it is that your union ought to be considered as a main prop of your liberty, and that the love of the one ought to endear to you the preservation of the other. . . .

In contemplating the causes which may disturb our union it occurs as matter of serious concern that any ground should have been furnished for characterizing parties by geographical discriminations–Northern and Southern–Atlantic and Western--whence designing men may endeavor to excite a belief that there is a real difference of local interests and views. One of the expedients of party to acquire influence within particular districts is to misrepresent the opinions and aims of other districts. You can not shield yourselves too much against the jealousies and heart burnings which spring from these misrepresentations; they tend to render alien to each other those who ought to be bound together by fraternal affection. . . .

James D. Richardson, ed., A Compilation of the Messages and Papers of the Presidents 1789-1908 (New York, 1908), I, 216-223.

I have already intimated to you the danger of parties in the State, with particular reference to the founding of them on geographical discriminations. Let me now take a more comprehensive view, and warn you in the most solemn manner against the baneful effects of the spirit of party, generally.

This spirit, unfortunately, is inseparable from our nature, having its root in the strongest passions of the human mind. It exists under different shapes in all governments, more or less stifled, controlled, or repressed; but in those of the popular form it is seen in its greatest rankness and is truly their worst enemy.

The alternate domination of one faction over another, sharpened by the spirit of revenge natural to party dissension, which in different ages and countries has perpetrated the most horrid enormities, is itself a frightful despotism. But this leads at length to a more formal and permanent despotism. The disorders and miseries which result gradually incline the minds of men to seek security and repose in the absolute power of an individual, and sooner or later the chief of some prevailing faction, more able or more fortunate than his competitors, turns this disposition to the purposes of his own elevation on the ruins of Public Liberty. . . .

[The spirit of party] serves always to distract the public councils and enfeeble the public administration. It agitates the community with ill-founded jealousies and false alarms; kindles the animosity of one part against another; foments occasionally riot and insurrection. It opens the door to foreign influence and corruption, which find a facilitated access to the government itself through the channels of party passion. Thus the policy and the will of one country are subjected to the policy and will of another. . . .

Observe good faith and justice towards all nations. Cultivate peace and harmony with all. . . .

In the execution of such a plan nothing is more essential than that permanent, inveterate antipathies against particular nations and passionate attachments for others be excluded, and that in place of them just and amicable feelings toward all should be cultivated. The nation which indulges toward another an habitual hatred or an habitual fondness is in some degree a slave. It is a slave to its animosity or to its affection, either of which is sufficient to lead it astray from its duty and its interest. . . .

Against the insidious wiles of foreign influence (I conjure you to believe me, fellow-citizens) the jealousy of a free people ought to be <u>constantly</u> awake, since history and experience prove that foreign influence is one of the most baneful foes of republican government. . . .

The great rule of conduct for us in regard to foreign nations is, in extending our commercial relations to have with them as little <u>political</u> connection as possible. So far as we have already formed engagements let them be fulfilled with perfect good faith. Here let us stop. . . .

Our detached and distant situation invites and enables us to pursue a different course. . . .

Why forego the advantages of so peculiar a situation? Why quit our own to stand upon foreign ground? Why, by interweaving our destiny with any part of Europe, entangle our peace and prosperity in toils of European ambition, rivalry, interest, humor, or caprice?

It is our true policy to steer clear of permanent alliances with any portion of the foreign world, so far, I mean, as we are now at liberty to do it; for let me not be understood as capable of patronizing infidelity to existing arrangements. . . .

Taking care always to keep ourselves by suitable establishments on a respectable defensive posture, we may safely trust to temporary alliances for extraordinary emergencies. . . .

There can be no greater error than to expect or calculate upon real favors from nation to nation. It is an illusion which experience must cure, which a just pride ought to discard.

## THOMAS JEFFERSON

What can one say in a few words about a man like Mr. Jefferson--an accomplished violinst, an amateur architect far better than most professionals, author of Virginia's separation of church and state, avid supporter of education, an expert agriculturist, author of the Declaration of Independence, founder of the Democratic Party, first Secretary of State, second Vice President, third and most intelligent of our Presidents! The following brief quotations from his writings reveal the innate genius of one of the truly unique men in Western Civilization.

(a) Letter to James Madison, September 6, 1789

It may be proved that no society can make a perpetual constitution, or even a perpetual law. The earth belongs always to the living generation. They may manage it then, and what proceeds from it, as they please, during their usufruct. They are masters too of their own persons, and consequently make govern them as they please.

(b) Letter of Edward Carrington, January 16, 1787

I am persuaded myself that the good sense of the people will always be found to be the best army. They may be led astray for a moment, but will soon correct themselves. The people are the only censors of their governors: and even their errors will tend to keep these to the true principles of their institution. To punish these errors too severely would be to suppress the only safeguard of the public liberty. The way to prevent these irregular interpositions of the people is to give them full information of their affairs thro' the channel of the public papers, and to contrive that those papers should penetrate the whole mass of the people. The basis of our governments being the opinion of the people, the very first object should be to keep that right; and were it left to me to decide whether we should have a government without newspapers, or newspapers without a government, I should not hesitate a moment to prefer the latter.

(c) Letter of Judge John Tyler, June 28, 1804

    No experiment can be more interesting than that we are now trying, and which we trust will end in establishing the fact, that man may be governed by reason and truth. Our first object should therefore be, to leave open to him all the avenues to truth. The most effectual hiterto found, is the freedom of the press. It is therefore, the first shut up by those who fear the investigation of their actions. The firmness with which the people have withstood the late abuses of the press, the discernment they have manifested between truth and falsehood, show that they may safely be trusted to hear everything true and false, and to form a correct judgment between them. As little is it necessary to impose on their senses, or dazzle their minds by pomp, splendor, or forms. Instead of this artificial, how much surer is that real respect, which results from the use of their reason, and the habit of bringing everything to the test of common sense.

(d) Letter of Dr. Benjamin Rush, September 23, 1800

    . . . The clergy [have] a very favorite hope of obtaining an establishment of a particular form of Christianity thro' the U.S.; and as every sect believes its own form the true one, every one perhaps hoped for his own, but especially the Episcopalians & Congregationalists. The returning good sense of our country threatens abortion to their hopes, & they believe that any portion of power confided to me, will be exerted in opposition to their schemes. And they believe rightly; for I have sworn upon the altar of god, eternal hostility against every form of tyranny over the mind of man.

(e) Letter to James Madison, December 20, 1787

    Above all things I hope the education of the common people will be attended to; convinced that on their good sense we may rely with the most security for the preservation of a due degree of liberty.

(f) Letter to John Tyler, May 26, 1810

    I have indeed two great measures at heart, without which no republic can maintain itself in strength. 1. That of general education, to enable every man to judge for himself what will secure or endanger his freedom. 2. To divide every county into hundreds, of such size that all the children of each will be within reach of a central school in it.

(g) Letter of John Wyche, May 19, 1809

    I always hear with pleasure of institutions for the promotion of knowledge among my countrymen. The people of every country are the only safe guardians of their own rights, and are the only instruments which can be used for their destruction. And certainly they would never consent to be so used were they no deceived. To avoid this, they should be instructed to a certain degree. I have often thought that nothing would do more extensive good at small expense than the establishment of a small circulating library in every county, to consist of a few well-chosen books, to be lent to the people of the county, under such regulations as would secure their safe return in due time.

(h) Letter to Benjamin Banneker, August 30, 1791

No body wishes more than I do to see such proofs as you exhibit, that nature has given to our black brethren, talents equal to those of the other colors of men, and that the appearance of a want of them is owing merely to the degraded condition of their existence, both in Africa & America. I can add with truth, that no body wishes more ardently to see a good system commenced for raising the condition both of their body & mind to what it ought to be, as fast as the imbecility of their present existence, and other circumstances which cannot be neglected, will admit.

(i) Letter to Edward Coles, August 25, 1814

The love of justice and the love of country plead equally the cause of these people, and it is a moral reproach to us that they should have pleaded it so long in vain, and should have produced not a single effort, nay I fear not much serious willingness to relieve them & ourselves from our present condition of moral & political reprobation. . . . Yet the hour of emancipation is advancing, in the march of time. It will come; and whether brought on by the generous energy of our own minds; or by the bloody process of St Domingo, excited and conducted by the power of our present enemy, if once stationed permanently within our Country, and offering asylum and arms to the oppressed, is a leaf of our history not yet turned over. As to the method by which this difficult work is to be effected, if permitted to be done by ourselves, I have seen no proposition so expedient on the whole, as that as emancipation of those born after a given day, and of their education and expatriation after a given age. This would give time for a gradual extinction of that species of labour & substitution of another, and lessen the severity of the shock which an operation so fundamental cannot fail to produce.

(j) Letter to Roger C. Weightman, June 24, 1826

. . . . Our fellow citizens, after half a century of experience and prosperity, continue to approve the choice we made. May it be to the world, what I believe it will be, (to some parts sooner, to others later, but finally to all,) the signal of arousing men to burst the chains under which monkish ignorance and superstition had persuaded them to bind themselves, and to assume the blessings and security of self-government. That form which we have substituted, restores the free right to the unbounded exercise of reason and freedom of opinion. All eyes are opened, or opening, to the rights of man. The general spread of the light of science has already laid open to every view the palpable truth, that the mass of mankind has not been born with saddles on their backs, nor a favored few booted and spurred, ready to ride them legitimately, by the grace of God. These are grounds of hope for others.

# ALEXANDER HAMILTON

Alexander Hamilton still stands as a symbol of conservative values. If his strident nationalism, elitist politics, and planned economics did not entirely square with American republicanism, Hamilton's views, nonetheless, contributed mightily to the development of the newborn United States of America. The following selections reflect some of Hamilton's strongly held views.

(a) Letter to Edward Stevens, November 11, 1769

Ned, my Ambition is prevalent that I contemn the grov'ling and condition of a Clerk or the like, to which my Fortune &c. condemns me and would willingly risk my life tho' not my Character to exalt my Station. Im confident, Ned that my Youth excludes me from any hopes of immediate Preferment nor do I desire it, but I mean to prepare the way for futurity. Im no Philosopher you see and may be jusly said to Build Castles in the Air. My Folly makes me ashamd and beg youll Conceal it, yet Neddy we have seen such Schemes successfull when the Projector is Constant I shall Conclude saying I wish there was a War.

(b) Letter to John Jay, November 26, 1775

In times of such commotion as the present, while the passions of men are worked up to an uncommon pitch there is great danger of fatal extremes. The same state of the passions which fits the multitude, who have not a sufficient stock of reason and knowledge to guide them, for opposition to tyranny and oppression, very naturally leads them to a contempt and disregard of all authority. The due medium is hardly to be found among the more intelligent, it is almost impossible among the unthinking populace. When the minds of these are loosened from their attachment to ancient establishments and courses, they seem to grow giddy and are apt more or less to run into anarchy. These principles, too true in themselves, and confirmed to me both by reading and my own experience, deserve extremely the attention of those, who have the direction of public affairs. In such tempestuous times, it requires the greatest skill in the political pilots to keep men steady and within proper bounds, on which account I am always more or less alarmed at every thing which is done of mere will and pleasure, without any proper authority. Irregularities I know are to be expected, but they are nevertheless dangerous and ought to be checked, by every prudent and moderate mean.

(c) Letter to Gouverneur Morris, May 19, 1777

To determine the qualifications proper for the chief executive Magistrate requires the deliberate wisdom of a select assembly, and cannot be safely lodged with the people at large. That instability is inherent in the nature of popular governments, I think very disputable; unstable democracy, is an epithet frequently in the mouths of politicians; but I believe that from a strict examination of the matter, from the records of history, it will be found that the fluctuation of governments in which the popular principle has borne a considerable sway, has proceeded from its being compounded with other principles and from its being made to operate in an improper channel.

Compound governments, though they may be harmonious in the beginning, will introduce distinct interests; and these interests will clash, throw the state into convulsions & produce a change or dissolution. When the deliberative or judicial powers are vested wholly or partly in the collective body of the people, you must expect error, confusion and instability. But a representative democracy, where the right of election is well secured and regulated & the exercise of the legislative, executive and judiciary authorities, is vested in select persons, chosen <u>really</u> and not <u>nominally</u> by the people, will in my opinion be most likely to be happy, regular and durable.

(d) Letter to James Duane, September 3, 1780

The fundamental defect is a want of power in Congress. It is hardly worth while to show in what this consists, as it seems to be universally acknowledged, or to point out how it has happened, as the only question is how to remedy it. It may however be said that it has originated from three causes--an excess of the spirit of liberty which has made the particular states show a jealousy of all power not in their own hands; and this jealousy has led them to exercise a right of judging in the last resort of the measures recommended by Congress, and of acting according to their own opinions of their propriety or necessity, a diffidence in Congress of their own powers, by which they have been timid and indecisive in their resolutions, constantly making concessions to the states, till they have scarcely left themselves the shadow of power; a want of sufficient means at their disposal to answer the public exigencies and of vigor to draw forth those means; which have occasioned them to depend on the states individually to fulfil their engagements with the army, and the consequence of which has been to ruin their influence and credit with the army, to establish its dependence on each state separately rather than <u>on them</u>, that is rather than on the whole collectively. . . .

But the confederation itself is defective and requires to be altered; it is neither fit for war, nor peace. The idea of an uncontrolable sovereignty in each state, over its internal police, will defeat the other powers given to Congress, and make our union feeble and precarious. . . .

The confederation gives the states individually too much influence in the affairs of the army; they should have nothing to do with it. The entire formation and disposal of our military forces ought to belong to Congress. It is an essential cement of the union; and it ought to be the policy of Congress to destroy all ideas of state attachments in the army and make it look up wholly to them.

(e) Remarks at Constitutional Convention, Philadelphia, June 18, 1787

All communities divide themselves into the few and the many. The first are the rich and well born, the other the mass of the people. The voice of the people has been said to be the voice of God; and however generally this maxim has been quoted and believed, it is not true in fact. The people are turbulent and changing; they seldom judge or determine right.

(f) Remarks at Constitutional Convention, Philadelphia, June 29, 1787

    No government could give us tranquillity and happiness at home, which did not possess sufficient stability and strength to make us respectable abroad. . . .

    Foreigners are jealous of our increasing greatness, and would rejoice in our distractions. . . . The sovereigns in Europe have. . . an anxiety for the **preservation** of our democratic governments, probably for no other reason, but **to keep** us weak. Unless your government is respectable, foreigners will **invade** your rights; and to maintain tranquility it must be respectable.

(g) The Federalist, Number 29

    **Standing** armies are dangerous to liberty.

(h) **Remarks at** Constitutional Ratification Convention, New York, June 21, 1788

    It **has been** observed, by an honorable gentleman, that a pure democracy, if it were **practicable**, would be the most perfect government. Experience has proved that no position in politics is more false than this. The ancient democracies, in which the people themselves deliberated, never possessed one feature of good government. Their very character was tyranny; their figure, deformity. When they assembled, the field of debate presented an ungovernable mob, not only incapable of deliberation, but prepared for every enormity

(i) Letter to George Washington, August 13, 1788

    I take it for granted, sir, you have concluded to comply with what will no doubt be the general call of your country in relation to the new government. You will permit me to say that it is indispensable you should lend yourself to its first operations. It is of little purpose to have introduced a system, if the weightiest influence is not given to its firm establishment in the outset.

(j) Letter to Jonathan Dayton, 1799

    An accurate view of the internal situation of the United States presents many discouraging reflections to the enlightened friends of our government and country. Notwithstanding the unexampled success of our public measures at home and abroad--notwithstanding the instructive comments afforded by the disastrous and disgusting scenes of the French Revolution--public opinion has not been ameliorated; sentiments dangerous to social happiness have not been diminished; on the contrary, there are symptoms which warrant the apprehension that among the most numerous class of citizens, errors of a very pernicious tendency have not only preserved but have extended their empire. Though some thing may have been gained on the side of men of information and property, more has probably been lost on that of persons of a different description. An extraordinary exertion of the friends of government, aided by circumstances of momentary impression, gave, in the last election for members of Congress, a more favorable countenance to some States than they had before worn; yet it is the belief of well-informed men that no real or desirable change has been wrought in those States. On the other hand, it is admitted by close observers that some of the parts of the Union which, in times past, have been the soundest, have of late exhibited signs of a gangrene begun and progressive.

It is likewise apparent that opposition to the government has acquired more system than formerly, is bolder in the avowal of its designs, less solicitous than it was to discriminate between the Constitution and the administration, and more open and more enterprising in its projects. The late attempt of Virginia and Kentucky to unite the State Legislatures in a direct resistance to certain laws of the Union can be considered in no other light than as an attempt to change the government.

(k) Letter to James McHenry, March 18, 1799

Beware, my dear sir, of magnifying a riot into an insurrection, by employing, in the first instance, an inadequate force. 'T is better far to err on the other side.
Whenever the government appears in arms, it ought to appear like a <u>Hercules</u>, and inspire respect by the display of strength. The consideration of expense is of no moment compared with the advantages of energy. 'T is true this is always a relative question, but 't is always important to make no mistake. I only offer a <u>principle</u> and a <u>caution</u>.

(1) Letter to James A Bayard, January 16, 1801

I admit that his [Jefferson's] politics are tinctured with fanaticism; that he is too much in earnest in his democracy; that he has been a mischievous enemy to the principal measures of our past administration; that he is crafty and persevering in his objects; that he is not scrupulous about the means of success, nor very mindful of truth, and that he is a contemptible hypocrite. But it is not true, as is alleged, that he is an enemy to the power of the Executive, or that he is for confounding all the powers in the House of Representatives. It is a fact which I have frequently mentioned, that, while we were in the administration together, he was generally for a large construction of the Executive authority and not backward to act upon it in cases which coincided with his views. Let it be added that in his theoretic ideas he has considered as improper the participations of the Senate in the Executive authority. I have more than once made the reflection that, viewing himself as the reversioner, he was solicitous to come into the possession of a good estate. Nor is it true that Jefferson is zealot enough to do any thing in pursuance of his principles which will contravene his popularity or his interest. He is as likely as any man I know to temporize-- to calculate what will be likely to promote his own reputation and advantage;. . .
As to Burr these things are admitted, and indeed cannot be denied, that he is a man of <u>extreme</u> and <u>irregular</u> ambition; that he is <u>selfish</u> to a degree which excludes all social affections, and that he is decidedly <u>profligate</u>.
The truth is, that Burr is a man of a very subtle imagination, and a mind of this make is rarely free from ingenious whimsies. Yet I admit that he has no fixed theory, and that his peculiar notions will easily give way to his interest. But is it a recommendation to have <u>no theory</u>? Can that man be a systematic or able statesman who has none? I believe not. <u>No general principles</u> will hardly work much better than erroneous ones.

(m) Letter to Gouveneur Morris, February 27, 1802

    Mine is an odd destiny. Perhaps no man in the United States has sacrificed or done more for the present Constitution than myself; and contrary to all my anticipations of its fate, as you know from the very beginning, I am still laboring to prop the fail and worthless fabric. Yet I have the murmurs of its friends no less than the curses of its foes for my reward. What can I do better than withdraw from the scene? Every day proves to me more and more, that this American world was not made for me.

(n) Letter to Theodore Sedgwick, July 10, 1804

    I will here express but one sentiment, which is, that dismemberment of our empire will be a clear sacrifice of great positive advantages without any counterbalancing good, administering no relief to our real disease, which is <u>democracy</u>, the poison of which, by a subdivision, will only be the more concentrated in each part, and consequently the more virulent.

## THE SEDITION ACT (1798)

    The political battle between the Democratic-Republican Party and the Federalist Party was reaching fever pitch by 1798. At that point the Federalists attempted to prevent the Jeffersonians from competing fairly in the upcoming campaign of 1800 by outlawing criticism of the administration of John Adams.

    Section 1. <u>Be it enacted by the Senate and House of Representatives of the United States of America, in Congress assembled</u>, That if any persons shall unlawfully combine or conspire together, with intent to oppose any measure or measures of the government of the United States, which are or shall be directed by proper authority, or to impede the operation of any law of the United States, or to intimidate or prevent any person holding a place or office in or under the government of United States, from undertaking, performing or executing his trust or duty; and if any person or persons, with intent as aforesaid, shall counsel, advise or attempt to procure any insurrection, riot, unlawful assembly, or combination, whether such conspiracy, threatening, counsel, advice, or attempt shall have the proposed effect or not, he or they shall be deemed guilty of a high misdemeanor, and on conviction, before any court of the United States having jurisdiction thereof, shall be punished by a fine not exceeding five thousand dollars, and by

---

United States <u>Statutes</u> at <u>Large</u>, 5th Congress, 2nd session, vol. I, Chap. 74, pp. 596-597.

imprisonment during a term not less than six months nor exceeding five years; and further, at the discretion of the court may be holden to find sureties for his good behaviour in such sum, and for such time, as the said court may direct.

Sec. 2. <u>And be it further enacted,</u> That if any person shall write, print, utter or publish, or shall cause or procure to be written, printed, uttered or published, or shall knowingly and willingly assist or aid in writing, printing, uttering or publishing any false, scandalous and malicious writing or writings against the government of the United States, or either house of the Congress of the United States, or the President of the United States, with intent to defame the said government, or either house of the said Congress, or the said President, or to bring them, or either of them, into contempt or disrepute; or to excite against them, or either or any of them, the hatred of the good people of the United States, or to stir up sedition within the United States, or to excite any unlawful combinations therein, for opposing or resisting any law or the United States, or any act of the President of the United States, done in pursuance of any such law, or of the powers in him vested by the constitution of the United States, or to resist, oppose, or defeat any such law of act, or to aid, encourage or abet any hostile designs of any foreign nation against the United States, their people or government, then such person, being thereof convicted before any court of the United States having jurisdiction thereof, shall be punished by a fine not exceeding two thousand dollars, and by imprisonment not exceeding two years.

Sec. 3. <u>And be it further enacted and declared,</u> That if any person shall be prosecuted under this act, for the writing or publishing any libel aforesaid, it shall be lawful for the defendant, upon the trial of the cause, to give in evidence in his defence, the truth of the matter contained in the publication charged as a libel. And the jury who shall try the cause, shall have a right to determine the law and the fact, under the direction of the court, as in other cases.

Sec. 4. <u>And be it further enacted,</u> That this act shall continue and be in force until the third day of March, one thousand eight hundred and one, and no longer: <u>Provided</u>, that the expiration of the act shall not prevent or defeat a prosecution and punishment of any offence against the law, during the time it shall be in force.

## <u>RED JACKET ON THE WHITE MAN'S RELIGION (1805)</u>

Red Jacket (Sagoyewatha) was a leader of the Seneca tribe--one of the Six Nations--in western New York. He rose to prominence largely on the basis of his powers of eloquence. He spoke often about the wrongs inflicted on his people by the white man. In 1805 a missionary from Massachusetts visited Buffalo and urged the Senecas to adopt Christianity. Red Jacket offered the following response.

---

Samuel G. Goodrich, <u>Lives of Celebrated American Indians</u> (New York, 1844), pp. 283-87.

Friend and brother; it was the will of the Great Spirit that we should meet together this day. He orders all things, and he has given us a fine day for our council. He has taken his garment from before the sun, and caused it to shine with brightness upon us; our eyes are opened, that we see clearly; our ears are unstopped, that we have been able to hear distinctly the words that you have spoken; for all these favors we thank the Great Spirit, and him only.

Brother, this council fire was kindled by you; it was at your request that we came together at this time; we have listened with attention to what you have said. You requested us to speak our minds freely; this gives us great joy, for we now consider that we stand upright before you, and can speak what we think; all have heard your voice, and all speak to you as one man; our minds are agreed.

Brother, you say you want an answer to your talk before you leave this place. It is right you should have one, as you are a great distance from home, and we do not wish to detain you; but we will first look back a little, and tell you what our fathers have told us, and what we have heard from the white people.

Brother, listen to what we say. There was a time when our forefathers owned this great island. Their seats extended from the rising to the setting sun. The Great Spirit had made it for the use of Indians. He had created the buffalo, the deer, and other animals for food. He made the bear and the beaver, and their skins served us for clothing. He had scattered them over the country, and taught us how to take them. He had caused the earth to produce corn for bread. All this he had done for his red children because he loved them. If we had any disputes about hunting grounds, they were generally settled without the shedding of much blood. But an evil day came upon us; your forefathers crossed the great waters, and landed on this island. Their numbers were small; they found friends, and not enemies; they told us they had fled from their own country for fear of wicked men, and come here to enjoy their religion. They asked for a small seat; we took pity on them, granted their request, and they sat down amongst us; we gave them corn and meat; they gave us poison in return. The white people had now found our country; tidings were carried back, and more came amongst us; yet we did not fear them, we took them to be friends; they called us brothers; we believed them, and gave them a larger seat. At length, their numbers had greatly increased; they wanted more land; they wanted our country. Our eyes were opened, and our minds became uneasy. Wars took place; Indians were hired to fight against Indians, and many of our people were destroyed. They also brought strong liquor among us; it was strong and powerful, and has slain thousands.

Brother, our seats were once large, and yours were very small; you have now become a great people, and we have scarcely a place left to spread our blankets; you have got our country, but are not satisfied; you want to force your religion upon us.

Brother, continue to listen. You say you are sent to instruct us how to worship the Great Spirit agreeably to his mind, and if we do not take hold of the religion which you white people teach, we shall be unhappy hereafter. You say that you are right, and we are lost; how do we know this to be true? We understand that your religion is written in a book; if it was intended for us as well as you, why has not the Great Spirit given it to us, and not only to us, but why did he not give to our forefathers the knowledge of that book, with the means of understanding it rightly? We only know what you tell us about it. How shall we know when to believe, being so often deceived by the white people?

Brother, you say there is but one way to worship and serve the Great Spirit; if there is but one religion, why do you white people differ so much about it? Why not all agree, as you can all read the book?

Brother, we do not understand these things. We are told that your religion was given to your forefathers, and has been handed down from father to son. We also have a religion which was given to our forefathers, and has been handed down to us their children. We worship that way. It teacheth us to be thankful for all the favors we receive; to love each other, and to be united. We never quarrel about religion.

Brother, the Great Spirit has made us all; but he had made a great difference between his white and red children; he has given us a different complexion, and different customs; to you he has given the arts; to these he has not opened our eyes; we know these things to be true. Since he has made so great a difference between us in other things, why may we not conclude that he has given us a different religion according to our understanding. The Great Spirit does right; he knows what is best for his children; we are satisfied.

Brother, we do not wish to destroy your religion, or take it from you; we only want to enjoy our own.

Brother, you say you have not come to get our land or our money, but to enlighten our minds. I will now tell you that I have been at your meetings, and saw you collecting money from the meeting. I cannot tell what this money was intented for, but suppose it was for your minister; and if we should conform to your way of thinking, perhaps you may want some from us.

Brother, we are told that you have been preaching to the white people in this place. These people are our neighbors; we are acquainted with them; we will wait a little while and see what effect your preaching has upon them. If we find it does them good, makes them honest and less disposed to cheat Indians, we will then consider again what you have said.

Brother, you have now heard our answer to your talk, and this is all we have to say at present. As we are going to part, we will come and take you by the hand, and hope the Great Spirit will protect you on your journey, and return you safe to your friends.


## HENRY CLAY ON WAR WITH GREAT BRITAIN (1810)

Henry Clay, colorful Kentucky orator and Speaker of the House of Representatives, was one of a new generation of political leaders known as the War Hawks. Republicans from the west and back country of the South, they fueled the drive for war with England, the invasion of Canada, and war against frontier Indians. President Madison, a Republican himself, could not turn a deaf ear to such tumultuous congressional warmongering as one sees in this speech of Clay's. Although opposed by Federalists and peace Republicans, war indeed was declared.

---

James F. Hopkins, ed., The Papers of Henry Clay (Lexington, KY, 1959), I, 449-452.

No man in the nation desires peace more than I. But I prefer the troubled ocean of war, demanded by the honor and independence of the country, with all its calamities, and desolations, to the tranquil, putrescent pool of ignominious peace. If we can accommodate our differences with one of the belligerents only, I should prefer that one to be Great Britain. But if with neither, and we are forced into a selection of our enemy, then am I for war with Britain; because I believe her prior in aggression and her injuries and insults to us were atrocious in character. . . .

But we are asked for the means of carrying on War; and those who oppose it triumphantly appeal to the vacant vaults of the treasury. With the unimpaired credit of the government, invigorated by a faithful observance of public engagements, and a rapid extinction of the debt of the revolution; with the boundless territories in the west, presenting a safe pledge for reimbursement of loans to any extent--is it not astonishing that despondency itself should disparage the resources of this country? . . .

Or, are we to be governed by the low, groveling parsimony of the counting room, and to cast up the actual pence in the drawer before we assert our inestimable rights? It is said, however, that no object is attainable by war with Britain. In its fortunes we are to estimate not only the benefit to be derived to ourselves, but the injury to be done the enemy. The conquest of Canada is in your power. I trust I shall not be deemed presumptuous when I state, what I verily believe, that the militia of Kentucky are alone competent to place Montreal and Upper Canada at your feet. Is it nothing to the British nation--is it nothing to the pride of her monarch to have the last of the immense North American possessions held by him in the commencement of his réign, wrested from his dominion? Is it nothing to us to extinguish the torch that lights up savage warfare? Is it nothing to acquire the entire fur trade connected with that country, and to destroy the temptation and the opportunity of violating your revenue and other laws? . . .

Another effect of war will be the re-production and cherishing of a martial spirit amongst us. Is there not danger that we shall become enervated by the spirit of avarice unfortunately so predominant? . . . a certain portion of military ardor (and this is what I desire) is essential to the protection of the country. The withered arm, and wrinkled brow of the illustrious founders of our freedom, are melancholy indications that they will shortly be removed from us. Their deeds of glory and renown will then be felt only through the cold medium of the historic page. We shall want the presence and living example of a new race of heroes to supply their place, and to animate us to preserve unviolated what they atchieved [sic].

# RESOLUTIONS OF THE HARTFORD CONVENTION (1815)

The Massachusetts legislature was responsible for sending invitations for the Hartford Convention in October, 1814. The delegates who attended represented Connecticut, Massachusetts, Rhode Island, New Hampshire, and Vermont. Although there were men who wished to force an open break with the federal government, luckily for the Union's sake moderates controlled the convention from the outset. These excerpts from the final report show the depth of discontent in New England with the war and the Democratic administration.

Resolved, That the following amendments of the constitution of the United States be recommended to the states represented as aforesaid, to be proposed by them for adoption by the state legislatures, and in such cases as may be deemed expedient by a convention chosen by the people of each state. . . .

First. Representatives and direct taxes shall be apportioned among the several states which may be included within this Union, according to their respective numbers of free persons, including those bound to serve for a term of years, and excluding Indians not taxed, and all other persons.

Second. No new state shall be admitted into the Union by Congress, in virtue of the power granted by the constitution, without the concurrence of two thirds of both houses.

Third. Congress shall not have power to lay any embargo on the ships or vessels of the citizens of the United States, in the ports or harbours thereof, for more than sixty days.

Fourth. Congress shall not have power, without the concurrence of two thirds of both houses, to interdict the commercial intercourse between the United States and any foreign nation, or the dependencies thereof.

Fifth. Congress shall not make or declare war, or authorize acts of hostility against any foreign nation, without the concurrence of two thirds of both houses, except such acts of hostility be in defence of the territories of the United States when actually invaded.

. Sixth. No person who shall hereafter be naturalized, shall be eligible as a member of the senate or house of representatives of the United States, nor capable of holding any civil office under the authority of the United States.

Seventh. The same person shall not be elected president of the United States a second time; nor shall the President be elected from the same state two terms of succession.

Resolved, That if the application of these states to the government of the United States, recommended in a foregoing resolution, should be unsuccessful, and peace should not be concluded, and the defence of these states should be neglected, as it has been since the commencement of the war, it will, in the opinion of this convention, be expedient for the legislatures of the several states to appoint delegates to another convention, to meet at Boston in the state of Massachusetts, on the third Thursday of June next, with such powers and instructions as the exigency of a crisis so momentous may require.

---

Theodore Dwight, <u>History of the Hartford Convention</u> (New York, 1833), pp. 377-378.

## JOHN C. CALHOUN ENDORSES FEDERAL FUNDING FOR INTERNAL IMPROVEMENTS (1817)

Calhoun is best known for his career in the 1830's and 1840's as a South Carolina advocate of a strict interpretation of the constitution, states' rights, nullification, Southern sectionalism and the "virtues" of slavery. But in his earlier career he was an ardent nationalist who felt the fortunes of all sections were interdependent. In the following speech he justifies federal expenditures for internal improvements.

Let it not be said that internal improvements may be wholly left to the enterprise of the states and of individuals. I know that much might justly be expected to be done by them; but in a country so new, and so extensive as ours, there is room enough for all the general and state governments and individuals, in which to exert their resources. But many of the improvements contemplated are on too great a scale for the resources of the states or individuals; and many of such a nature, that the rival jealousy of the states, if left alone, might prevent. They require the resources and the general superintendence of this government to effect and complete them . . . .

In many respects, no country of equal population and wealth, possesses equal materials of power with ours. The people, in muscular power, in hardy and enterprising habits, and in lofty and gallant courage, are surpassed by none. In one respect, and in my opinion, in one only, are we materially weak. We occupy a surface prodigiously great in proportion to our numbers. The common strength is brought to bear with great difficulty on the point that may be menaced by an enemy. It is our duty, then, as far as in the nature of things it can be effected, to counteract this weakness. Good roads and canals, judiciously laid out, are the proper remedy. In the recent war, how much did we suffer for the want of them! Besides the tardiness and the consequential inefficacy of our military movements, to what an increased expense was the country put for the article of transportation alone! In the event of another war, the saving in this particular would go far towards indemnifying us for the expense of constructing the means of transportation. . . .

But, on this subject of national power, what can be more important than a perfect unity in every part, in feelings and sentiments? And what can tend more powerfully to produce it, than overcoming the effects of distance? No country enjoying freedom, ever occupied any thing like as great an extent of country as this Republic. One hundred years ago, the most profound philosophers did not believe it to be even possible. They did not suppose it possible that a pure republic could exist on as great a scale even as the island of Great Britain . . . .

We are great, and rapidly--I was about to say fearfully--growing. This is our pride and our danger--our weakness and our strength. Little does he deserve to be entrusted with the liberties of this people who does not raise his mind to these truths. We are under the most imperious obligation to counteract every tendency to disunion. . . . Whatever impedes the intercourse

---

Robert L. Meriwether, ed., The Papers of John C. Calhoun (Columbia, 1959), I, 400-403.

of the extremes with this, the centre of the republic, weakens the union. The more enlarged the sphere of commercial circulation, the more extended that of social intercourse; the more strongly are we bound together; the more inseparable are our destinies. Those who understand the human heart best, know how powerfully distance tends to break the sympathies of our nature. Nothing, not even dissimilarity of language, tends more to estrange man from man. Let us then bind the Republic together with a perfect system of roads and canals. Let us conquer space. It is thus the most distant parts of the republic will be brought within a few days' travel of the centre; it is thus that a citizen of the West will read the news of Boston still moist from the press. The mail and the press are the nerves of the body politic. By them, the slightest impression made on the most remote parts is communicated to the whole system; and the more perfect the means of transportation, the more rapid and true the vibration . . . .

Such, then, being the obvious advantages of internal improvements, why should the House hesitate to commence the system? I understand there are, with some members, consitutional objections. . . . It is mainly urged that the Congress can only apply the public money in execution of the (Constitution's) enumerated powers. I am no advocate for refined arguments on the Constitution. The instrument was not intended as a thesis for the logician to exercise his ingenuity on. It ought to be construed with plain, good sense; and what can be more express than the Constitution on this very point?

## McCULLOCH v. MARYLAND (1819)

Of all the major principles set forth by Chief Justice John Marshall, none was more important than the paramountcy of the federal government over the states. The debate over the constitutionality of the Bank of the United States was divisive, and helped to form the first political party system in the young nation. The issue of the Bank continued to occasion controversy for decades, but in 1819 it provided an opportunity for John Marshall to issue a ruling of exceptional significance for the relationship between the states and the federal government. Marshall's decision also went far to establish the implied powers doctrine of constitutional interpretation. The case involves both the constitutionality of the Bank, and whether the state of Maryland could tax a branch of that Bank.

---

McCulloch v. Maryland, 4 Wheaton 316 (1819).

That the power of taxation is one of vital importance; that it is retained by the states; that it is not abridged by the grant of a similar power to the government of the Union; that it is to be concurrently exercised by the two governments: are truths which have never been denied. But such is the paramount character of the Constitution that its capacity to withdraw any subject from the action of even this power is admitted. The states are expressly forbidden to lay any duties on imports or exports, except what may be absolutely necessary for executing their inspection laws . . . . the same paramount character would seem to restrain . . . . a state from such other exercise of this power as is in its nature incompatible with, and repugnant to, the constitutional laws of the Union. A law absolutely repugnant to another, as entirely repeals that other as if express terms of repeal were used.

On this ground the counsel for the Bank place its claim to be exempted from the power of a state to tax its operations. There is no express provision for the case, but the claim has been sustained on a principle which so entirely pervades the Constitution, is so intermixed with the materials which compose it, so interwoven with its web, so blended with its texture, as to be incapable of being separated from it without rending it into shreds.

This great principle is, that the Constitution, and the laws made in pursuance thereof, are supreme; that they control the constitution and laws of the respective states, and cannot be controlled by them. From this, which may be almost termed an axiom, other propositions are deduced as corollaries, . . . These are: 1st. that a power to create implies a power to preserve. 2d. That a power to destroy, if wielded by a different hand, is hostile to, and incompatible with these powers to create and to preserve. 3d. That where this repugnancy exists, that authority which is supreme must control, not yield to that over which it is supreme . . . .

That the power to tax involves the power to destroy; that the power to destroy may defeat and render useless the power to create; that there is a plain repugnance, in conferring on one government a power to control the constitutional measures of another. . . .are propositions not to be denied. . . . If we apply the principle for which the state of Maryland contends, to the constitution generally, we shall find it capable of changing totally the character of that instrument. We shall find it capable of arresting all the measures of the government, and of prostrating it at the foot of the states. The American people have declared their constitution, and the laws made in pursuance thereof, to be supreme; and this principle would transfer the supremacy, in fact, to the states.

If the states may tax one instrument, employed by the government in the execution of its powers, they may tax any and every other instrument. They may tax the mail; they may tax the mint; they may tax patent rights; they may tax the papers of the custom-house; they may tax judicial process; they may tax all the means employed by the government, to an excess which would defeat all the ends of government. This was not intended by the American people. They did not design to make their government dependent on the states . . . .

The question is, in truth, a question of supremacy; and if the right of the states to tax the means employed by the general government be conceded, the declaration that the Constitution, and the laws made in pursuance thereof, shall be the supreme law of the land, is empty and unmeaning declaration.

## THOMAS JEFFERSON ON THE MISSOURI QUESTION (1820)[1]

Thomas Jefferson was badly depressed by the controversy which had developed over the admission of Missouri to statehood. He believed that the quarrel involved a struggle for power by northern politicians who had stirred up and "fanaticized" the people for political reasons. But whatever the true motives behind the fight which had occurred, Jefferson wrote Congressman John Holmes that he was convinced that the ensuing quarrel was a terrible omen for the nation's future.

[T]his momentous question, like a fire-bell in the night, awakened and filled me with terror. I considered it at once as the knell of the Union. It is hushed, indeed, for the moment. But this is a reprieve only, not a final sentence. A geographical line, coinciding with a marked principle, moral and political, once conceived and held up to the angry passions of men, will never be obliterated; and every new irritation will mark it deeper and deeper. I can say, with conscious truth, that there is not a man on earth who would sacrifice more than I would to relieve us from this heavy reproach, in any _practicable_ way. The cession of that kind of property, for so it is misnamed, is a bagatelle which would not cost me a second thought, if, in that way, a general emancipation and _expatriation_ could be effected; and, gradually, and with due sacrifices, I think it might be. But as it is, we have the wolf by the ears, and we can neither hold him, nor safely let him go. Justice is in one scale, and self-preservation in the other.


## THE MONROE DOCTRINE (1823)[2]

Neither the British nor the Americans (for different reasons) wanted the Holy Alliance to intrude in the affairs of South America. The United States declined a British offer to make a joint pronouncement on the subject, and President James Monroe, instead, set forth the principles of American foreign policy that would forever bear his name. The Monroe Doctrine has no legal standing; it is simply a statement which has been much used (and abused) down to the present day.

At the proposal of the Russian Imperial Government, made through the minister of the Emperor residing here, a full power and instructions have been transmitted to the minister of the United States at St. Petersburg to arrange by amicable negotiation the respective rights and interests of the two nations on the northwest coast of this continent. A similar proposal had been made by

---

[1] Thomas Jefferson, Letter to John Holmes, April 22, 1820.

[2] James D. Richardson, ed., _A Compilation of the Messages and Papers of the Presidents_ (New York, 1897), II, 778, 786-88.

His Imperial Majesty to the Government of Great Britain, which has likewise been acceded to. The Government of the United States has been desirous by this friendly proceeding of manifesting the great value which they have invariably attached to the friendship of the Emperor and their solicitude to cultivate the best understanding with his Government. In the discussions to which this interest has given rise and in the arrangements by which they may terminate the occasion has been judged proper for asserting, as a principle in which the rights and interests of the United States are involved, that the American continents, by the free and independent condition which they have assumed and maintain, are henceforth not to be considered as subjects for further colonization by any European powers. . . .

Of events in that quarter of the globe [Europe], with which we have so much intercourse and from which we derive our origin, we have always been anxious and interested spectators. The citizens of the United States cherish sentiments the most friendly in favor of the liberty and happiness of their fellow-men on that side of the Atlantic. In the wars of the European powers in matters relating to themselves we have never taken any part, nor does it comport with our policy so to do. It is only when our rights are invaded or seriously menaced that we resent injuries or make preparation for our defense. With the movements in this hemisphere we are of necessity more immediately connected, and by causes which must be obvious to all enlightened and impartial observers. The political system of the allied powers is essentially different in this respect from that of America. This difference proceeds from that which exists in their respective Governments; and to the defense of our own, which has been achieved by the loss of so much blood and treasure, and matured by the wisdom of their most enlightened citizens, and under which we have enjoyed unexampled felicity, this whole nation is devoted. We owe it, therefore, to candor and to the amicable relations existing between the United States and those powers to declare that we should consider any attempt on their part to extend their system to any portion of this hemisphere as dangerous to our peace and safety. With the existing colonies or dependencies of any European power we have not interfered and shall not interfere. But with the Governments who have declared their independence and maintained it, and whose independence we have, on great consideration and on just principles, acknowledged, we could not view any interposition for the purpose of oppressing them, or controlling in any other manner their destiny, by any European power in any other light than as the manifestation of an unfriendly disposition toward the United States. In the war between those new Governments and Spain we declared our neutrality at the time of their recognition, and to this we have adhered, and shall continue to adhere, provided no change shall occur which, in the judgment of the competent authorities of this Government, shall make a corresponding change on the part of the United States indispensable to their security.

The late events in Spain and Portugal shew that Europe is still unsettled. Of this important fact no stronger proof can be adduced than that the allied powers should have thought it proper, on any principle satisfactory to themselves, to have interposed by force in the internal concerns of Spain. To what extent such interposition may be carried, on the same principle, is a question in which all independent powers whose governments differ from theirs are interested, even those most remote, and surely none more so than the United States. Our policy in regard to Europe, which was adopted at an early stage of the wars which have so long agitated that quarter of the globe, nevertheless remains the same, which is, not to interfere in the internal concerns of any of its powers; to consider the government *de facto* as the legitimate government for us; to cultivate friendly relations with it, and to preserve those relations by a frank, firm, and manly policy, meeting in all instances the just claims of every power, submitting to injuries from none. But in regard to those continents circumstances are eminently and conspicuously different. It is impossible that the allied powers should extend their political system to any portion of either continent without endangering our peace and happiness; nor can anyone believe that our southern brethren, if left to themselves, would adopt it of their own accord. It is equally impossible, therefore, that we should behold such interposition in any form with indifference. If we look to the comparative strength and resources of Spain and those new Governments, and their distance from each other, it must be obvious that she can never subdue them. It is still the true policy of the United States to leave the parties to themselves, in the hope that other powers will pursue the same course.

## PRINCE METTERNICH ON THE MONROE DOCTRINE (1824)

Prince Clemens von Metternich, Austrian foreign minister, was a principal architect of the European peace (or "concert") fashioned after the defeat of Napoleon in 1815. Profoundly conservative (to the point of being reactionary), Metternich insisted on a balance of power and a restoration of the legitimate seats of authority challenged by the French Revolution: aristocracy, monarchy, and conservative Christianity. His own dread of nationalism and revolution found international expression in the Holy Alliance, dominated by Austria, Russia, and Prussia. The Holy Alliance was pledged to oppose revolution anywhere it occurred, and to Metternich, America's bold endorsement of Latin American revolutions against Spanish rule was alarming. It seems odd today that a nation which, in the late twentieth century, stands in staunch opposition to Communist and other revolutions should itself have been so feared for the contagion of its revolution.

These United States of America, which we have seen arise and grow, and which during their too short youth already meditated projects which they dared not then avow, have suddenly left a sphere too narrow for their ambition, and have astonished Europe by a new act of revolt, more unprovoked, fully as audacious, and no less dangerous than the former. They have distinctly and clearly announced their intention to set not only power against power, but, to express it more exactly, altar against altar. In their indecent declarations they have cast blame and scorn on the institutions of Europe most worthy of

---

From <u>A History of the Monroe Doctrine</u> by Dexter Perkins. Copyright (c) 1963 by Dexter Perkins. By permission of Little, Brown and Company.

respect, on the principles of its greatest sovereigns, on the whole of those measures which a sacred duty no less than an evident necessity has forced our government to adopt to frustrate plans most criminal. In permitting themselves these unprovoked attacks, in fostering revolutions wherever they show themselves, in regretting those which have failed, in extending a helping hand to those which seem to prosper, they lend new strength to the apostles of sedition, and reanimate the courage of every conspirator. If this flood of evil doctrines and pernicious examples should extend over the whole of America, what would become of our religious and political institutions, of the moral force of our governments, and of that conservative system which has saved Europe from complete dissolution?

## THE INAUGURATION OF ANDREW JACKSON (1829)

Andrew Jackson was carried into the White House on a rising tide of democracy, and he enthusiastically cultivated his image of a man of the people, won earlier by his victory at the Battle of New Orleans and his invasion of Florida. The inaugural ceremony of 1829 reflected an awareness by Jackson and his Democratic party of the growing importance of the common man, but from an aristocrat's point of view neither the election of 1828 nor the subsequent inauguration had much to recommend them. Margaret Bayard Smith, a Washington society woman, recorded her impression of the inaugural ceremony and her fear of democracy.

I left the rest of this sheet for an account of the inauguration. It was not a thing of detail of a succession of small incidents. No, it was one grand whole, an imposing and majestic spectacle and to a reflective mind one of moral sublimity. Thousands and thousands of people, without distinction of rank, collected in an immense mass round the Capitol, silent, orderly and tranquil, with their eyes fixed on the front of that edifice, waiting the appearance of the President in the portico. The door from the Rotunda opens, preceded by the marshals, surrounded by the Judges of the Supreme Court, the old man with his grey locks, that crown of glory, advances, bows to the people, who greet him with a shout that rends the air, the Cannons, from the heights around, from Alexandria and Fort Warburton proclaim the oath he has taken and all the hills reverberate the sound. It was grand,--it was sublime! An almost breathless silence, succeeded and the multitude was still,-- listening to catch the sound of his voice, tho' it was so low, as to be heard only by those nearest to him. After reading his speech, the oath was administered to him by the Chief Justice. The Marshal presented the Bible.

---

Margaret Bayard Smith, The First Forty Years of Washington Society, ed. by Gaillard Hunt (New York, 1906), pp. 290-296.

The President took it from his hands, pressed his lips to it, laid it reverently down, then bowed again to the people--Yes, to the people in all their majesty. And had the spectacle closed here, even Europeans must have ackowledged that a free people, collected in their might, silent and tranquil, restrained solely by a moral power, without a shadow around of military force, was majesty, rising to sublimity, and far surpassing the majesty of Kings and Princes, surrounded with armies and glittering in gold. But I will not anticipate, but will give you an account of the inauguration in more detail. The whole of the preceding day, immense crowds were coming into the city from all parts, lodgings could not be obtained, and the newcomers had to go to George Town, which soon overflowed and others had to go to Alexandria. I was told the Avenue and adjoining streets were so crowded on Tuesday afternoon that it was difficult to pass.

A national salute was fired early in the morning, and ushered in the 4th of March. By ten oclock the Avenue was crowded with carriages of every description, from the splendid Barronet and coach, down to waggons and carts, filled with women and children, some in finery and some in rags, for it was the people's President, and all would see him . . . . Even from a distance he could be discerned from those who accompanied him, for he only was uncovered [hatless] (the servant in the presence of his Sovereign, the People). . . . [After the inauguration speech] with difficulty he made his way through the Capitol and down the hill to the gateway that opens on the avenue. Here for a moment he was stopped. The living mass was impenetrable. After a while a passage was opened, and he mounted his horse which had been provided for his return (for he had walked to the Capitol) then such a cortege as followed him! Countrymen, farmers, gentlemen, mounted and dismounted, boys, women and children, black and white . . . . [At the President's house] what a scene did we witness! The Majesty of the People had disappeared, and a rabble, a mob, of boys, negros, women, children, scrambling fighting, romping. What a pity what a pity! No arrangements had been made no police officers placed on duty and the whole house had been inundated by the rabble mob. We came too late. The President, after having been literally nearly pressed to death and almost suffocated and torn to pieces by the people in their eagerness to shake hands with Old Hickory, had retreated through the back way of south front and had escaped to his lodgings at Gadsby's. Cut glass and china to the amount of several thousand dollars had been broken in the struggle to get the refreshments, punch and other articles had been carried out in tubs and buckets, but had it been in hogsheads it would have been insufficient, ice-creams, and cake and lemonade, for 20,000 people, for it is said that number were there, tho' I think the estimate exaggerated. Ladies fainted, men were seen with bloody noses and such a scene of confusion took place as is impossible to describe,--those who got in could not get out by the door again, but had to scramble out of windows. At one time, the President who had retreated and retreated until he was pressed against the wall, could only be secured by a number of gentlemen forming round him and making a kind of barrier of their own bodies, and the pressure was so great that Col Bomford who was one said that at one time he was afraid they should have been pushed down, or on the President. It was then the windows were thrown open, and the torrent found an outlet, which otherwise might have proved fatal.

This concourse had not been anticipated and therefore not provided against. Ladies and gentlemen, only had been expected at this Levee, not the people en masse. But it was the People's day, and the People's President and the People would rule. God grant that one day or other, the People, do not put down all rule and rulers. I fear, enlightened Freemen as they are, they will be found, as they have been found in all ages and countries where they get the Power in their hands, that of all tyrants, they are the most ferocious, cruel and despotic.

## THE SOUTH CAROLINA PROTEST AGAINST THE TARIFF OF 1828 (1828)

After the passage of the Tariff of 1828--the "Tariff of Abominations"--Vice-President John C. Calhoun wrote an attack on the tariff entitled the "South Carolina Exposition and Protest," in which he outlined the theory of nullification. The Protest, which followed Calhoun's Exposition, was adopted by the legislature of South Carolina.

The Senate and House of Representatives of South Carolina, now met and sitting in General Assembly--through the Honorable William Smith, and the Honorable Robert Y. Hayne, their representatives in the Senate of the United States, do, in the name and on behalf of the good people of the said Commonwealth, solemnly protest against the system of protecting duties lately adopted by the Federal Government, for the following reasons:
 1. Because the good people of this Commonwealth believe that the powers of Congress were delegated to it in trust for the accomplishment of certain specified objects which limit and control them, and that every exercise of them for any other purposes is a violation of the Constitution as unwarrantable as the undisguised assumption of substantive independent powers not granted or expressly withheld.
 2. Because the power to lay duties on imports is, and in its very nature can be, only a means of effecting objects specified by the constitution; since no free government, and least of all a government of enumerated powers, can of right impose any tax (any more than a penalty,) which is not at once justified by public necessity, and clearly within the scope and purview of the social compact, and since the right of confining appropriations of the public money to such legitimate and constitutional objects, is as essential to the liberties of the people, as their unquestionable privilege to be taxed only by their own consent.
 3. Because they believe that the Tariff Law, passed by Congress at its last session, and all other acts of which the principal object is the protection of manufactures, or any other branch of domestic industry--if they be considered as the exercise of a supposed power in Congress, to tax the people at its own good will and pleasure, and to apply the money raised to objects not specified in the Constitution--is a violation of these fundamental principles, a breach of a well defined trust and a perversion of the high powers vested in the Federal Government for Federal purposes only.

---

Clyde N. Wilson and W. Edwin Hemphill, eds., The Papers of John C. Calhoun (Columbia, SC, 1977), X, 535-539.

4. Because such acts considered in the light of a regulation of commerce are equally liable to objection--since although the power to regulate commerce, may like other powers, be exercised so as to protect domestic manufactures, yet it is clearly distinguishable from a power to do so <u>eo nomine</u>, both in the nature of the thing and in the common acceptation of the terms; and because the confounding of them would lead to the most extravagant results, since the encouragement of domestic industry implies an absolute control over all the interests, resources and pursuits of a people, and is inconsistent with the idea of any other than a simple consolidated government.

5. Because from the contemporaneous exposition of the Constitution, in the numbers of the Federalist, (which is cited only because the Supreme Court has recognized its authority,) it is clear that the power to regulate commerce was considered by the convention as only incidentally connected with the encouragement of agriculture and manufactures; and because the power of laying imposts and duties on imports, was not understood to justify in any case a prohibition of foreign commodities, except as a means of extending commerce by coercing foreign nations to a fair reciprocity in their intercourse with us, or for some bona fide commercial purpose.

6. Because that whilst the power to protect manufactures is no where expressly granted to Congress, nor can be considered as necessary and proper to carry into effect any specified power, it seems to be expressly reserved to the States by the tenth section of the first article of the Constitution.

7. Because even admitting Congress to have a constitutional right to protect manufactures by the imposition of the duties or by regulations of commerce, designed principally for that purpose, yet a Tariff of which the operation is grossly unequal and oppressive, is such an abuse of power, as is incompatible with the principles of a free government and the great ends of civil society, justice and equality of rights and protection.

8. Finally, because South Carolina, from her climate, situation, and peculiar institutions, is, and must ever continue to be, wholly dependent upon agriculture and commerce, not only for her prosperity, but for her very existence as a state--because the valuable products of her soil--the blessings by which Divine Providence seems to have designed to compensate for the great disadvantages under which she suffers in other respects--are among the very few that can be cultivated with any profit by slave labor--and if by the loss of her foreign commerce, these products should be confined to an inadequate market, the fate of this fertile State would be poverty and utter desolation--her citizens in despair would emigrate to more fortunate regions, and the whole frame and constitution of her civil polity be impaired and deranged, if not dissolved entirely.

Deeply impressed with these considerations, the Representatives of the good people of this Commonwealth, anxiously desiring to live in peace with their fellow citizens, and to do all that in them lies to preserve and perpetuate the union of the States and liberties of which it is the surest pledge--but feeling it to be their bounden duty to expose and to resist all encroachments upon the true spirit of the Constitution, lest an apparant acquiescence in the system of protecting duties should be drawn into precedent, do, in the name of the Commonwealth of South Carolina, claim to enter upon the journals of the [U.S.] Senate, their protest against it as unconstitutional, oppressive, and unjust.

# ANDREW JACKSON ON NULLIFICATION (1831)

When the state of South Carolina adopted an Ordinance of Nullification against the 1828 "Tariff of Abominations," President Andrew Jackson responded quickly and forcefully in the following proclamation. As Jackson asked in a private letter at about this same time, "can any one of common sense believe the absurdity that. . . a state has right to. . .nullify the laws of the union. . . [without] our constitution [becoming] a rope of sand. . . ."

The ordinance is founded, not on the indefeasible right of resisting acts which are plainly unconstitutional and too oppressive to be endured, but on the strange position that any one State may not only declare an act of Congress void, but prohibit its execution; that they may do this consistently with the Constitution; that the true construction of that instrument permits a State to retain its place in the Union and yet be bound by no other of its laws than those it may choose to consider as constitutional. It is true, they add, that to justify this abrogation of a law it must be palpably contrary to the Constitution; but it is evident that to give the right of resisting laws of that description, coupled with the uncontrolled right to decide what laws deserve that character, is to give the power of resisting all laws; for as by the theory there is no appeal, the reasons alleged by the State, good or bad, must prevail. If it should be said that public opinion is a sufficient check against the abuse of this power, it may be asked why it is not deemed a sufficient guard against the passage of an unconstitutional act by Congress? There is, however, a restraint in this last case which makes the assumed power of a State more indefensible, and which does not exist in the other. There are two appeals from an unconstitutional act passed by congress--one to the judiciary, the other to the people and the States. There is no appeal from the State decision in theory, and the practical illustration shows that the courts are closed against an application to review it, both judges and jurors being sworn to decide in its favor. But reasoning on this subject is superfluous when our social compact, in express terms, declares that the laws of the United States, its Constitution, and treaties made under it are the supreme law of the land, and, for greater caution, adds "that the judges in every State shall be bound thereby, anything in the constitution or laws of any State to the contrary notwithstanding." And it may be asserted without fear of refutation that no federative government could exist without a similar provision. Look for a moment to the consequence. If South Carolina considers the revenue laws unconstitutional and has a right to prevent their execution in the port of Charleston, there would be a clear constitutional objection to their collection in every other port; and no revenue could be collected anywhere, for all imposts must be equal . . . .

If this doctrine had been established at an earlier day, the Union would have been dissolved in its infancy . . . .

I consider, then, the power to annul a law of the United States, assumed by one State, incompatible with the existence of the Union, contradicted expressly by the letter of the Constitution, unauthorized by its spirit, inconsistent with every principle on which it was founded, and destructive of the great object for which it was formed.

James D. Richardson, ed., A Compilation of the Messages and Papers of the Presidents (Washington, D.C., 1908), II, 651-656.

After this general view of the leading principle, we must examine the particular application of it which is made in the ordinance.

The preamble rests its justification on these grounds: It assumes as a fact that the obnoxious laws, although they purport to be laws for raising revenue, were in reality intended for the protection of manufactures, which purpose it asserts to be unconstitutional; that the operation of these laws is unequal; that the amount raised by them is greater than is required by the wants of the Government; and, finally, that the proceeds are to be applied to objects unauthorized by the Constitution. . . .The first virtually acknowledges that the law in question was passed under a power expressly given by the Constitution to lay and collect imposts; but its constitutionality is drawn in question from the motives of those who passed it. However apparent this purpose may be in the present case, nothing can be more dangerous than to admit the position that an unconstitutional purpose entertained by the members who assent to a law enacted under a constitutional power shall make the law void. For how is that purpose to be ascertained?. . . Admit this doctrine, and you give to the States an uncontrolled right to decide, and every law may be annulled under this pretext. If, therefore, the absurd and dangerous doctrine should be admitted that a State may annul an unconstitutional law, or one that it deems such, it will not apply to the present case.

The next objection is that the laws in question operate unequally. This objection may be made with truth to every law that has been or can be passed. The wisdom of man never yet contrived a system of taxation that would operate with perfect equality. If the unequal operation of a law makes it unconstitutional, and if all laws of that description may be abrogated by any State for that cause, then, indeed, is the Federal Constitution unworthy of the slightest effort for its preservation. . . .

The Constitution declares that the judicial powers of the United States extend to cases arising under the laws of the United States, and that such laws, the Constitution, and treaties shall be paramount to the State constitutions and laws. The judiciary act prescribes the mode by which the case may be brought before a court of the United States by appeal when a State tribunal shall decide against this provision of the Constitution. The ordinance declares there shall be no appeal--makes the State law paramount to the Constitution and laws of the United States, forces judges and jurors to swear that they will disregard their provisions, and even makes it penal in a suitor to attempt relief by appeal. It further declares that it shall not be lawful for the authorities of the United States or of that State to enforce the payment of duties imposed by the revenue laws within its limits.

Here is a law of the United States, not even pretended to be unconstitutional, repealed by the authority of a small majority of the voters of a single State. Here is a provision of the Constitution which is solemnly abrogated by the same authority.

On such expositions and reasonings the ordinance grounds not only an assertion of the right to annul the laws of which it complains, but to enforce it by a threat of seceding from the Union if any attempt is made to execute them.

This right to secede is deduced from the nature of the Constitution, which, they say, is a compact between sovereign States who have preserved their whole sovereignty and therefore are subject to no superior; that because they made the compact they can break it when in their opinion it has been departed from by the other States. Fallacious as this course of reasoning is, it enlists State pride and finds advocates in the honest prejudices of those who have not studied the nature of our Government sufficiently to see the radical error on which it rests . . . .

The Constitution of the United States, then, forms a <u>government</u>, not a league; and whether it be formed by compact between the States or in any other manner, its character is the same. It is a Government in which all the people are represented, which operates directly on the people individually, not upon the States; they retained all the power they did not grant. But each State, having expressly parted with so many powers as to constitute, jointly with the other States, a single nation, cannot, from that period, possess any right to secede, because such secession does not break a league, but destroys the unity of a nation; and any injury to that unity is not only a breach which would result from the contravention of a compact, but it is an offense against the whole Union. To say that any State may at pleasure secede from the Union is to say that the United States are not a nation, because it would be a solecism to contend that any part of a nation might dissolve its connection with the other parts, to their injury or ruin, without committing any offense. Secession, like any other revolutionary act, may be morally justified by the extremity of oppression; but to call it a constitutional right is confounding the meaning of terms, and can only be done through gross error or to deceive those who are willing to assert a right, but would pause before they made a revolution or incur the penalties consequent on a failure. . . .

An attempt, by force of arms, to destroy a government is an offense, by whatever means the constitutional compact may have been formed: and such government has the right by the law of self-defense to pass acts for punishing the offender, unless that right is modified, restrained, or resumed by the constitutional act. In our system, although it is modified in the case of treason, yet authority is expressly given to pass all laws necessary to carry its powers into effect, and under this grant provision has been made for punishing acts which obstruct the due administration of the laws . . . .

This, then, is the position in which we stand: A small majority of the citizens of one State in the Union have elected delegates to a State convention; that convention has ordained that all the revenue laws of the United States must be repealed, or that they are no longer a member of the Union. The governor of that State has recommended to the legislature the raising of an army to carry the secession into effect, and that he may be empowered to give clearances to vessels in the name of the State. No act of violent opposition to the laws has yet been committed, but such a state of things is hourly apprehended. And it is the intent of this instrument to <u>proclaim</u>, not only that the duty imposed on me by the Constitution "to take care that the laws be faithfully executed" shall be performed to the extent of the powers already vested in me by law, or of such others as the wisdom of Congress shall devise and intrust to me for that purpose, but to warn the citizens of South Carolina who have been deluded into an opposition to the laws of the danger they will incur by obedience to the illegal and disorganizing ordinance of the convention; to exhort those who have refused to support it to persevere in their determination to uphold the Constitution and laws of their country; and to point out to all the perilous situation into which the good people of that State have been led, and that the course they are urged to pursue is one of ruin and disgrace to the very State whose rights they affect to support.

If your leaders could succeed in establishing a separation, what would be your situation? Are you united at home? Are you free from the apprehension of civil discord, with all its fearful consequences? Do our neighboring republics, every day suffering some new revolution or contending with some new insurrection, do they excite your envy? But the dictates of a high duty oblige me solemnly to announce that you cannot succeed. The laws of the United States must be executed. I have no discretionary power on the subject; my duty is emphatically pronounced in the Constitution. Those who told you that you might peaceably prevent their execution deceived you; they could not have been deceived themselves. They know that a forcible opposition could alone prevent the execution of the laws, and they know that such opposition must be repelled. Their object is disunion. But be not deceived by names. Disunion by armed force is treason. Are you really ready to incure its guilt? If you are, on the heads of the instigators of the act be the dreadful consequences; on their heads be the dishonor, but on yours may fall the punishment. On your unhappy State will inevitably fall all the evils of the conflict you force upon the Government of your country . . . .

Having the fullest confidence in the justness of the legal and constitutional opinion of my duties which as been expressed, I rely with equal confidence on your undivided support in my determination to execute the laws, to preserve the Union by all constitutional means, to arrest, if possible, by moderate and firm measures the necessity of a recourse to force; and if it be the will of Heaven that the recurrence of its primeval curse on man for the shedding of a brother's blood should fall upon our land, that it be not called down by any offensive act on the part of the United States.

Fellow-citizens, the momentous case is before you. On your undivided support of your Government depends the decision of the great question it involves--whether your sacred Union will be preserved and the blessing it secures to us as one people shall be perpetuated . . . .

May the Great Ruler of Nations grant that the signal blessings with which He has favored ours may not, by the madness of party or personal ambition, be disregarded and lost; and may His wise providence bring those who have produced this crisis to see the folly before they feel the misery of civil strife, and inspire a returning veneration for that Union which, if we may dare to penetrate His designs, He has chosen as the only means of attaining the high destinies to which we may reasonably aspire.


ANDREW JACKSON ON THE NATIONAL BANK (1832)

As part of a ruse amidst the usual turmoil of a presidential election year, supporters of the Second National Bank of the United States (B.U.S.) persuaded the head of the Bank, Nicholas Biddle, to apply in 1832 for a renewal of the Bank's charter, which would not expire until 1835. Congress approved Biddle's request, and the bill was sent to President Andrew Jackson. Henry Clay and his supporters fully expected Jackson, whose hatred

---

U.S. Congress, 22nd Cong., 1st sess., July 10, 1832, <u>Register</u> of <u>Debates</u>, vol. III, Appendix, pp. 73-79.

for the National Bank was well known, to veto the bill, but they believed that by doing so Jackson would lose enough political support to swing the 1832 election to Clay. Jackson did not disappoint his opponents in attaching a fierce veto message to the bill. Thus, although the first part of the anti-Jackson scheme proceeded according to plan, the second part went awry-- Jackson was re-elected.

    The bill "to modify and continue" the act entitled " An act to incorporate the subscribers to the Bank of the United States," was presented to me on the 4th of July instant. Having considered it with that solemn regard to the principles of the constitution which the day was calculated to inspire, and come to the conclusion that it ought not to become a law, I herewith return it to the Senate, in which it originated, with my objections.
    A Bank of the United States is, in many respects, convenient for the Government, and useful to the people. Entertaining this opinion, and deeply impressed with the belief that some of the powers and privileges possessed by the existing bank are unauthorized by the constitution, subversive of the rights of the States, and dangerous to the liberties of the people, I felt it my duty, at an early period of my administration, to call the attention of Congress to the practicability of organizing an institution combining all its advantages, and obviating these objections. I sincerely regret that, in the act before me, I can perceive none of those modifications of the bank charter which are necessary, in my opinion, to make it compatible with justice, with sound policy, or with the constitution of our country.
    The present corporate body, denominated the President, Directors, and Company of the Bank of the United States, will have existed, at the time this act is intended to take effect, twenty years. It enjoys an exclusive privilege of banking under the authority of the General Government, a monopoly of its favor and support, and, as a necesary consequence, almost a monopoly of the foreign and domestic exchange. The powers, privileges, and favors bestowed upon it in the original charter, by increasing the value of the stock far above its par value, operated as a gratuity of many millions to the stockholders. . . .
    The act before me proposes another gratuity to the holders of the same stock, and in many cases to the same men, of at least seven millions more. . . . More than eight millions of the stock of this bank are held by foreigners. By this act the American republic proposes virtually to make them a present of some millions of dollars. . . .
    Every monopoly, and all exclusive privileges, are granted at the expense of the public, which ought to receive a fair equivalent. The many millions which this act proposes to bestow on the stockholders of the existing bank, must come directly or indirectly out of the earnings of the American people. . . .
    But this act does not permit competition in the purchase of this monopoly. It seems to be predicated on the erroneous idea that the present stockholders have a prescriptive right, not only to the favor, but to the bounty of the government. It appears that more than a fourth part of the stock is held by foreigners, and the residue is held by a few hundred of our citizens, chiefly of the richest class. For their benefit does this act exclude the whole American people from competition in the purchase of this monopoly, and dispose of it for many millions less than it is worth. . . .

It has been urged as an argument in favor of rechartering the present bank, that calling in its loans will produce great embarrassment and distress. The time allowed to close its concerns is ample; and if it has been well managed, its pressure will be light, and heavy only in case its management has been bad. If, therefore, it shall produce distress, the fault will be its own, and it would furnish a reason against renewing a power which has been so obviously abused. . . .

The modifications of the existing charter, proposed by this act, are not such, in my view, as make it consistent with the rights of the States, or the liberties of the people. . . .

As little stock is held in the West, it is obvious that the debt of the people in that section to the bank is principally a debt to the Eastern and foreign stockholders; that the interest they pay upon it is carried into the Eastern States and into Europe; and that it is a burden upon their industry, and a drain of their currency, which no country can bear without inconvenience and occasional distress. . . .

Is there no danger to our liberty and independence in a bank that, in its nature, has so little to bind it to our country? The president of the bank has told us that most of the State banks exist by its forbearance. Should its influence become concentred, as it may under the operation of such an act as this in the hands of a self-elected directory, whose interests are identified with those of the foreign stockholder, will there not be cause to tremble for the purity of our elections in peace, and for the independence of our country in war? Their power would be great whenever they might choose to exert it; but if this monopoly were regularly renewed every fifteen or twenty years, on terms proposed by themselves, they might seldom in peace put forth their strength to influence elections or control the affairs of the nation. But if any private citizen or public functionary should interpose to curtail its powers, or prevent a renewal of its privileges, it cannot be doubted that he would be made to feel its influence.

Should the stock of the bank principally pass into the hands of the subjects of a foreign country, and we should unfortunately become involved in a war with that country, what would be our condition? Of the course which would be pursued by a bank almost wholly owned by the subjects of a foreign Power, and managed by those whose interests, if not affections, would run in the same direction, there can be no doubt. All its operations within would be in aid of the hostile fleets and armies without: controlling our currency, receiving our public moneys, and holding thousands of our citizens in dependence, it would be more formidable and dangerous than the naval and military power of the enemy. . . .

It is maintained by the advocates of the bank, that its constitutionality, in all its features, ought to be considered as settled by precedent, and by the decision of the Supreme Court. To this conclusion I cannot assent. Mere precedent is a dangerous source of authority, and should not be regarded as deciding questions of constitutional power, except where the acquiescence of the people and the States can be considered as well settled. So far from this being the case on this subject, an argument against the bank might be based on precedent. One Congress, in 1791, decided in favor of a bank; another, in 1811, decided against it. One Congress, in 1815, decided against a bank; another, in 1816, decided in its favor. Prior to the present Congress, therefore, the precedents drawn from that source were equal. If we resort to the States, the expressions of legislative, judicial, and executive opinions against the bank have been, probably, to those in its favor, as four to one. There is nothing in precedent, therefore, which, if its authority were admitted, ought to weigh in favor of the act before me. . . .

The bonus which is exacted from the bank, is a confession, upon the face of the act, that the powers granted by it are greater than are "necessary" to its character as a fiscal agent. . . .

It is, therefore, for "exclusive privileges and benefits," conferred for their own use and emolument, and not for the advantage of the Government, that a bonus is exacted. These surplus powers, for which the bank is required to pay, cannot be "necessary" to make it the fiscal agent of the treasury. If they were, the exaction of a bonus for them would not be "proper."

It is maintained by some that the bank is a means of executing the constitutional power "to coin money, and regulate the value thereof." Congress have established a mint to coin money, and passed laws to regulate the value thereof. The money so coined, with its value so regulated, and such foreign coins as Congress may adopt, are the only currency known to the constitution. But if they have other power to regulate the currency, it was conferred to be exercised by themselves, and not to be transferred to a corporation. If the bank be established for that purpose, with a charter unalterable without its consent, Congress have parted with their power for a term of years, during which the consitution is a dead letter. It is neither necessary nor proper to transfer its legislative power to such a bank, and therefore unconstitutional. . . .

There are no necessary evils in Government. Its evils exist only in its abuses. If it would confine itself to equal protection, and, as Heaven does its rains, shower its favors alike on the high and the low, the rich and the poor, it would be an unqualified blessing. In the act before me there seems to be a wide and unnecessary departure from these just principles.

Nor is our Government to be maintained, or our Union preserved, by invasions of the rights and powers of the several States. In thus attempting to make our General Government strong, we make it weak. Its true strength consists in leaving individuals and States, as much as possible, to themselves; in making itself felt, not in its power, but in its beneficence-- not in its control, but in its protection--not in binding the States more closely to the centre, but leaving each to move, unobstructed, in its proper orbit.

Experience should teach us wisdom. Most of the difficulties our Government now encounters, and most of the dangers which impend over our Union, have sprung from an abandonment of the legitimate objects of Government by our national legislation, and the adoption of such principles as are embodied in this act. Many of our rich men have not been content with equal protection and equal benefits, but have besought us to make them richer by act of Congress. By attempting to gratify their desires, we have, in the results of our legislation, arrayed section against section, interest against interest, and man against man, in a fearful commotion, which threatens to shake the foundations of our Union. It is time to pause in our career, to review our principles, and, if possible, revive that devoted spirit of patriotism and spirit of compromise which distinguished the sages of the revolution and the fathers of our Union. If we cannot, at once, in justice to interests vested under improvident legislation, make our Government what it ought to be, we can, at least, take a stand against all new grants of monopolies and exclusive privileges, against any prostitution of our

Government to the advancement of the few at the expense of the many, and in favor of compromise and gradual reform in code of laws and system of political economy.

## GEORGE CATLIN ON THE NORTH AMERICAN INDIAN (1839)

Between 1832 and 1839, George Catlin travelled among the Indian tribes from the Mississippi River westward to the Rocky Mountains. As the self-styled "historian" of the Plains Indians, Catlin visited 48 tribes and amassed a portfolio of over 500 oil paintings. At the end of his journey, Catlin offered this prediction.

The peculiar condition in which we are obliged to contemplate these most unfortunate people at this time--hastening to destruction and extinction, as they evidently are, lays an uncompromising claim upon the sympathies of the civilized world, and gives a deep interest and value to such records as are truly made--setting up, and perpetuating from the life, their true native character and customs.

If the great family of North American Indians were all dying by a scourge or epidemic of the country, it would be natural, and a virtue, to weep for them; but merely to sympathize with them (and but partially to do that) when they are dying at our hands, and rendering their glebe [land] to our possession, would be to subvert the simplest law of Nature, and turn civilized man, with all his boasted virtues, back to worse than savage barbarism.

Justice to a nation who are dying, need never be expected from the hands of their destroyers; and where injustice and injury are visited upon the weak and defenceless, from ten thousand hands--from Governments--monopolies and individuals--the offence is lost in the inseverable iniquity in which all join, and for which nobody is answerable, unless it be for their respective amounts, at a final day of retribution.

Long and cruel experience has well proved that it is impossible for enlightened Governments or money-making individuals to deal with these credulous and unsophisticated people, without the sin of injustice; but the humble biographer or historian, who goes amongst them from a different motive, may come out of their country with his hands and his conscience clean, and himself an anomaly, a white man dealing with Indians, and meting out justice to them; which I hope it may be my good province to do with my pen and my brush, with which, at least, I will have the singular and valuable satisfaction of having done them no harm. . . .

The present condition of these once numerous people, contrasted with what it was, and what it is soon to be, is a subject of curious interest, as well as some importance, to the civilized world--a subject well entitled to the attention, and very justly commanding the sympathies of, enlightened

---

George Catlin, Letters and Notes on the Manners, Customs, and Conditions of the North American Indians (London, 1844), II, Letter 58.

communities. There are abundant proofs recorded in the history of this country, and to which I need not at this time more particularly refer, to shew that this very numerous and respectable part of the human family, which occupied the different parts of North America, at the time of its first settlement by the Anglo-Americans, contained more than fourteen millions, who have been reduced since that time, and undoubtedly in consequence of that settlement, to something less than two millions!

This is a startling fact, and one which carries with it, if it be the truth, other facts and their results, which are equally startling, and such as every inquiring mind should look into. The first deduction that the mind draws from such premises, is the rapid declension of these people, which must at that rate be going on at this day; and sooner or later, lead to the most melancholy result of their final extinction.

Of this sad termination of their existence, there need not be a doubt in the minds of any man who will read the history of their former destruction; contemplating them swept already from two-thirds of the Continent; and who will then travel as I have done, over the vast extent of Frontier, and witness the modes by which the poor fellows are falling, whilst contending for their rights, with acquisitive white men. Such a reader, and such a traveller, I venture to say, if he has not the heart of a brute, will shed tears for them; and be ready to admit that their character and customs, are at <u>this time</u>, a subject of interest and importance, and rendered peculiarly so from the facts that they are dying <u>at the hands</u> of their Christian neighbours; and, from all past experience, that there will probably be no effectual plan instituted, that will save the remainder of them from a similar fate. As they stand at this day, there may be four or five hundred thousand in their primitive state; and a milion and a half, that may be said to be semi-civilized, contending with the sophistry of white men, amongst whom they are timidly and unsuccessfuly endeavouring to hold up their heads, and aping their modes; whilst they are swallowing their poisons, and yielding their lands and their lives, to the superior tact and cunning of their merciless cajolers. . . .

For the Christian and philanthropist, in any part of the world, there is enough, I am sure, in the character, condition, and history of these unfortunate people, to engage his sympathies—for the Nation, there is an unrequited account of sin and injustice that sooner or later will call for <u>national retribution</u>—and for the American citizens, who live, every where proud of their growing wealth and their luxuries, over the bones of these poor fellows, who have surrendered their hunting-grounds and their lives, to the enjoyment of their cruel dispossessors, there is a lingering terror yet, I fear, for the reflecting minds, whose mortal bodies must soon take their humble places with their red, but injured brethren, under the same glebe; to appear and stand, at last, with guilt's shivering conviction, amidst the myriad ranks of accusing spirits, that are to rise in their own fields, at the final day of resurrection!

# DAVID WALKER'S APPEAL (1829)[1]

David Walker was a free black born in 1785 in North Carolina. He moved to Boston in the 1820's, declaring that he could no longer bear being surrounded by slavery. There he penned <u>The Appeal</u>, a bloody call for the slaves to seize their freedom. Walker's assertion that God would be with them because their cause was just was the first major attack on the South's schizophrenic posture of Bible in one hand and bullwhip in the other. The response of Dixie was electric--Southern legislatures went to fantastic lengths to suppress the pamphlet.

Get the blacks started, and if you do not have a gang of tigers and lions to deal with, I am a deceiver of the blacks and of the whites. . . . If you commence, make sure work--do not trifle, for they will not trifle with you--they want us for their slaves, and think nothing of murdering us in order to subject us to that wretched condition--therefore, if there is an <u>attempt</u> made by us, kill or be <u>killed</u>. Now, I ask you, had you not rather be killed than to be a slave to a tyrant, who take the life of your mother, wife, and dear little children? Look upon your mother, wife and children, and answer God Almighty; and believe this, that it is no more harm for you to kill a man, who is trying to kill you, than it is for you to take a drink of water when thirsty. . . .

I pray that the Lord may undeceive my ignorant brethren, and permit them to throw away pretensions, and seek after the substance of learning. . . . For coloured people to acquire learning in this country, makes tyrants quake and tremble on their sandy foundation. . . . Do you suppose one man of good sense and learning would submit himself, his father, mother, wife and children, to be slaves to a wretched man like himself, who, instead of compensating him for his labours, chains, hand-cuffs and beats him and family almost to death?. . . No! no! he would cut his devilish throat from ear to ear, and well do slave-holders know it. The bare name of educating the coloured people, scares our cruel oppressors almost to death. . . . The whites shall have enough of the blacks, yet, as true as God sits on his throne in Heaven.


# THE REACTION TO THE NAT TURNER INSURRECTION (1831)[2]

The revolt in Southampton County, Virginia, unleashed a paroxysm of fear that swept through the South in a frightful fashion. After a decade of unease and mounting slave restlessness, Nat Turner's revolt had such a

---

[1] David Walker, <u>The Appeal</u> (Boston, 1829), pp. 25-26, 31-32.

[2] "The Effects of David Walker's <u>Appeal</u> and Nat Turner's Insurrection on North Carolina," Derris L. Raper unpublished Master's Thesis, University of North Carolina, 1969, pp. 53-55.

devastating effect on the mind of the South that some historians believe it caused something akin to a collective nervous breakdown. The following passages deal with various reactions to the Virginia insurrection within the state of North Carolina.

A prominent North Carolinian described the state of things in a letter to the Governor. He had witnessed great mental stress among the females. "Many ladies fled to the woods and remained out all night, several of whom with their children have since been extremely sick." There had been several false alarms which had done much damage psychologically, and had even resulted in the deaths of three North Carolinians. Thomas Weston, an old and respectable farmer, was literally frightened to death when a false alarm was given by a man from Northampton. Borland had also heard of two other deaths in the same manner a little distance from Murfreesboro.

In order to demonstrate what the state of several neighborhoods had been because of such alarms, Borland related the one that he himself had experienced. He had been in a house where a dozen or so ladies had assembled for safety, when a man rode up in great haste and informed them that a considerable number of Negroes were within two miles of their house. "The immediate cries of the women, as to what they should do for safety, and the frantic distress depicted in each face, gave me feelings, I have not words to express." They remained in this state of fear and anxiety for about thirty minutes before a messenger arrived and told them it was a false alarm.

During the excitement several incidents occurred in the Murfreesboro area which indicated the state of the public mind. A slave from Ahosky Ridge had obtained a forged pass and attempted to go through Murfreesboro on his way to Southampton, having told another Negro before he left home that there would be a war between the black and white people. He was shot by the town guard. "They then cut off his head, stuck it on a pole, and planted the pole at the cross streets . . . ." The body was thrown in "the bottom." On the same day a lady and her children were heading for town when her driver "behaved imprudently" and frightened her. When she reached town, the driver was put to death. Another Negro had been caught travelling through the country in woman's dress and had been thrown in jail.

On September 12, 1831, word reached Wilmington that two hundred blacks were within twenty miles of Wilmington. Curtis recorded vividly, "Bless me! now the explosion has taken place indeed and the women (some of them he-woman) are in a desperate taking." Venturing out to discover the truth he found "fear and despair, what confusion! The women were all flying or fled with their trinkets and mattresses to the garrison." When Curtis reached the garrison, he found 120 women packed in a small dwelling . . . half dead with fear. One was stretched out on a mattress in the hysterics, a number fainted, and one was jabbering nonsense in a fit of derangement. A few men too noticed with tremulous voices, and solemn visages, pacing back and forth in fearful anxiety. Hang 'em! thought I." Curtis found that nor arrangements had been made for the night so he returned home. He believed that his was the only family outside of the garrison. He considered the whole affair a contemptible fuss caused by a lack of reason and judgment, but he was sure that " . . . . few eyes will close in this town tonight."

The whole available white population of Wilmington had been put under arms when they received the report that the blacks were just outside of the city. The excitement was painful as they waited many hours expecting an attack. Four blacks were shot without trial and their heads placed on poles in different parts of the town--"a measure indispensable to the safety of the community," declared the Wilmington Cape Fear Recorder. Charlotte Hooper, the mother of John De Berniere Hooper, a tutor and professor at the University of North Carolina, wrote her son that he would be shocked when he saw in the papers that the state of excitement which had existed for some time had been so great that it had " . . . . led to the execution of four men in a manner which would gladly have been avoided; but four viler more disbolical wretches never suffered the penalty of their crimes." Ironically she recorded that although the patrols were very vigilant, there had not occurred " . . . . any instance of violence or unnecessary severity."

Thousands of militia were under arms, notwithstanding " . . . . that not a single party of negroes, nay, not a single individual (had) been found in arms or in rebellion . . . . " Slaves were imprisoned wholesale, and the jail was crowded with the accused. The town was strongly guarded and nearly all the citizens were under arms almost constantly for eleven days. Charlotte Hooper asserted that "we are all . . . . much exhausted in mind by anxiety and apprehension. I get very little sleep tho [sic] told the town is so well guarded it cannot be unsafe in any part of it."

## WILLIAM LLOYD GARRISON ON THE ABOLITION OF SLAVERY (1831)

> Garrison's well-earned reputation as a radical abolitionist was enhanced enormously when he began publishing the inflammatory weekly, The Liberator. Widely denounced in the South for his uncompromising assaults on slavery, Garrison offended Northern conservatives as well, and helped to generate the sort of internecine antagonism that eventually made the Civil War possible.

During my recent tour for the purpose of exciting the minds of the people by a series of discourses on the subject of slavery, every place that I visited gave fresh evidence of the fact, that a greater revolution in public sentiment was to be effected in the free states--and particularly in New England--than at the South. I found contempt more bitter, opposition more active, detraction more relentless, prejudice more stubborn, and apathy more frozen, than among slave-owners themselves. Of course, there were individual exceptions to the contrary. This state of things afflicted, but did not dishearten me. I determined, at every hazard, to lift up the standard of emancipation in the eyes of the nation, within sight of Bunker Hill and in the birthplace of liberty. That standard is now unfurled; and long may it float, unhurt by the spoliations of time or the missiles of a desperate foe--yea, till every chain be broken, and every bondman set free! Let Southern oppressors tremble--let their secret abettors tremble--let their Northern apologists tremble--let all the enemies of the persecuted blacks tremble. . . .

Quoted in William Lloyd Garrison, 1805-1879: The Story of His Life Told By His Children (New York, 1885) I, 224-225.

Assenting to the "self-evident truth" maintained in the American Declaration of Independence, "that all men are created equal, and endowed by their Creator with certain inalienable rights--among which are life, liberty, and the pursuit of happiness," I shall strenuously contend for the immediate enfranchisement of our slave population. In Park-Street Church, on the Fourth of July, 1829, in an address on slavery, I unreflectingly assented to the popular but pernicious doctrine of <u>gradual</u> abolition. I seize this opportunity to make a full and unequivocal recantation, and thus publicly to ask pardon of my God, of my country, and of my brethren the poor slaves, for having uttered a sentiment so full of timidity, injustice, and absurdity. . . .

I am aware that many object to the severity of my language; but is there not cause for severity? I <u>will be</u> as harsh as truth, and as uncompromising as justice. On this subject, I do not wish to think or speak, or write, with moderation. No! no! Tell a man whose house is on fire to giver a moderate alarm; tell him to moderately rescue his wife from the hands of the ravisher; tell the mother to gradually extricate her babe from the fire into which it has fallen; but urge me not to use moderation in a cause like the present. I am in earnest--I will not equivocate--I will not excuse--I will not retreat a single inch--AND I WILL BE HEARD. The apathy of the people is enough to make every statue leap from its pedestal, and to hasten the resurrection of the dead.

It is pretended, that I am retarding the cause of emancipation by the coarseness of my invective and the precipitancy of my measures. <u>The charge is not true</u>. On this question my influence,--humble as it is,--is felt at this moment to a considerable extent, and shall be felt in coming years--not perniciously, but beneficially--not as a curse, but as a blessing; and posterity will bear testimony that I was right.


## <u>ALEXIS de TOCQUEVILLE ON THE NEGRO RACE IN THE UNITED STATES (1835)</u>

This perceptive young Frenchmen visited the United States in 1831, travelling seven thousand miles around the country in nine months. Upon his return to France he wrote <u>Democracy in America,</u> one of the most lucid evaluations of America and the Americans ever published. His observations are so acute and accurate that his analyses of our character and the workings of our democracy seem just as true today as in 1835. A century and a half later there is still no rival to Alexis de Tocqueville.

---

Alexis de Tocqueville, <u>Democracy in America</u> (New York, 1904), I, 383-385.

Turning my attention to the United States of our own day, I plainly see that in some parts of the country the legal barrier between the two races is tending to come down, but not that of mores: I see that slavery is in retreat, but the prejudice from which it arose is immovable.

In that part of the Union where the Negroes are no longer slaves, have they come closer to the whites? Everyone who has lived in the United States will have noticed just the opposite.

Race prejudice seems stronger in those states that have abolished slavery than in those where it still exists, and nowhere is it more intolerant than in those states where slavery was never known.

It is true that in the North of the Union the law allows legal marriages between Negroes and whites, but public opinion would regard a white man married to a Negro woman as disgraced, and it would be very difficult to quote an example of such an event.

In almost all the states where slavery has been abolished, the Negroes have been given electoral rights, but they would come forward to vote at the risk of their lives. When oppressed, they can bring an action at law, but they will find only white men among their judges. It is true that the laws make them eligible as jurors, but prejudice wards them off. The Negro's son is excluded from the school to which the European's child goes. In the theaters he cannot for good money buy the right to sit by his former master's side; in the hospitals he lies apart. He is allowed to worship the same God as the white man but must not pray at the same altars. He has his own clergy and churches. The gates of heaven are not closed against him, but his inequality stops only just short of the boundaries of the other world. When the Negro is no more, his bones are cast aside, and some difference in condition is found even in the equality of death.

So the Negro is free, but he cannot share the rights, pleasures, labors, griefs, or even the tomb of him whose equal he has been declared; there is nowhere where he can meet him, neither in life nor in death.

In the South, where slavery still exists, less trouble is taken to keep the Negro apart: they sometimes share the labors and the pleasures of the white men; people are prepared to mix with them to some extent; legislation is more harsh against them, but customs are more tolerant and gentle.

In the South the master has no fear of lifting the slave up to his level, for he knows that when he wants to he can always throw him down into the dust. In the North the white man no longer clearly sees the barrier that separates him from the degraded race, and he keeps the Negro at a distance all the more carefully because he fears lest one day they be confounded together.

Among the Americans of the South, Nature sometimes, reclaiming her rights, does for a moment establish equality between white and black. In the North pride silences even the most imperious of human passions. Perhaps the northern American might have allowed some Negro woman to be the passing companion of his pleasures, had the legislators declared that she could not hope to share his nuptial bed; but she can become his wife, and he recoils in horror from her.

Thus it is that in the United States the prejudice rejecting the Negroes seems to increase in proportion to their emancipation, and inequality cuts deep into mores as it is effaced from the laws.

But if the relative position of the two races inhabiting the United States is as I have described it, why is it that the Americans have abolished slavery in the North of the Union, and why have they kept it in the South and aggravated its rigors?

The answer is easy. In the United States people abolish slavery for the sake not of the Negroes but of the white men.

## JOHN L. O'SULLIVAN ON MANIFEST DESTINY (1845)

John L. O'Sullivan was an editor whose Democratic, expansionist views impelled him to write the following editorial in defense of the annexation of Texas in *The United States Magazine and Democratic Review*. O'Sullivan coined the phrase "Manifest Destiny," whose mid-nineteenth-century meaning becomes clear below. But the spirit of Manifest Destiny can be traced at least as far back as the New England Puritans, and as far forward as U.S. foreign policy in the years since 1945.

It is time now for opposition to the Annexation of Texas to cease, . . .

Texas is now ours. Already, before these words are written, her Convention has undoubtedly ratified the acceptance, by her Congress, of our proffered invitation into the Union; and made the requisite changes in her already republican form of constitution to adapt it to its future federal relations. Her star and her stripe may already be said to have taken their place in the glorious blazon of our common nationality; and the sweep of our eagle's wing already includes within its circuit the wide extent of her fair and fertile land . . . .

Why, were other reasoning wanting, it surely is to be found, found abundantly, in the manner in which other nations have undertaken to intrude themselves into it, between us and the proper parties to the case, in a spirit of hostile interference against us, for the avowed object of thwarting our policy and hampering our power, limiting our greatness and checking the fulfillment of our manifest destiny to overspread the continent allotted by Providence for the free development of our yearly multiplying millions. . . .

It is wholly untrue, and unjust to ourselves, the pretence that the Annexation has been a measure of spoilation, unrightful and unrighteous--of military conquest under forms of peace and law--of territorial aggrandizement at the expense of justice, and justice due by a double sanctity to the weak. This view of the question is wholly unfounded, and has been before so amply refuted in these pages, as well as in a thousand other modes, that we shall not again dwell upon it. The independence of Texas was complete and absolute. It was in independence, not only in fact but of right. No obligation of duty towards Mexico tended in the least degree to restrain our right to effect the desired recovery of the fair province once our own--whatever motives of policy might have prompted a more deferential consideration of her feelings and her pride, as involved in the question. If Texas became peopled with an American population, it was by no contrivance of our government, but on the express invitation of that of Mexico herself; accompanied with such guaranties of State independence, and the maintenance of a federal system analogous to our

---

John L. O'Sullivan, "Annexation," *The United States Magazine and Democratic Review*, XVII (July/August, 1845), 5-9.

own, as constituted a compact fully justifying the strongest measures of redress on the part of those afterwards deceived in this guaranty, and sought to be enslaved under the yoke imposed by its violation. She was released, rightfully and absolutely released, from all Mexican allegiance, or duty of cohesion to the Mexican political body, by the acts and fault of Mexico herself, and Mexico alone. There never was a clearer case. It was not revolution; it was resistance to revolution; and resistance under such circumstances as left independence the necessary resulting state, caused by the abandonment of those with whom her former federal association had existed. What then can be more preposterous than all this clamor by Mexico and the Mexican interest, against Annexation, as a violation of any rights of hers, any duties of ours? . . . .

Nor is there any just foundation of the charge that Annexation is a great pro-slavery measure--calculated to increase and perpetuate that institution. Slavery had nothing to do with it . . . .

Texas has been absorbed into the Union in the inevitable fulfilment of the general law which is rolling our population westward; the connexion of which with that ratio of growth in population which is destined within a hundred years to swell our numbers to the enormous population of <u>two hundred and fifty millions</u> (if not more), is too evident to leave us in doubt of the manifest design of Providence in regard to the occupation of this continent. It was disintegrated from Mexico in the natural course of events, by a process perfectly legitimate on its own part, blameless on ours; and in which all the censures due to wrong, perfidy and folly, rest on Mexico alone. And possessed as it was by a population which was in truth but a colonial detachment from our own, and which was still bound by myriad ties of the very heartstrings to its old relations, domestic and political, their incorporation into the Union was not only inevitable, but the most natural, right and proper thing in the world--and it is only astonishing that there should be any among ourselves to say it nay . . . .

California will, probably, next fall away from the loose adhesion which, in such a country as Mexico, holds a remote province in a slight equivocal kind of dependence on the metropolis. Imbecile and distracted, Mexico never can exert any real governmental authority over such a country. The impotence of the one and the distance of the other, must make the relation one of virtual independence; unless, by stunting the province of all natural growth, and forbidding that immigration which can alone develop its capabilities and fulfil the purposes of its creation, tyranny may retain a military dominion which is no government in the legitimate sense of the term. In the case of California this is now impossible. The Anglo-Saxon foot is already on its borders. Already the advance guard of the irresistible army of Anglo-Saxon emigration has begun to pour down upon it, armed with the plough and the rifle, and marking its trail with schools and colleges, courts and representative halls, mills and meeting-houses. A population will soon be in actual occupation of California, over which it will be idle for Mexico to dream of dominion. They will necessarily become independent. All this without agency of our government, without responsibility of our people--in the natural flow of events, the spontaneous working of principles, and the adaptation of the tendencies and wants of the human race to the elemental circumstances in the midst of which they find themselves placed. And they will have a right to independence--to self-government--to the possession of the homes conquered from the wilderness by their own labors and dangers, sufferings and sacrifices--a better and a truer right than the artificial title of sovereignty in Mexico a thousand miles distant, inheriting from Spain a title good only against those who have none better. Their right to independence will be the natural right of self-government belonging to any community strong enough to maintain it--distinct in position, origin and character, and free from any mutual obligations of membership of a common political body, binding it to others by the duty of loyalty and compact of public faith. This will be their title to independence; and by this title, there can be no doubt that the population now fast streaming down upon California will both assert and maintain that independence . . . .

Away, then, with all idle French talk of <u>balances of power</u> on the American Continent.

## JAMES K. POLK ON THE WAR WITH MEXICO (1846)

President Polk was determined that the United States should have the disputed area between Texas and Mexico--peacefully if possible, by war if necessary. When his diplomatic efforts failed, Polk ordered General Zachary Taylor to proceed with Mexican troops into the territory which both Mexico and the United States claimed. The ensuing bloodshed led Polk to request that Congress declare war against Mexico.

May 11, 1846

The existing state of the relations between the United States and Mexico renders it proper that I should bring the subject to the consideration of Congress. . . .

In my message at the commencement of the present session I informed you that upon the earnest appeal both of the Congress and convention of Texas I had ordered an efficient military force to take a position "between the Nueces and the Del Norte." This had become necessary to meet a threatened invasion of Texas by the Mexican forces, for which extensive military preparations had been made. The invasion was threatened solely because Texas had determined, in accordance with a solemn resolution of the Congress of the United States, to annex herself to our Union, and under these circumstances it was plainly our duty to extend our protection over her citizens and soil.

This force was concentrated at Corpus Christi, and remained there until after I had received such information from Mexico as rendered it probable, if not certain, that the Mexican Government would refuse to receive our envoy.

Meantime Texas, by the final action of our Congress, had become an integral part of our Union. The Congress of Texas, by its act of December 19, 1836, had declared the Rio del Norte to be the boundary of that Republic. Its jurisdiction had been extended and exercised beyond the Nueces. The country between that river and the Del Norte had been represented in the Congress and in the convention of Texas, had thus taken part in the act of annexation itself, and is now included within one of our Congressional districts. Our own Congress had, moreover, with great unanimity, by the act approved December 31, 1845, recognized the country beyond the Nueces as a part of our

---

James D. Richardson, ed., <u>A Compilation of the Messages and Papers of the Presidents</u> (New York, 1897), VI, 2287-93.

territory by including it within our own revenue system, and a revenue officer to reside within that district has been appointed by and with the advice and consent of the Senate. It became, therefore, of urgent necessity to provide for the defense of that portion of our country. Accordingly, on the 13th of January last instructions were issued to the general in command of these troops to occupy the left bank of the Del Norte. This river, which is the southwestern boundary of the State of Texas, is an exposed frontier. From this quarter invasion was threatened; upon it and in its immediate vicinity, in the judgment of high military experience, are the proper stations for the protecting forces of the Government. In addition to this important consideration, several others occurred to induce this movement. Among these are the facilities afforded by the ports at Brazos Santiago and the mouth of the Del Norte for the reception of supplies by sea, the stronger and more healthful military positions, the convenience for obtaining a ready and a more abundant supply of provisions, water, fuel, and forage, and the advantages which are afforded by the Del Norte in forwarding supplies to such posts as may be established in the interior and upon the Indian frontier.

The movement of the troops to the Del Norte was made by the commanding general under positive instructions to abstain from all aggressive acts toward Mexico or Mexican citizens and to regard the relations between that Republic and the United States as peaceful unless she should declare war or commit acts of hostility indicative of a state of war. He was specially directed to protect private property and respect personal rights. . . .

The Mexican forces at Matamoras assumed a belligerent attitude, and on the 12th of April General [Pedro] Ampudia, then in command, notified General Taylor to break up his camp within twenty-four hours and to retire beyond the Nueces River, and in the event of his failure to comply with these demands announced that arms, and arms alone, must decide the question. But no open act of hostility was committed until the 24th of April. On that day General [Mariano] Arista, who had succeeded to the command of the Mexican forces, communicated to General Taylor that "he considered hostilities commenced and should prosecute them." A party of dragoons of 63 men and officers were on the same day dispatched from the American camp up the Rio del Norte, on its left bank, to ascertain whether the Mexican troops had crossed or were preparing to cross the river, "became engaged with a large body of these troops, and after a short affair, in which some 16 were killed and wounded, appear to have been surrounded and compelled to surrender" . . . .

Our commerce with Mexico has been almost annihilated. . . . Had we acted with vigor in repelling the insults and redressing the injuries inflicted by Mexico at the commencement, we should doubtless have escaped all the difficulties in which we are now involved. . . .

But now, after reiterated menaces, Mexico has passed the boundary of the United States, has invaded our territory and shed American blood upon the American soil. She has proclaimed that hostilities have commenced, and that the two nations are now at war.

As war exists, and, notwithstanding all our efforts to avoid it, exists by the act of Mexico herself, we are called upon by every consideration of duty and patriotism to vindicate with decision the honor, the rights, and the interests of our country.

Anticipating the possibility of a crisis like that which has arrived, instructions were given in August last, "as a precautionary measure" against invasion or threatened invasion, authorizing General Taylor, if the emergency required, to accept volunteers, not from Texas only, but from the States of Louisiana, Alabama, Mississippi, Tennessee, and Kentucky, and corresponding letters were addressed to the respective governors of those States. These instructions were repeated, and in January last, soon after the incorporation of "Texas into our Union of States," General Taylor was further "authorized by the President to make a requisition upon the executive of that State for such of its militia force as may be needed to repel invasion or to secure the country against apprehended invasion." On the 2d day of March he was again reminded, "in the event of the approach of any considerable Mexican force, promptly and efficiently to use the authority with which he was clothed to call to him such auxiliary force as he might need". . . .

In further vindication of our rights and defense of our territory, I invoke the prompt action of Congress to recognize the existence of the war, and to place at the disposition of the Executive the means of prosecuting the war with vigor, and thus hastening the restoration of peace. To this end I recommend that authority should be given to call into the public service a large body of volunteers to serve for not less than six or twelve months unless sooner discharged. A volunteer force is beyond question more efficient than any other description of citizen soldiers, and it is not to be doubted that a number far beyond that required would readily rush to the field upon the call of their country. I further recommend that a liberal provision be made for sustaining our entire military force and furnishing it with supplies and munitions of war.

## ABRAHAM LINCOLN ON THE MEXICAN WAR (1847)

Lincoln's major speech of his first term in Congress was a supremely partisan oration designed to fasten guilt for the war directly on President Polk. The speech took the form of lawyer's interrogatories, demanding that Polk reveal the exact "spot" where American blood had first been spilled. Unfortunately for Lincoln the war soon came to an end, and the Illinois Democratic papers ranted at him for his "treasonable assault" against the President. One paper dubbed him "spotty Lincoln" and predicted that he would die of the spotted fever. Even many of his own Whig Party were upset with him.

Whereas the President of the United States, in his message of May 11, 1846, has declared that "the Mexican Government not only refused to receive him, [the envoy of the United States,] or listen to his propositions, but, after a long-continued series of menaces, have at last invaded our territory and shed the blood of our fellow-citizens on our own soil:

And again, in his message of December 8, 1846, that "we had ample cause of war against Mexico long before the breaking out of hostilities; but even then we forbore to take redress into our own hands untill Mexico herself became the aggressor, by invading our soil in hostile array and shedding the blood of our citizens:"

The Congressional Globe, 30th Cong., 1st sess., December 22, 1847, p. 64.

And yet again, in his message of December 7, 1847, that the Mexican Government refused even to hear the terms of adjustment which he [our minister of peace] was authorized to propose, and finally, under wholly unjustifiable pretexts, involved the two countries in war, by invading the territory of the State of Texas, striking the first blow, and shedding the blood of our citizens on our own soil:"

And whereas this House is desirous to obtain a full knowledge of all the facts which go to establish whether the particular spot on which the blood of our citizens was so shed was or was not at that time our own soil; Therefore,

Resolved by the House of Representatives, That the President of the United States be respectfully requested to inform the House --

1st. Whether the spot on which the blood of our citizens was shed, as in his messages declared, was or was not within the territory of Spain, at least after the treaty of 1819, untill the Mexican revolution.

2nd. Whether the spot is or is not within the territory which was wrested from Spain by the revolutionary Government of Mexico.

3rd. Whether that spot is or is not within a settlement of people, which settlement has existed ever since long before the Texan revolution, and untill its inhabitants fled before the approach of the United States army.

4th. Whether that settlement is or is not isolated from any and all other settlements by the Gulf and the Rio Grande on the south and west, and by wide uninhabited regions on the north and east.

5th. Whether the people of that settlement, or a majority of them, or any of them, have ever submitted themselves to the government or laws of Texas or of the United States, by consent or by compulsion either by accepting office, or voting at elections, or paying tax, or serving on juries, or having process served upon them, or in any other way . . . .

8th. Whether the military force of the United States was or was not sent into that settlement after General Taylor had more than once intimated to the War Department that, in his opinion, no such movement was necessary to the defence or protection of Texas.

## JAMES RUSSELL LOWELL ON THE MEXICAN WAR (1848)

Massachusetts poet James Russell Lowell, like other abolitionists, opposed the Mexican War. Lowell could not alter American foreign policy, but he did speak for many New Englanders who protested the power of the South in the Union. The following selection is taken from a long work, The Biglow Papers I, which links slavery and the Mexican War and abhors both. The speaker in the poem is one Hosea Biglow, who expresses his feelings after having been approached by a recruiting sergeant in Boston.

---

James Russell Lowell, The Poetical Works of James Russell Lowell (Boston, 1915), pp. 173-175.

'T would n't suit them Southun fellers,
    They're a dreffle graspin' set,
We must ollers blow the bellers
    Wen they want their irons het;
May be it's all right ez preachin',
    But _my_ narves it kind o' grates,
Wen I see the overreachin'
    O' them nigger-drivin' States. . . .

Ez fer war, I call it murder,—
    There you hev it plain an' flat;
I don't want to go no furder
    Than my Testyment fer that;
God hez sed so plump an' fairly,
    It's ez long ez it is broad,
An you've gut to git up airly
    Ef you want to take in God.

'Taint your eppyletts an' feathers
    Make the thing a grain more right;
'Taint afollerin' your bell-wethers
    Will excuse ye in His sight;
Ef you take a sword an' dror it,
    An' go stick a feller thru,
Guv'ment aint to answer for it,
    God 'll send the bill to you.

Wut 's the use o' meeting'-goin'
    Every Sabbath, wet or dry,
Ef it 's right to go amowin'
    Feller-men like oats an' rye?
I dunno but wut it 's pooty
    Trainin' round in bobtail coats,—
But it 's curus Christian dooty
    This 'ere cuttin' folks's throats.

They may talk o' Freedom's airy
    Tell they 're pupple in the face,—
It's a grant gret cemetary
    Fer the barthrights of our race;
They jest want this Californy
    So 's to lug new slave-states in
To abuse ye, an' to scorn ye,
    An' to plunder ye like sin.

Aint it cute to see a Yankee
    Take sech everlastin' pains,
All to git the Devil's thankee
    Helpin' on 'em weld their chains?
Wy, it's jest ez clear ez figgers,
    Clear ez one an' one make two,
Chaps thet make black slaves o' niggers
    Want to make wite slaves o' you.

Tell ye jest the eend I 've come to
    Arter cipherin' plaguy smart,
An' it makes a handy sum, tu,
    Any gump could larn by heart;
Laborin' man an' laborin' woman
    Hev one glory an' one shame.
Ev'y thin' thet's done inhuman
    Injers all on 'em the same.

'Taint by turnin' out to hack folks
    You 're agoin' to git your right,
Nor by lookin' down on black folks
    Coz you 're put upon by wite;
Slavery aint o' nary color,
    'Taint the hide thet makes it wus,
All it keers fer in a feller
    'S jest to make him fill its pus. . . .

Massachusetts, God forgive her,
    She 's akneelin' with the rest,
She, thet ough' to ha' clung ferever
    In her grand old eagle-nest;
She thet ough' to stand so fearless
    Wile the wracks are round her hurled,
Holdin' up a beacon peerless
    To the oppressed of all the world!

"I'll return ye good fer evil
    Much ez we frail mortils can,
But I wun't go help the Devil
    Makin' man the cus o' man;
Call me coward, call me traiter,
    Jest ez suits your mean idees,—
Here I stand a tyrant-hater,
    An' the friend o' God an' Peace!"

Ef I 'd *my* way I hed ruther
    We should go to work an' part,—
They take one way, we take t' other,—
    Guess it would n't break my heart;
Man hed ough' to put asunder
    Them thet God has noways jined;
An' I should n't gretly wonder
    Ef there 's thousands o' my mind.

# JOHN TYLER ON THE CHINA TRADE (1843)

In 1784, merchants from Philadelphia and Boston entered a joint commercial venture by outfitting a ship, Empress of China, to sail to China. The enterprise returned a profit of 25% and thereby set the pattern for American trade with China (which some have called the "Myth of the China Market"). Many European powers, too, sought to reap the benefits of trade--and power--in China. The British, in particular, tried to pry open the China markets. After much bloodshed, the British forced China in 1842 to make several concessions, including access to five so-called "treaty ports" and the principle of extraterritoriality (which mocked China's sovereignty by extending the British legal system to British subjects in China). President John Tyler and the State Department, fearful that a British monopoly in China would foreclose any American trade opportunities there, selected Caleb Cushing to gain through diplomacy the same advantages the British had earned through force.

I hope your health is good. China is a great empire, extending over a great part of the world. The Chinese are numerous. You have millions and millions of subjects. The twenty-six United States are as large as China, though our people are not so numerous. The rising sun looks upon the great mountains and great rivers of China. When he sets, he looks upon rivers and mountains equally large in the United States. Our territories extend from one great ocean to the other; and on the west we are divided from your dominions only by the sea. Leaving the mouth of one of our great rivers, and going constantly.

Now, my words are, that the Governments of two such great countries should be at peace. It is proper, and according to the will of Heaven, that they should respect each other, and act wisely. I therefore send to your Court Caleb Cushing, one of the wise and learned men of this country. On his first arrival in China, he will inquire for your health. He has then strict orders to go to your great city of Pekin, and there to deliver this letter. He will have with him secretaries and interpreters.

The Chinese love to trade with our people, and to sell them tea and silk, for which our people pay silver, and sometimes other articles. But if the Chinese and the Americans will trade, there should be rules, so that they shall not break your laws nor our laws. Our minister, Caleb Cushing, is authorized to make a treaty to regulate trade. Let it be just. Let there be no unfair advantage on either side. Let the people trade not only at Canton, but also at Amoy, Ning-po, Shang-hai, Fu-chow, and all such other places as may offer profitable exchanges both to China and the United States, provided they do not break your laws nor our laws. We shall not take the part of evil-doers. We shall not uphold them that break your laws. Therefore, we doubt not that you will be pleased that our messenger of peace, with this

---

United States, Congress, Senate, Executive Document 457, 28th Cong., 2nd sess., vol. VIII, No. 138, p. 8.

letter in his hand, shall come to Peking, and there deliver it; and that your great officers will, by your order, make a treaty with him to regulate affairs of trade--so that nothing may happen to disturb the peace between China and America. Let the treaty be signed by your own imperial hand. It shall be signed by mine, by the authority of our great council, the Senate.

And so may your health be good, and may peace reign. . . .

Your good friend,

John Tyler


## THE UNITED STATES ON OPENING RELATIONS WITH JAPAN (1852)

American diplomatic successes in China spurred hopes of building a similar relationship with Japan. In 1852, Commodore Matthew C. Perry received these instructions.

[Acting Secretary of State C. M. Conrad to Secretary of the Navy John P. Kennedy, November 5, 1852]
Since the islands of Japan were first visited by European nations, efforts have constantly been made by the various maritime powers to establish commercial intercourse with a country whose large population and reputed wealth hold out great temptations to mercantile enterprise. Portugal was the first to make the attempt, and her example was followed by Holland, England, Spain, and Russia; and finally by the United States. All these attempts, however, have thus far been unsuccessful; the permission enjoyed for a short period by the Portugese to trade with the islands, and that granted to Holland to send annually a single vessel to the port of Nagasaki, hardly deserving to be considered exceptions to this remark.

China is the only country which caries on any considerable trade with these islands.

So rigorously is this system of exclusion carried out, that foreign vessels are not permitted to enter their ports in distress, or even to do an act of kindness to their own people. . . .

When vessels are wrecked or driven ashore on the islands their crews are subjected to the most cruel treatment. . . .

Every nation has undoubtedly the right to determine for itself the extent to which it will hold intercourse with other nations. The same law of nations, however, which protects a nation in the exercise of this right imposes upon her certain duties which she cannot justly disregard. Among these duties none is more imperative than that which requires her to succor and relieve those persons who are cast by the perils of the ocean upon her shores. . . .

That the civilized nations of the world should for ages have submitted to such treatment by a weak and semi-barbarous people, can only be accounted for on the supposition that, from the remoteness of the country, instances of such treatment were of rare occurrence, and the difficulty of chastising it very great. . . .

---

U.S. Congress, Senate, Executive Document 34, 33rd Cong., 2d sess., Serial 751, pp. 4-9.

Recent events--the navigation of the ocean by steam, the acquisition and rapid settlement by this country of a vast territory on the Pacific, the discovery of gold in that region, the rapid communication established across the isthmus which separates the two oceans--have practically brought the countries of the east in closer proximity to our own; although the consequences of these events have scarcely begun to be felt, the intercourse between them has already greatly increased, and no limits can be assigned to its future extension. . . .

The objects sought by this government are--

1. To effect some permanent arrangement for the protection of American seamen and property wrecked on these islands, or driven into their ports by stress of weather.

2. The permission to American vessels to enter one or more of their ports in order to obtain supplies of provisions, water, fuel, &c., or, in case of disasters, to refit so as to enable them to prosecute their voyage.

It is very desirable to have permission to establish a depot for coal, if not on one of the principal islands, at least on some small uninhabited one, of which, it is said, there are several in their vicinity.

3. The permission to our vessels to enter one or more of their ports for the purpose of disposing of their cargoes by sale or barter. . . .

The next question is, how are the above mentioned objects to be attained?

It is manifest, from past experience, that arguments or persuasion addressed to this people, unless they be seconded by some imposing manifestation of power, will be utterly unavailing.

You will, therefore, be pleased to direct the commander of the squadron to proceed, with his whole force, to such point on the coast of Japan as he may deem most advisable, and there endeavor to open a communication with the government, and, if possible, to see the emperor in person, and deliver to him the letter of introduction from the President with which he is charged. He will state that he has been sent across the ocean by the President to deliver that letter to the emperor, and to communicate with his government on matters of importance to the two countries. That the President entertains the most friendly feeling towards Japan, but has been surprised and grieved to learn, that when any of the people of the United States go, of their own accord, or are thrown by the perils of the sea within the dominions of the emperor, they are treated as if they were his worst enemies. . . .

If, after having exhausted every argument and every means of persuasion, the commodore should fail to obtain from the government any relaxation of their system of exclusion, or even any assurance of humane treatment of our ship-wrecked seamen, he will then change his tone, and inform them in the most unequivocal terms that it is the determination of this government to insist, that hereafter all citizens or vessels of the United States that may be wrecked on their coasts, or driven by stress of weather into their harbors shall, so long as they are compelled to remain there, be treated with humanity; and that if any acts of cruelty should hereafter be practised upon citizens of this country, whether by the government or by the inhabitants of Japan, they will be severely chastised. In case he should succeed in obtaining concessions on any of the points above mentioned, it is desirable that they should be reduced into the form of a treaty, for negotiating which he will be furnished with the requisite powers. . . .

In his intercourse with this people, who are said to be proud and vindictive in their character, he should be courteous and conciliatory, but at the same time, firm and decided. He will, therefore, submit with patience and forbearance to acts of discourtesy to which he may be subjected, by a people to whose usages it will not do to test by our standard of propriety, but at the same time, will be careful to do nothing that may compromise in their eyes, his own dignity, or that of the country. He will, on the contrary, do everything to impress them with a just sense of the power and greatness of this country, and to satisfy them that its past forbearance has been the result, not of timidity, but of a desire to be on friendly terms with them.

### RALPH WALDO EMERSON ON REFORM (1842)

Transcendentalists like Ralph Waldo Emerson encouraged people to use their intuition to determine ethical standards. By transcending, or going beyond, mere logic or tradition, people were led along a natural course to the spirit of reform. For Emerson, reform meant the removal of obstacles to human progress and the development of each individual. But if reform held a noble purpose for Emerson, he was less patient with the reformers.

The present age will be marked by its harvest of projects, for the reform of domestic, civil, literary, and ecclesiastical institutions. . . . These movements are on all accounts important; they not only check the special abuses to which they address themselves, but they educate the conscience and the intellect of the people. How can such a question as the Slave trade be agitated for forty years by all the Christian nations, without throwing great light on ethics into the general mind? The fury, with which the slave-trader defends every inch of his bloody deck, and his howling auction-platform, is a trumpet to alarm the ear of mankind, to wake the dull, and drive all neutrals to take sides, and listen to the argument and the verdict which justice shall final pronounce. . . .

There is a perfect chain,--see it, or see it not,--of reforms emerging from the surrounding darkness, each cherishing some part of the general idea, and all must be seen, in order to do justice to any one. Seen in this their natural connexion, they are sublime. The conscience of the Age demonstrates itself in this effort to raise the life of man by putting it in harmony with his idea of the Beautiful and the Just. The history of reform is always identical; it is the comparison of the idea with the fact. Our modes of living are not agreeable to our imagination. . . . Is there a necessity that the works of man should be sordid? Perhaps not.--Out of this fair idea in the mind springs forever the effort at the Perfect. It is the testimony of the soul in man to a fairer possibility of life and manners, which agitates society every day with the offer of some new amendment. If we would make more strict inquiry concerning its origin, we find ourselves rapidly approaching

---

R.W. Emerson, "Lectures on the Times," The Dial, III (July, 1842), 6-13.

the inner boundaries of thought, that term where speech becomes silence, and science conscience. For the origin of all reform is in that mysterious fountain of the moral sentiment in man, which, amidst the natural ever contains the supernatural for men. That is new and creative. That is alive. That alone can make a man other than he is. Here or nowhere resides unbounded energy, unbounded power. . . .

So much for the Reforms; but we cannot say as much for the Reformers. Beautiful is the impulse and the theory; the practice is less beautiful. The Reformers affirm the inward life, but they do not trust it, but use outward and vulgar means. They do not rely on precisely that strength which wins me to their cause; not on love, not on a principle, but on men, on multitudes, on circumstances, on money, on party; that is, on fear, on wrath, and pride. The love which lifted men to the sight of these better ends, was the true and best distinction of this time, the disposition to trust a principle more than a material force. . . .

The Reforms have their high origin in an ideal justice, but they do not retain the purity of an idea. They are quickly organized in some low, inadequate form, and present no more poetic image to the mind, than the evil tradition which they reprobated. They mix the fire of the moral sentiment with personal and party heats, with measureless exaggerations, and the blindness that prefers some darling measure to justice and truth. Those, who are urging with most ardor what are called the greatest benefits of mankind, are narrow, self-pleasing, conceited men, and affect us as the insane do. They bite us, and we run mad also. I think the work of the reformer as innocent as other work that is done around him; but when I have seen it near, I do not like it better. It is done in the same way, it is done profanely, not piously; by management, by tactics, and clamor. It is a buzz in the ear. I cannot feel any pleasure in sacrifices which display to me such partiality of character. . . .

This then is our criticism on the reforming movement; that it is in its origin divine; in its management and details timid and profane.


## HENRY DAVID THOREAU ON CIVIL DISOBEDIENCE (1848)

Transcendentalist Henry David Thoreau spent a night in jail for refusing to pay his taxes. His act of civil disobedience is explained in this classic essay. The two principal moral issues that engaged his conscience--slavery and the Mexican War--were specific to Thoreau's generation, but the issues that he raises are not. All societies--certainly all free ones--must deal with the questions of the relationship of the individual to the state, the protection of minority opinion, and the role of conscience in political behavior. Thoreau's manifesto transcends his own era to provide some forthright, and very controversial, answers.

---

Henry David Thoreau, "Civil Disobedience," in The Writings of Henry David Thoreau (New York, 1906), IV, 356-387.

I heartily accept the motto, "That government is best which governs least;". . . The government itself, which is only the mode which the people have chosen to execute their will, is equally liable to be abused and perverted before the people can act through it. Witness the present Mexican war, the work of comparatively a few individuals using the standing government as their tool; . . .

. . . the practical reason why, when the power is once in the hands of the people, a majority are permitted, and for a long period continue, to rule is not because they are most likely to be in the right, nor because this seems fairest to the minority, but because they are physically the strongest. . . . Can there not be a government in which majorities do not virtually decide right and wrong, but conscience?--in which majorities decide only those questions to which the rule of expediency is applicable?. . . It is not desirable to cultivate a respect for the law, so much as for the right. . . . Law never made men a whit more just; and, by means of their respect for it, even the well-disposed are daily made the agents of injustice. A common and natural result of an undue respect for law is, that you may see a file of soldiers, colonel, captain, corporal, privates, powder-monkeys, and all, marching in admirable order over hill and dale to the wars, against their wills, ay, against their common sense and consciences, which makes it very steep marching indeed, and produces a palpitation of the heart. They have no doubt that it is a damnable business in which they are concerned; they are all peaceably inclined. . . .they are as likely to serve the devil, without intending it, as God. . . .

How does it become a man to behave toward this American government to-day? I answer, that he cannot without disgrace be associated with it. I cannot for an instant recognize that political organization as my government which is the slave's government also. . . .

. . . a people, as well as an individual, must do justice, cost what it may. If I have unjustly wrested a plank from a drowning man, I must restore it to him though I drown myself. . . . This people must cease to hold slaves, and to make war on Mexico, though it cost them their existence as a people. . . .

It is not a man's duty, as a matter of course, to devote himself to the eradiction of any, even the most enormous, wrong; he may still properly have other concerns to engage him; but it is his duty, at least, to wash his hands of it, and, if he gives it no thought longer, not to give it practically his support. If I devote myself to other pursuits and contemplations, I must first see, at least, that I do not pursue them sitting upon another man's shoulders. . . .

Unjust laws exist: shall we be content to obey them, or shall we endeavor to amend them, and obey them until we have succeeded, or shall we transgress them at once? . . .

If the injustice is part of the necessary friction of the machine of government, let it go, let it go: perchance if will wear smooth,--certainly the machine will wear out. . . .but if it is of such a nature that it requires you to be the agent of injustice to another, then, I say, break the law. Let your life be a counter-friction to stop the machine. What I have to do is to see, at any rate, that I do not lend myself to the wrong which I condemn.

As for adopting the ways which the State has provided for remedying the evil, I know not of such ways. They take too much time, and a man's life will be gone. . .

I do not hesitate to say, that those who call themselves Abolitionists should at once effectually withdraw their support, both in person and property, from the government of Massachusetts, and not wait til they constitute a majority of one, before they suffer the right to prevail through them. I think that it is enough if they have God on their side, without waiting for that other one. Moreover, any man more right than his neighbors constitutes a majority of one already. . . .

But even suppose blood should flow. Is there not a sort of blood shed when the conscience is wounded? Through his wound a man's real manhood and immortality flow out, and he bleeds to an everlasting death. I see this blood flowing now. . . .

Webster never goes behind government, and so cannot speak with authority about it. . . . Still, his quality is not wisdom, but prudence. . . . He well deserves to be called, as he has been called, the Defender of the Constitution. . . . His leaders are the men of '87. "I have never made an effort," he says, "and never propose to make an effort; I have never countenanced an effort, to disturb the arrangement as originally made, by which the various States came into the Union." Still thinking of the sanction which the Constitution gives to slavery, he says, "Because it was a part of the original compact,--let it stand." . . .

They who know of no purer sources of truth, who have traced up its stream no higher, stand, and wisely stand, by the Bible and the Constitution, and drink at it there with reverence and humility; but they who behold where it comes trickling into this lake or that pool, gird up their loins once more, and continue their pilgrimage toward its fountain-head. . . . There will never be a really free and enlightened State until the State comes to recognize the individual as a higher and independent power, from which all its own power and authority are derived, and treats him accordingly. I please myself with imagining a State at last which can afford to be just to all men, and to treat the individual with respect as a neighbor; which even would not think it inconsistent with its own repose if a few were to live aloof from it, not meddling with it, nor embraced by it, who fulfilled all the duties of neighbors and fellow-men.

DECLARATION OF SENTIMENTS AT SENECA FALLS (1848)

The American feminist movement separated from the abolition movement in the 1840s. The first women's rights convention was held in 1848 in Seneca Falls, New York, and was led by Lucretia Mott and Elizabeth Cady Stanton. The convention adopted this aggressive and far-ranging declaration of sentiments, paraphrasing Thomas Jefferson for some very shrewd reasons. Only since the 1960s have American women defined their legitimate rights in as broad terms as one sees in this declaration, and only since the 1960s have women been able to achieve much of the equality demanded in 1848.

Elizabeth Cady Stanton, Susan B. Anthony, and Matlida Joslyn Gage, eds., History of Woman Suffrage (Rochester, 1889), I, 70-71.

When, in the course of human events, it becomes necessary for one portion of the family of man to assume among the people of the earth a position different from that which they have hitherto occupied, but one to which the laws of nature and of nature's God entitle them, a decent respect to the opinions of mankind requires that they should declare the causes that impel them to such a course.

We hold these truths to be self-evident: that all men and women are created equal; that they are endowed by their Creator with certain inalienable rights; that among these are life, liberty, and the pursuit of happiness; that to secure these rights governments are instituted, deriving their just powers from the consent of the governed. Whenever any form of government becomes destructive of these ends, it is the right of those who suffer from it to refuse allegiance to it, and to insist upon the institution of a new government, laying its foundation on such principles, and organizing its powers in such form, as to them shall seem most likely to effect their safety and happiness. Prudence, indeed, will dictate that governments long established should not be changed for light and transient causes; and accordingly all experience hath shown that mankind are more disposed to suffer, while evils are sufferable, than to right themselves by abolishing the forms to which they were accustomed. But when a a long train of abuses and usurpations, pursuing invariably the same object evinces a design to reduce them under absolute despotism, it is their duty to throw off such government, and to provide new guards for their future security. Such has been the patient sufferance of the women under this government, and such is now the necessity which constrains them to demand the equal station to which they are entitled.

The history of mankind is a history of repeated injuries and usurpations on the part of man toward woman, having in direct object the establishment of an absolute tyranny over her. To prove this, let facts be submitted to a candid world.

He has never permited her to exercise her inalienable right to the elective franchise.

He has compelled her to submit to laws, in the formation of which she had no voice.

He has withheld from her rights which are given to the most ignorant and degraded men--both natives and foreigners.

Having deprived her of this first right of a citizen, the elective franchise, thereby leaving her without representation in the halls of legislation, he has oppressed her on all sides.

He has made her, if married, in the eye of the law, civilly dead.

He has taken from her all right in property, even to the wages she earns.

He has made her, morally, an irresponsible being, as she can commit many crimes with impunity, provided they be done in the presence of her husband. In the covenant of marriage, she is compelled to promise obedience to her husband, he becoming, to all intents and purposes, her master--the law giving him power to deprive her of her liberty, and to administer chastisement.

He has so framed the laws of divorce, as to what shall be the proper causes, and in case of separation, to whom the guardianship of the children shall be given, as to be wholly regardless of the happiness of women--the law, in all cases, going upon a false supposition of the supremacy of man, and giving all power into his hands.

After depriving her of all rights as a married woman, if single, and the owner of property, he has taxed her to support a government which recognizes her only when her property can be made profitable to it.

He has monopolized nearly all the profitable employments, and from those she is permitted to follow, she receives but a scanty remuneration. He closes against her all the avenues to wealth and distinction which he considers most honorable to himself. As a teach of theology, medicine, or law, she is not known.

He has denied her the facilities for obtaining a thorough education, all colleges being closed against her.

He allows her in Church, as well as State, but a subordinate position, claiming Apostolic authority for her exclusion from the ministry, and, with some exceptions, from any public participation in the affairs of the Church.

He has created a false public sentiment by giving to the world a different code of morals for men and women, by which moral delinquencies which exclude women from society, are not only tolerated, but deemed of little account in man.

He has usurped the prerogative of Jehovah himself, claiming it as his right to assign for her a sphere of action, when that belongs to her conscience and to her God.

He has endeavored, in every way that he could, to destroy her confidence in her own powers, to lessen her self-respect, and to make her willing to lead a dependent and abject life.

Now, in view of this entire disfranchisement of one-half the people of this country, their social and religious degradation--in view of the unjust laws above mentioned, and because women do feel themselves aggrieved, oppressed, and fraudulently deprived of their most sacred rights, we insist that they have immediate admission to all the rights and privileges which belong to them as citizens of the United States.

In entering upon the great work before us, we anticipate no small amount of misconception, misrepresentation, and ridicule; but we shall use every instrumentality within our power to effect our object. We shall employ agents, circulate tracts, petition the State and National legislatures, and endeavor to enlist the pulpit and the press in our behalf. We hope this Convention will be followed by a series of Conventions embracing every part of the country.


JOHN C. CALHOUN ON THE COMPROMISE OF 1850 (March 4, 1850)

The quarrel over the status of the lands seized from Mexico had convulsed Congress and the country for five long years. Finally Henry Clay had proposed an eight point compromise. Everyone then awaited anxiously the opinion of two other elder statesmen, Calhoun and Webster, hoping that their support would guarantee an end to the struggle. Unfortunately Mr. Calhoun's harsh response was not what a weary nation had wished to hear.

The Congressional Globe, 31st Cong., 1st sess., pp. 451-455.

I have, Senators, believed from the first that the agitation of the subject of slavery would, if not prevented by some timely and effective measure, end in disunion. Entertaining this opinion, I have, on all proper occasions, endeavored to call the attention of both the two great measure to prevent so great a disaster, but without success. The agitation has been permitted to proceed, with almost no attempt to resist it, until it has reached a point when it can no longer be disguised or denied that the Union is in danger. You have thus had forced upon you the greatest and the gravest question that can ever come under your consideration--How can the Union be preserved?. . .

There is but one way by which it can with any certainty; and that is, by a full and final settlement, on the principle of justice, of all the questions at issue between the two sections. The South asks for justice, simple justice, and less she ought not to take. She has no compromise to offer, but the constitution; and no concession or surrender to make. She has already surrendered so much that she has little left to surrender. Such a settlement would go to the root of the evil, and remove all cause of discontent, by satisfying the South, that she could remain honorably and safely in the Union, and thereby restore the harmony and fraternal feelings between the sections, which existed anterior to the Missouri agitation. Nothing else can, with any certainty, finally and for ever settle the questions at issue, terminate agitation, and save the Union.

But can this be done? Yes, easily; not by the weaker party, for it can of itself do nothing--not even protect itself--but by the stronger. The North has only to will it to accomplish it--to do justice by conceding to the South an equal right in the acquired territory, and to do her duty by causing the stipulations relative to fugitive slaves to be faithfully fulfilled--to cease the agitation of the slave question, and to provide for the insertion of a provision in the constitution, by an amendment, which will restore to the South, in substance, the power she possessed of protecting herself, before the equilibrium between the sections was destroyed by the action of this Government. There will be no difficulty in devising such a provision--one that will protect the South, and which, at the same time, will improve and strengthen the Government, instead of impairing and weakening it.

But will the North agree to this? It is for her to answer the question. But, I will say, she cannot refuse, if she has half the love of the Union which she professes to have, or without justly exposing herself to the charge that her love of power and aggrandizement is far greater than her love of the Union. At all events, the responsibility of saving the Union rests on the North, and not on the South. The South cannot save it by any act of hers, and the North may save it without any sacrifice, whatever, unless to do justice, and to perform her duties under the constitution, should be be regarded by her as a sacrifice.

It is time, Senators, that there should be an open and manly avowal on all sides, as to what is intended to be done. If the question is not now settled, it is uncertain whether it ever can hereafter be; and we, as the representatives of the States of this Union, regarded as governments, should come to a distinct understanding as to our respective views, in order to ascertain whether the great questions at issue can be settled or not. If you, who represent the stronger portion, cannot agree to settle them on the broad principle of justice and duty, say so; and let the States we both represent agree to separate and part in peace. If you are unwilling we should part in peace, tell us so; and we shall know what to do, when you reduce the question to submission or resistance. If you remain silent, you will compel us to infer by your acts what you intend. In that case, California will become the test question. If you admit her, under all the difficulties that oppose her admission, you compel us to infer that you intend to exclude us from the whole of the acquired territories, with the intention of destroying, irretrievably, the equilibrium between the two sections. We would be blind not to perceive in that case, that your real objects are power and aggrandizement, and infatuated not to act accordingly.

I have now, Senators, done my duty in expressing my opinions fully, freely, and candidly, on this solemn occasion. In doing so, I have been governed by the motives which have governed me in all the stages of the agitation of the slavery question since its commencement. I have exerted myself, during the whole period, to arrest it, with the intention of saving the Union, if it could be done; and if it could not, to save the section where it has pleased Providence to cast my lot, and which I sincerely believe has justice and the constitution on its side. Having faithfully done my duty to the best of my ability, both to the Union and my section, throughout this agitation, I shall have the consolation, let what will come, that I am free from all responsibility.


## DANIEL WEBSTER ON THE COMPROMISE OF 1850 (March 7, 1850)

> While Calhoun's angry words had only exacerbated an already difficult situation, Webster presented an emotional plea for conciliation in an attempt to mediate between the North and South. Sadly, during the two remaining years of his life, Webster would be vilified by the abolitionists for his conciliatory stance which they labelled a sell out to the slaveholders.

Mr. President,--I wish to speak to-day, not as a Massachusetts man, nor as a northern man, but as an American, and a member of the Senate of the United States. It is fortunate that there is a Senate of the United States; a body not yet moved from propriety, not lost to a just sense of its own dignity and its own high responsibilities, and a body to which the country looks, with confidence, for wise, moderate, patriotic, and healing counsels. It is not to be denied that we live in the midst of strong agitations, and are surrounded by very considerable dangers to our institutions and government. The imprisoned winds are let loose. The East, the West, the North, and the stormy South, all combine to throw the whole sea into commotion, to toss its billows to the skies, and disclose its profoundest depths. I do not affect to regard myself, Mr. President, as holding, or as fit to hold, the helm in this combat with the political elements; but I have a duty to perform, and I mean to perform it with fidelity--not without a sense of existing dangers, but not without hope. I have a part to act, not for my own security or safety, for I am looking out for no fragment upon which to float away from the wreck, if

---

The Congressional Globe, 31st Cong., 1st sess., pp. 480-483.

wreck there must be, but for the good of the whole, and the preservation of the whole; and there is that which will keep me to my duty during this struggle, whether the sun and the stars shall appear, or shall not appear for many days. I speak to-day for the preservation of the Union. "Hear me for my cause." I speak to-day, out of a solicitous and anxious heart, for the restoration to the country of that quiet and that harmony which make the blessings of this union so rich and so dear to us all. These are the topics that I propose to myself to discuss; these are the motives, and the sole motives, that influence me in the wish to communicate my opinions to the Senate and the country; and if I can do anything, however little, for the promotion of these ends, I shall have accomplished all that I desire. . . .

Mr. President, I should much prefer to have heard, from every member on this floor, declarations of opinion that this Union could never be dissolved, than the declaration of opinion that in any case, under the pressure of circumstances, such a dissolution was possible. I hear with pain, and anguish, and distress, the word secession, especially when it falls from the lips of those who are eminently patriotic, and known to the country, and known all over the world, for their political services. Secession! Peaceable secession! Sir, your eyes and mine are never destined to see that miracle. The dismemberment of this vast country without convulsion! The breaking up of the fountains of the great deep without ruffling the surface! Who is foolish--I beg every body's pardon--as to expect to see any such thing? Sir, he who sees these States, now revolving in harmony around a common centre, and expects to see them quit their places and fly off without convulsion, may look the next hour to see the heavenly bodies rush from their spheres, and jostle against each other in the realms of space, without producing the crush of the universe. There can be no such thing as a peaceable secession. Peaceable secession is an utter impossibility. Is the great Constitution under which we live--covering this whole country--is it to be thawed and melted away by secession, as the snows on the mountain melt under the influence of a vernal sun--disappear almost unobserved, and die off? No, sir! No, sir! I will not state what might produce the disruption of the states; but, sir, I see it as plainly as I see the sun in heaven--I see that disruption must produce such a war as I will not describe, in its twofold characters. . . .

Sir, I may express myself too strongly, perhaps--but some things, some moral things, are almost as impossible, as other natural or physical things; and I hold the idea of a separation of these States--those that are free to form one government, and those that are slaveholding to form another--as a moral impossibility. We could not separate the States by any such line, if we were to draw it. We could not sit down here to-day and draw a line of separation, that would satisfy any five men in the country. There are natural causes that would keep and tie us together, and there are social and domestic relations which we could not break if we would, and which we should not, if we could. Sir, nobody can look over the face of this country at the present moment--nobody can see where its population is the most dense and growing--without being ready to admit, and compelled to admit, that ere long, America will be in the valley of the Mississippi. . . .

And now, Mr. President, instead of speaking of the possibility or utility of secession, instead of dwelling in these caverns of darkness, instead of groping with those ideas so full of all that is horrid and horrible, let us come out into the light of day; let us enjoy the fresh air of liberty and union; let us cherish those hopes which belong to us; let us devote ourselves to those great objects that are fit for our consideration and our action; let us raise our conceptions to the magnitude and the importance of the duties that devolve upon us; let our comprehension be as broad as the country for which we act, our aspirations as high as its certain destiny; let us not be pigmies in a case that calls for men. Never did there devolve, on any generation of men, higher trusts than now devolve upon us for the preservation of this Constitution and the harmony and peace of all who are destined to live under it. Let us make our generation one of the strongest and brightest links in that golden chain which is destined, I fully believe, to grapple the people of all the States to this Constitution, for ages to come.

### THE FUGITIVE SLAVE ACT (1850)

As part of "the Compromise of 1850," Congress agreed to pass a new fugitive slave law to replace the eighteenth-century version. (Article IV of the Constitution had called for a fugitive slave law, and one was duly passed in 1793.) This new law was supposed to call for stricter enforcement, especially by anti-slave states in the North and West. Ironically, the law, passed in 1850, was so harsh that it generated abolitionist spirit among formerly moderate segments outside the South.

Sec. 5. . .That it shall be the duty of all marshals and deputy marshals to obey and execute all warrants and precepts issued under the provisions of this act, when to them directed; and should any marshal or deputy marshal refuse to receive such warrant, or other process, when tendered, or to use all proper means diligently to execute the same, he shall, on conviction thereof, be fined in the sum of one thousand dollars, . . . [and] shall be liable, on this official bond, to be prosecuted for the benefit of such claimant, for the full value of the service or labor of said fugitive in the State, Territory, or District whence he escaped: . . .

Sec. 6. . .That when a person held to service or labor in any State or Territory of the United States, has heretofore or shall hereafter escape into another State or Territory of the United States, the person or persons to whom such service or labor may be due . . . . may pursue and reclaim such fugitive person. . . . In no trial or hearing under this act shall the testimony of such alleged fugitive be admitted in evidence; . . .

Sec. 7. . .That any person who shall knowingly and willingly obstruct, hinder, or prevent such claimant. . . from arresting such a fugitive from service or labor,. . . or shall rescue, or attempt to rescue, such fugitive from service or labor, from the custody of such claimant. . .or shall aid, abet, or assist such person so owing service or labor as aforesaid, directly or indirectly, to escape from such claimant, . . .or shall harbor or conceal such fugitive, so as to prevent the discovery and arrest of such person. . . shall, for either of said offences, be subject to a fine not exceeding one thousand dollars, and imprisonment not exceeding six months. . .and shall moreover forfeit and pay, by way of civil damages to the party injured by such illegal conduct, the sum of one thousand dollars, for each fugitive so lost.

U.S. Statutes at Large, IX (Sept. 18, 1850), 462-464.

# GEORGE FITZHUGH, CANNIBALS ALL! OR, SLAVES WITHOUT MASTERS (1857)

By the 1850s Calhoun and other Southerners had moved from the defense of slavery as a "necessary evil" to the argument that it was a "positive good." As criticism of the South's "peculiar institution" mounted, Southern writers advanced a variety of arguments affirming the virtues of the slave system. George Fitzhugh, a Virginia aristocrat, certainly believed that the best defense was an aggressive offense.

We are, all, North and South, engaged in the White Slave Trade, and he who succeeds best, is esteemed most respectable. It is far more cruel than the Black Slave Trade, because it exacts more of its slaves, and neither protects nor governs them. We boast that it exacts more when we say, "that the <u>profits</u> made from employing free labor are greater than those from slave labor.". . . But we not only boast that the White Slave Trade is more exacting and fraudulent (in fact, though not in intention,) than Black Slavery; but we also boast, that it is more cruel, in leaving the laborer to take care of himself and family out of the pittance which skill or capital have allowed him to retain. When the day's labor is ended, he is free, but is overburdened with the cares of family and household, which make his freedom an empty and delusive mockery. But his employer is really free, and may enjoy the profits made by others' labor, without a care, or a trouble, as to their well-being. The negro slave is free, too, when the labors of the day are over, and free in mind as well as body; for the master provides food, raiment, house, fuel, and everything else necessary to the physical well-being of himself and family. The master's labors commence just when the slave's end. No wonder men should prefer white slavery to capital, to negro slavery, since it is more profitable, and is free from all the cares and labors of black slave-holding. . . .

[W]hite slave-holding is much more respectable than negro slavery--for the master works nearly as hard for the negro as he for the master. But you, my virtuous, respectable reader, exact three thousand dollars per annum from white labor (for your income is the product of white labor) and make not one cent of return in any form. You retain your capital, and never labor, and yet live in luxury on the labor of others. Capital commands labor, as the master does the slave. Neither pays for labor; but the master permits the slave to retain a larger allowance from the proceeds of his own labor, and hence "free labor is cheaper than slave labor." You, with the command over labor which your capital gives you, are a slave owner--a master, without the obligations of a master. They who work for you, who create your income, are slaves, without the rights of slaves. Slaves without a master! Whilst you were engaged in amassing your capital, in seeking to become independent, you were in the White Slave Trade . . . .

The negro slaves of the South are the happiest, and, in some sense, the freest people in the world. The children and the aged and infirm work not at all, and yet have all the comforts and necessaries of life provided for them.

---

George Fitzhugh, <u>Cannibals All! or Slaves Without Masters</u>, ed. by C. Vann Woodward (Cambridge, MA, 1960), pp. 15-20.

They enjoy liberty, because they are oppressed neither by care nor labor. The women do little hard work, and are protected from the despotism of their husbands by their masters. The negro men and stout boys work, on the average, in good weather, not more than nine hours a day. The balance of their time is spent in perfect abandon. Besides, they have their Sabbaths and holidays. White men, with so much of license and liberty, would die of ennui; but negroes luxuriate in corporeal and mental repose. With their faces upturned to the sun, they can sleep at any hour; and quiet sleep is the greatest of human enjoyments. "Blessed be the man who invented sleep." 'Tis happiness in itself--and results from contentment with the present, and confident assurance of the future. We do not know whether free laborers ever sleep. They are fools to do so; for, whilst they sleep, the wily and watchful capitalist is devising means to ensnare and exploitate them. The free laborer must work or starve. He is more of a slave than the negro, because he works longer and harder for less allowance than the slave, and has no holiday, because the cares of life with him begin when its labors end. He has no liberty, and not a single right. . . .

Your capital will not bring you an income of a cent, nor supply one of your wants, without labor. Labor is indispensable to give value to property, and if you owned everything else, and did not own labor, you would be poor. But fifty thousand dollars means, and is, fifty thousand dollars worth of slaves. You can command, without touching on that capital, three thousand dollars' worth of labor per annum. You could do no more were you to buy slaves with it, and then you would be cumbered with the cares of governing and providing for them. You are a slaveholder now, to the amount of fifty thousand dollars, with all the advantages, and none of the cares and responsibilities of a master.

"Property in man" is what all are struggling to obtain. Why should they not be obliged to take care of man, their property, as they do of their horses and their hounds, their cattle and their sheep. Now, under the delusive name of liberty, you work him "from morn to dewy eve"--from infancy to old age-- then turn him out to starve. You treat your horses and hounds better. Capital is a cruel master. The free slave trade, the commonest, yet the cruellest of trades.


CHARLES SUMNER ON THE KANSAS QUESTION (1856)

Charles Sumner was a well known abolitionist senator from Massachusetts. On May 19 and 20, 1856, he rose in the Senate and delivered an extremely lengthy, rambling, abusive speech entitled "The Crime Against Kansas." He attacked his opponents so vituperatively that it would lead to his being physically assaulted inside the Senate chamber several days later.

---

Appendix to the Congressional Globe, 34th Cong., 1st sess., pp. 529-530.

Against this Territory. . . .a crime has been committed, which is without example in the records of the past. Not in plundered provinces or in the cruelties of selfish governors will you find its parallel. . . .

But the wickedness which I now begin to expose is immeasurably aggravated by the motive which prompted it. Not in any common lust for power did this uncommon tragedy have its origin. It is the rape of a virgin Territory, compelling it to the hateful embrace of Slavery; and it may be clearly traced to a depraved longing for a new slave State, the hideous offspring of such a crime, in the hope of adding to the power of Slavery in the National Government. Yes, sir, when the whole world, alike Christian and Turk, is rising up to condemn this wrong, and to make it a hissing to the nations, here in our Republic, <u>force</u>-ay, sir, FORCE--has been openly employed in compelling Kansas to this pollution, and all for the sake of political power. There is the simple fact, which you will vainly attempt to deny, but which in itself presents an essential wickedness that makes other public crimes seem like public virtues. . . .

. . .I must say something of a general character, particularly in response to what has fallen from Senators who have raised themselves to eminence on this floor in championship of human wrongs; I mean the Senator from South Carolina, [Mr. Butler,] and the Senator from Illinois, [Mr. Douglas,] who, though unlike as Don Quixote and Sancho Panza, yet, like this couple, sally forth together in the same adventure. I regret much to miss the elder Senator from his seat; but the cause, against which he has run a tilt, with such activity of animosity, demands that the opportunity of exposing him should not be lost; and it is for the cause that I speak. The Senator from South Carolina has read many books of chivalry, and believes himself a chivalrous knight, with sentiments of honor and courage. Of course he has chosen a mistress to whom he has made his vows, and who, through ugly to others, is always lovely to him; through polluted in the sight of the world, is chaste in his sight--I mean the harlot, Slavery. For her, his tongue is always profuse in words. Let her be impeached in character, or any proposition be made to shut her out from the extension of her wantonness, and no extravagance of manner or hardihood of assertion is then too great for this Senator. The frenzy of Don Quixote, in behalf of his wench, Dulcinea del Toboso, is all surpassed. The asserted rights of slavery, which shock equality of all kinds, are cloaked by a fantastic claim of equality. If the slave States cannot enjoy what, in mockery of the great fathers of the Republic, he misnames equality under the Constitution--in other words, the full power in the National Territories to compel fellow-men to unpaid toil, to separate husband and wife, and to sell little children at the auction block-- then, sir, the chilvaric Senator will conduct the State of South Carolina out of the Union! Heroic knight! Exalted Senator! A second Moses comes for a second exodus!

## DRED SCOTT v. SANFORD (1857)

In 1787 Congress, by the Northwest Ordinance, prohibited slavery in the Northwest territory, and the new Congress ratified that prohibition after the Constitution went into effect. In 1820, Congress similarly prohibited slavery in the territories of the United States north of the line marking the southern boundary of Missouri. But with the acquisition of new lands from Mexico in the 1840s there arose two questions that would ultimately split the Union asunder. Would there be slavery in the new territories, and who would make that determination? Apologists for slavery now argued that Congress had no power to prohibit slavery there. Stephen Douglas and the 1850 compromise approved "popular sovereignty," whereby local residents would decide yea or nay. Free soilers insisted that slavery be utterly prohibited from expanding into the territories; of course the abolitionists concurred. In the important case excerpted here the Supreme Court, sympathetic to the south, deals with these issues. Dred Scott was a slave who argued that since his master had taken him to a territory defined as free soil by the Missouri Compromise, he had been freed. The counter argument was that a slave, as property, could be moved anywhere in the U.S., for property rights are protected under the 5th Amendment. The Supreme Court deals with Dred Scott's citizenship, slaves as property, and the competence of Congress to exclude slavery from the territories. The Court's decision demolished the popular sovereignty, free soil, and abolitionist positions, and aroused cries of outrage from Republicans and others in the North. The Dred Scott decision had a devastating effect on North-South relations, which were rapidly deteriorating in this crisis decade of the 1850s.

Held, that the plaintiff in error could not be and was not a citizen of the State of Missouri, within the meaning of the Constitution of the United States, and consequently was not entitled to sue in its courts.

The legislation and histories of the times, and the language used in the Declaration of Independence, show that neither the class of persons who had been imported as slaves, nor their descendants, whether they had become free or not, were then acknowledged as part of the people, nor intended to be included in the general words used in that instrument.

The descendants of Africans who were imported into this country and sold as slaves, when they shall become emancipated, or who are born of parents who had become free before their birth, are not citizens of a state in the sense in which the word "citizen" is used in the Constitution of the United States.

The enslaved African race was not intended to be included in, and formed no part of, the people who framed and adopted the Declaration of Independence.

---

Dred Scott v. John F. A. Sandford, 19 Howard 393 (1857). The official court record misspells the name of Scott's owner.

When the framers of the Constitution were conferring special rights and privileges upon the citizens of a state in every other part of the Union, it is impossible to believe that these rights and privileges were intended to be extended to the negro race.

The words of the Constitution should be given the meaning they were intended to bear, when that instrument was framed and adopted.

Where the court has decided against the jurisdiction of the Circuit Court on a plea of abatement, it has still the right to examine any question presented by exception or by the record, and may reverse the judgment for errors committed, and remand the case to the Circuit Court for it to dismiss the case for want of jurisdiction.

The right of property in a slave is distinctly and expressly affirmed in the Constitution.

The Act of Congress which prohibited a citizen from holding and owning property of this kind in the territory of the United States north of the line therein mentioned (thirty-six degrees thrity minutes north latitude), is not warranted by the Constitution, and is therefore void.

Neither Dred Scott himself, nor any of his family were made free by being carried into such territory: even if they had been carried there by their owner with the intention of becoming permanent residents.


## JOHN BROWN'S LAST WORDS (1859)

Evaluations of the life and death of John Brown are as dramatic in their disagreement as Brown himself was in his life. A martyred hero to some, an insane rabble-rouser to others, at least this can be said of Brown: he was instrumental in bringing about the violent, bloody conflict that he believed was necessary to purge America of the taint of slavery. He handed the following sentence to one of his guards on the morning of his execution.

Charlestown, Va, 2d, December, 1859.

I John Brown am now quite certain that the crimes of this guilty, land: will never be purged away; but with Blood. I had as I now think: vainly flattered myself that without verry much bloodshed; it might be done.

---

Louis Ruchames, ed., A John Brown Reader (New York, 1959), p. 159.

## SOUTH CAROLINA'S DECLARATION OF THE CAUSES OF SECESSION (1860)

> In December, 1860, the legislature of South Carolina revoked that state's allegiance to the United States Constitution and left the Union. The following is the explanation for their decision.

The people of the State of South Carolina in Convention assembled, on the 2d day of April, A.D. 1852, declared that the frequent violations of the Constitution of the United States by the Federal Government, and its encroachments upon the reserved rights of the States, fully justified this State in their withdrawal from the Federal Union; but in deference to the opinions and wishes of the other Slaveholding States, she forbore at that time to exercise this right. Since that time these encroachments have continued to increase, and further forbearance ceases to be a virtue.

And now the State of South Carolina having resumed her separate and equal place among nations, deems it due to herself, to the remaining United States of America, and to the nations of the world, that she should declare the immediate cause which have led to this act . . . .

In 1787, Deputies were appointed by the States to revise the articles of Confederation; and on 17th September 1787, these Deputies recommended, for the adoption of the States, the Articles of Union, known as the Constitution of the United States . . . .

Thus was established, by compact between the States, a Government with defined objects and powers, limited to the express words of the grant . . . . We hold that the Government thus established is subject to the two great principles asserted in the Declaration of Independence; and we hold further, that the mode of its formation subjects it to a third fundamental principle, namely, the law of compact. We maintain that in every compact between two or more parties, the obligation is mutual; that the failure of one of the contracting parties to perform a material part of the agreement, entirely releases the obligation of the other; and that, where no arbiter is provided, each party is remitted to his own judgment to determine the fact of failure, with all its consequences.

In the present case, that fact is established with certainty. We assert that fourteen of the States have deliberately refused for years past to fulfil their constitutional obligations, and we refer to their own statutes for the proof.

The Constitution of the United States, in its fourth Article, provides as follows:

"No person held to service or labor in one State under the laws thereof, escaping into another, shall, in consequence of any law or regulation therein, be discharged from such service or labor, but shall be delivered up, on claim of the party to whom such service or labor may be due."

The stipulation was so material to the compact that without it that compact would not have been made. The greater number of the contracting parties held slaves, and they had previously evinced their estimate of the value of such a stipulation by making it a condition in the Ordinance for the government of the territory ceded by Virginia, which obligations, and the laws of the General Government, have ceased to effect the objects of the Constitution. The States of Maine, New Hampshire, Vermont, Massachusetts, Connecticut, Rhode Island, New York, Pennsylvania, Illinois, Indiana,

---

Frank Moore, ed., The Rebellion Record: A Diary of American Events (New York, 1867), I, 3-4.

Michigan, Wisconsin and Iowa, have enacted laws which either nullify the acts of Congress, or render useless any attempt to execute them . . . . Thus the constitutional compact has been deliberately broken and disregarded by the non-slaveholding States; and the consequence follows that South Carolina is released from her obligation . . . .

We affirm that these ends for which this Government was instituted have been defeated, and the Government itself has been destructive of them by the action of the non-slaveholding States. Those States have assumed the right of deciding upon the propriety of our domestic institutions; and have denied the rights of property established in fifteen of the States and recognized by the Constitution; they have denounced as sinful the institution of Slavery; they have permitted the open establishment among them of societies, whose avowed object is to disturb the peace of and eloin the property of the citizens of other States. They have encouraged and assisted thousands of our slaves to leave their homes; and those who remain, have been incited by emissaries, books, and pictures, to servile insurrection.

For twenty-five years this agitation has been steadily increasing, until it has now secured to its aid the power of the common Government. Observing the <u>forms</u> of the Constitution, a sectional party has found within that article establishing the Executive Department, the means of subverting the Constitution itself. A geographical line has been drawn across the Union, and all the States north of that line have united in the election of a man to the high office of President of the United States whose opinions and purposes are hostile to Slavery. He is to be intrusted with the administration of the common Government, because he has declared that that "Government cannot endure permanently half slave, half free," and that the public mind must rest in the belief that Slavery is in the course of ultimate extinction.

This sectional combination for the subversion of the Constitution has been aided, in some of the States , by elevating to citizenship persons who, by the supreme law of the land, are incapable of becoming citizens; and their votes have been used to inaugurate a new policy, hostile to the South, and destructive of its peace and safety.

On the 4th of March next this party will take possession of the Government. It has announced that the South shall be excluded from the common territory, that the Judicial tribunal shall be made sectional, and that a war must be waged against Slavery until it shall cease throughout the United States.

The guarantees of the Constitution will then no longer exist; the equal rights of the States will be lost. The Slaveholding States will no longer have the power of self-government, or self-protection, and the Federal Government will have become their enemy.

Sectional interest and animosity will deepen the irritation; and all hope of remedy is rendered vain, by the fact that the public opinion at the North has invested a great political error with the sanctions of a more erroneous religious belief.

We, therefore, the people of South Carolina, by our delegates in Convention assembled, appealing to the Supreme Judge of the world for the rectitude of our intentions, have solemnly declared that the Union heretofore existing between this States and the other States of North America is dissolved, and that the State of South Carolina has resumed her position among the nations of the world, as separate and independent state, with full power of levy war, conclude peace, contract alliances, establish commerce, and to do all other acts and things which independent States may of right do.

## ALEXANDER STEPHENS COMMENTS ON THE CONFEDERACY (1861)[1]

Though Georgia's Alexander Stephens had opposed secession, he bowed to his state's decision, and was chosen the Vice President of the new Confederate States of America. In this speech, given in Savannah less than a month before Fort Sumter, Stephens comments on the C.S.A. constitution and slavery's part in it.

The new constitution has put at rest, forever, all the agitating questions relating to our peculiar institution--African slavery, as it exists amongst us--the proper status of the Negro in our form of civilization. This was the immediate cause of the late rupture and present revolution. Jefferson in his forecast has anticipated this as the "rock upon which the old Union would split." He was right. What was conjecture with him, is now a realized fact. But whether he fully comprehended the great truth upon which that rock stood and stands may be doubted. The prevailing ideas entertained by him and most of the leading statesmen at the time of the formation of the old constitution, were that the enslavement of the African was in violation of the laws of nature; that it was wrong in principle, socially, morally, and politically. It was an evil they knew not well how to deal with, but the general opinion of the men of that day was that, somehow or other in the order of Providence, the institution would be evanescent and pass away. This idea, though not incorporated in the constitution, was the prevailing idea at the time . . . . Those ideas, however, were fundamentally wrong. They rested upon the assumption of the equality of the races . . . .

Our new government is founded upon exactly the opposite idea; its foundations are laid, its corner-stone rests upon the great truth that the negro is not equal to the white man; that slavery--subordination to the superior race--is his natural and normal condition. (Applause.)

This, our new government, is the first, in the history of the world, based upon this great physical, philosophical, and moral truth.


## WILLIAM H. SEWARD ON THE TRENT AFFAIR (1861)[2]

The seizure of two Confederate diplomats and their secretaries (James M. Mason, John Slidell, E.J. MacFarland, and George Eustis) from the British ship Trent by the Union produced a serious crisis in

---

[1] Henry Cleveland, Alexander H. Stephens in Public and Private With Letters and Speeches, Before, During, and Since the War (Philadelphia, 1866), p. 721.

[2] U.S. Navy Department, Official Records of the Union and Confederate Navies in the War of the Rebellion (Washington, D.C., 1894), I, Series I, 177-187.

relations between Washington and London. President Lincoln was caught between alienating public support (the Union naval commander, Charles Wilkes, earned widespread approval for his actions) and risking a diplomatic rupture--or worse--with the British. Yet, the law of the sea clearly supported the British position that Wilkes had acted illegally. Lincoln skillfully arranged the return of the four Confederates. The crisis was resolved peacefully, owing in large measure to the built-in delay in simply exchanging communications (it took anywhere from 7-18 days for mail service between London and the eastern United States).

[Seward to Lord Lyons (British Minister), December 26, 1861]

The British Government has rightly conjectured what it is now my duty to state, that Captain Wilkes, in conceiving and executing the proceeding in question, acted upon his own suggestions of duty, without any direction or instruction, or even foreknowledge of it, on the part of this Government. No direction had been given to him or any other naval officer to arrest the four persons named, or any of them, on the <u>Trent</u>, or on any other British vessel, or on any other neutral vessel, at the place where it occurred or elsewhre. The British Government will justly infer from these facts that the United States no only have had no purpose, but even no thought, of forcing into discussion the question which has arisen, or any other which could affect in any way the sensibilities of the British nation.

It is true that a round shot was fired by the <u>San Jacinto</u> from her pivot gun when the <u>Trent</u> was distantly approaching; but as the facts have been reported to this Government, the shot was nevertheless intentionally fired in a direction so obviously divergent from the course of the <u>Trent</u> as to be quite as harmless as a blank shot, while it should be regarded as a signal. . . .

It had been settled by correspondence that the United States and Great Britain, mutually recognized, as applicable to this local strife, these two articles of the declaration made by the Congress of Paris, in 1856, viz, that the neutral or friendly flag should cover enemy's goods not contraband of war, and that neutral goods not contraband of war are not liable to capture under an enemy's flag. These exceptions of contraband from favor were a negative acceptance by the parties of the rule hitherto everywhere recognized as a part of the law of nations, that whatever is contraband is liable to capture and confiscation in all cases. . . .

Your lordship will now perceive that the case before us, . . . was undertaken as a simple, legal, and customary belligerent proceeding by Captain Wilkes to arrest and capture a neutral vessel engaged in carrying contraband of war for the use and benefit of the insurgents.

The question before us is, whether this proceeding was authorized by and conducted according to the law of nations. It involves the following enquiries. . . .

I address myself to the first inquiry, namely; Were the four persons mentioned, and their supposed dispatches, contraband?

Maritime law so generally deals, as its professors say, <u>in rem</u>, that is, with property, and so seldom with persons that it seems a straining of the term "contraband" to apply it to them. But persons as well as property may become contraband, since the word means broadly "contrary to proclamation, prohibited, illegal, unlawful." All writers and judges pronounce naval or military persons in the service of the enemy contraband. . . .

The second enquiry is, whether Captain Wilkes had a right, by the law of nations, to detain and search the Trent. . . .

Whatever disputes have existed concerning a right of visitation or search in time of peace none, it is supposed, has existed in modern times about the right of a belligerent in time of war to capture contraband in neutral and even friendly merchant vessels and of the right of visitation and search in order to determine whether they are neutral and are documented as such according to law of nations. . . .

The third question is, whether Captain Wilkes exercised the right of search in a lawful and proper manner. If any doubt hung over this point, as the case was presented in the statement of it adopted by the British Government, I think it must already have passed away before the modification of that statement which I have already submitted.

I proceed to the fourth enquiry, namely, having found the suspected contraband of war on board the Trent, had Captain Wilkes a right to capture the same? Such a capture is the chief, if not the only, recognized object of the permitted visitation and search. . . . The law is so very liberal in this respect that when contraband is found on board a neutral vessel, not only is the contraband forfeited, but the vessel which is the vehicle of its passage or transportation, being tainted, also becomes contraband, and is subject to capture and confiscation.

Only the fifth question remains, namely, did Captain Wilkes exercise the right of capturing the contraband in conformity with the law of nations?

It is just here that the difficulties of the case begin.

What is the manner which the law of nations prescribes for disposing of the contraband when you have found and seized it on board of the neutral vessel? The answer would be easily found if the question were, what shall you do with the contraband vessel? You must take or send her into a convenient port and subject her to a judicial prosecution there in admiralty, which will try and decide the questions of belligerency, neutrality, contraband, and capture. So again you would promptly find the same answer if the question were, what is the manner of proceeding prescribed by the law of nations in regard to the contraband, if it be property, or things, or material, or pecuniary value? But the question here concerns the mode of procedure in regard, not to the vessel that was carrying the contraband, nor yet the contraband things which worked the forfeiture of the vessel, but to contraband persons. . . .

While the law authorities were found silent, it was suggested at an early day by this Government that you should take the captured persons into a convenient port and institute judicial proceedings there to try the controversy. But only courts of admiralty have jurisdiction in maritime cases, and these courts have formulas to try only claims to contraband chattels, but none to try claims concerning contraband persons. The courts can entertain no proceedings and render no judgment in favor of or against the alleged contraband men. . . .

In the present case Captain Wilkes, after capturing the contraband persons and making prize of the Trent, in what seems to us a perfectly lawful manner, instead of sending her into port released her from the capture and permitted her to proceed with her whole cargo upon her voyage. He thus effectually prevented the judicial examination which might otherwise have occurred.

If now the capture of the contraband persons and the capture of the contraband vessel are to be regarded not as two separable or distinct transactions under the law of nations, but as one transaction, one capture only, then it follows that the capture in this case was left unfinished, or was abandoned. . . .

I trust that I have shown to the satisfaction of the British Government . . . that what has happened has been simply an inadvertency, consisting in a departure by a naval officer, free from any wrongful motive, from a rule uncertainly established, and probably by the several parties concerned either imperfectly understood or entirely unknown. For this error the British Government has right to expect the same reparation that we, as an independent state, should expect from Great Britain or from any other friendly nation in a similar case.

I have not been unaware that in examining this question I have fallen into an argument for what seems to be the British side of it against my own country, but I am relieved from all embarrassment on that subject. I had hardly fallen into that line of argument when I discovered that I was really defending and maintaining, not an exclusively British interest, but an old honored and cherished American cause, not upon British authorities, but upon principles that constitute a large portion of the distinctive policy by which the United States have developed the resources of a continent, and thus becoming a considerable maritime power, have won the respect and confidence of many nations. . . .

If I decide this case in favor of my own Government I must disallow its most cherished principles and reverse and forever abandon its essential policy. The country can not afford the sacrifice. If I maintain those principles and adhere to that policy, I must surrender the case itself. It will be seen, therefore, that his Government could not deny the justice of the claim presented to us in this respect upon its merits. We are asked to do to the British nation just what we have always insisted all nations ought to do to us. . . .

The four persons in question are now held in military custody at Fort Warren, in the State of Massachusetts. They will be cheerfully liberated. Your lordship will please indicate a time and place for receiving them.

## ABRAHAM LINCOLN

His contemporaries sometimes took Abraham Lincoln for an unsophisticated, rather simpleminded politician whom they could manipulate to their advantage. Instead, they encountered a complex, introspective, and extremely capable statesman. But posterity seems to have fallen into a similar error of oversimplifying Lincoln: this time to venerate him as the Great Emancipator, the friend of the freed slave, and the savior of the Union. Just who was the real Abraham Lincoln, and what were his beliefs about slavery, race relations, and political realities? The following selections will provide some answers, but will also reveal the depth and complexity of the sixteenth president. Through him, one may see something of the tangled roots of the Civil War.

a.  Letter to a friend on equality, 1855[1]

I am not a Know-Nothing. That is certain. How could I be? How can any one who abhors the oppression of negroes, be in favor of degrading classes of white people? Our progress in degeneracy appears to me to be pretty rapid. As a nation, we began by declaring that "all men are created equal." We now practically read it "all men are create equal, except negroes." When the Know-Nothings get control, it will read "all men are created equal, except negroes, and foreigners, and catholics." When it comes to this I should prefer emigrating to some country where they make no pretence of loving liberty--to Russia, for instance, where despotism can be taken pure, and without the base alloy of hypocracy [sic].

b.  Statement on equality, 1858[2]

I hold that. . . there is no reason in the world why the negro is not entitled to all the natural rights enumerated in the Declaration of Independence, the right to life, liberty and the pursuit of happiness. [Loud cheers.] I hold that he is as much entitled to these as the white man. I agree with Judge Douglas he is not my equal in many respects--certainly not in color, perhaps not in moral or intellectual endowment. But in the right to eat the bread, without leave of anybody else, which his own hand earns, he is my equal and the equal of Judge Douglas, and the equal of every living man. [Great applause.]

c.  Statement on Republican principles, 1858[3]

The Republican party. . . hold that this government was instituted to secure the blessings of freedom, and that slavery is an unqualified evil to the negro, to the white man, to the soil, and to the State. Regarding it an evil, they will not molest it in the States where it exists; they will not overlook the constitutional guards which our forefathers have placed around it; they will do nothing which can give proper offence to those who hold slaves by legal sanction; but they will use every constitutional method to prevent the evil from becoming larger and involving more negroes, more white men, more soil, and more States in its deplorable consequences. They will, if possible, place it where the public mind shall rest in the belief that it is in course of ultimate peaceable extinction, in God's own good time. And to this end they will, if possible, restore the government to the policy of the fathers--the policy of preserving the new territories from the baneful influence of human bondage, as the Northwestern territories were sought to be preserved by the ordinance of 1787 and the compromise act of 1820. They will oppose, in all its length and breadth, the modern Democratic idea that slavery is as good as freedom, and ought to have room for expansion all over the continent, if people can be found to carry it. . . .

---

[1] Letter to his friend, Joshua Speed, August 24, 1855.

[2] Speech on August 21, 1858 at Ottawa, Illinois, during Lincoln-Douglas debates.

[3] Speech on September 11, 1858 at Edwardsville, Illinois, during the Lincoln-Douglas debates.

Now, when by all these means you have succeeded in dehumanizing the negro; when you have put him down, and made it forever impossible for him to be but as the beasts of the field; when you have extinguished his soul, and placed him where the ray of hope is blown out in darkness like that which broods over the spirits of the damned; are you quite sure the demon which you have roused will not turn and rend you? What constitutes the bulwark of our own liberty and independence? It is not our frowning battlements, our bristling sea coasts, the guns of our war steamers, or the strength of our gallant and disciplined army. These are not our reliance against a resumption of tyranny in our fair land. All of them may be turned against our liberties, without making us stronger or weaker for the struggle. Our reliance is in the love of liberty which God has planted in our bosoms. Our defense is in the preservation of the spirit which prizes liberty as the heritage of all men, in all lands, every where. Destroy this spirit, and you have planted the seeds of despotism around your own doors. Familiarize yourselves with the chains of bondage, and you are preparing your own limbs to wear them. Accustomed to trample on the rights of those around you, you have lost the genius of your own independence, and become the fit subjects of the first cunning tyrant who rises. And let me tell you, all these things are prepared for you with the logic of history, if the elections shall promise that the next Dred Scott decision and all future decisions will be quietly acquiesced in by the people.

d. Statement on racial equality, 1858[1]

I am not, nor ever have been in favor of bringing about in any way the social and political equality of the white and black races, [applause]--that I am not nor ever have been in favor of making voters or jurors of negroes, nor of qualifying them to hold office, nor to intermarry with white people; and I will say in addition to this that there is a physical difference between the white and black races which I believe will for ever forbid the two races living together on terms of social and political equality. And inasmuch as they cannot so live, while they do remain together there must be the position of superior and inferior, and I as much as any other man am in favor of having the superior position assigned to the white race. I say upon this occasion I do not perceive that because the white man is to have the superior position the negro should be denied everything. I do not understand that because I do not want a negro woman for a slave I must necessarily want her for a wife. [Cheers and laughter.] My understanding is that I can just let her alone. . . . I will add to this that I have never seen to my knowledge a man, woman or child who was in favor of producing a perfect equality, social and political, between negroes and white men.

e. Letter on Jeffersonian principles, 1859[2]

Bearing in mind that about seventy years ago, two great political parties were first formed in this country, that Thomas Jefferson was the head of one of them, and Boston the head-quarters of the other, it is both curious

---

[1] Speech on September 18, 1858 at Charleston, Illinois, during the Lincoln-Douglas debates.

[2] Letter to Henry L. Pierce and Others, April 6, 1859, regretting that he cannot attend a Jefferson's birthday celebration.

and interesting that those supposed to descend politically from the party opposed to Jefferson, should now be celebrating his birth-day in their own original seat of empire, while those claiming political descent from him have nearly ceased to breathe his name everywhere.

Remembering too, that the Jefferson party were formed upon their supposed superior devotion to the personal rights of men, holding the rights of property to be secondary only, and greatly inferior, and then assuming that the so-called democracy of to-day, are the Jefferson, and their opponents, the anti-Jefferson parties, it will be equally interesting to note how completely the two have changed hands as to the principle upon which they were originally supposed to be be divided.

The democracy of to-day hold the liberty of one man to be absolutely nothing, when in conflict with another man's right of property. Republicans, on the contrary, are for both the man and the dollar; but in case of conflict, the man before the dollar. . . .

This is a world of compensations; and he who would be no slave, must consent to have no slave. Those who deny freedom to others, deserve it not for themselves; and, under a just God, can not long retain it.

All honor to Jefferson--to the man who, in the concrete pressure of a struggle for national independence by a single people, had the coolness, forecast, and capacity to introduce into a merely revolutionary document, an abstract truth, applicable to all men and all times, and so to embalm it there, that to-day, and in all coming days, it shall be a rebuke and a stumbling-block to the very harbingers of re-appearing tyrany [sic] and oppression.

f. Statement to blacks on the merits of recolonization, 1862

Your race are suffering, in my judgment, the greatest wrong inflicted on any people. But even when you cease to be slaves, you are yet far removed from being placed on an equality with the white race. You are cut off from many of the advantages which the other race enjoy. The aspiration of men is to enjoy equality with the best when free, but on this broad continent, not a single man of your race is made the equal of a single man of ours. Go where you are treated the best, and the ban is still upon you.

I do not propose to discuss this, but to present it as a fact with which we have to deal. I cannot alter it if I would. It is a fact, about which we all think and feel alike, I and you. We look to our condition, owing to the existence of the two races on this continent. I need not recount to you the effects upon white men, growing out of the institution of Slavery. I believe in its general evil effects on the white race. See our present condition--the country engaged in war!--our white men cutting one another's throats, none knowing how far it will extend; and then consider what we know to be the truth. But for your race among us there could not be war, although many men engaged on either side do not care for you one way or the other. Nevertheless, I repeat, without the institution of Slavery and the colored race as a basis, the war could not have an existence.

It is better for us both, therefore, to be separated. . . . I suppose one of the principal difficulties in the way of colonization is that the free colored man cannot see that his comfort would be advanced by it. . . .

---

Lincoln's Address to a Deputation of Negroes, reported in the New York Tribune, August 15, 1862.

One reason for an unwillingness to do so is that some of you would rather remain within reach of the country of your nativity. I do not know how much attachment you may have toward our race. It does not strike me that you have the greatest reason to love them. But still you are attached to them at all events.

The place I am thinking about having for a colony is in Central America. It is nearer to us than Liberia--

g. Letter responding to the criticisms of Horace Greeley, 1862[1]

I would save the Union. I would save it the shortest way under the Constitution. The sooner the national authority can be restored; the nearer the Union will be "the Union as it was." If there be those who would not save the Union, unless they could at the same time <u>save</u> slavery, I do not agree with them. If there be those who would not save the Union unless they could at the same time <u>destroy</u> slavery, I do not agree with them. My paramount object in this struggle is to save the Union, and is not either to save or to destroy slavery. If I could save the Union without freeing <u>any</u> slave I would do it, and if I could save it by freeing <u>all</u> the slaves I would do it; and if I could save it by freeing some and leaving others alone I would also do that. What I do about slavery, and the colored race, I do because I believe it helps to save the Union; and what I forbear, I forbear because I do <u>not</u> believe it would help to save the Union. . . .

I have here stated my purpose according to my view of <u>official</u> duty; and I intend no modification of my oft-expressed <u>personal</u> wish that all men every where could be free.

## ABRAHAM LINCOLN, SECOND INAUGURAL ADDRESS (1865)[2]

Lincoln embarked on his second administration just six weeks before his assassination. He was both ill and depressed in these last weeks, and subject to grim forebodings. His second inaugural address was short, full of sadness and weariness, but also of determination and certainty that some great and holy purpose was being served by the suffering America was enduring. The introspective, compassionate, and even spiritual tone of the address seems unexpected for a commander-in-chief in wartime, but it reflects Lincoln's character and his state of mind in March of 1865.

---

[1] Letter to Horace Greeley, August 22, 1862.

[2] James D. Richardson, ed., <u>A Compilation of the Messages and Papers of the Presidents</u> (Washington, D.C., 1908), VI, 276-277.

FELLOW-COUNTRYMEN: At this second appearing to take the oath of the Presidential office there is less occasion for an extended address than there was at the first. Then a statement somewhat in detail of a course to be pursued seemed fitting and proper. Now, at the expiration of four years, during which public declarations have been constantly called forth on every point and phase of the great contest which still absorbs the attention and engrosses the energies of the nation, little that is new could be presented. The progress of our arms, upon which all else chiefly depends, is as well known to the public as to myself, and it is, I trust, reasonably satisfactory and encouraging to all. With high hope for the future, no prediction in regard to it is ventured.

On the occasion corresponding to this four years ago all thoughts were anxiously directed to an impending civil war. All dreaded it, all sought to avert it. While the inaugural address was being delivered from this place, devoted altogether to <u>saving</u> the Union without war, insurgent agents were in the city seeking to <u>destroy</u> it without war--seeking to dissolve the Union and divide effects by negotiation. Both parties deprecated war, but one of them would <u>make</u> war rather than let the nation survive, and the other would <u>accept</u> war rather than let it perish, and the war came.

One-eighth of the whole population were colored slaves, not distributed generally over the Union, but localized in the southern part of it. These slaves constituted a peculiar and powerful interest. All knew that this interest was somehow the cause of the war. To strengthen, perpetuate, and extend this interest was the object for which the insurgents would rend the Union even by war, while the Government claimed no right to do more than to restrict the territorial enlargement of it. Neither party expected for the war the magnitude or the duration which it has already attained. Neither anticipated that the <u>cause</u> of the conflict might cease with or even before the conflict itself should cease. Each looked for an easier triumph, and a result less fundamental and astounding. Both read the same Bible and pray to the same God, and each invokes His aid against the other. It may seem strange that any men should dare to ask a just God's assistance in wringing their bread from the sweat of other men's faces, but let us judge not, that we be not judged. The prayers of both could not be answered. That of neither has been answered fully. The Almighty has His own purposes. "Woe unto the world because of offenses; for it must needs to that offenses come, but woe to that man by whom the offense cometh." If we shall suppose that American slavery is one of those offenses which, in the providence of God, must needs come, but which, having continued through His appointed time, He now wills to remove, and that He gives to both North and South this terrible war as the woe due to those by whom the offense came, shall we discern therein any departure from those divine attributes which the believers in a living God always ascribe to Him? Fondly do we hope, fervently do we pray, that this mighty scourge of war may speedily pass away. Yet, if God wills that it continue until all the wealth piled by the bondsman's two hundred and fifty years of unrequited toil shall be sunk, and until every drop of blood drawn with the lash shall be paid by another drawn with the sword, as was said three thousand years ago, so still it must be said "the judgments of the Lord are true and righteous altogether."

With malice toward none, with charity for all, with firmness in the right as God gives us to see the right, let us strive on to finish the work we are in, to bind up the nation's wounds, to care for him who shall have borne the battle and for his widow and his orphan, to do all which may achieve and cherish a just and lasting peace among ourselves and with all nations.

## GENERAL ROBERT E. LEE'S FAREWELL TO HIS ARMY (1865)[1]

Through three years of shortages of men and supplies General Lee had demonstrated exceptional military leadership. The overwhelming numerical superiority of the enemy and the lack of Confederate resources had finally brought defeat. At Appomattox he took his final leave of the men, for many of whom Lee himself had become the sole reason for their continuing the struggle.

After four years of arduous service, marked by unsurpassed courage and fortitude, the Army of Northern Virginia has been compelled to yield to overwhelming numbers and resources. I need not tell the survivors of so many hard-fought battles, who have remained steadfast to the last, that I have consented to his result from no distrust of them: but, feeling that valour and devotion could accomplish nothing that could compensate for the loss that would have attended the continuation of the contest, I have determined to avoid the useless sacrifice of those whose past services have endeared them to their countrymen. By the terms of the agreement, officers and men can return to their homes and remain there until exchanged. You will take with you the satisfaction that proceeds from the consciousness of duty faithfully performed; and I earnestly pray that a merciful God will extend to you His blessing and protection. With an increasing admiration of your constancy and devotion to your country, and a grateful remembrance of your kind and generous consideration of myself, I bid you an affectionate farewell.

## JEFFERSON DAVIS ON LINCOLN'S ASSASSINATION (1881)[2]

On Good Friday, 1865, Abraham Lincoln was assassinated. While the North mourned his death, many in the South expressed their joy. The President of the Confederacy, Jefferson Davis, was in flight to evade capture by Union forces, but he had a different reaction to the news. These comments, made sixteen years later, may or may not indicate Davis's true feelings in 1865, but they reflect a perceptive awareness--in hindsight at least--of the consequences of Lincoln's death for Reconstruction.

We arrived at Charlotte on April 18, 1865, and I there received, at the moment of dismounting, a telegram from General Breckinridge announcing, on information received from General Sherman, that President Lincoln had been assassinated. An influential citizen of the town, who had come to welcome me,

---

[1] R. E. Lee, Recollections and Letters of General Robert E. Lee (New York, 1924), pp. 153-154.

[2] Jefferson Davis, The Rise and Fall of the Confederate Government (New York, 1881), II, 683-684.

was standing near me, and, after remarking to him in a low voice that I had received sad intelligence, I handed the telegram to him. Some troopers encamped in the vicinity had collected to see me; they called to the gentleman who had the dispatch in his hand to read it, no doubt supposing it to be army news. He complied with their request, and a few, only taking in the fact but not appreciating the evil it portended, cheered, as was natural at news of the fall of one they considered their most powerful foe. The man who invented the story of my having read the dispatch with exultation, had free scope for his imagination, as he was not present, and had no chance to know whereof he bore witness, even if there had been any foundation of truth for his fiction.

For an enemy so relentless in the war for our subjugation, we could not be expected to mourn; yet, in view of its political consequences, it could not be regarded otherwise than as a great misfortune to the South. He had power over the Northern people, and was without personal malignity toward the people of the South. His successor was without power in the North, and the embodiment of malignity toward the Southern people, perhaps the more so because he had betrayed and deserted them in the hour of their need.

## EDMUND G. ROSS ON THE IMPEACHMENT OF ANDREW JOHNSON (1896)

> Executive power inevitably grows during wartime, but once war is over the normal restraints upon executive power in a constitutional system reexert themselves. Congress after the Civil War went so far as to seek the impeachment of Andrew Johnson, not only as a reaction to the power Lincoln had wielded during the war, but in an effort to remove a Chief Executive who did not support Radical Republician Reconstruction policies. The pretext for the impeachment effort was Johnson's violation of the Tenure of Office Act. Radicals, who had an overwhelming majority in both Houses, and who had gone so far as to choose a cabinet for the anticipated President Benjamin Wade, were unable to convince all Republicans in the Senate of the merits of their enterprise. One dissenting Republican, Edmund Ross of Kansas, later wrote about the impeachment.

For the first time in the history of the government, practically eighty years, the President of the United States was at the bar of the Senate, by virtue of a constitutional warrant, on an accusation of the House of Representatives of high crimes and misdemeanors in office, and his conviction and expulsion from office demanded in the name of all the people. . . .

Upon the closing of the hearing--even prior thereto, and again during the few days of recess that followed, the Senate had been carefully polled,

---

Edmund G. Ross, History of the Impeachment of Andrew Johnson (New York, 1896), pp. 133-172.

and the prospective vote of every member from whom it was possible to procure a committal, ascertained and registered in many a private memoranda. There were fifty-four members--all present. According to these memoranda, the vote would stand eighteen for acquittal, thirty-five for conviction--one less than the number required by the Constitution to convict. What that one vote would be, and could it be had, were anxious queries, of one to another, especially among those who had set on foot the impeachment enterprise and staked their future control of the government upon its success. Given for conviction and upon sufficient proofs, the President must step down and out of his place, the highest and most honorable and honoring in dignity and sacredness of trust in the constitution of human government, a disgraced man and a political pariah. If so cast upon insufficient proofs or from partisan considerations, the office of President of the United States would be degraded--cease to be a co-ordinate branch of the Government, and ever after subordinated to the legislative will. It would have practically revolutionized our splendid political fabric into a partisan Congressional autocracy. A political tragedy was imminent.

On the other hand, that vote properly given for acquittal, would at once free the Presidential office from imputed dishonor and strengthen our triple organization and distribution of powers and responsibilities. It would preserve the even tenor and courses of administration, and effectively impress upon the world a conviction of the strength and grandeur of Republican institutions in the hands of a free and enlightened people. . . .

It was plain that a single vote would be sufficient to turn the scales either way--to evict the President from his great office to go the balance of his life's journey with the brand of infamy upon his brow, or be relieved at once from the obloquy the inquisitors had sought to put upon him--and more than all else, to keep the honorable roll of American Presidents unsmirched before the world, despite the action of the House. . . .

Mr. Ross, of Kansas, was the fifth Republican Senator to vote "Not Guilty." Representing an intensely Radical constituency--entering the Senate but a few months after the close of a three years enlistment in the Union Army and not unnaturally imbued with the extreme partisan views and prejudices against Mr. Johnson then prevailing--his predilections were sharply against the President, and his vote was counted upon accordingly. But he had sworn to judge the defendant not by his political or personal prejudices, but by the facts elicited in the investigation. In his judgment those facts did not sustain the charge. . . .

[The articles of impeachment] failed because of their innate weakness. Failed because they proved nothing. Failed because not a single allegation of the entire indictment was or could be proven or tortured into an impeachable offense. Not a remark made by the President or an act performed in all the long and bitter controversy that had subsisted between himself and Congress could be brought nearer to the impeachment mark, in fact, few if any of them so near, as had been the every day rule in the House of Representatives during the previous two years in their treatment of the President. Yet nobody thought of impeaching members of the House for their every day personal vituperations against him.

Bill after bill had been offered in Congress, and law after law enacted, with apparently the sole purpose of hampering the Constitutional authority and functions of the President--even the assumption of Executive powers and judicial functions by Congress--the not remote purpose of which seemed to be his entrapment into some measure of resistance upon which could be based an indictment. The House seemed to be literally "lying in wait" for him, with traps set on every side for his ensnarement. . . .

When [attempts to persuade Ross] seemed to fail of the desired effect, more direct and, it was hoped, more effective methods were resorted to. The beleaguered Senator was reminded that the applicant represented the united sentiment of the people of the State from which he held his Senatorial seat-- that they demanded Mr. Johnson's conviction and removal--that that demand could not be safely denied, trifled with, or delayed; and that if money was wanted, to use the language of a notorious inquisitor of the House, Mr. Butler, speaking of the possibility of securing a designated vote for Impeachment--"tell the d-----d scoundrel that if he wants money, there is a bushel of it here to be had!" Mr. Butler's message was delivered.

So desperate were the inquisitors, and so close the certainty of the vote, that even a project of kidnapping a Senator under the pretense of taking a trip to Baltimore for much needed rest, where, if the terms to be there proffered were refused, a vacancy was to be created--by assassination, if necessary--then a recess of the Senate to afford time for the appointment by the Governor of that Senator's State of a successor who would vote for the Impeachment of the President--was entered upon and its execution attempted. But the trip to Baltimore for "rest" was not taken.

These are not pleasant facts to contemplate, but they somewhat conspicuously characterized the conditions of that time, and illustrate the real nature of the impeachment scheme. . . .

[T]he Republican majority of the Senate placed themselves and their party in the attitude of prosecutors in the case--instead of judges sworn to give the President an impartial trial and judgment that their course had the appearance, at least, of a conspiracy to evict the President for purely partisan purposes, regardless of testimony or the facts of the case--that public animosity against Mr. Johnson had been manufactured throughout the North by wild and vicious misrepresentations for partisan effect--that practically the entire Republican Party machinery throughout the country was bent to the work of prosecution. They party cry was "Crucify him!" "Convict him anyway, and try him afterwards!" With rare exceptions, the Republican Party of the country, press and people, were a unit in this insensate cry. . . .

There can be but one conclusion from these premises, established by the record of the trial--that the entire proceeding, from its inception in the House of Representatives to its conclusion in the Senate, was a thoroughly partisan prosecution on the part of the majority in both Houses, and that the country was saved from the shameful spectacle, and the dangerous consequences of such a proceeding, by the intervention and self-sacrifice of a few gentlemen who proposed to respect the obligation of their oath, and give Mr. Johnson, so far as in their power, a fair trial and judgment--and not having had such a trial--to give him the benefit of what he claimed he could prove in his own behalf and was not permitted to--and a verdict of "Not Guilty," regardless of consequences to themselves. . . .

The power of impeachment and removal becomes . . . a two-edged sword, which must be handled with consummate judgment and skill, and resort thereto had only in the gravest emergencies and for causes so clearly manifest as to preclude the possibility of partisan divisions or partisan judgments thereon. Otherwise, too ready resort to impeachment must inevitably establish and bring into common use a new and dangerous remedy for the cure of assumed political ills which have their origin only in partisan differences as to methods of administration. It would become an engine of partisan intolerance for the punishment and ostracism of political opponents, under the operation of which the great office of Chief Magistrate must inevitably lose its dignity, and decline from its Constitutional rank as a co-ordinate department of the Government, and its occupant no longer the political head and Chief Executive of the Nation, except in name.

It was in that sense, and to a pointed degree, that in the impeachment and trial of Andrew Johnson the quality of coordination of the three great Departments of Government--the Executive, Legislative, and Judicial--was directly involved--the House of Representatives as prosecutor--the President as defendant--the Senate sitting as the trial court in which the Chief Justice represented the judicial department as presiding officer. . . .

In a large sense, the American system of politics and of government was on trial, quite as much as was Andrew Johnson. The extreme element of American politics was in absolute control in the House of Representatives, and practically so, in the Senate. The impeachment and removal of the President on unsubstantiated, or even remotely doubtful charges, simply because of a disagreement between himself and Congress as to the method of treating a great public emergency, would have introduced a new and destructive practice into our political system. . . .

History affords too many illustrations of that tendency to decadence and disruption from disregard of the proper and necessary checks and balances in the distribution and equalization of the powers of government, to permit us to doubt what the final end would have been had the President been removed on the unsubstantiated accusation preferred by the House of Representatives. Our peculiar system of political government--a Democratic Republic--passed the danger point of its history in that hour.

## THADDEUS STEVENS AND THE NEW YORK TIMES ON RECONSTRUCTION (1865)

Northerners who had united in wishing to see the defeat of the Confederacy and the restoration of the Union did not agree on how the fallen South should be treated. The issue of how to reconstruct the South consumed the energies of politicians for over 20 years, beginning in 1865. Here we see two opposing viewpoints. Thaddeus Stevens's punitive attitude and far-reaching plans were voiced in a speech given in Lancaster, Pennsylvania, and represent the Radical Republican stand. The New York Times sees the task of Reconstruction in a very different light.

The New York Times, September 10 and 15, 1865.

(a) Thaddeus Stevens

[W]e hold it to be the duty of the government to inflict condign punishment on the rebel belligerents, and so weaken their hands that they can never again endanger the Union; and so reform their municipal institutions as to make them republican in spirit as well as in name.

We especially insist that the property of the chief rebels should be seized and appropriated to the payment of the National debt, caused by the unjust and wicked war which they instigated. . . .

[R]eformation must be effected; the foundation of their institutions, both political, municipal and social, must be broken up and relaid, or all our blood and treasure have been spent in vain. This can only be done by treating and holding them as a conquered people. . . . As a conquered territory, Congress would have full power to legislate for them. . . . They would be held in a territorial condition until they are fit to form State Constitutions, republican in fact, not in form only, and ask admission into the Union as new States. . . .

The whole fabric of Southern society must be changed, and never can it be done if this opportunity is lost. Without this, this government can never be, as it never has been, a true republic. Heretofore, it had more the features of aristocracy than of democracy. The Southern States have been despotisms, not governments of the people. . . .

But we can have [no excuse] if we do not thoroughly eradicate slavery and render it forever impossible in this republic. The slave power made war upon the nation. They declared the "more perfect Union" dissolved--solemnly declared themselves a foreign nation, alien to this republic; for four years were in fact what they claimed to be. We accepted war. We have conquered them, and as a conquered enemy we can give them laws; can abolish all their municipal institutions and form new ones. If we do not make those institutions fit to last through generations of freemen, a heavy curse will be on us. . . .

Is then all lost? Is this great conquest to be in vain? That will depend upon the virtue and intelligence of the next Congress.

(b) The New York Times

The defeated Southerners meet their calamity in a . . . manly style. They show in their defeat, as they did in their struggle,--courage, desperate tenacity of purpose, and that high-spirited readiness to meet all the responsibilities of their conduct, which never fails to command the respect of the world.

It may not be wholly in keeping with this courageous temper, that quite a number of these persons, on reading the speech of Hon. Thad. Stevens, have abandoned their business projects and gone home discouraged. They say they cannot face the desolation which his plans propose for the South. . . .

True, Mr. S. is a prominent and influential public man. . . . But as a public man he belongs rather to the past than the future. He is universally known to be extreme in all his views, sometimes to the verge of eccentricity;. . .

The people of the North are not revengeful. They have never hated the South. Even in the midst of the war they have cherished kindly sentiments toward the people they were compelled to fight; and now that the war is over, they have no thought or wish to crush a fallen foe. For they know perfectly well that the people of the South must come to be our friends,--that as the nation is one, so have all its people a common welfare,--only to be secured by common sentiments of respect and of mutual regard. . . . The great mass of the

Northern people, without regard to party, will sustain, heartily and vigorously, the policy of the President. They went into the war reluctantly, but they have fought it out victoriously; and they accept the extirpation of slavery, the perpetuation of the Union, the increased consideration and respect which we enjoy abroad, and the self-reliance and courage which it has developed at home, as equivalent for the sufferings, burdens and sacrifices it has involved.

BENJAMIN TILLMAN ON THE NEGRO (1907)

Benjamin Ryan Tillman ("Pitchfork Ben") became a United States Senator from South Carolina in 1895 with a reputation for flaming words and bad manners. He expressed his opinions loudly and often crudely on a variety of subjects, and especially so on the Negro question. Unlike his Southern aristocratic predecessors in the Senate who had given lip service to the prevailing democratic doctrines while glossing over the fact that South Carolina blacks were actually bound in political and social servitude, Tillman stated openly and frankly that the Negro should be held in subjugation.

It was then that "we shot them;" it was then that "we killed them;" it was then that "we stuffed ballot boxes." After the troops came and told us, "You must stop this rioting," we had decided to take the government away from men so debased as were the negroes--I will not say baboons; I never have called them baboons; I believe they are men, but some of them are so near akin to the monkey that scientists are yet looking for the missing link. . . .

[T]he white women of the South are in a state of siege; the greatest care is exercised that they shall at all times where it is possible not be left alone or unprotected, but that can not always and in every instance be the case. That Senator's daughter undertakes to visit a neighbor or is left home alone for a brief while. Some lurking demon who has watched for the opportunity seizes her; she is choked or beaten into insensibility and ravished, her body prostituted, her purity destroyed, her chastity taken from her, and a memory branded on her brain as with a red-hot iron to haunt her night and day as long as she lives. . . . And shall such a creature, because he has the semblance of a man, appeal to the law? Shall men coldbloodedly stand up and demand for him the right to have a fair trial and be punished in the regular course of justice? So far as I am concerned he has put himself outside the pale of the law, human and divine. He has sinned against the Holy Ghost. He has invaded the holy of holies. He has struck civilization a blow, the most deadly and cruel that the imagination can conceive. It is idle to

---

U.S. Congress, Senate, 59th Cong., 2nd sess., January 21, 1907, Congressional Record, XLI, 1440-1441.

reason about it; it is idle to preach about it. Our brains reel under the staggering blow and hot blood surges to the heart. Civilization peels off us, any and all of us who are men, and we revert to the original savage type whose impulse under any and all such circumstances has always been to "kill! kill! kill!". . . I have three daughters, but, so help me God, I had rather find either one of them killed by a tiger or a bear and gather up her bones and bury them, conscious that she had died in the purity of her maidenhood, than to have her crawl to me and tell me the horrid story that she had been robbed of the jewel of her womanhood by a black fiend. The wild beast would only obey the instinct of nature, and we would hunt him down and kill him just as soon as possible.

## THE VIOLENT SIDE OF AMERICAN RACISM

In the 1890s there were hundreds of vicious attacks upon black Americans, the majority occurring in the South. The decade witnessed over one thousand lynchings, as well as other deadly forms of punishment. Far from abating by 1900, racism was at a peak as the nation entered the Twentieth Century. At the same time that cries for restrictions against "undesirable" immigrants were increasing in the North, Jim Crow segregation laws were passed in the South to keep Negroes "in their place." Blacks who failed to observe legal and social pressures might find themselves victims of mob action, as is clearly shown in the following two tragic cases.

(a) Inch by inch the Negro was fairly cooked to death. Every few minutes fresh leaves were tossed on the funeral pyre until the blaze had passed the Negro's waist . . . . Even after the flesh had dropped away from his legs and the flames were leaping toward his face, Lowry retained consciousness . . . . Once or twice he attempted to pick up the hot ashes in his hands and thrust them in his mouth in order to hasten death.

As the flames were eating away his abdomen, a member of the mob stepped forward and saturated the body with gasoline. It was then only a few minutes until the Negro had been reduced to ashes.

(b) When the two Negroes were captured, they were tied to trees and while the funeral pyres were being prepared they were forced to suffer the most fiendish tortures. The blacks were forced to hold out their hands while one finger at a time was chopped off. The fingers were distributed as souveniers. The ears of the murderers were cut off. Holbert was beaten severely, his skull was fractured, and one of his eyes, knocked out with a stick, hung by a shred from the socket. . . . The most excruciating form of punishment consisted in the use of a large corkscrew in the hands of some of the mob. This instrument was bored into the flesh of the man and woman, in the arms, legs and body, and then pulled out, the spirals tearing out big pieces of raw, quivering flesh every time it was withdrawn.

---

Walter White, Rope and Faggot: A Biography of Judge Lynch (New York, 1969), pp. 24, 35-36.

## PLESSY v. FERGUSON (1896)

The retreat from Reconstruction culminated in the 1890s with the near-total disfranchisement of blacks in the South and passage of "Jim Crow" segregation laws. In 1890 Louisiana passed an "Act to Promote the Comfort of Passengers," requiring railroad companies to provide "separate but equal" cars for its white and black passengers, and prescribing criminal penalties for the violation of the law. Homer Plessy, who was one-eighth black, was arrested for riding in a white railroad car. His lawyers argued that the statute violated the 13th Amendment, which prohibited slavery and involuntary servitude, and the 14th Amendment, which extended citizenship and the equal protection of the laws to blacks as well as whites. The court's ruling here is the clarion justification for legal racial discrimination and was not reversed until 1954. Justice Henry Billings Brown delivered the Court's opinion; Justice John Marshall Harlan of Kentucky was the sole dissenter.

Justice Brown
A statute which implies merely a legal distinction between the white and colored races--a distinction which is founded in the color of the two races, and which must always exist so long as white men are distinguished from the other race by color--has no tendency to destroy the legal equality of the two races, or re-establish a state of involuntary servitude. . . .

The object of the [14th] Amendment was undoubtedly to enforce the absolute equality of the two races before the law, but in the nature of things it could not have been intended to abolish distinctions based upon color, or to enforce social, as distinguished from political, equality, or a commingling of the two races upon terms unsatisfactory to either. Laws permitting, and even requiring their separation in places where they are liable to be brought into contact do not necessarily imply the inferiority of either race to the other, and have been generally, if not universally, recognized as within the competency of the state legislatures in the exercise of their police power. . . .

We consider the underlying fallacy of the plaintiff's argument to consist in the assumption that the enforced separation of the two races stamps the colored race with a badge of inferiority. If this be so, it is not by reason of anything found in the act, but solely because the colored race chooses to put that construction upon it. . . . The argument also assumes that social prejudices may be overcome by legislation, and that equal rights cannot be secured to the negro except by an enforced commingling of the two races. We cannot accept this proposition. If the two races are to meet on terms of social equality, it must be the result of natural affinities, a mutual appreciation of each other's merits and a voluntary consent of

---

Plessy v. Ferguson, 163 U.S. 537 (1896).

individuals. . . . Legislation is powerless to eradicate racial instincts or to abolish distinctions based upon physical differences, and the attempt to do so can only result in accentuating the difficulties of the present situation. If the civil and political rights of both races be equal, one cannot be inferior to the other civilly or politically. If one race be inferior to the other socially, the Constitution of the United States cannot put them upon the same plane.

Justice Harlan, dissenting:

The 13th Amendment. . . . not only struck down the institution of slavery as previously existing in the United States, but it prevents the imposition of any burdens or disabilities that constitute badges of slavery or servitude. . . . [and] it was followed by the 14th Amendment, which added greatly to the dignity and glory of American citizenship, and to the security of personal liberty, . . .

These notable additions to the fundamental law were welcomed by the friends of liberty throughout the world. They removed the race line from our governmental systems. . . .

The white race deems itself to be the dominant race in this country. And so it is, in prestige, in achievements, in education, in wealth, and in power. . . . But in view of the Constitution, in the eye of the law, there is in this country no superior, dominant, ruling class of citizens. There is no caste here. Our Constitution is color-blind, and neither knows nor tolerates classes among citizens. In respect of civil rights, all citizens are equal before the law. The humblest is the peer of the most powerful. The law regards man as man, and takes no account of his surroundings or of his color when his civil rights as guaranteed by the supreme law of the land are involved. It is therefore to be regretted that this high tribunal, the final expositor of the fundamental law of the land, has reached the conclusion that it is competent for a state to regulate the enjoyment of their civil rights solely upon the basis of race.

In my opinion, the judgment this day rendered will, in time, prove to be quite as pernicious as the decision made by this tribunal in the <u>Dred Scott Case</u>. . . . The destinies of the two races in this country are indisollubly linked together, and the interests of both require that the common government of all shall not permit the seeds of race hate to be planted under the sanction of law. What can more certainly arouse race hate, what more certainly create and perpetuate a feeling of distrust between these races, than state enactments which, in fact, proceed on the ground that colored citizens are so inferior and degraded that they cannot be allowed to sit in public coaches occupied by white citizens? That, as all will admit, is the real meaning of such legislation as was enacted in Louisiana.

The sure guaranty of the peace and security of each race is the clear, distinct, unconditional recognition by our governments, national and state, of every right that inheres in civil freedom, and of the equality before the law of all citizens of the United States, without regard to race. . . .

We boast of the freedom enjoyed by our people above all other peoples. But it is difficult to reconcile that boast with a state of the law which, practically, puts the brand of servitude and degradation upon a large class of our fellow citizens,--our equals before the law. The thin disguise of "equal" accommodations for passengers in railroad coaches will not mislead any one, nor atone for the wrong this day done.

[ARTICLE VI.] In deciding the matters submitted to the Arbitrators, they shall be governed by the following three rules, which are agreed upon by the high contracting parties as rules to be taken as applicable to the case, and by such principles of international law not inconsistent therewith as the Arbitrators shall determine to have been applicable to the case.

[RULES.] A neutral Government is bound--

First, to use due diligence to prevent the fitting out, arming, or equipping, within its jurisdiction, of any vessel which it has reasonable ground to believe is intended to cruise or to carry on war against a Power with which it is at peace; and also to use like diligence to prevent the departure from its jurisdiction of any vessel intended to cruise or carry on war as above, such vessel having been specially adapted, in whole or in part, within such jurisdiction, to warlike use.

Secondly, not to permit or suffer either belligerent to make use of its ports or waters as the base of naval operations against the other, or for the purpose of the renewal or augmentation of military supplies or arms, or the recruitment of men.

Thirdly, to exercise due diligence in its own ports and waters, and, as to all persons within its jurisdiction, to prevent any violation of the foregoing obligations and duties.

Her Britannic Majesty has commanded her High Commissioners and Plenipotentiaries to declare that Her Majesty's Government cannot assent to the foregoing rules as a statement of principles of international law which were in force at the time when the claims mentioned in Article I arose, but that Her Majesty's Government, in order to evince its desire of strengthening the friendly relations between the two countries and of making satisfactory provision for the future, agrees that in deciding the questions between the two countries arising out of those claims, the Arbitrators should assume that Her Majesty's Government had undertaken to act upon the principles set forth in these rules.

And the high contracting parties agree to observe these rules as between themselves in future, and to bring them to the knowledge of other maritime Powers, and to invite them to accede to them. . . .

[ARTICLE XI.] The high contracting parties engage to consider the result of the proceedings of the tribunal of arbitration and of the board of Assessors, should such board be appointed, as a full, perfect, and final settlement of all the claims hereinbefore referred to; and further engage that every such claim, whether the same may or may not have been presented to the notice of, made, preferred, and laid before the tribunal or board, shall, from and after the conclusion of the proceedings of the tribunal or board, be considered and treated as finally settled, barred, and thenceforth inadmissible.

# BOOKER T. WASHINGTON ON THE FUTURE OF BLACKS IN AMERICA (1895)

> Booker T. Washington earned prominence as a spokesman for blacks during the difficult era of adjustment following Reconstruction, a time when racism was rampant in America. His conviction that salvation for blacks lay in education and employment was well received among whites, who saw in it little threat to white economic, political, and social supremacy. Washington, founder of Tuskegee Institute, a technical college for blacks in Alabama, offered the following advice to whites and blacks alike in his famous Atlanta Exposition Address. Even President Grover Cleveland congratulated him on the speech.

Our greatest danger is that in the great leap from slavery to freedom we may overlook the fact that the masses of us are to live by the productions of our hands, and fail to keep in mind that we shall prosper in proportion as we learn to dignify and glorify common labour and put brains and skill into the common occupations of life; shall prosper in proportion as we learn to draw the line between the superficial and the substantial, the ornamental gewgaws of life and the useful. No race can prosper till it learns that there is as much dignity in tilling a field as in writing a poem. It is at the bottom of life we must begin, and not at the top. Nor should we permit our grievances to overshadow our opportunities.

To those of the white race who look at the incoming of those of foreign birth and strange tongue and habits for the prosperity of the South, were I permitted I would repeat what I say to my own race, "Cast down your bucket where you are." Cast it down among the eight millions of Negroes whose habits you know, whose fidelity and love you have tested in days when to have proved treacherous meant the ruin of your firesides. Cast down your bucket among these people who have, without strikes and labour wars, tilled your fields, cleared your forests, built your railroads and cities, and brought forth treasures from the bowels of the earth, and helped make possible this magnificent representation of the progress of the South. Casting down your bucket among my people, helping and encouraging them as you are doing on these grounds, and to education of head, hand, and heart, you will find that they will buy your surplus land, make blossom the waste places in your fields, and run your factories. While doing this, you can be sure in the future, as in the past, that you and your families will be surrounded by the most patient, faithful, law-abiding, and unresentful people that the world has seen. As we have proved our loyalty to you in the past, in nursing your children, watching by the sick-bed of your mothers and fathers, and often following them with tear-dimmed eyes to their graves, so in the future, in our humble way, we shall stand by you with a devotion that no foreigner can approach, ready to lay down our lives, if need be, in defence of yours, interlacing our industrial, commercial, civil, and religious life with yours in a way that shall make the interests of both races one. In all things that are purely social we can be as separate as the fingers, yet one as the hand in all things essential to mutual progress. . . .

The wisest among my race understand that the agitation of questions of social equality is the extremest folly, and that progress in the enjoyment of

---

Booker T. Washington, <u>Up From Slavery</u> (New York, 1901), pp. 111-115.

all the privileges that will come to us must be the result of severe and constant struggle rather than of artificial forcing. No race that has anything to contribute to the markets of the world is long in any degree ostracized. It is important and right that all privileges of the law be ours, but it is vastly more important that we be prepared for the exercises of these privileges. The opportunity to earn a dollar in a factory just now is worth infinitely more than the opportunity to spend a dollar in an opera-house.

## W. E. B. Du BOIS ON SEGREGATION (1903)

W. E. B. Du Bois was a sociologist and historian who earned his Ph.D. from Harvard. In his writings he firmly opposed the accommodationist views of Booker T. Washington, and he offered blacks alternative leadership and ideals by calling for full, immediate, and unconditional equality for the black race. A founder of the pro-equality Niagara Movement, Du Bois was also instrumental in the creation in 1910 of the National Association for the Advancement of Colored People (NAACP), whose periodical he edited. Du Bois's ideas seem far less radical today than they did at the beginning of this century.

Mr. Washington represents in Negro thought the old attitude of adjustment and submission; but adjustment at such a peculiar time as to make his programme unique. This is an age of unusual economic development, and Mr. Washington's programme naturally takes an economic cast, becoming a gospel of Work and Money to such an extent as apparently almost completely to overshadow the higher aims of life. Moreover, this is an age when the more advanced races are coming in closer contact with the less developed races, and the race-feeling is therefore intensified; and Mr. Washington's programme practically accepts the alleged inferiority of the Negro races. Again, in our own land, the reaction from the sentiment of war time has given impetus to race-prejudice against Negroes, and Mr. Washington withdraws many of the high demands of Negroes as men and American citizens. In other periods of intensified prejudice all the Negro's tendency of self-assertion has been called forth; at this period a policy of submission is advocated. . . .
. . . it has been claimed that the Negro can survive only through submission. Mr. Washington distinctly asks that black people give up, at least for the present, three things, --
First, political power,
Second, insistence on civil rights,
Third, higher education of Negro youth,--
and concentrate all their energies on industrial education, the accumulation of wealth, and the conciliation of the South. This policy has been courageously and insistently advocated for over fifteen years, and has been triumphant for perhaps ten years. As a result of this tender of the palm-branch, what has been the return? In these years there have occurred:

---

W. E. Burghardt Du Bois, "Of Mr. Booker T. Washington and Others," in The Souls of Black Folk: Essays and Sketches (Chicago, 1903), pp. 50-52, 58-59.

1. The disfranchisement of the Negro.
2. The legal creation of a distinct status of civil inferiority for the Negro.
3. The steady withdrawal of aid from institutions for the higher training of the Negro.

These movements are not, to be sure, direct results of Mr. Washington's teachings; but his propaganda has, without a shadow of doubt, helped their speedier accomplishment. The question then comes: Is it possible, and probable, that nine millions of men can make effective progress in economic lines if they are deprived of political rights, made a servile caste, and allowed only the most meagre chance for developing their exceptional men? If history and reason give any distinct answer to these questions, it is an emphatic No. And Mr. Washington thus faces the triple paradox of his career:

1. He is striving nobly to make Negro artisans business men and property-owners; but it is utterly impossible, under modern competitive methods, for workingmen and property-owners to defend their rights and exist without the right of suffrage.
2. He insists on thrift and self-respect, but at the same time counsels a silent submission to civic inferiority such as is bound to sap the manhood of any race in the long run.
3. He advocates common-school and industrial training, and depreciates institutions of higher learning; but neither the Negro common-schools, nor Tuskegee itself, could remain open a day were it not for teachers trained in Negro colleges, or trained by their graduates. . . .

His doctrine has tended to make the whites, North and South, shift the burden of the Negro problem to the Negro's shoulders and stand aside as critical and rather pessimistic spectators; when in fact the burden belongs to the nation, and the hands of none of us are clean if we bend not our energies to righting these great wrongs.

The South ought to be led, by candid and honest criticism, to assert her better self and do her full duty to the race she has cruelly wronged and is still wronging. The North--her co-partner in guilt--cannot salve her conscience by plastering it with gold. We cannot settle this problem by diplomacy and suaveness, by "policy" alone. If worse come to worst, can the moral fibre of this country survive the slow throttling and murder of nine millions of men?

The black men of America have a duty to perform, a duty stern and delicate,--a forward movement to oppose a part of the work of their greatest leader. So far as Mr. Washington preaches Thrift, Patience, and Industrial Training for the masses, we must hold up his hands and strive with him, rejoicing in his honors and glorying in the strength of this Joshua called of God and of man to lead the headless host. But so far as Mr. Washington apologizes for injustice, North or South, does not rightly value the privilege and duty of voting, belittles the emasculating effects of caste distinctions, and opposes the higher training and ambition of our brighter minds,--so far as he, the South, or the Nation, does this,--we must unceasingly and firmly oppose them. By every civilized and peaceful method we must strive for the rights which the world accords to men, clinging unwaveringly to those great words which the sons of the Fathers would fain forget: "We hold these truths to be self-evident: That all men are created equal; that they are endowed by their Creator with certain unalienable rights; that among these are life, liberty, and the pursuit of happiness."

## GEORGE A. CUSTER ON THE AMERICAN INDIAN (1872)

General George Armstrong Custer made no secret of his contempt for the American Indian. The image of the noble red man, as portrayed in American literature, particularly galled Custer.

It is to be regretted that the character of the Indian as described in [James Fenimore] Cooper's interesting novels is not the true one. But as, in emerging from childhood into the years of a maturer age, we are often compelled to cast aside many of our earlier illusions and replace them by beliefs less inviting but more real, so we, as a people, with opportunities enlarged and facilities for obtaining knowledge increased, have been forced by a multiplicity of causes to study and endeavor to comprehend thoroughly the character of the red man. So intimately has he become associated with the Government as ward of the nation, and so prominent a place among the questions of national policy does the much mooted "Indian question" occupy, that it behooves us no longer to study this problem from works of fiction, but to deal with it as it exists in reality. Stripped of the beautiful romance with which we have been so long willing to envelop him, transferred from the inviting pages of the novelist to the localities where we are compelled to meet with him, in his native village, on the war path, and when raiding upon our frontier settlements and lines of travel, the Indian forfeits his claim to the appellation of the "noble red man." We see him as he is, and, so far as all knowledge goes, as he ever has been, a savage in every sense of the word; not worse, perhaps, than his white brother would be similarly born and bred, but one whose cruel and ferocious nature far exceeds that of any wild beast of the desert. That this is true no one who has been brought into intimate contact with the wild tribes will deny. Perhaps there are some who, as members of peace commissions or as wandering agents of some benevolent society, may have visited these tribes or attended with them at councils held for some pacific purpose, and who, by passing through the villages of the Indian while at peace, may imagine their opportunities for judging of the Indian nature all that could be desired. But the Indian, while he can seldom be accused of indulging in a great variety of wardrobe, can be said to have a character capable of adapting itself to almost every occasion. He has one character, perhaps his most serviceable one, which he preserves carefully, and only airs it when making his appeal to the Government or its agents for arms, ammunition, and license to employ them. This character is invariably paraded, and often with telling effect, when the motive is a peaceful one. Prominent chiefs invited to visit Washington invariably don this character, and in their "talks" with the "Great Father" and other less prominent personages they successfuly contrive to exhibit but this one phase. Seeing them under these or similar circumstances only, it is not surprising that by many the Indian is looked upon as a simple-minded "son of nature," desiring nothing beyond the privilege of roaming and hunting over the vast unsettled wilds of the West, inheriting and asserting but few native rights, and never trespassing upon the rights of others. This view is equally erroneous with that which regards the Indian as a creature possessing the human form but divested of all other

---

George A. Custer, <u>My Life on the Plains</u> (New York, 1881), pp. 11-16.

attributes of humanity, and whose traits of character, habits, modes of life, disposition, and savage customs disqualify him from the exercise of all rights and privileges, even those pertaining to life itself. Taking him as we find him, at peace or at war, at home or abroad, waiving all prejudices, and laying aside all partiality, we will discover in the Indian a subject for thoughtful study and investigation. In him we will find the representative of a race whose origin is, and promises to be, a subject forever wrapped in mystery; a race incapable of being judged by the rules or laws applicable to any other known race of men; one between which and civilization there seems to have existed from time immemorial a determined and unceasing warfare--a hostility so deep-seated and inbred with the Indian character, that in the exceptional instances where the modes and habits of civilization have been reluctantly adopted, it has been at the sacrifice of power and influence as a tribe, and the more serious loss of health, vigor, and courage as individuals. . . .

Inseparable from the Indian character, wherever he is to be met with, is his remarkable taciturnity, his deep dissimulation, the perseverance with which he follows his plans of revenge or conquest, his concealment and apparent lack of curiosity, his stoical courage when in the power of his enemies, his cunning, his caution, and last, but not least, the wonderful power and subtlety of his senses. . . .

In studying the Indian character, while shocked and disgusted by many of his traits and customs, I find much to be admired, and still more of deep and unvarying interest. To me Indian life, with its attendant ceremonies, mysteries, and forms, is a book of unceasing interest. Grant that some of its pages are frightful, and, if possible, to be avoided, yet the attraction is none the weaker. Study him, fight him, civilize him if you can, he remains still the object of your curiosity, a type of man peculiar and undefined, subjecting himself to no known law of civilization, contending determinedly against all efforts to win him from his chosen mode of life. He stands in the group of nations solitary and reserved, seeking alliance with none, mistrusting and opposing the advances of all. Civilization may and should do much for him, but it can never civilize him.


CHIEF JOSEPH ON FIGHTING NO MORE (1877)

In 1877, soldiers under the command of General O. O. Howard pursued a band of Nez Perce Indians led by Chief Joseph. After a long and bloody chase, Howard finally trapped Joseph in Montana--just 30 miles from the Canadian border, where the Indians might have found refuge. Relying on earlier promises to return the Nez Perce to their homeland in Oregon, Joseph reluctantly decided to surrender.

See General O. O. Howard's report to General of the Army, William T. Sherman, in U. S. War Department, Report to the Secretary of War [George W. McCrary], 1877, vol. I, contained in U. S. Congress, 45 Cong., 1st sess., Executive Documents, 1877-1878, II, Serial 1794, p. 630.

Tell General Howard I know his heart. What he told me before I have in my heart. I am tired of fighting. Our chiefs are killed. Looking Glass is dead. Too-hul-hul-sote is dead. He old men are all dead. It is the young men who say yes or no. He who led on the young men is dead. It is cold and we have no blankets. The little children are freezing to death. My people, some of them, have run away to the hills, and have no blankets, no food; no one knows where they are--perhaps freezing to death. I want to have time to look for my children and see how many of them I can find. Maybe I shall find them among the dead. Hear me, my chiefs. I am tired; my heart is sick and sad. From where the sun now stands I will fight no more forever.

## THE TREATY OF WASHINGTON (1871)

After the Civil War, the United States maintained claims against the British for damages, indirect as well as direct, caused by ships built in Britain which became part of the Confederate navy (especially the Alabama and the Florida). Americans and British argued about the claims without result until 1871. That year the two countries agreed in the Treaty of Washington to a procedure which would settle their differences without resorting to the use of force.

[ARTICLE I.] Whereas differences have arisen between the Government of the United States and the Government of Her Britannic Majesty, and still exist, growing out of the acts committed by the several vessels which have given rise to the claims generically known as the "Alabama Claims:"

And whereas Her Britannic Majesty has authorized her High Commissioners and Plenipotentiaries to express, in a friendly spirit, the regret felt by Her Majesty's Government for the escape, under whatever circumstances, of the Alabama and other vessels from British ports, and for the depredations committed by those vessels:

Now, in order to remove and adjust all complaints and claims on the part of the United States, and to provide for the speedy settlement of such claims which are not admitted by Her Britannic Majesty's Government, the high contracting parties agree that all the said claims, growing out of acts committed by the aforesaid vessels, and generically known as the "Alabama Claims," shall be referred to a tribunal of arbitration to be composed of five Arbitrators, to be appointed in the following manner, that is to say: One shall be named by the President of the United States; one shall be named by Her Britanic Majesty; His Majesty the King of Italy shall be requested to name one; the President of the Swiss Confederation shall be requested to name one; and His Majesty the Emperor of Brazil shall be requested to name one. . . .

---

U. S. Department of State, Treaties and Conventions Concluded Between the United States of America and Other Powers Since July 4, 1776 (Washington, D.C, 1889), pp. 478-93.

# ANDREW CARNEGIE ON THE GOSPEL OF WEALTH (1889)

A Scottish immigrant and himself an example of a life that began with rags and progressed to riches in the steel business, Andrew Carnegie typified the captain of industry in late nineteenth-century America. Carnegie was also an able apologist for the accumulation of wealth. He argued that vast wealth, far from representing wickedness and greed, was socially useful. As a philanthropist, Carnegie endowed libraries, institutes to promote teaching, science, and international peace, and the concert hall in New York that bears his name. Carnegie further held that inequality in society was the inevitable and essential companion of progress towards higher civilization.

The problem of our age is the proper administration of wealth, that the ties of brotherhood may still bind together the rich and poor in harmonious relationship. The conditions of human life have not only been changed, but revolutionized, within the past few hundred years. In former days there was little difference between the dwelling, dress, food, and environment of the chief and those of his retainers. . . . The contrast between the palace of the millionaire and the cottage of the laborer with us to-day measures the change which has come with civilization. This change, however, is not to be deplored, but welcomed as highly beneficial. It is well, nay, essential, for the progress of the race that the houses of some should be homes for all that is highest and best in literature and the arts, and for all the refinements of civilization, rather than that none should be so. Much better this great irregularity than universal squalor. . . .

The "good old times" were not good old times. Neither master nor servant was as well situated then as to-day. A relapse to old conditions would be disastrous to both--not the least so to him who serves--and would sweep away civilization with it. . . .

In the manufacture of products we have the whole story. . . . To-day the world obtains commodities of excellent quality at prices which even the preceding generation would have deemed incredible. . . . The poor enjoy what the rich could not before afford. What were the luxuries have become the necessaries of life. The laborer has now more comforts than the farmer had a few generations ago. The farmer has more luxuries than the landlord had, and is more richly clad and better housed. The landlord has books and pictures rarer and appointments more artistic than the king could then obtain.

The price we pay for this salutary change is, no doubt, great. We assemble thousands of operatives in the factory, and in the mine, of whom the employer can know little or nothing, and to whom he is little better than a myth. All intercourse between them is at an end. Rigid castes are formed, and, as usual, mutual ignorance breeds mutural distrust. Each caste is without sympathy with the other, and ready to credit anything disparaging in

---

Andrew Carnegie, The Gospel of Wealth and Other Timely Essays, ed. by Edward C. Kirkland (Cambridge, MA, 1962), pp. 14-17.

regard to it. Under the law of competition, the employer of thousands is forced into the strictest economies, among which the rates paid to labor figure prominently, and often there is friction between the employer and the employed, between capital and labor, between rich and poor. Human society loses homogeneity.

The price which society pays for the law of competition, like the price it pays for cheap comforts and luxuries, is also great; but the advantages of this law are also greater still than its cost--for it is to this law that we owe our wonderful material development, which brings improved conditions in its train. But, whether the law be benign or not, we must say of it, as we say of the change in the conditions of men to which we have referred: It is here; we cannot evade it; no substitutes for it have been found; and while the law may be sometimes hard for the individual, it is best for the race, because it insures the survival of the fittest in every department. We accept and welcome, therefore, as conditions to which we must accommodate ourselves, great inequality of environment; the concentration of business, industrial and commercial, in the hands of a few; and the law of competition between these, as being not only beneficial, but essential to the future progress of the race. Having accepted these, it follows that there must be great scope for the exercise of special ability in the merchant and in the manufacturer who has to conduct affairs upon a great scale. That this talent for organization and management is rare among men is proved by the fact that it invariably secures enormous rewards for its possessor, no matter where or under what laws or conditions. . . . for able men soon create capital; in the hands of those without the special talent required, capital soon takes wings. Such men become interested in firms or corporations using millions; . . . the great manufacturing or commercial concern which does not earn at least interest upon its capital soon becomes bankrupt. It must either go forward or fall behind;. . . It is a law, as certain as any of the others named, that men possessed of this peculiar talent for affairs, under the free play of economic forces must, of necessity, soon be in receipt of more revenue than can be judiciously expended upon themselves; and this law is as beneficial for the race as the others.

Objections to the foundations upon which society is based are not in order, because the condition of the race is better with these than it has been with any other which has been tried.


WILLIAM GRAHAM SUMNER ON SOCIAL WELFARE (1914)

Son of an English immigrant, self-made man, William Graham Sumner studied in Germany and England and was ordained an Episcopal priest before he assumed his duties as Professor of Political and Social Science at Yale. By 1876 he had become converted to Social Darwinism through

---

William Graham Sumner, "The Challenge of Facts," in The Challenge of Facts and Other Essays ed. by Albert Galloway Keller (New Haven: Yale University Press, 1914), pp. 17-18, 23-25, 51-52.

the writings of Herbert Spencer, and he revised his own sociology in light of the new doctrines of evolution and natural selection in society. In this essay Sumner not only argues for Social Darwinism as an explanation for how society evolves, but as a guide in assessing the merits of schemes of social reform.

Man is born under the necessity of sustaining the existence he has received by an onerous struggle against nature, both to win what is essential to his life and to ward off what is prejudicial to it. He is born under a burden and a necessity. Nature holds what is essential to him, but she offers nothing gratuitously. He may win for his use what she holds, if he can. . . . For any real satisfaction, labor is necessary to fit the products of nature for human use. In this struggle every individual is under the pressure of the necessities for food, clothing, shelter, fuel, and every individual brings with him more or less energy for the conflict necessary to supply his needs. The relation, therefore, between each man's needs and each man's energy, or "individualism," is the first fact of human life.

It is not without reason, however, that we speak of a "man" as the individual in question, for women (mothers) and children have special disabilities for the struggle with nature, and these disabilities grow greater and last longer as civilization advances. The perpetuation of the race in health and vigor and its success as a whole in its struggle to expand and develop human life on earth, therefore, require that the head of the family shall, by his energy, be able to supply not only his own needs, but those of the organisms which are dependent upon him. . . .

Liberty means the security given to each man that, if he employs his energies to sustain the struggle on behalf of himself and those he cares for, he shall dispose of the product exclusively as he chooses. . . .

The struggle for existence is aimed against nature. It is from her niggardly hand that we have to wrest the satisfactions for our needs, but our fellow-men are our competitors for the meager supply. Competition, therefore, is a law of nature. Nature is entirely neutral; she submits to him who most energetically and resolutely assails her. She grants her rewards to the fittest, therefore, without regard to other considerations of any kind. If, then, there be liberty, men get from her just in proportion to their works, and their having and enjoying are just in proportion to their being and their doing. Such is the system of nature. If we do not like it, and if we try to amend it, there is only one way in which we can do it. We can take from the better and give to the worse. We can deflect the penalties of those who have done ill and throw them on those who have done better. We can take the rewards from those who have done better and give them to those who have done worse. We shall thus lessen the inequalities. We shall favor the survival of the unfittest, and we shall accomplish this by destroying liberty. Let it be understood that we cannot go outside of this alternative: liberty, inequality, survival of the fittest; not-liberty, equality, survival of the unfittest. The former carries society forward and favors all its best members; the latter carries society downwards and favors all its worst members. . . .

Whatever assails that right [of private property], or goes in the direction of making it still more uncertain whether the industrious man can dispose of the fruits of his industry for his own interests exclusively, tends directly towards violence, bloodshed, poverty, and misery. . . .

Industry, self-denial, and temperance are the laws of prosperity for men and states; without them advance in the arts and in wealth means only corruption and decay through luxury and vice. With them progress in the arts and increasing wealth are the prime conditions of an advancing civilization which is sound enough to endure. The power of the human race to-day over the conditions of prosperous and happy living are sufficient to banish poverty and misery if it were not for folly and vice. . . .

The socialist or philanthropist who nourishes them [the poor] in their situation and saves them from the distress of it is only cultivating the distress which he pretends to cure.

## RUSSELL CONWELL ON "ACRES OF DIAMONDS" (1915)

Protestant Christianity was never of one mind on the subject of wealth. On the one hand, it was supposed to be nearly impossible for the rich man to enter the Kingdom of Heaven, but on the other hand, the Protestant Reformation had deep roots in a rising business-oriented middle class which, as in the case of New England Puritans, saw wealth as a presumptive sign of God's blessing. During the gilded age business virtually became a religion, and religion often served the purposes of business. It is said that Baptist preacher Russell Conwell delivered this sermon thousands of times.

Now then, I say again that the opportunity to get rich, to attain unto great wealth, is here in Philadelphia now, within the reach of almost every man and woman who hears me speak to-night, and I mean just what I say. . . . [T]he men and women sitting here, who found it difficult perhaps to buy a ticket to this lecture or gathering to-night, have within their reach "acres of diamonds," opportunities to get largely wealthy. . . .

I say that you ought to get rich, and it is your duty to get rich. How many of my pious brethren say to me, "Do you, a Christian minister, spend your time going up and down the country advising young people to get rich, to get money?" "Yes, of course I do." They say, "Isn't that awful! Why don't you preach the gospel instead of preaching about man's making money?" "Because to make money honestly is to preach the gospel." That is the reason. The men who get rich may be the most honest men you find in the community.

"Oh," but says some young man here to-night, "I have been told all my life that if a person has money he is very dishonest and dishonorable and mean and contemptible." My friend, that is the reason why you have none, because you have that idea of people. The foundation of your faith is altogether false. . . .

Says another young man, "I hear sometimes of men that get millions of dollars dishonestly." Yes, of course you do, and so do I. But they are so rare a thing in fact that the newspapers talk about them all the time as a matter of news until you get the idea that all the other rich men got rich dishonestly.

---

Russell H. Conwell, <u>Acres</u> <u>of</u> <u>Diamonds</u> (New York, 1915), pp. 17-22.

My friends, you take and drive me--if you furnish the auto--out into the suburbs of Philadelphia, and introduce me to the people who own their homes around this great city, those beautiful homes with gardens and flowers, those magnificent homes so lovely in their art, and I will introduce you to the very best people in character as well as in enterprise in our city, and you know I will. A man is not really a true man until he owns his own home, and they that own their homes are made more honorable and honest and pure, and true and economical and careful, by owning the home. . . .

Money is power, and you ought to be reasonably ambitious to have it. You ought because you can do more good with it than you could without it. Money printed your Bible, money builds your churches, money sends your missionaries, and money pays your preachers, and you would not have many of them, either, if you did not pay them. I am always willing that my church should raise my salary, because the church that pays the largest salary always raises it the easiest. You never knew an exception to it in your life. The man who gets the largest salary can do the most good with the power that is furnished to him. Of course he can if his spirit be right to use it for what it is given to him.

I say, then, you ought to have money. If you can honestly attain unto riches in Philadelphia, it is your Christian and godly duty to do so. It is an awful mistake of these pious people to think you must be awfully poor in order to be pious.

Some men say, "Don't you sympathize with the poor people?" Of course I do, or else I would not have been lecturing these years. I won't give in but what I sympathize with the poor, but the number of poor who are to be sympathized with is very small. To sympathize with a man whom God has punished for his sins, thus to help him when God would still continue a just punishment, is to do wrong, no doubt about it, and we do that more than we help those who are deserving. While we should sympathize with God's poor--that is, those who cannot help themselves--let us remember there is not a poor person in the United States who was not made poor by his own shortcomings, or by the shortcomings of some one else. It is all wrong to be poor anyhow. Let us give in to that argument and pass that to one side.

A gentleman gets up back there, and says, "Don't you think there are some things in this world that are better than money?" Of course I do, but I am talking about money now. Of course there are some things higher than money. Oh yes, I know by the grave that has left me standing alone that there are some things in this world that are higher and sweeter and purer than money. Well do I know there are some things higher and grander than gold. Love is the grandest thing on God's earth, but fortunate the lover who has plenty of money. Money is power, money is force, money will do good as well as harm. In the hands of good men and women it could accomplish, and it has accomplished, good.

## WALTER RAUSCHENBUSCH ON REFORM DARWINISM (1907)

Analyzing the debates over social issues during the late Nineteenth Century, one is reminded of "Alice-Through-the Looking-Glass"; that is, participants were using the same words to support widely differing positions. For example, the term "Social Darwinism" was used unflinchingly to describe the most brutal implications of the process known as "Survival of the Fittest." On the other hand, the same term--often called "Reform Darwinism" for purposes of distinction--was invoked to justify social reform. In general, these reformers believed that by helping each other the entire human race would progress (and therefore "evolve" along the lines of Darwin's original theory). No voice in favor of reform in this era was louder, or more influential, than that of Walter Rauschenbusch, a New York City minister, who maintained that the principles of Christianity applied to a modern, technological-urban society.

[The Church] should be swiftest to awaken to every undeserved suffering, bravest to speak against every wrong, and strongest to rally the moral foces of the community against everything that threatens the better life among men. . . .

Other organizations may conceivably be indifferent when confronted with the chronic or acute poverty of our cities. The Christian Church cannot. The very name of "Christian" would turn into an indictment if it did not concern itself in the situation in some way. . . .

Few churches have the resources and leadership to undertake institutional work on a large scale, but most churches in large cities have some institutional features, and all pastors who are at willing to do it have institutional work thrust on them. They have to care for the poor. Those of us who passed through the last great industrial depression will never forget the procession of men out of work, out of clothes, out of shoes, and out of hope. They wore down our threshold, and they wore away our hearts. This is the stake of the churches in modern poverty. They are buried at times under stream of human wreckage. They are turned aside constantly from their more spiritual functions to "serve tables." They have a right, therefore, to inquire who is unloading this burden of poverty and suffering upon them by underpaying, exhausting, and maiming the people. . . .

"Don't mix business and religion." "Business is business." These common maxims express the consciousness that there is a radical divergence between the two domains of life, and that the Christian rules of conduct would forbid many common transactions of business and make success in it impossible. Thus life is cut into two halves, each governed by a law opposed to that of the other, and the law of Christ is denied even the opportunity to gain control of business. . . .

---

Walter Rauschenbusch, Christianity and The Social Crisis (New York, 1924), pp. 287, 304-305, 313, 322-323, 410-411, 418, 422.

In our own country we are still at the parting of the ways. Our social movement is still in its earliest stages. The bitterness and anger of their fight has not eaten into the heart of the working classes as it has abroad. Many of them are still ready to make their fight in the name of God and Christ, though not of the Church. . . . Some of the favorite speakers and organizers of the socialists in our country are former Christian ministers, who use their power of ethical and religious appeal. In Labor Lyceums and similar gatherings, ministers are often invited as speakers, though perhaps quite as much in the hope of converting them as with a desire to hear what they have to say. The divorce between the new class movement and the old religion can still be averted.

[T]he Christian idealists must not make the mistake of trying to hold the working class down to the use of moral suasion only, or be repelled when they hear the brute note of selfishness and anger. The class struggle is bound to be transferred to the field of politics in our country in some form. It would be folly if the working class failed to use the leverage which their political power gives them. The business class has certainly never failed to use political means to further its interests.

The championship of social justice is almost the only way left open to a Christian nowadays to gain the crown of martyrdom.

If at this juncture we can rally sufficient religious faith and moral strength to snap the bonds of evil and turn the present unparalleled economic and intellectual resources of humanity to the harmonious development of a true social life, the generations yet unborn will mark this as the great day of the Lord for which the ages waited, and count us blessed for sharing in the apostolate that proclaimed it.


JACOB RIIS ON SLUMS AND THE URBAN POOR (1890)

How the Other Half Lives is a landmark book, both in journalism and in reform. Danish immigrant Jacob Riis here provides a vivid portrait and analysis of urban life in the gilded age, calling America's attention to poverty and suffering in the cities. This newspaperman's book provided both evidence of the severe human costs of the industrial age and a rallying cry for large-scale social action in the name of humanity. As an early "muckraker," Riis believed that the "power of the fact is the mightiest lever of this or any day," and he campaigned untiringly for the urban middle class to fulfill its social and moral obligations to poor people whose humanity was not fundamentally different from their own, but whose slum environment had debased them.

Jacob Riis, How the Other Half Lives: Studies Among the Tenements of New York (New York, 1901), pp. 43-47, 168-171.

Suppose we look into one [tenement]? No.--Cherry Street. Be a little careful, please! The hall is dark and you might stumble over the children pitching pennies back there. Not that it would hurt them; kicks and cuffs are their daily diet. They have little else. Here where the hall turns and dives into utter darkness is a step, and another, another. A flight of stairs. You can feel your way, if you cannot see it. Close? Yes! What would you have? All the fresh air that ever enters these stairs comes from the hall door that is forever slamming, and from the windows of dark bedrooms that in turn receive from the stairs their sole supply of the elements God meant to be free, but man deals out with such niggardly hand. That was a woman filling her pail by the hydrant you just bumped against. The sinks are in the hallway, that all the tenants may have access--and all be poisoned alike by their summer stenches. Hear the pump squeak! It is the lullaby of tenement house babes. In summer, when a thousand thirsty throats pant for a cooling drink in this block, it is worked in vain. But the saloon, whose open door you passed in the hall, is always there. The smell of it has followed you up. Here is a door. Listen! That short hacking cough, that tiny, helpless wail- -what do they mean? They mean that the soiled bow of white you saw on the door downstairs will have another story to tell--Oh! a sadly familiar story--before the day is at an end. The child is dying with measles. With half a chance it might have lived; but it had none. That dark bedroom killed it. . . .

[W]e grope our way up the stairs and down from floor to floor, listening to the sounds behind the closed doors--some of quarelling, some of coarse songs, more of profanity. They are true. When the summer heats comes with their suffering they have meaning more terrible than words can tell. Come over here. Step carefully over this baby--it is a baby, spite of its rags and dirt--under these iron bridges called fire escapes, but loaded down, despite the incessant watchfulness of the firemen, with broken household goods, with washtubs and barrels, over which no man could climb from a fire. This gap between dingy brick walls is the yard. That strip of smoke-colored sky up there is the heaven of these people. Do you wonder the name does not attract them to the churches? That baby's parents live in the rear tenement here. She is at least as clean as the steps we are now climbing. There are plenty of houses with half a hundred such in. The tenement is much like the one in front we just left, only fouler, closer, darker--we will not say more cheerless. The word is a mockery. A hundred thousand people lived in rear tenements in New York last year. Here is a room neater than the rest. The woman, a stout matron with hard lines of care in her face, is at the washtub. "I try to keep the childer clean," she says, apologetically, but with a hopeless glance around. The spice of hot soapsuds is added to the air already tainted with the smell of boiling cabbage, of rags and uncleanliness all about. It makes an overpowering compound. . . .

What sort of an answer, think you, would come from these tenements to the question "Is life worth living?" were they heard at all in the discussion? It may be that this, cut from the last report but one of the Association for the Improvement of the Condition of the Poor, a long name for a weary task, has a suggestion of it: "In the depth of winter the attention of the Association was called to a Protestant family living in a garret in a miserable tenement in Cherry Street. The family's condition was most deplorable. The man, his wife, and three small children shivering in one room through the roof of which the pitiless winds of winter whistled. The room was almost barren of furniture; the parents slept on the floor, the elder children in boxes, and the baby was swung in an old shawl attached to the rafters by cords by way of a hammock. The father, a seaman, had been obliged to give up that calling because he was in consumption, and was unable to provide either bread or fire for his little ones."

Perhaps this may be put down as an exceptional case, but one that came to my notice some months ago in a Seventh Ward tenement was typical enough to escape that reproach. There were nine in the family: husband, wife, an aged grandmother, and six children; honest, hardworking Germans, scrupulously neat, but poor. All nine lived in two rooms, one about ten feet square that served as parlor, bedroom, and eating room, the other, a small half room made into a kitchen. The rent was seven dollars and a half a month, more than a week's wages for the husband and father, who was the only breadwinner in the family. That day the mother had thrown herself out of the window, and was carried up from the street dead. She was "discouraged," said some of the other women from the tenement, who had come in to look after the children while a messenger carried the news to the father at the shop. . . .

That ignorance plays its part, as well as poverty and bad hygienic surroundings, in the sacrifice of life is of course inevitable. They go usually hand in hand. A message came one day last spring summoning me to a Mott Street tenement in which lay a child dying from some unknown disease. With the "charity doctor" I found the patient on the top floor, stretched upon two chairs in a dreadfully stifling room. She was gasping in the agony of peritonitis that had already written its death sentence on her wan and pinched face. The whole family, father, mother, and four ragged children, sat around looking on with the stony resignation of helpless despair that had long since given up the fight against fate as useless. A glance around the wretched room left no doubt as to the cause of the child's condition. "Improper nourishment," said the doctor, which, translated to suit the place, meant starvation. The father's hands were crippled from lead poisoning. He had not been able to work for a year. A contagious disease of the eyes, too long neglected, had made the mother and one of the boys nearly blind. The children cried with hunger. They had not broken their fast that day, and it was then near noon. For months the family had subsisted on two dollars a week from the priest, and a few loaves and a piece of corned beef which the sisters sent them on Saturday. The doctor gave direction for the treatment of the child, knowing that it was possible only to alleviate its sufferings until death should end them, and left some money for food for the rest. An hour later, when I returned, I found them feeding the dying child with ginger ale, bought for two cents a bottle at the pedlar's cart down the street. A pitying neighbor had proposed it as the one thing she could think of as likely to make the child forget its misery. There was enough in the bottle to go round to the rest of the family. In fact, the wake had already begun; before night it was under way in dead earnest.

Every once in a while a case of downright starvation gets into the newspapers and makes a sensation. But this is the exception. Were the whole truth known, it would come home to the community with a shock that would rouse it to a more serious effort than the spasmodic undoing of its purse strings. I am satisfied from my own observation that hundreds of men, women, and children are every day slowly starving to death in the tenements with my medical friend's complaint of "improper nourishment." Within a single week I have had this year [some] cases of insanity, provoked directly by poverty and want. One was that of a mother who in the middle of the night got up to murder her child, who was crying for food; another was the case of an Elizabeth Street truck driver whom the newspapers never heard of. With a family to provide for, he had been unable to work for many months. There was neither food, nor a scrap of anything upon which money could be raised, left in the house; this mind gave way under the combined physical and mental suffering.

## LESTER FRANK WARD ON A PLANNED SOCIETY (1897)

A pioneering American sociologist, Lester Frank Ward, argued against Spencer's theories and the do-nothing laissez-faire view of the role of government. He insisted on the conscious manipulation of forces toward desired ends ("the organization of human happiness") through a welfare state which integrated scientific methods with a democratic base. One historian called Ward "the St. Augustine of the American cult of science."

There are those who maintain that civilization can only be achieved through the action of the individual, unconscious of the end, doing that which will conduce to the end. The present state of progress is adduced as proof that this is the necessary result. But while it is admitted that this has resulted in some parts of the world and in past history, it must be denied that the effect has been beneficial in all parts of the world or wholly so in any part, and also that any guaranty exists that it will continue indefinitely to be so, even where the actual benefits have been greatest. It can also be legitimately argued that much greater benefits might be secured if society were the conscious agent and had its improvement for its clearly perceived end. . . .

But the most important factor in the environment of any species is its organic environment. The hardest pressure that is brought to bear upon it comes from the living things in the midst of which it lives, and though paradoxical, it is those beings which most resemble it that crowd it most severely. The least advantage gained by one species from a favorable change of structure tends to make it spread and infringe upon others, and soon to acquire, if not strenuously resisted, a complete monopoly of all things that are required for its support. Any other species that consumes the same elements must, unless equally vigorous, be crowded out. This is the true meaning of the survival of the fittest. It is essentially a process of competition, but it is competition in its purest form, wholly unmixed with either moral or intellectual elements, which is never the case with competition in human society.

The prevailing idea is wholly false which claims that it is the fittest possible that survive in this struggle. The effect of competition is to prevent any form from attaining its maximum development, and to maintain a certain comparatively low level of development for all forms that succeed in surviving. . . .

Competition, therefore, not only involves the enormous waste which has been described, but it prevents the maximum development, since the best that can be attained under its influence is far inferior to that which is easily attained by the artificial, i.e., the rational and intelligent, removal of that influence.

---

L. F. Ward, The Psychic Factors of Civilization (Boston, 1897), pp. 96-331.

Hard as it seems to be for modern philosophers to understand this, it was one of the first truths that dawned upon the human intellect. Consciously or unconsciously it was felt from the very outset that the mission of mind was to grapple with the law of competition and as far as possible to resist and defeat it. This iron law of nature, as it may be appropriately called (Ricardo's "iron law of wages" is only one manifestation of it), was everywhere found to lie athwart the path of human progress, and the whole upward struggle of rational man, whether physical, social or moral, has been with this tyrant of nature--the law of competition. And in so far as he has progressed at all beyond the purely animal stage he has done so through triumphing little by little over this law and gaining somewhat the mastery in this struggle. . . .

Competition between industrial associations, or corporations, follows the law of competition among rational beings in general, and is only a brief transition stage, to be quickly followed by further combination. Just as competition among individuals soon resulted in that combination by which corporations were formed, so competition between corporations soon results in the amalgamation of all in any one industry into one great compound corporation, now commonly under the form of a "trust." This process of compound cooperation does not stop until the whole product of the given industry is controlled by a single body of men. Such a body thus acquires absolute power over the price of the commodity produced, the only limit being that of the maximum profit that it can be made to yield. . . .

But when mind enters into the contest the character of competition is at first completely changed, and later competition itself is altogether crushed out, and while it is still the strong that survive it is a strength which comes from indirection, from deceptions, artfulness, cunning, and shrewdness, necessarily coupled with stunted moral qualities, and largely aided by the accident of position. In no proper sense is it true that the fittest survive. If this were their only function it is evident that brains would be a positive detriment to society. Pure animal competition would be far better. . . .

[But] competition is growing more and more aggressive, heated, and ephemeral. Combination is growing more and more universal, powerful and permanent. This is the result of the most complete <u>laissez faire</u> policy. The paradox therefore is that <u>individual freedom can only come through social regulation</u>. The cooperative effects of the rule of mind which annihilate competition can only be overcome by that still higher form of cooperation which shall stay the lower form and set free the normal faculties of man. Free competition that shall be both innocent and beneficial may be secured to a limited extent in this way and in no other way. . . .

There is one power and only one that is greater than that which now chiefly rules society. That power is society itself. There is one form of government that is stronger than autocracy or aristocracy or democracy, or even plutocracy, and that is <u>sociocracy</u>.

The individual has reigned long enough. The day has come for society to take its affairs into its own hands and shape its own destinies. The individual has acted as best he could. He has acted in the only way he could. With a consciousness, will, and intellect of his own he could do nothing else than pursue his natural ends. . . .

For a long time to come social action must be chiefly negative and be confined to the removal of evils that exist, such as have been pointed out in these pages, but a positive stage will ultimately be reached in which society will consider and adopt measures for its own advancement.

# PEOPLE'S PARTY PLATFORM (1892)

> With both major political parties unwilling or unable to address the major problems of farmers and laborers, the Farmers' Alliance created in 1892 a new political organization--the People's Party. Calling themselves Populists, the party adopted a platform dealing directly with the grievances of the ignored millions of America's "producing classes."

The conditions which surround us best justify our co-operation! We meet in the midst of a nation brought to the verge of moral, political, and material ruin. Corruption dominates the ballot box, the Legislatures, the Congress, and touches even the ermine of the Bench. The people are demoralized; most of the States have been compelled to isolate the voters at the polling places to prevent universal intimidation or bribery. The newspapers are largely subsidized or muzzled, public opinion silenced, business prostrated, our homes covered with mortgages, labor impoverished, and the land concentrating in the hands of capitalists. The urban workmen are denied the right of organization for self-protection, imported pauperized labor beats down their wages, a hireling standing army, unrecognized by our laws, is established to shoot them down, and they are rapidly degenerating into European conditions. The fruits of the toil of millions are boldly stolen to build up colossal fortunes for a few, unprecedented in the history of mankind, and the possessors of these in turn despise the Republic and endanger liberty. From the same prolific womb of governmental injustice we breed the two great classes--tramps and millionaires.

The national power to create money is appropriated to enrich bondholders; a vast public debt payable in legal tender currency, has been funded into gold-bearing bonds, thereby adding millions to the burdens of the people.

Silver, which has been accepted as coin since the dawn of history, has been demonetized to add to the purchasing power of gold of decreasing the value of all forms of property as well as human labor, and the supply of currency is purposely abridged to fatten usurers, bankrupt enterprise and enslave industry.

A vast conspiracy against mankind has been organized on two continents, and it is rapidly taking possession of the world. If not met and overthrown at once it forebodes terrible social convulsions, the destruction of civilization, or the establishment of an absolute despotism.

We have witnessed, for more than a quarter of a century, the struggles of the two great political parties for power and plunder, while grievous wrongs have been inflicted upon the suffering people. We charge that the controlling influences dominating both these parties have permitted the existing dreadful conditions to develop without serious effort to prevent or restrain them.

---

Edward McPherson, _A Hand-Book of Politics for 1892_ (Washington, 1892), pp. 269-271.

[OLD PARTIES TREATED AS ONE.] Neither do they now promise us any substantial reform. They have agreed together to ignore, in the coming campaign, every issue but one. They propose to drown the outcries of a plundered people with the uproar of a sham battle over the tariff, so that capitalists, corporations, national banks, rings, trusts, watered stock, the demonetization of silver and the oppressions of the usurers may all be lost sight of. They propose to sacrifice our homes, lives and children, on the altar of mammon; to destroy the multitude in order to secure corruption funds from the millionaires.

Assembled on the anniversary of the birthday of the nation, and filled with the spirit of the grand general and chieftain who established our independence, we seek to restore the Government of the Republic to the hands of the "plain people" with which class it originated. We assert our purposes to be identical with the purposes of the National Constitution, to form a more perfect Union and establish justice, insure domestic tranquility, provide for the common defense, promote the general welfare and secure the blessings of liberty for ourselves and our posterity.

We declare that this Republic can only endure as a free government while built upon the love of the whole people for each other and for the nation; that it cannot be pinned together by bayonets; that the civil war is over and that every passion and resentment which grew out of it must die with it, and that we must be in fact, as we are in name, one united brotherhood of freedom.

[FARMERS' DEMANDS.] Our country finds itself confronted by conditions for which there is no precedent in the history of the world; our annual agricultural productions amount to billions of dollars in value, which must within a few weeks or months be exchanged for billions of dollars' worth of commodities consumed in their production; the existing currency supply is wholly inadequate to make this exchange; the results are falling prices, the formation of combines and rings, the impoverishment of the producing class. We pledge ourselves that, if given power, we will labor to correct these evils by wise and reasonable legislation, in accordance with the terms of our platform.

We believe that the powers of government--in other words, of the people--should be expanded (as in the case of the postal service) as rapidly and as far as the good sense of an intelligent people and the teachings of experience shall justify, to the end that oppression, injustice and poverty, shall eventually cease in the land.

While our sympathies as a party of reform are naturally upon the side of every proposition which will tend to make men intelligent, virtuous and temperate, we nevertheless regard these questions--important as they are--as secondary to the great issues now pressing for solution, and upon which not only our individual prosperity, but the very existence of free institutions depend; and we ask all men to first help us to determine whether we are to have a Republic to administer, before we differ as to the conditions upon which it is to be administered; believing that the forces of reform this day organized will never cease to move forward, until every wrong is righted, and equal rights and equal privileges securely established for all the men and women of this country. We declare, therefore,

[PERPETUAL LABOR UNION.] First--That the union of the labor forces of the United States this day consummated shall be permanent and perpetual; may its spirit enter into all hearts for the salvation of the Republic, and the uplifting of mankind.

[WEALTH FOR WORKERS.] Second--Wealth belongs to him who creates it, and every dollar taken from industry without an equivalent is robbery. "If any will not work, neither shall he eat." The interests of rural and civic labor are the same; their enemies are identical.

[OWNERSHIP OF RAILWAYS.] Third--We believe that the time has come when the railroad corporations will either own the people or the people must own the railroads; and should the Government enter upon the work of owning and managing all railroads, we should favor an amendment to the Constitution by which all persons engaged in the Government service shall be placed under a civil service regulation of the most rigid character, so as to prevent the increase of the power of the national administration by the use of of such additional Government employees.

[FINANCE.] 1st. We demand a national currency, safe, sound and flexible, issued by the General Government only, a full legal tender for all debts public and private, and that without the use of banking corporations; a just, equitable and efficient means of distribution direct to the people at a tax not to exceed 2 per cent. per annum, to be provided as set forth in the Sub-Treasury plan of the Farmers' Alliance, or a better system; also by payments in discharge of its obligations for public improvements.

(A) We demand free and unlimited coinage of silver and gold at the present legal ratio of 16 to 1.

(B) We demand that the amount of circulating medium be speedily increased to not less than $50 per capita.

(C) We demand a graduated income tax.

(D) We believe that the money of the country should be kept as much as possible in the hands of the people, and hence we demand that all State and National revenues shall be limited to the necessary expenses of the Government, economically and honestly administered.

(E) We demand that Postal Savings Banks be established by the Government for the safe deposit of the earnings of the people and to facilitate exchange.

[TRANSPORTATION.] 2d. Transportation being a means of exchange and a public necessity, the government should own and operate the railroads in the interest of the people.

The telegraph and telephone, like the post office system, being a necessity for the transmission of news, should be owned and operated by the Government in the interest of the people.

[LAND.] 3d. The land, including all the natural sources of wealth, is the heritage of the people and should not be monopolized for speculative purposes, and alien ownership of land should be prohibited. All land now held by railroads and other corporations in excess of their actual needs, and all lands now owned by aliens, should be reclaimed by the Government and held for actual settlers only.

The following supplementary resolutions, not to be incorporated in the platform, come from the Committee on Resolutions and were adopted, as follows:

[THE SUPPLEMENTARY PLATFORM.] Whereas, Other questions have been presented for our consideration, we hereby submit the following, not as a part of the platform of the People's Party, but as resolutions expressive of the sentiment of this Convention:

1. Resolved, That we demand a free ballot and a fair count in all elections, and pledge ourselves to secure it to every legal voter without Federal intervention, through the adoption by the States of the unperverted Australian or secret ballot system.

2. That the revenue derived from a graduated income tax should be applied to the reduction of the burden of taxation now resting upon the domestic industries of this country.

3. That we pledge our support to fair and liberal pensions to ex-Union soldiers and sailors.

4. That we condemn the fallacy of protecting American labor under the present system, which opens our ports to the pauper and criminal classes of the world, and crowds out our wage-earners; and we denounce the present ineffective laws against contract labor, and demand the further restriction of undesirable immigration.

5. That we cordially sympathize with the efforts of organized workingmen to shorten the hours of labor, and demand a rigid enforcement of the existing eight-hour law on Government work, and ask that a penalty clause be added to the said law.

6. That we regard the maintenance of a large standing army of mercenaries, known as the Pinkerton system, as a menace to our liberties, and we demand its abolition; and we condemn the recent invasion of the Territory of Wyoming by the hired assassins of plutocracy, assisted by Federal officers.

7. That we commend to the favorable consideration of the people and the reform press the legislative system known as the initiative and referendum.

8. That we favor a constitutional provision limiting the office of President and Vice-President to one term, and providing for the election of Senators of the United States by a direct vote of the people.

9. That we oppose any subsidy or national aid to any private corporation for any purpose.

10. That this convention sympathizes with the Knights of Labor, and their righteous contest with the tyrannical combine of clothing manufacturers of Rochester, and declare it to be the duty of all who hate tyranny and oppression, to refuse to purchase the goods made by the said manufacturers, or to patronize any merchants who sell such goods. . . .


## WILLIAM JENNINGS BRYAN, THE "CROSS OF GOLD" SPEECH (1896)

> At the Democratic Party convention of 1896 there were a number of potential presidential candidates. William Jennings Bryan, only thirty-six years of age, delivered one of the most famous of all American political speeches and thereby gained the nomination for himself.

The humblest citizen in all the land, when clad in the armor of a righteous cause, is stronger than all the hosts of error. I come to speak to you in defense of a cause as holy as the cause of liberty--the cause of humanity. . . .

---

W. J. Bryan, The First Battle: A Story of the Campaign of 1896 (Chicago, 1896), pp. 199-206.

Never before in the history of this country has there been witnessed such a contest as that through which we have just passed. Never before in the history of American politics has a great issue been fought out as this issue has been, by the voters of a great party. On the fourth of March, 1895, a few Democrats, most of them members of Congress, issued an address to the Democrats of the nation, asserting that the money question was the paramount issue of the hour; declaring that a majority of the Democratic party had the right to control the action of the party on this paramount issue; and concluding with the request that the believers in the free coinage of silver in the Democratic party should organize, take charge of, and control the policy of the Democratic party. Three months later, at Memphis, an organization was perfected, and the silver Democrats went forth openly and courageously proclaiming their belief, and declaring that, if successful, they would crystallize into a platform the declaration which they had made. Then began the conflict. With a zeal approaching the zeal which inspired the crusaders who followed Peter the Hermit, our silver Democrats went forth from victory unto victory until they are now assembled, not to discuss, not to debate, but to enter up the judgment already rendered by the plain people of this country. . . .

Ah, my friends, we say not one word against those who live upon the Atlantic coast, but the hardy pioneers who have braved all the dangers of the wilderness, who have made the desert to blossom as the rose--the pioneers away out there, who rear their children near to Nature's heart, where they can mingle their voices with the voices of the birds--out there where they have erected schoolhouses for the education of their young, churches where they praise their Creator, and cemeteries where rest the ashes of their dead--these people, we say, are as deserving of the consideration of our party as any people in this country. It is for these that we speak. We do not come as aggressors. Our war is not a war of conquest; we are fighting in the defense of our homes, our families, and posterity. We have petitioned, and our petitions have been scorned; we have entreated, and our entreaties have been disregarded; we have begged, and they have mocked when our calamity came. We beg no longer; we entreat no more; we petition no more. We defy them. . . .

And now, my friends, let me come to the paramount issue. If they ask us why it is that we say more on the money question than we say upon the tariff question, I reply that, if protection has slain its thousands, the gold standard has slain its tens of thousands. If they ask us why we do not embody in our platform all the things that we believe in, we reply that when we have restored the money of the Constitution all other necessary reforms will be possible; but that until this is done there is no other reform that can be accomplished. . . .

We go forth confident that we shall win. Why? Because upon the paramount issue of this campaign there is not a spot of ground upon which the enemy will dare to challenge battle. If they tell us that the gold standard is a good thing, we shall point to their platform and tell them that their platform pledges the party to get rid of the gold standard and substitute bimetallism. If the gold standard is a good thing, why try to get rid of it? I call your attention to the fact that some of the very people who are in this convention today and who tell us that we ought to declare in favor of international bimetallism--thereby declaring that the gold standard is wrong and that the principle of bimetallism is better--these very people four months ago were open and avowed advocates of the gold standard, and were then telling us that we could not legislate two metals together, even with the aid of all the world. If the gold standard is a good thing, we ought to declare in favor of its retention and not in favor of abandoning it; and if the gold standard is a bad thing why should we wait until other nations are willing to help us to get go? Here is the line of battle, and we care not upon which issue they force the fight. . . .

There are two ideas of government. There are those who believe that, if you will only legislate to make the well-to-do prosperous, their prosperity will leak through on those below. The Democratic idea, however, has been that if you legislate to make the masses prosperous, their prosperity will find its way up through every class which rests upon them.

You come to us and tell us that the great cities are in favor of the gold standard; we reply that the great cities rest upon our broad and fertile prairies. Burn down your cities and leave our farms, and your cities will spring up again as if by magic; but destroy our farms and the grass will grow in the streets of every city in the country. . . .

If they say bimetallism is good, but that we cannot have it until other nations help us, we reply that, instead of having a gold standard because England has, we will restore bimetallism and then let England have bimetallism because the United States has it. If they dare to come out in the open field and defend the gold standard as a good thing, we will fight them to the uttermost. Having behind us the producing masses of this nation and the world, supported by the commercial interests, the laboring interests, and the toilers everywhere, we will answer their demand for a gold standard by saying to them: You shall not press down upon the brow of labor this crown of thorns, you shall not crucify mankind upon a cross of gold.


## RICHARD OLNEY ON THE VENEZUELAN BOUNDARY DISPUTE (July 20, 1895)

> In 1895, the boundary dispute between Venezuela and British Guiana, which had lingered for over fifty years, became more heated with the British seizure of a post (and customs house) in Nicaragua and a forceful public relations campaign by Venezuela. "Twisting the lion's tail" proved a popular pastime in American politics, and President Grover Cleveland felt pressure to take the British to task for violating the Monroe Doctrine. With Cleveland's approval, Secretary of State Richard Olney sent a stiff warning to the British via U.S. Ambassador Thomas E. Bayard about the boundary dispute. Olney's "bombshell" reflected the surging expansionism in American society during the 1890's, particularly the unapologetic, martial spirit of the day known as "jingoism."

The important features of the existing situation, as shown by the foregoing recital, may be briefly stated.

---

U. S. Department of State, Papers Relating to the Foreign Relations of the United States, 1895 (Washington, D.C., 1896), Part I, pp. 545-62.

parties is right and which wrong--it is certainly within its right to demand that the truth shall be ascertained. Being entitled to resent and resist any sequestration of Venezuelan soil by Great Britain, it is necessarily entitled to know whether such sequestration has occurred or is now going on. . . .

If it were possible to point to a boundary which both parties had ever agreed or assumed to be such either expressly or tacitly, the demand that territory conceded by such line to British Guiana should be held not to be in dispute might rest upon a reasonable basis. But there is no such line. The territory which Great Britain insists shall be ceded to her as a condition of arbitrating her claim to other territory has never been admitted to belong to her. It has always and consistently been claimed by Venezuela. . . .

She says to Venezuela, in substance: "You can get none of the debatable land by force, because you are not strong enough; you can get none by treaty, because I will not agree; and you can take your chance of getting a portion by arbitration, only if you first agree to abandon to me such other portion as I may designate". . . . It seems therefore quite impossible that this position of Great Britain should be assented to by the United States, or that, if such position be adhered to with the result of enlarging the bounds of British Guiana, it should not be regarded as amounting, in substance, to an invasion and conquest of Venezuelan territory.

In these circumstances, the duty of the President appears to him unmistakable and imperative. Great Britain's assertion of title to the disputed territory combined with her refusal to have that title investigated being a substantial appropriation of the territory to her own use, not to protest and give warning that the transaction will be regarded as injurious to the interests of the people of the United States as well as oppressive in itself would be to ignore an established policy with which the honor and welfare of this country are closely identified. While the measures necessary or proper for the vindication of that policy are to be determined by another branch of the Government, it is clearly for the Executive to leave nothing undone which may tend to render such determination unnecessary.

You are instructed, therefore, to present the foregoing views to Lord Salisbury by reading to him this communication (leaving with him a copy should he so desire), and to reinforce them by such pertinent considerations as will doubtless occur to you. They call for a definite decision upon the point whether Great Britain will consent or will decline to submit the Venezuelan boundary question in its entirety to impartial arbitration. It is the earnest hope of the President that the conclusion will be on the side of arbitration, and that Great Britain will add one more to the conspicuous precedents she has already furnished in favor of that wise and just mode of adjusting international disputes. If he is to be disappointed in that hope, however--a result not to be anticipated and in his judgment calculated to greatly embarrass the future relations between this country and Great Britain--it is his wish to be made acquainted with the fact at such early date as will enable him to lay the whole subject before Congress in his next annual message.

## JOSIAH STRONG ON U.S. EXPANSIONISM (1885)

During the late Nineteenth Century, many Americans began to look beyond the borders of the United States in search of empire. Many motives stimulated this "outward thrust," but two of the strongest were Social Darwinism (including all its racist implications) and the so-called missionary impulse. Ministers like Josiah Strong took comfort in a grand design which seemed to favor both Anglo-Saxons and Christians.

It is not necessary to argue to those for whom I write that the two great needs of mankind, that all men may be lifted up into the light of the highest Christian civilization are first a pure spiritual Christianity, and, second, civil liberty. Without controversy, these are the forces which, in the past, have contributed most to the elevation of the human race, and they must continue to be, in the future, the most efficient ministers to its progress. It follows, then, that the Anglo-Saxon, as the great representative of these two ideas, the depositary of these two greatest blessings, sustains peculiar relations to the world's future, is divinely commissioned to be, in a peculiar sense, his brother's keeper. Add to this the fact of his rapidly increasing strength in modern times, and we have well nigh a demonstration of his destiny. . . . And the expansion of this race has been no less remarkable than its multiplication. In one century the United States has increased its territory ten-fold, while the enormous acquisition of foreign territory by Great Britain--and chiefly within the last hundred years--is wholly unparalleled in history. This mighty Anglo-Saxon race, though comprising only one-fifteenth part of mankind, now rules more than one-third of the earth's surface, and more than one-fourth of its people. And if this race, while growing from 6,000,000 to 100,000,000, thus gained possession of a third portion of the earth, is it to be supposed that when it numbers 1,000,000,000, it will lose the disposition, or lack the power to extend its sway?. . .

It is not unlikely that, before the close of the next century, this race will outnumber all the other civilized races of the world. Does it not look as if God were not only preparing in our Anglo-Saxon civilization the die with which to stamp the peoples of the earth, but as if he were also massing behind that die the mighty power with which to press it? My confidence that this race is eventually to give its civilization to mankind is not based on mere numbers--China forbid! I look forward to what the world has never yet seen united in the same race; viz., the greatest numbers, and the highest civilization. . . .

It may be easily shown, and is of no small significance, that the two great ideas [civil liberty and christianity] of which the Anglo-Saxon is the exponent are having a fuller development in the United States than in Great Britain. There the union of Church and State tends strongly to paralyze some of the members of the body of Christ. Here there is no such influence to destroy spiritual life and power. Here, also, has been evolved the form of government consistent with the largest possible civil liberty. Furthermore,

---

Josiah Strong, Our Country (New York, 1885), pp. 159-80.

it is significant that the marked characteristics of this race are being here emphasized most. Among the most striking features of the Anglo-Saxon is his money-making power--a power of increasing importance in the widening commerce of the world's future. . . . [A]lthough England is by far the richest nation of Europe, we have already oustripped her in the race after wealth, and we have only begun the development of our vast resources.

Again, another marked characteristic of the Anglo-Saxon is what may be called an instinct or genius for colonizing. His unequaled energy, his indomitable perseverance, and his personal independence, made him a pioneer. He excels all others in pushing his way into new countries. It was those in whom this tendency was strongest that came to America, and this inherited tendency has been further develped by the westward sweep of successive generations across the continent. So noticeable has this characteristic become that English visitors remark it. Charles Dickens once said that the typical American would hesitate to enter heaven unless assured that he could go further west.

Again, nothing more manifestly distinguishes the Anglo-Saxon than his intense and persistent energy; and he is developing in the United States an energy which, in eager activity and effectiveness, is peculiarly American. This is due partly to the fact that Americans are much better fed than Europeans, and partly to the undeveloped resources of a new country, but more largely to our climate, which acts as a constant stimulus. . . . Moreover, our social institutions are stimulating. In Europe the various ranks of society are, like the strata of the earth, fixed and fossilized. There can be no great change without a terrible upheaval, a social earthquake. Here society is like the waters of the sea, mobile; . . . Our aristocracy, unlike that of Europe, is open to all comers. Wealth, position, influence, are prizes offered for energy; and every farmer's boy, every apprentice and clerk, every friendless and penniless immigrant, is free to enter the lists. Thus many causes co-operate to produce here the most forceful and tremendous energy in the world.

What is the significiance of such facts? These tendencies infold the future; they are the mighty alphabet with which God writes his prophecies. May we not, by a careful laying together of the letters, spell out something of his meaning? It seems to me that God, with infinite wisdom and skill, is training the Anglo-Saxon race for an hour sure to come in the world's future. Heretofore there has always been in the history of the world a comparatively unoccupied land westward, into which the crowded countries of the East have poured their surplus populations. But the widening waves of migration, which millenniums ago rolled east and west from the valley of the Euphrates, meet to-day on our Pacific coast. There are no more new worlds. The unoccupied arable lands of the earth are limited, and will soon be taken. The time is coming when the pressure of population on the means of subsistence will be felt here as it is now felt in Europe and Asia. Then will the world enter upon a new stage of its history--<u>the final competition of races, for which the Anglo-Saxon is being schooled.</u> Long before the thousand millions are here, the mighty <u>centrifugal</u> tendency, inherent in this stock and strengthened in the United States, will assert itself. Then this race of unequaled energy, with all the majesty of numbers and the might of wealth behind it--the representative, let us hope, of the largest liberty, the purest Christianity, the highest civilization--having developed peculiarly aggressive traits calculated to impress its institutions upon mankind, will spread itself over the earth. If I read not amiss, this powerful race will move down upon Mexico, down upon Central and South America, out upon the islands of the sea, over upon Africa and beyond. And can any one doubt that the result of this competition of races will be the "survival of the fittest"?. . . To this result no war of extermination is needful; the contest is not one of arms, but of vitality and of civilization. . . . Every civilization has its destructive and preservative elements. The Anglo-Saxon race would speedily decay but for the salt of Christianity. Bring savages into contact with our civilization, and its destructive forces become operative at once, while years are necessary to render effective the saving influences of Christian instruction. Moreover, the pioneer wave of our civilization carries with it more scum than salt. Where there is one missionary, there are hundreds of miners or traders or adventurers ready to debauch the native. Whether the extinction of inferior races before the advancing Anglo-Saxon seems to the reader sad or otherwise, it certainly appears probable. I know of nothing except climatic conditions to prevent this race from populating Africa as it has peopled North America. And those portions of Africa which are unfavorable to Anglo-Saxon life are less extensive than was once supposed. The Dutch Boers, after two centuries of life there, are as hardy as any race on earth. The Anglo-Saxon has established himself in climates totally diverse--Canada, South Africa, and India--and, through several generations, has preserved his essential race characteristics. He is not, of course, superior to climatic influences; but, even in warm climates, he is likely to retain his aggressive vigor long enough to supplant races already enfeebled. . . .

Is there room for reasonable doubt that this race, unless devitalized by alcohol and tobacco, is destined to dispossess many weaker races, assimilate others, and mold the remainder, until, in a very true and important sense, it has Anglo-Saxonized mankind?

## THE De LOME LETTER (1898)

The newspapers controlled by William Randolph Hearst were decided advocates of American expansionism. Early in 1898, with war fever rising in the U.S., Hearst's New York Journal obtained and published a private letter, written by the Spanish Minister in Washington, Depuy De Lome.

His Excellency Don Jose Canalejas. . . .

The situation here remains the same. Everything depends on the political and military outcome in Cuba. The prologue of all this, in this second stage (phase) of the war, will end the day when the colonial cabinet shall be appointed and we shall be relieved in the eyes of this country of a part of the responsibility for what is happening in Cuba, while the Cubans, whom these people think so immaculate, will have to assume it.

---

U. S. Department of State, Papers Relating to the Foreign Relations of the United States, 1898 (Washington, D.C., 1901), pp. 1007-8.

Until then, nothing can be clearly seen, and I regard it as a waste of time and progress, by a wrong road, to be sending emissaries to the rebel camp, or to negotiate with the autonomists who have as yet no legal standing, or to try to ascertain the intentions and plans of this Government. The [Cuban] refugees will keep on returning one by one, as they do so will make their way into the sheepfold, while the leaders in the field will gradually come back. Neither the one nor the other class had the courage to leave in a body and they will not be brave enough to return in a body.

The message has been a disillusionment to the insurgents, who expected something different; but I regard it as bad (for us).

Besides the ingrained and inevitable bluntness (groseria) with which is repeated all that the press and public opinion in Spain have said about Weyler, it once more shows what McKinley is, weak and a bidder for the admiration of the crowd, besides being a would-be politician (politicastro) who tries to leave a door open behind himself while keeping on good terms with the jingoes of his party.

Nevertheless, whether the practical results of it [the message] are to be injurious and adverse depends only upon ourselves.

I am entirely of your opinions; without a military end of the matter nothing will be accomplished in Cuba, and without a military and political settlement there will always be the danger of encouragement being given to the insurgents by a part of the public opinion if not by the Government.

I do not think sufficient attention has been paid to the part England is playing.

Nearly all the newspaper rabble that swarms in your hotels are Englishmen, and while writing for the Journal they are also correspondents of the most influential journals and reviews of London. It has been so ever since this thing began. As I look at it, England's only object is that the Americans should amuse themselves with us and leave her alone, and if there should be a war, that would the better stave off the conflict which she dreads but which will never come about.

It would be very advantageous to take up, even if only for effect, the question of commercial relations, and to have a man of some prominence sent hither in order that I may make use of him here to carry on a propaganda among the Senators and others in opposition to the junta and to try to win over the refugees.

So, Amblard is coming. I think he devotes himself too much to petty politics, and we have got to do something very big or we shall fail.

Adela returns your greeting, and we all trust that next year you may be a messenger of peace and take it as a Christmas gift to poor Spain.


## HENRY M. TELLER ON THE ANNEXATION OF CUBA (1898)

As the Senate debated a proposal to recognize the independence of Cuba, Senator Henry M. Teller of Colorado saw fit to offer an amendment which would clarify, especially for the European powers, the true intentions of the United States. Teller, however, made clear that his proposal--the so-called Teller Amendment--applied only to Cuba and not to "other islands."

---

U. S. Congress, Senate, 55th Cong., 2d sess., April 16, 1898, Congressional Record, XXXI, 3954.

First. That the people of the Island of Cuba are, and of right ought to be, free and independent, and that the Government of the United States hereby recognizes the Republic of Cuba as the true and lawful Government of that island.

Second. That it is now apparent that Spain can not maintain her control of Cuba against the republician government of that island. The war now existing between the Government of Spain and the Republic of Cuba, as now conducted, is destructive of the interests of the people of Cuba, and injurious to the interests of the United States, and has created a condition in that island that can no longer be endured.

The only hope of relief and repose from such a condition is the enforced pacification of Cuba by the withdrawal of the land and naval forces of Spain from that island; it is, therefore, the duty of the United States to demand, and the Government of the United States does hereby demand, that the Government of Spain at once withdraw its land and naval forces from Cuba and Cuban waters. If Spain fails or refuses to accede to such demand, it will be the duty of the Government of the United States in defense of its interests and in the interest of humanity to take such measures as shall put an immediate stop to the war in Cuba, hereby disclaiming any disposition or intention to exercise jurisdiction or control over said island except for the pacification thereof and a determination when that is accomplished to leave the government and control of the island to the people thereof.

Resolved, That the President is hereby authorized and directed to take at once such steps as may be necessary to terminate hostilities in the Island of Cuba and to secure to the people of that island an independent republican government by the people thereof; and the President is authorized and directed to use, if necessary, the land and naval forces of the United States for the purpose of carrying this joint resolution into effect.

## ALBERT J. BEVERIDGE ON THE "LARGE POLICY" OF EXPANSIONISM (1900)

Few voices in favor of American expansion were raised with as much zeal and eloquence as that of Albert J. Beveridge. The Senator from Indiana remained steady in his determination to see the United States become the dominant power in the world.

Mr. President, the times call for candor. The Philippines are ours forever, "territory belonging to the United States," as the Constitution calls them. And just beyond the Philippines are China's illimitable markets. We will not retreat from either. We will not repudiate our duty in the archipelago. We will not abandon our opportunity in the Orient. We will not

---

U. S. Congress, Senate, 56th Cong., 1st sess., January 9, 1900, Congressional Record, XXXIII, 704-12.

renounce our part in the mission of our race, trustee, under God, of the civilization of the world. And we will move forward to our work, not howling out regrets like slaves whipped to their burdens, but with gratitude for a task worthy of our strength, and thanksgiving to Almighty God that He has marked us as His chosen people, henceforth to lead in the regeneration of the world.

This island empire is the last land left in all the oceans. If it should prove a mistake to abandon it, the blunder once made would be irretrievable. If it proves a mistake to hold it, the error can be corrected when we will. Every other progressive nation stands ready to relieve us.

But to hold it will be no mistake. Our largest trade henceforth must be with Asia. The Pacific is our ocean. More and more Europe will manufacture the most it needs, secure from its colonies the most it consumes. Where shall we turn for consumers of our surplus? Geography answers the question. China is our natural customer. She is nearer to us than to England, Germany, or Russia, the commercial powers of the present and the future. They have moved nearer to China by securing permanent bases on her borders. The Philippines give us a base at the door of all the East.

Lines of navigation from our ports to the Orient and Australia; from the Isthmian Canal to Asia; from all Oriental ports to Australia, converage at and separate from the Philippines. They are a self-supporting, dividend-paying fleet, permanently anchored at a spot selected by the stragegy of Providence, commanding the Pacific. And the Pacific is the ocean of the commerce of the future. Most future wars will be conflicts for commerce. The power that rules the Pacific, therefore, is the power that rules the world. And, with the Philippines, that power is and will forever be the American Republic.

China's trade is the mightiest commercial fact in our future. Her foreign commerce was $285,738,300 in 1897, of which we, her neighbor, had less than 9 per cent, of which only a little more than half was merchandise sold to China by us. We ought to have 50 per cent, and we will. And China's foreign commerce is only beginning. . . .

That statesman commits a crime against American trade--against the American grower of cotton and wheat and tobacco, the American manufacturer of machinery and clothing--who fails to put America where she may command that trade. Germany's Chinese trade is increasing like magic. She has established ship lines and secured a tangible foothold on China's very soil. Russia's Chinese trade is growing beyond belief. She is spending the revenues of the Empire to finish her railroad into Pekin itself, and she is in physical possession of the imperial province of Manchuria. Japan's Chinese trade is multiplying in volume and value. She is bending her energy to her merchant marine, and is located along China's very coast; but Manila is nearer China than Yokohama is. The Philippines command the commercial situation of the entire East. . . . And yet American statesmen plan to surrender this commercial throne of the Orient where Providence and our soldier's lives have placed us. When history comes to write the story of that suggested treason to American supremacy and therefore to the spread of American civilization, let her in mercy write that those who so proposed were merely blind and nothing more.

But if they did not command China, India, the Orient, the whole Pacific for purposes of offense, defense, and trade, the Philippines are so valuable in themselves that we should hold them. . . .

National prestige, national propinquity, these and commercial activity are the elements of commercial success. The Philippines give the first; the character of the American people supply the last. It is a providential conjunction of all the elements of trade, of duty, and of power. If we are willing to go to war rather than let England have a few feet of frozen Alaska, which affords no market and commands none, what should we not do rather than let England, Germany, Russia, or Japan have all the Philippines? And no man on the spot can fail to see that this would be their fate if we retired. . . .

It will be hard for Americans who have not studied them to understand the people. They are a barbarous race modified by three centuries of contact with a decadent race. The Filipino is the South Sea Malay, put through a process of three hundred years of superstition in religion, dishonesty in dealing, disorder in habits of industry, and cruelty, caprice, and corruption in government. It is barely possible that 1,000 men in all the archipelago are capable of self-government in the Anglo-Saxon sense. . . .

Two years ago there was no land in all the world which we could occupy for any purpose. Our commence was daily turning toward the Orient and geography and trade developments made necessary our commercial empire over the Pacific. And in that ocean we had no commercial, naval, or military base. To-day we have one of the three great ocean possessions of the globe, located at the most commanding commercial, naval, and military points in the eastern seas, within hail of India, shoulder to shoulder with China, richer in its own resources than any equal body of land on the entire globe, and peopled by a race which civilization demands shall be improved. Shall we abandon it?. . .

But, Senators, it would be better to abandon this combined garden and Gibraltar of the Pacific, and count our blood and treasure already spent a profitable loss, than to apply any academic arrangement of self-government to these children. They are not capable of self-government. How could they be? They are not of a self-governing race. They are Orientals, Malays, instructed by Spaniards in the latter's worst estate. . . .

What alchemy will change the oriental quality of their blood and set the self-governing currents of the American puring through their Malay veins? How shall they, in the twinkling of an eye, be exalted to the heights of self-governing peoples which required a thousand years for us to reach, Anglo-Saxon though we are?. . .

Mr President, self-government and internal development have been the dominant notes of our first century; administration and the development of other lands will be the dominant notes of our second century. And administration is as high and holy a function as self-government, just as the care of a trust estate is as sacred an obligation as the management of our own concerns. . . .

The Declaration of Independence does not forbid us to do our part in the regeneration of the world. . . . It was written by self-governing men for self-governing men.

It was written by men who, for a century and a half, had been experimenting in self-government on this continent, and whose ancestors for hundreds of years before had been gradually developing toward that high and holy estate. The Declaration applies only to people capable of self-government. How dare any man prostitute this expression of the very elect of self-governing peoples to a race of Malay children of barbarism, schooled in Spanish methods and ideas? And you, who say the Declaration applies to all men, how dare you deny its application to the American Indian? And if you deny it to the Indian at home, how dare you grant it to the Malay abroad?. . .

The ocean does not separate us from the field of our duty and endeavor--it joins us, an established highway needing no repair, and landing us at any point desired. The seas do not separate the Philippine Islands from us or from each other. The seas are highways through the archipelago, which would cost hundreds of millions of dollars to construct if they were land instead of water. Land may separate men from their desire, the ocean never. . . .

There is in the ocean no constitutional argument against the march of the flag, for the oceans, too, are ours. With more extended coast lines than any nation of history; with a commerce vaster than any other people ever dreamed of, and that commerce as yet only in its beginnings; with naval traditions equaling those of England or of Greece, and the work of our Navy only just begun; with the air of the ocean in our nostrils and the booodj of a sailor ancestry in our veins; with the shores of all the continents calling us, the great Republic before I die will be the acknowledged lord of the world's high seas. And over them the Republic will hold dominion, by virtue of the strength God has given it, for the peace of the world and the betterment of man.

No: the oceans are not limitations of the power which the Constitution expressly gives Congress to govern all territory the nation may acquire. The Constitution declares that "Congress shall have power to dispose of and make all needful rules and regulations respecting the territory belonging to the United States." Not the Northwest Territory only; not Louisiana or Florida only; not territory on this continent only, but any territory anywhere belonging to the nation. . . .

Mr. President, this question is deeper than any question of party politics; deeper than any question of the isolated policy of our country even; deeper even than any question of constitutional power. It is elemental. It is racial. God has not been preparing the English-speaking and Teutonic peoples for a thousand years for nothing but vain and idle self-contemplation and self-admiration. No! He has made us the master organizers of the world to establish system where chaos reigns. He has given us the spirit of progress to overwhelm the forces of reaction throughout the earth. He has made us adepts in government that we may administer government among savage and senile peoples. Were it not for such a force as this the world would relapse into barbarism and night. And of all our race He has marked the American people as His chosen nation to finally lead in the regeneration of the world. This is the divine mission of America, and it holds for us all the profit, all the glory, all the happiness possible to man. We are trustees of the world's progess, guardians of its righteous peace.


WILLIAM GRAHAM SUMNER ON THE CONQUEST OF THE UNITED STATES BY SPAIN (1899)

It may seem ironic that someone like William Graham Sumner, who fully accepted the brutal competitive theory of Social Darwinism in domestic affairs, argued forcefully against American participation in the

---

William Graham Sumner, The Conquest of the United States by Spain (Boston, 1899), pp. 1, 7, 9-10, 12, 19, 23-25, 27-28, 32.

international competition for empire. Yet Sumner believed that if the country were to become entangled with inferior races and breeds the evolution of the United States (the "fittest") would be unnecessarily tainted and hindered.

During the last year the public has been familiarized with descriptions of Spain and of Spanish methods of doing things until the name of Spain has become a symbol for a certain well-defined set of notions and policies. On the other hand, the name of the United States has always been, for all of us, a symbol for a state of things, a set of ideas and traditions, a group of views about social and political affairs. Spain was the first, for a long time the greatest, of the modern imperialistic states. The United States, by its historical origin, its traditions and its principles, is the chief representative of the revolt and reaction against that kind of a state. I intend to show that, by the line of action now proposed to us, which we call expansion and imperialism, we are throwing away some of the most important elements of the American symbol, and are adopting some of the most important elements of the Spanish symbol. We have beaten Spain in a military conflict, but we are submitting to be conquered by her on the field of ideas and policies. Expansionism and imperialism are nothing but the old philosophies of national prosperity which have brought Spain to where she now is. Those philosophies appeal to national vanity and national cupidity. They are seductive, especially upon the first view and the most superficial judgment, and therefore it cannot be denied that they are very strong for popular effect. They are delusions, and they will lead us to ruin unless we are hard-headed enough to resist them. . . .

There is a set of men who have always been referred to, in our Northern States, for the last thirty years, with especial disapproval. They are those Southerners who, in 1861, did not believe in secession, but, as they said, "Went with their States." They have been condemned for moral cowardice. Yet within a year it has become almost a doctrine with us that patriotism requires that we should hold our tongues whenever our rulers choose to engage in war, although our interests, our institutions, our most sacred traditions, and our best established maxims may be trampled underfoot. There is no doubt that moral courage is the virtue which is more needed than any other in the modern democratic state, and that truckling to popularity is the worst political vice. The press, the platform, and the pulpit have all fallen under this vice, and there is evidence that the university also, which ought to be the last citadel of truth, is succumbing to it likewise. I have no doubt that the conservative classes of this country will yet look back with great regret to their acquiescence in the events of 1898 and the doctrines and precedents which have been silently established. Let us be well assured that self-government is not a matter of flags and Fourth of July orations, nor yet of strife to get offices. External vigilance is the price of that as of every other political good. The perpetuity of self-government depends on the sound political sense of the people, and sound political sense is a matter of habit and practice. We can give it up and we can take instead pomp and glory. . . .

We assume that what we like and practise, and what we think better, must come as a welcome blessing to Spanish-Americans and Filipinos. This is grossly and obviously untrue. They hate our ways. They are hostile to our ideas. Our religion, language, institutions, and manners offend them. They like their own ways, and if we appear amongst them as rulers, there will be social discord on all the great departments of social interest. The most important thing which we shall inherit from the Spaniards will be the task of suppressing rebellions. If the United States takes out of the hands of Spain her mission, on the ground that Spain is not executing it well, and if this nation, in its turn, attempts to be school-mistress to others, it will shrivel up into the same vanity and self-conceit of which Spain now presents an example. To read our current literature one would think that we were already our current literature one would think that we were already well on the way to it. Now, the great reason why all these enterprises, which begin by saying to somebody else: We know what is good for you, better than you know yourself, and we are going to make you do it--are false and wrong, is that they violate liberty; or, to turn the same statement into other words: the reason why liberty, of which we Americans talk so much, is a good thing, is, that it means leaving people to live out their own lives in their own way, while we do the same. If we believe in liberty, as an American principle, why do we not stand by it? Why are we going to throw it away to enter upon a Spanish policy of dominion and regulations? . . .

There are plenty of people in the United States to-day who regard negroes as human beings, perhaps, but of a different order from white men, so that the ideas and social arrangements of white men cannot be applied to them with propriety. Others feel the same way about Indians. This attitude of mind, wherever you meet with it, is what causes tyranny and cruelty. It is this disposition to decide offhand that some people are not fit for liberty and self-government which gives relative truth to the doctrine that all men are equal, and, inasmuch as the history of mankind has been one long story of the abuse of some by others (who, of course, smoothed over their tyranny by some beautiful doctrines of religion, or ethics, or political philosophy, which proved that it was all for the best good of the oppressed), therefore the doctrine that all men are equal has come to stand as one of the corner-stones of the temple of justice and truth. It was set up as a bar to just this notion that we are so much better than others that it is liberty for them to be governed by us.

The conclusion of this branch of the subject is that it is fundamentally antagonistic to our domestic system to hold dependencies which are unfit to enter into the Union. Our system cannot be extended to take them in, or adjusted to them to keep them out without sacrificing its integrity. If we take in dependencies, which, as we now agree, are not fit to come in as States, there will be constant political agitation to admit them as States, for such agitation will be fomented by any party which thinks that it can win votes in that way. It was an enormous blunder in statecraft to engage in a war which was sure to bring us into this predicament. . . .

Everywhere you go on the Continent of Europe at this hour you see the conflict between militarism and industrialism. You see the expansion of industrial power pushed forward by the energy, hope, and thrift of men, and you see the development arrested, diverted, crippled, and defeated by measures which are dictated by military considerations. At the same time the press is loaded down with discussions about political economy, political philosophy, and social policy. They are discussing poverty, labor, socialism, charity, reform, and social ideals, and are boasting of enlightenment and progress, at the same time that the things which are done are dictated not by these considerations, but by military interests. It is militarism which is eating up all the products of science and art, defeating the energy of the population, and wasting its savings. It is militarism which forbids the people to give their attention to the problems of their own welfare, and to give their strength to the education and comfort of their children. It is militarism which is combating the grand efforts of science and art to ameliorate the struggle for existence. . . .

Now what will hasten the day when our present advantages will wear out, and when we shall come down to the conditions of the older and densely populated nations? The answer is: war, debt, taxation, diplomacy, a grand governmental system, pomp, glory, a big army and navy, lavish expenditures, political jobbery,--in a word, imperialism. . . .

Three years ago we were ready to fight Great Britain to make her arbitrate a quarrel which she had with Venezuela. The question about the Maine was the fittest subject for arbitration that ever arose between two nations, and we refused to listen to such a proposition. Three years ago, if you had said that any proposition put forth by anybody was "English," he might have been mobbed in the streets. Now the English are our beloved friends, and we are going to try to imitate them and adopt their way of doing things. They are encouraging us to go into difficulties, first because our hands will be full and we will be unable to interfere elsewhere, and secondly, because if we are in difficulties we shall need allies, and they think that they will be our first choice as such. Some of our public journals have been pouring out sentimental drivel for years about arbitration, but last summer they turned around and began to pour out sentimental drivel about the benefits of war. We congratulate ourselves all the time on the increased means of producing wealth, and then we take the opposite fit and commit some great folly in order to prove that there is something grander than the pursuit of wealth. Three years ago we were on the verge of a law to keep immigrants out who were not good enough to be in with us. Now we are going to take in 8,000,000 barbarians and semi-barbarians, and we are paying $20,000,000 to get them. For thirty years the negro has been in fashion. He has had political value, and has been petted. Now we have made friends with the Southerners. They and we are hugging each other. We are all united. The negro's day is over. He is out of fashion. We cannot treat him one way and the Malays, Tagals, and Kanakas another way. A Southern senator two or three days ago thanked an expansionist senator from Connecticut for enunciating doctrines which proved that, for the last thirty years, the Southerners have been right all the time, and his inference was incontrovertible. . . . .

My patriotism is of the kind which is outraged by the notion that the United States never was a great nation until in a petty three months' campaign it knocked to pieces a poor, decrepit, bankrupt old state like Spain. To hold such an opinion as that is to abandon all American standards, to put shame and scorn on all that our ancestors tried to build up here, and to go over to the standards of which Spain is a representative.

## AMERICAN ANTI-IMPERIALIST LEAGUE PLATFORM (1899)

Opponents of American imperialism invoked several different arguments, which ranged from the most humane to the most selfish. As a result, the anti-imperialists reflected a broad range of viewpoints, and they had very little in common. One could scarcely imagine people such as Andrew Carnegie and William Graham Sumner on the one hand and Samuel Gompers and Carl Schurz on the other hand working together for any appreciable length of time. Nevertheless, in late 1898, the Anti-Imperialist League formed. The following year, with an eye on the presidential campaign of 1900, the League adopted the following platform.

We hold that the policy known as imperialism is hostile to liberty and tends toward militarism, an evil from which it has been our glory to be free. We regret that it has become necessary in the land of Washington and Lincoln to reaffirm that all men, of whatever race or color, are entitled to life, liberty and the pursuit of happiness. We maintain that governments derive their just powers from the consent of the governed. We insist that the subjugation of any people is "criminal aggression" and open disloyalty to the distinctive principles of our Government.

We earnestly condemn the policy of the present National Administration in the Philippines. It seeks to extinguish the spirit of 1776 in those islands. We deplore the sacrifice of our soldiers and sailors, whos bravery deserves admiration even in an unjust war. We denounce the slaughter of the Filipinos as a needless horror. We protest against the extension of American sovereignty by Spanish methods.

We demand the immediate cessation of the war against liberty, begun by Spain and continued by us. We urge that Congress be promptly convened to announce to the Filipinos our purpose to concede to them the independence for which they have so long fought and which of right is theirs.

The United States have always protested against the doctrine of international law which permits the subjugation of the weak by the strong. A self-governing state cannot accept sovereignty over an unwilling people. The United States cannot act upon the ancient heresy that might makes right.

Imperialists assume that with the destruction of self-government in the Philippines by American hands, all opposition here will cease. This is a grievous error. Much as we abhor the war of "criminal aggression" in the Philippines, greatly as we regret that the blood of the Filipinos on American hands, we more deeply resent the betrayal of American institutions at home. The real firing line is not in the suburbs of Manila. The foe is of our own household. The attempt of 1861 was to divide the country. That of 1899 is to destroy its fundamental principles and noblest ideals.

Whether the ruthless slaughter of the Filipinos shall end next month or next year is but an incident in a contest that must go on until the Declaration of Independence and the Constitution of the United States are rescued from the hands of their betrayers. Those who dispute about standards of value while the foundation of the Republic is undermined will be listened to as little as those who would wrangle about the small economies of the household while the house is on fire. The training of a great people for a century, the aspiration for liberty of a vast immigration are forces that will hurl aside those who in the delirium of conquest seek to destroy the character of our institutions.

We deny that the obligation of all citizens to support their Government in times of grave National peril applies to the present situation. If an Administration may with impunity ignore the issues upon which it was chosen, deliberately create a condition of war anywhere on the face of the globe, debauch the civil service for spoils to promote the adventure, organize a truth-suppressing censorship and demand of all citizens a suspension of judgment and their unanimous support while it chooses to continue the fighting, representative government itself is imperiled. . . .

We hold, with Abraham Lincoln, that "no man is good enough to govern another man without the other's consent. When the white man governs himself, that is self-government, but when he governs himself and also governs another man, that is more than self-government--that is despotism. Our reliance is in the love of liberty which God has planted in us. Our defense is in the spirit which prizes liberty as the heritage of all men in all lands. Those who deny freedom to others deserve it not for themselves, and under a just God cannot long retain it."

## WILLIAM McKINLEY ON THE ANNEXATION OF THE PHILIPPINE ISLANDS (1898)

> Once the United States found itself in military possession of the Philippine Islands during the Spanish-American War, a decision had to be made about what to do with them. President McKinley offered an explanation about the source of his inspiration in making that decision.

I have been criticized a good deal about the Philippines, but I don't deserve it. The truth is I didn't want the Philippines, and when they came to us, as a gift from the gods, I did not know what to do with them. When the Spanish War broke out, Dewey was at Hong-kong, and I ordered him to go to Manila and to capture or destroy the Spanish fleet, and he had to; because, if defeated, he had no place to refit on that side of the globe, and if the Dons were victorious, they would likely cross the Pacific and ravage our Oregon and California coasts. And so he had to destroy the Spanish fleet, and did it! But that was as far as I thought then.

When next I realized that the Philippines had dropped into our laps, I confess I did not know what to do with them. I sought counsel from all sides--Democrats as well as Republicans--but got little help. I thought first we would take only Manila; then Luzon; then other islands, perhaps, also. I walked the floor of the White House night after night until midnight; and I am not ashamed to tell you, gentlemen, that I went down on my knees and prayed Almighty God for light and guidance more than one night. And one night late it came to me this way--I don't know how it was, but it came: (1) That we could not give them back to Spain--that would be cowardly and dishonorable; (2) that we could not turn them over to France or Germany-our commercial rivals in the Orient--that would be bad business and discreditable; (3) that

---

Quoted in Charles S. Olcott, The Life of William McKinley (Boston, 1916), II, 109-11.

we could not leave them to themselves--they were unfit for self-government--and they would soon have anarchy and misrule there worse than Spain's was; and (4) that there was nothing left for us to do but to take them all, and to educate the Filipinos, and uplift and civilize and Christianize them, and by God's grace do the very best we could by them, as our fellowmen for whom Christ also died. And then I went to bed, and went to sleep, and slept soundly, and the next morning I sent for the chief engineer of the War Department (our map-maker), and I told him to put the Philippines on the map of the United States, and there they are, and there they will stay while I am president!

## THE PLATT AMENDMENT (1901)

Despite the Teller Amendment, many American expansionists wanted to annex Cuba following the Spanish-American War. They feared that inept Cuban leadership or the chronic instability in Cuba might somehow attract a European power and thereby jeopardize U. S. interests. To reduce that risk and to uphold at least the letter (if not the spirit) of the Teller Amendment, Senator Orville H. Platt of Connecticut offered an amendment to an Army appropriations bill in 1901. The Platt Amendment virtually reduced Cuba to the status of an American protectorate. With much pressure from Washington, Cuba incorporated the language of the Platt Amendment in its 1901 constitution; two years later, the same wording found its way into a treaty between the United States and Cuba.

That in fulfillment of the declaration contained in the joint resolution approved April 20, 1898, entitled "For the recognition of the independence of the people of Cuba, demanding that the Government of Spain relinquish its authority and government in the island of Cuba, and to withdraw its land and naval forces from Cuba and Cuban waters, and directing the President of the United States to use the land and naval forces of the United States to carry these resolutions into effect," the President is hereby authorized to "leave the government and control of the island of Cuba to its people" so soon as a government shall have been established in said island under a constitution which, either as a part thereof or in an ordinance appended thereto, shall define the future relations of the United States with Cuba, substantially as follows:

---

U. S. Congress, Senate, February 25, 1901, <u>Congressional Record</u>, XXXIV, 2954.

I. That the government of Cuba shall never enter into any treaty or other compact with any foreign power or powers which will impair or tend to impair the independence of Cuba, nor in any manner authorize or permit any foreign power or powers to obtain by colonization or for military or naval purposes or otherwise lodgment in or control over any portion of said island.

II. That said government shall not assume or contract any public debt to pay the interest upon which and to make reasonable sinking-fund provision for the ultimate discharge of which the ordinary revenues of the island, after defraying the current expenses of government, shall be inadequate.

III. That the government of Cuba consents that the United States may exercise the right to intervene for the preservation of Cuban independence, the maintenance of a government adequate for the protection of life, property, and individual liberty, and for discharging the obligations with respect to Cuba imposed by the treaty of Paris on the United States, now to be assumed and undertaken by the government of Cuba.

IV. That all acts of the United States in Cuba during its military occupancy thereof are ratified and validated, and all lawful rights acquired thereunder shall be maintained and protected.

V. That the government of Cuba will execute, and as far as necessary extend, the plans already devised or other plans to be mutually agreed upon, for the sanitation of the cities of the island, to the end that a recurrence of epidemic and infectious diseases may be prevented, thereby assuring protection to the people and commerce of Cuba, as well as to the commerce of the southern ports of the United States and the people residing therein.

VI. That the Isle of Pines shall be omitted from the proposed constitutional boundaries of Cuba, the title thereto being left to future adjustment by treaty.

VII. That to enable the United States to maintain the independence of Cuba, and to protect the people thereof, as well as for its own defense, the government of Cuba will sell or lease to the United States lands necessary for coaling or naval stations at certain specified points, to be agreed upon with the President of the United States.

VIII. That by way of further assurance the government of Cuba will embody the foregoing provisions in a permanent treaty with the United States.


## THEODORE ROOSEVELT ON THE PANAMA CANAL (1904)

When Colombia refused to cooperate with United States' efforts to negotiate a treaty to allow construction of a canal through Panama (a province of Colombia), President Roosevelt was incensed, calling the Colombians variously "jackrabbits," "contemptible little creatures," and "greedy little anthropoids." When Panama rose in revolt, with the comfort and some aid from the U.S., Roosevelt was elated that the U.S. had been spared the need to

---

James D. Richardson, ed., *A Compilation of the Messages and Papers of the Presidents* (Washington, D.C., 1908), X, 696-701.

intervene more directly. Secretary of State John Hay quickly negotiated a Panamanian treaty, which he privately admitted was "very satisfactory, vastly advantageous to the United States, and we confess, with what face we can muster, not so advantageous to Panama." There were critics of the actions of the U.S., however, and this is how "TR" answered them.

We, in effect, policed the Isthmus in the interest of its inhabitants and of our own national needs, and for the good of the entire civilized world. Failure to act as the Administration acted would have meant great waste of life, great suffering, great destruction of property; all of which was avoided by the firmness and prudence with which Commander Hubbard [of the <u>Nashville</u>] carried out his orders and prevented either party from attacking the other. Our action was for the peace both of Colombia and of Panama. It is earnestly to be hoped that there will be no unwise conduct on our part which may encourage Colombia to embark on a war which cannot result in her gaining control of the Isthmus, but which may cause much bloodshed and suffering.

I hesitate to refer to the injurious insinuations which have been made of complicity by this Government in the revolutionary movement in Panama. They are as destitute of foundation as of propriety. The only excuse for my mentioning them is the fear lest unthinking persons might mistake for acquiescence the silence of mere self-respect. I think proper to say, therefore, that no one connected with this Government had any part in preparing, inciting, or encouraging the late revolution on the Isthmus of Panama, and that save from the reports of our military and naval officers, given above, no one connected with this Government had any previous knowledge of the revolution except such as was accessible to any person of ordinary intelligence who read the newspapers and kept up a current acquaintance with public affairs.

By the unanimous action of its people, without the firing of a shot-- with a unanimity hardly before recorded in any similar case--the people of Panama declared themselves an independent Republic. Their recognition by this Government was based upon our action in ordinary cases. I have not denied, nor do I wish to deny, either the validity or the propriety of the general rule that a new state should not be recognized as independent till it has shown its ability to maintain its independence. This rule is derived from the principle of non-intervention, and as a corollary of that principle has generally been observed by the United States. But, like the principle from which it is deduced, the rule is subject to exceptions; and there are in my opinion clear and imperative reasons why a departure from it was justified and even required in the present instance. These reasons embrace, first, our treaty rights; second, our national interests and safety; and, third, the interests of collective civilization . . . .

In all the range of our international relations, I do not hesitate to affirm that there is nothing of greater or more pressing importance than the construction of an interoceanic canal. Long acknowledged to be essential to our commercial development, it has become, as the result of the recent extension of our territorial dominion, more than ever essential to our national self-defense . . . .

I confidently maintain that the recognition of the Republic of Panama was an act justified by the interests of collective civilization. If ever a government could be said to have received a mandate from civilization to effect an object the accomplishment of which wad demanded in the interest of mankind, the United States holds that position with regard to the interoceanic canal.

## THE ROOSEVELT COROLLARY TO THE MONROE DOCTRINE (1904-1905)

South American countries which defaulted on their debts to the European powers soon found their customs houses seized by the creditors until full restitution had been made. American leaders grew anxious that such episodes might one day lead a European power to establish a permanent foothold in the Western Hemisphere. The bankruptcy of the Dominican Republic in 1904 seemed to furnish yet another occasion for European intervention (as had occurred the year before in Venezuela). Seeking to forestall action by the European powers in the Dominican Republic, President Theodore Roosevelt hit upon a new twist to the Monroe Doctrine.

(a) Annual Message, December 6, 1904

It is not true that the United States feels any land hunger or entertains any projects as regards the other nations of the Western Hemisphere save such as are for their welfare. All that this country desires is to see the neighboring countries stable, orderly, and prosperous. Any country whose people conduct themselves well can count upon our hearty friendship. If a nation shows that it knows how to act with reasonable efficiency and decency in social and political matters, if it keeps order and pays its obligations, it need fear no interference from the United States. Chronic wrongdoing, or an impotence which results in a general loosening of the ties of civilized society, may in America, as elsewhere, ultimately require intervention by some civilized nation, and in the Western Hemisphere the adherence of the United States to the Monroe Doctrine may force the United States, however reluctantly, in flagrant cases of such wrongdoing or impotence, to the exercise of an international police power. If every country washed by the Caribbean Sea would show the progress in stable and just civilization which with the aid of the Platt amendment Cuba has shown since our troops left the island, and which so many of the republics in both Americas are constantly and brilliantly showing, all question of interference by this Nation with their affairs would be at an end. Our interests and those of our southern neighbors are in reality identical. They have great natural riches, and if within their borders the reign of law and justice obtains, prosperity is sure to come to them. While they thus obey the primary laws of civilized society they may rest assured that they will be treated by us in a spirit of cordial and helpful sympathy. We would interfere with them only in the last resort, and then only if it became evident that their inability of unwillingness to do justice at home and abroad had violated the rights of the United States or had

---

James D. Richardson, ed., Messages and Papers of the Presidents (New York, 1897), XVI, 6923-6925, 6994-6996.

invited foreign aggression to the detriment of the entire body of American nations. It is a mere truism to say that every nation, whether in America or anywhere else, which desires to maintain its freedom, its independence, must ultimately realize that the right of such independence can not be separated from the responsibility of making good use of it.

In asserting the Monroe Doctrine, in taking such steps as we have taken in regard to Cuba, Venezuela, and Panama, and in endeavoring to circumscribe the theater of war in the Far East, and to secure the open door in China, we have acted in our own interest as well as in the interest of humanity at large. There are, however, cases in which, while our own interests are not greatly involved, strong appeal is made to our sympathies. . . . Nevertheless there are occasional crimes committed on so vast a scale and of such peculiar horror as to make us doubt whether it is not our manifest duty to endeavor at least show our dispproval of the deed and our sympathy with those who have suffered by it. The cases must be extreme in which such a course is justifiable. . . . But in exteme cases action may be justifiable and proper. What form the action shall take must depend upon the circumstances of the case; that is, upon the degree of the atrocity and upon our power to remedy it.

(b) Annual Message, December 5, 1905

One of the most effective instruments for peace is the Monroe Doctrine as it has been and is being gradually developed by this Nation and accepted by other nations. No other policy could have been as efficient in promoting peace in the Western Hemisphere and in giving to each nation thereon the chance to develop along its own lines. If we had refused to apply the doctrine to changing conditions it would now be completely outworn, would not meet any of the needs of the present day, and, indeed, would probably by this time have sunk into complete oblivion. It is useful at home, and is meeting with recognition abroad because we have adapted our application of it to meet the growing and changing needs of the hemisphere. When we announce a policy such as the Monroe Doctrine we thereby commit ourselves to the consequences of the policy, and those consequences from time to time alter. It is out of the question to claim a right and yet shirk the responsibility for its exercise. Not only we, but all American republics who are benefited by the existence of the doctrine, must recognize the obligations each nation is under as regards foreign peoples no less than its duty to insist upon its own rights.

That our rights and interests are deeply concerned in the maintenance of the doctrine is so clear as hardly to need argument. This is especially true in view of the construction of the Panama Canal. As a mere matter of self-defense we must exercise a close watch over the approaches to this canal; and this means that we must be thoroughly alive to our interests in the Caribbean Sea.

There are certain essential points which must never be forgotten as regards the Monroe Doctrine. In the first place we must as a Nation make it evident that we do not intend to treat it in any shape or way as an excuse for aggrandizement on our part at the expense of the republics to the south. We must recognize the fact that in some South American countries there has been much suspicion lest we should interpret the Monroe Doctrine as in some way inimical to their interests, and we must try to convince all the other nations of this continent once and for all that no just an orderly Government has anything to fear from us. There are certain republics to the south of us which have already reached such a point of stability, order, and prosperity that they themselves, though as yet hardly consciously, are among the guarantors of this doctrine. These republics we now meet not only on a basis of entire equality, but in a spirit of frank and respectful friendship, which we hope is mutual. If all of the republics to the south of us will only grow as those to which I allude have already grown, all need for us to be the especial champions of the doctrine will disappear, for no stable and growing American Republic wishes to see some great non-American military power acquire territory in its neighborhood. All that this country desires is that the other republics on this continent shall be happy and prosperous; and they cannot be happy and properous unless they maintain order within their boundaries and behave with a just regard for their obligations toward outsiders. It must be understood that under no circumstances will the United States use the Monroe Doctrine as a cloak for territorial aggression. We desire peace with all the world, but perhaps most of all with the other peoples of the American Continent. There are, of course, limits to the wrongs which any self-respecting nation can endure. It is always possible that wrong actions toward this Nation, or toward citizens of this Nation, in some State unable to keep order among its own people, unable to secure justice from outsiders, and unwilling to do justice to those outsiders who treat it well, may result in our having to take action to protect our rights; but such action will not be taken with a view to territorial aggression, and it will be taken at all only with extreme reluctance and when it has become evident that every other resource has been exhausted.

Moreover, we must make it evident that we do not intend to permit the Monroe Doctrine to be used by any nation on this Continent as a shield to protect it from the consequences of its own misdeeds against foreign nations. If a republic to the south of us commits a tort against a foreign nation, such as an outrage against a citizen of that nation, then the Monroe Doctrine does not force us to interfere to prevent punishment of the tort, save to see that the punishment does not assume the form of territorial occupation in any shape. The case is more difficult when it refers to a contractual obligation. Our own Government has always refused to enforce such contractual obligations on behalf of its citizens by an appeal to arms. It is much to be wished that all foreign governments would take the same view. But they do not; and in consequence we are liable at any time to be brought face to face with disagreeable alternatives. On the one hand, this country would certainly decline to go to war to prevent a foreign government from collecting a just debt; on the other hand, it is very inadvisable to permit any foreign power to take possession, even temporarily, of the custom houses of an American Republic in order to enforce the payment of its obligations; for such temporary occupation might turn into a permanent occupation. The only escape from these alternatives may at any time be that we must ourselves undertake to bring about some arrangement by which so much as possible of a just obligation shall be paid. It is far better that this country should put through such an arrangement, rather than allow any foreign country to undertake it. To do so insures the defaulting republic from having to pay debt of an improper character under duress, while it also insures honest creditors of the republic from being passed by in the interest of dishonest or grasping creditors. Moreover, for the United States to take such a position offers the only possible way of insuring us against a clash with some foreign power. The position is, therefore, in the interest of peace as well as in the interest of justice. It is of benefit to our people; it is of benefit to foreign peoples; and most of all it is really of benefit to the people of the country concerned.

This brings me to what should be one of the fundamental objects of the Monroe Doctrine. We must ourselves in good faith try to help upward toward peace and order those of our sister republics which need such help.

## McCLURE'S MAGAZINE ON PATRIOTISM (1905)

Some Americans questioned the motives of the social critics and reformers. Were they troublemakers, or misguided innocents? This editorial in <u>McClure's Magazine</u>, one of the leading voices for reform, sought to provide the answer.

For many months now our editorial mail has been heavy with letters inspired by Miss Tarbell's "History of the Standard Oil" and the articles by Mr. Steffens on municipal corruption. Most of these letters show that our purpose is understood. That is encouraging. Some of them call our attention to other corporations as bad as the Standard Oil or to cities or towns or villages as bad as St. Louis, Minneapolis, or Pittsburg. That also is encouraging. We chose the Standard Oil because it is the standard great business concern, and we are laying before the whole country the local disgrace of particular cities because each is the tale of a thousand cities. In these two series is the one great story of a common condition--corruption. That our readers see this is encouraging.

But some of the letters sound the note of despair. The writers cannot see what is to be done about it all. They want the cure before the diagnosis is complete, and they turn in their pessimism to some panacea that has not been tested. One of these writers, a distinguished and patriotic man, high in the public service, and no socialist, points to "socialism as the coming 'ism.'" He is mistaken. The coming "ism" is not Socialism; the coming "ism" is Patriotism.

If we did not believe that we should not have the heart to go on telling the truth. Patriotism is no child's play. It is easy enough in war, when all our friends recognize our courage, and physical pain or death is the only penalty. But the patriotism of peace,--with Society, often with your friends against you, with possible business failure before and the comfort of your family behind you,--that is hard, and that is patriotism. It is saying that if you cannot without bribery have a law passed to help your business, you will not have your business helped; that, if you know that a friend is corrupting your officials or that your party is undermining the institutions of your country, you will fight,--not for your friend or for your party, but for your country,--just as you would against a foreign enemy in war when the crowd is all with you. This takes courage.

But let us tell the weaklings and the short-sighted that we shall not join them in despair so long as we can read such chapters of the Standard Oil story as that of the fight the people and the newspapers of this country waged against the South Improvement Company, the first of Mr. Rockefeller's trust creations. No matter that the fight was lost, so long as the same spirit is alive to-day--in such men as Joseph W. Folk, of Missouri, and in the body of the citizens of Minneapolis. While there are such daily patriots, there will be patriotism to do the day's work without drums.

"Patriotism," <u>McClure's Magazine</u> (July, 1903), XXI, 335-336.

We shall proceed with the story of the Standard Oil and of the cities. In this, our July number, we print the most depressing of our city articles, that on Philadelphia, and we regard it as peculiarly appropriate reading for the glorious Fourth of July, the Anniversary of the Declaration of Independence, which was adopted one hundred and twenty-seven years ago in Philadelphia. For the new patriotism is not that which shuts its eyes and boasts, fires rockets and fails to vote. It is that which sees the truth, faces and fights any enemy of the country, at home or abroad, or in any disguise. And if we can finally persuade our readers to recognize as traitors some of the great men among us who have succeeded by means of boodling and are excused because of success, we shall have achieved our purpose. At any rate we shall try it. We propose when we have got well acquainted with them and their methods and excuses, to turn from the poor, miserable, petty traitors who sell out their country, to the "respectable," leading men, who buy it;-- from the bribed to the bribers.

A briber is a traitor. He may be a captain of industry, he may be a United States Senator, he may be a philanthropist. If he has won his fortune by bribery, the cost of his success is the undermining of the institutions of his country. He is not an "example to youth"; he is a corrupter of youth, a corrupter of everything he touches and everybody he inspires. He is an Enemy of the Republic. The only force that can stop him is PATRIOTISM.


## UPTON SINCLAIR ON THE MEATPACKING INDUSTRY (1905)

No one did more to prick the conscience of the vast American middle class about the staggering social, political, and economic injustices facing this nation than did the group of young writers called the "muckrakers." One of the best of them was Upton Sinclair. The Jungle, his book about the evil and corruption in the meatpacking houses, produced an enormous public outcry which led to the prompt enactment of the Pure Food and Drug Act of 1906.

Jonas had told them how the meat that was taken out of pickle would often be found sour, and how they would rub it up with soda to take away the smell, and sell it to be eaten on free-lunch counters; also of all the miracles of chemistry which they performed, giving to any sort of meat, fresh or salted, whole or chopped, any color and any flavor and any odor they chose. In the pickling of hams they had an ingenious apparatus, by which they saved time and increased the capacity of the plant--a machine consisting of a hollow needle attached to a pump; by plunging this needle into the meat and working with his foot a man could fill a ham with pickle in a few seconds. And yet, in spite of this, there would be hams found spoiled, some of them with an odor so bad that a man could hardly bear to be in the room with them. To pump into

---

Upton Sinclair, The Jungle (New York, 1960), pp. 135-137. From The Jungle by Upton Sinclair. Copyright 1905, 1906, 1933 by Upton Sinclair. Reprinted by permission of Viking Penguin Inc.

these the packers had a second and much stronger pickle which destroyed the odor--a process known to the workers as "giving them thirty per cent". . . .

There was never the least attention paid to what was cut up for sausage; there would come all the way back from Europe old sausage that had been rejected, and that was mouldy and white--it would be dosed with borax and glycerine, and dumped into the hoppers, and made over again for home consumption. There would be meat that had tumbled out on the floor, in the dirt and sawdust, where the workers had tramped and spit uncounted billions of consumption germs. There would be meat stored in great piles in rooms; and the water from leaky roofs would drip over it, and thousands of rats would race about on it. It was too dark in these storage places to see well, but a man could run his hand over these piles of meat and sweep off handfuls of the dried dung of rats. These rats were nuisances, and the packers would put poisoned bread out for them, they would die, and then rats, bread, and meat would go into the hoppers together. This is no fairy story and no joke; the meat would be shovelled into carts, and the man who did the shoveling would not trouble to lift out a rat even when he saw one--there were things that went into the sausage in comparison with which a poisoned rat was a tidbit. There was no place for the men to wash their hands before they ate their dinner, and so they made a practice of washing them in the water that was to be ladled into the sausage. There were the butt-ends of smoked meat, and the scraps of corned beef, and all the odds and ends of the waste of the plants, that would be dumped into old barrels in the cellar and left there . . . . In the barrels would be dirt and rust and old nails and stale water--and cart load after cart load of it would be taken up and dumped into the hoppers with fresh meat, and sent out to the public's breakfast. Some of it they would make into "smoked" sausage--but as the smoking took time, and was therefore expensive, they would call upon their chemistry department, and preserve it with borax and color it with gelatine to make it brown. All of their sausage came out of the same bowl, but when they came to wrap it they would stamp some of it "special," and for this they would charge two cents more a pound.

### THE PROGRESSIVE PARTY PLATFORM (1912)

When the Republican National Convention of 1912 rebuffed Teddy Roosevelt's candidacy for Presidential nomination, T.R. bolted the party and formed the Progressive Party ("Bull Moose" Party). The platform of the new third party created by T.R. and his followers was the most advanced statement of reform issued in the 1912 election, and served as an agenda for reform in the U.S. in the coming years.

<u>The New York Times</u>, August 8, 1912, pp. 2-3.

The conscience of the people in a time of grave National problems has called into being a new party, born of the Nation's awakened sense of justice.

We of the Progressive Party here dedicate ourselves to the fulfillment of the duty laid upon us by our fathers to maintain that government of the people, by the people, and for the people, whose foundations they laid . . . .

[The Old Parties.] Political parties exist to secure responsible government and to execute the will of the people. From these great tasks both of the old parties have turned aside. Instead of instruments to promote the general welfare, they have become the tools of corrupt interests which us them impartially to serve their selfish purposes. Behind the ostensible government sits enthroned an invisible government, owing no allegiance and acknowledging no responsibility to the people. To destroy this invisible government, to dissolve the unholy alliance between corrupt business and corrupt politics is the first task of the statesmanship of the day.

The deliberate betrayal of its trust by the Republican Party, the fatal incapacity of the Democratic Party to deal with the new issues of the new time, have compelled the people to forge a new instrument of government through which to give effect to their will in laws and institutions. Unhampered by tradition, uncorrupted by power, undismayed by the magnitude of the task, the new party offers itself as the instrument of the people to sweep away old abuses, to build a new and nobler commonwealth . . . .

[The Rule of the People.] In particular, the party declares for direct primaries for the nomination of State and National officers, for nation-wide preferential primaries for candidates for the presidency, for the direct election of United States Senators by the people, and we urge on the States the policy of the short ballot, with responsibility to the people, secured by the initiative, referendum, and recall . . . .

[Equal Suffrage.] The Progressive Party, believing that no people can justly claim to be a true democracy which denies political rights on account of sex, pledges itself to the task of securing equal suffrage to men and women alike.

[Corrupt Practices.] We pledge our party to legislation that will compel strict limitation of all campaign contributions and expenses, and detailed publicity of both, before as well as after primaries and elections.

[Publicity and Public Service.] We pledge our party to legislation compelling the registration of lobbyists, publicity of committee hearings, except on foreign affairs, and recording of all votes in committee, and forbidding Federal appointees from holding office in State or National political organizations, or taking part as officers or delegates in political conventions for the nomination of elective State or National officials.

[The Courts.] The Progressive Party demands such restriction of the power of the courts as shall leave to the people the ultimate authority to determine fundamental questions of social welfare and public policy. To secure this end it pledges itself to provide:

(1) That when an act, passed under the police power of the State, is held unconstitutional under the State Constitution by the courts, the people, after an ample interval for deliberation, shall have an opportunity to vote on the question whether they desire the act to become law, notwithstanding such decision.

(2) That every decision of the highest appellate court of a State, declaring an act of the Legislature unconstitutional on the ground of its violation of the Federal Constitution, shall be subject to the same review by the Supreme Court of the United States as is now accorded to decisions sustaining such legislation.

[Administration of Justice.] We believe that the issuance of injunctions in cases arising out of labor disputes should be prohibited when such injunctions would not apply when no labor disputes existed.

We believe also that a person cited for contempt in labor disputes, except when such contempt was committed in the actual presence of the court or so near thereto as to interfere with the proper administration of justice, should have a right to trial by jury.

[Social and Industrial Justice.] The supreme duty of the Nation is the conservation of human resources through an enlightened measure of social and industrial justice. We pledge ourselves to work unceasingly in State and Nation for:

Effective legislation, looking to the prevention of industrial accidents, occupational diseases, overwork, involuntary unemployment, and other injurious effects incident to modern industry.

The fixing of minimum safety and health standards for the various occupations, and the exercise of the public authority of State and Nation, including the Federal Control over inter-State commerce, and the taxing power, to maintain such standards.

The Prohibition of Child Labor.

Minimum wage standards for working women, to provide a "living wage" in all industrial occupations.

The general prohibition of night work for women, and the establishment of an eight-hour day for women and young persons.

One day's rest in seven for all wage workers.

The eight-hour day in continuous twenty-four-hour industries.

The abolition of the convict contract labor system.

Substituting a system of prison production for Governmental consumption only.

And the application of prisoner's earnings to the support of their dependent families.

Publicity as to wages, hours and conditions of labor.

Full reports upon industrial accidents and diseases, and the opening to public inspection of all tallies, weights, measures and check systems on labor products.

[Currency.] The issue of currency is fundamentally a Government function, and the system should have as basic principles soundness and elasticity. The control should be lodged with the Government, and should be protected from domination or manipulation by Wall Street or any special interests.

We are opposed to the so-called Aldrich Currency bill because its provisions would place our currency and credit system in private hands, not subject to effective public control . . . .

[Conservation.] We believe that the remaining forests, coal and oil lands, water powers, and other natural resources, still in State or National control (except agricultural lands) are more likely to be wisely conserved and utilized for the general welfare if held in the public hands. In order that consumers and producers, managers and workmen, now and hereafter, need not pay toll to private monopolies of power and raw material, we demand that such resources shall be retained by the State or Nation, and opened to immediate use under laws which will encourage development and make to the people a moderate return for benefits conferred.

## WOODROW WILSON, FIRST INAUGURAL ADDRESS (1913)

Woodrow Wilson was swept into the Presidency by the election of 1912, in which the clearest victor was Progressivism. This is his first inaugural address, and it reflects many of the sources of Progressivism, along with many of its ambiguities. And it certainly offers evidence of the righteous, crusading nature of the Progressive movement.

We see that in many things that life is very great. It is incomparably great in its material aspects, in its body of wealth, in the diversity and sweep of its energy, in the industries which have been conceived and built up by the genius of individual men and the limitless enterprise of groups of men. It is great, also, very great, in its moral force. Nowhere else in the world have noble men and women exhibited in more striking forms the beauty and the energy of sympathy and helpfulness and counsel in their efforts to rectify wrong, alleviate suffering, and set the weak in the way of strength and hope. We have built up, moreover, a great system of government, which has stood through a long age as in many respects a model for those who seek to set liberty upon foundations that will endure against fortuitous change, against storm and accident. Our life contains every great thing, and contains it in rich abundance.
  But the evil has come with the good, and much fine gold has been corroded. With riches has come inexcusable waste. We have squandered a great part of what we might have used, and have not stopped to conserve the exceeding bounty of nature, without which our genius for enterprise would have been worthless and impotent, scorning to be careful, shamefully prodigal as well as admirably efficient. We have been proud of our industrial achievements, but we have not hitherto stopped thoughtfully enough to count the human cost, the cost of lives snuffed out, of energies overtaxed and broken, the fearful physical and spiritual cost to the men and women and children upon whom the dead weight and burden of it all has fallen pitilessly the years through. The groans and agony of it all had not yet reached our ears, the solemn, moving undertone of our life, coming up out of the mines and factories and out of every home where the struggle had its intimate and familiar seat. With the great Government went many deep secret things which we too long delayed to look into and scrutinize with candid, fearless eyes. The great Government we loved has too often been made use of for private and selfish purposes, and those who used it had forgotten the people.
  At last a vision has been vouchsafed us of our life as a whole. We see the bad with the good, the debased and decadent with the sound and vital. With this vision we approach new affairs. Our duty is to cleanse, to reconsider, to restore, to correct the evil without impairing the good, to purify and humanize every process of our common life without weakening or sentimentalizing it. There has been something crude and heartless and unfeeling in our haste to succeed and be great. Our thought has been "Let every man look out for himself, let every generation look out for itself,"

---

James D. Richardson, ed., <u>A Compilation of the Messages and Papers of the Presidents</u> (New York, 1897), XVIII, 7868-7871.

while we reared giant machinery which made it impossible that any but those who stood at the levers of control should have a chance to look out for themselves. We had not forgotten our morals. We remembered well enough that we had set up a policy which was meant to serve the humblest as well as the most powerful, with an eye single to the standards of justice and fair play, and remembered it with pride. But we were very heedless and in a hurry to be great.

We have come now to the sober second thought. The scales of heedlessness have fallen from our eyes. We have made up our minds to square every process of our national life again with the standards we so proudly set up at the beginning and have always carried at our hearts. Our work is a work of restoration.

We have itemized with some degree of particularity the things that ought to be altered, and here are some of the chief items: A tariff which cuts us off from our proper part in the commerce of the world, violates the just principles of taxation, and makes the Government a facile instrument in the hands of private interests; a banking and currency system based upon the necessity of the Government to sell its bonds fifty years ago and perfectly adapted to concentrating cash and restricting credits; an industrial system which, take it on all its sides, financial as well as administrative, holds capital in leading strings, restricts the liberties and limits the opportunities of labor, and exploits without renewing or conserving the natural resources of the country; a body of agricultural activities never yet given the efficiency of great business undertakings or served as it should be through the instrumentality of science taken directly to the farm, or afforded the facilities of credit best suited to its practical needs; watercourses undeveloped, waste places unreclaimed, forests untended, fast disappearing without plan or prospect of renewal, unregarded waste heaps at every mine. We have studied as perhaps no other nation has the most effective means of production, but we have not studied cost or economy as we should either as organizers of industry, as statesmen, or as individuals.

Nor have we studied and perfected the means by which government may be put at the service of humanity, in safeguarding the health of the Nation, the health of its men and its women and its children, as well as their rights in the struggle for existence. This is no sentimental duty. The firm basis of government is justice, not pity. These are matters of justice. There can be no equality of opportunity, the first essential of justice in the body politic, if men and women and children be not shielded in their lives, their very vitality, from the consequences of great industrial and social processes which they cannot alter, control, or singly cope with. Society must see to it that it does not itself crush or weaken or damage its own constituent parts. The first duty of law is to keep sound the society it serves. Sanitary laws, pure-food laws, and laws determining conditions of labor which individuals are powerless to determine for themselves are intimate parts of the very business of justice and legal efficiency . . . .

This is the high enterprise of the new day: To lift everything that concerns our life as a Nation to the light that shines from the hearthfire of everyman's conscience and vision of the right. It is inconceivable that we should do this as partisans; . . . Justice, and only justice, shall always be our motto. . . .

The Nation has been deeply stirred, stirred by a solemn passion, stirred by the knowledge of wrong, of ideals lost, of government too often debauched and made an instrument of evil. The feelings with which we face this new age of right and opportunity sweep across our heartstrings like some air out of God's own presence, where justice and mercy are reconciled and the judge and the brother are one. . . .

This is not a day of triumph; it is a day of dedication. Here muster not the forces of party, but the forces of humanity. Men's hearts wait upon us; men's lives hang in the balance; men's hopes call upon us to say what we will do. Who shall live up to the great trust? Who dares fail to try? I summon all honest men, all patriotic, all forward-looking men, to my side. God helping me, I will not fail them, if they will but counsel and sustain me!

## WILSON ON THE SINKING OF THE LUSITANIA (1915)

Within one week after a German U-boat sank the Lusitania on May 7, 1915, the United States sent a protest to Germany. When President Woodrow Wilson found the German response less than satisfactory, he prepared a second, sharper note of protest. In fact, Secretary of State William Jennings Bryan considered the protest note so harshly worded that it amounted to an ultimatum to Germany. Bryan resigned rather than send this note, which went to Berlin on June 9, 1915, over the signature of Bryan's eventual successor, Robert Lansing.

Your excellency's note, in discussing the loss of American lives resulting from the sinking of the steamship Lusitania, adverts at some length to certain information which the Imperial German Government has received with regard to the character and outfil of that vessel, and your excellency expresses the fear that this information may not have been brought to the attention of the Government of the United States. It is stated in the note that the Lusitania was undoubtedly equipped with masked guns, supplied with trained gunners and special ammunition, transporting troops from Canada, carrying a cargo not permitted under the laws of the United States to a vessel also carrying passengers, and serving, in virtual effect, as an auxiliary to the naval forces of Great Britain. Fortunately, these are matters concerning which the Government of the United States is in a position to give the Imperial German Government official information. Of the facts alleged in your excellency's note, if true, the Government of the United States would have been bound to take official cognizance in performing its recognized duty as a neutral power and in enforcing its national laws. It was its duty to see to it that the Lusitania was not armed for offensive action, that she was not serving as a transport, that she did not carry a cargo prohibited by the statutes of the United States, and that, if in fact she was a naval vessel of Great Britain, she should not receive clearance as a merchantman; and it performed that duty and enforced its statutes with scrupulous vigilance through its regularly constituted officials. It is able, therefore, to assure the Imperial German Government that it has been misinformed. If the Imperial

---

U. S. Department of State, Papers Relating to the Foreign Relations of the United States, 1915, Supplement, The World War (Washington, D.C., 1928) pp. 436-438.

German Government should deem itself to be in possession of convincing evidence that the officials of the Government of the United States did not perform these duties with thoroughness, the Government of the United States sincerely hopes that it will submit that evidence for consideration.

Whatever may be the contentions of the Imperial German Government regarding the carriage of contraband of war on board the <u>Lusitania</u> or regarding the explosion of the material by the torpedo, it need only be said that in the view of this Government these contentions are irrelevant to the question of the legality of the methods used by the German naval authorities in sinking the vessel.

But the sinking of passenger ships involves principles of humanity which throw into the background any special circumstances of detail that may be throught to affect the cases, principles which lift it, as the Imperial German Government will no doubt be quick to recognize and acknowledge, out of the class of ordinary subjects of diplomatic discussion or of international controversy. Whatever be the other facts regarding the <u>Lusitania,</u> the principal fact is that a great steamer, primarily and chiefly a conveyance for passengers, and carrying more than a thousand souls who had no part or lot in the conduct of the war, was torpedoed and sunk without so much as a challenge or a warning, and that men, women, and children were sent to their death in circumstances unparalleled in modern warfare. The fact that more than one hundred American citizens were among those who perished made it the duty of the Government of the United States to speak of these things and once more, with solemn emphasis, to call the attention of the Imperial German Government to the grave responsibility which the Government of the United States conceives that it has incurred in this tragic occurrence, and to the indisputable principle upon which that responsibility rests. The Government of the United States is contending for something much greater than mere rights of property or privileges of commerce. It is contending for nothing less high and sacred than the rights of humanity, which every Government honors itself in respecting and which no Government is justified in resigning on behalf of those under its care and authority. Only her actual resistance to capture or refusal to stop when ordered to do so for the purpose of visit could have afforded the commander of the submarine any justification for so much as putting the lives of those on board the ship in jeopardy. This principle the Government of the United States understands the explicit instructions issued on August 3, 1914, by the Imperial German Admirality to its commanders at sea to have recognized and embodied, as do the naval codes of all other nations, and upon it every traveler and seaman had a right to depend. It is upon this principle of humanity as well as upon the law founded upon this principle that the United States must stand.

The Government of the United States is happy to observe that your excellency's note closes with the intimation that the Imperial German Government is willing, now as before, to accept the good offices of the United States in an atempt to come to an understanding with the Government of Great Britain by which the character and conditions of the war upon the sea may be changed. The Government of the United States would consider it a privilege thus to serve its friends and the world. It stands ready at any time to convey to either Government any intimation or suggestion the other may be willing to have it convey and cordially invites the Imperial German Government to make use of its services in this way at its convenience. The whole world is concerned in anything that may bring about even a partial accommodation of interests or in any way mitigate the terrors of the present distressing conflict. . . .

The Government of the United States can not admit that the proclamation of a war zone from which neutral ships have been warned to keep away may be made to operate as in any degree an abbreviation of the rights either of American shipmasters or of American citizens bound on lawful errands as passengers on merchant ships of belligerent nationality. It does not understand the Imperial German Government to question those rights. It understands it, also, to accept as established beyond question the principle that the lives of noncombatants can not lawfully or rightfully be put in jeopardy by the capture or destruction of an unresisting merchantman, and to recognize the obligation to take sufficient precaution to ascertain whether a suspected merchantman is in fact of belligerent nationality or is in fact carrying contraband of war under a neutral flag. The Government of the United States therefore deems it reasonable to expect that the Imperial German Government will adopt the measures necessary to put these principles into practice in respect of the safeguarding of American lives and American ships, and asks for assurances that this will be done.

### GERMANY ON SUBMARINE WARFARE (1915)

Germany, of course, held far different views about the legitimacy of submarine warfare. The German Foreign Minister set forth his country's side of the argument in a note to Washington on July 8, 1915.

The Imperial Government has learned with satisfaction from the note how earnestly the Government of the United States is concerned in seeing the principles of humanity realized in the present war. Also, this appeal meets with full sympathy in Germany, and the Imperial Government is quite willing to permit its statements and decisions in the case under consideration to be governed by the principles of humanity just as it has done always. . . .

If in the present war the principles which should be the ideal of the future have been traversed more and more the longer its duration, the German Government has no guilt therein.

It is known to the American Government how Germany's adversaries, by completely paralyzing peaceable traffic between Germany and the neutral countries, have aimed from the very beginning, and with increasing lack of consideration, at the destruction, not so much of the armed forces, as the life of the German nation, repudiating in so doing all the rules of international law and disregarding all the rights of neutrals. . . . Just as was the case with the Boers, the German people is now to be given the choice of perishing from starvation, with its women and children, or of relinquishing its independence.

---

U. S. Department of State, Papers Relating to the Foreign Relations of the United States, 1915, Supplement, The World War (Washington, D.C., 1928), pp. 463-466.

While are enemies thus loudly and openly have proclaimed war without mercy until our utter destruction, we are conducting war in self-defense for our national existence and for the sake of peace of assured permanency. We have been obliged to adopt submarine warfare to meet the declared intentions of our enemies and the method of warfare adopted by them in contravention of international law. . . .

However, the American Government will also understand and appreciate that in the fight for existence which has been forced upon Germany by its adversaries and announced by them, it is the sacred duty of the Imperial Government to do all within its power to protect and to save the lives of German subjects. If the Imperial Government were derelict in these, its duties, it would be guilty before God and history of the violation of those principles of the highest humanity which are the foundation of every national existence.

The case of the Lusitania shows with horrible clearness to what jeopardizing of human lives the manner of conducting war employed by our adversaries leads. In most direct contradiction of international law, all distinctions between merchantmen and war vessels have been obliterated by the order to British merchantmen to arm themselves and to ram submarines, and the promise of rewards therefor; and neutrals who use merchantmen as travelers have thereby been exposed in an increasing degree to all the dangers of war. If the commander of the German submarine which destroyed the Lusitania had caused the crew and travelers to put out in boats before firing the torpedo, this would have meant the sure destruction of his own vessel. After the experiences in the sinking of smaller and less seaworthy vessels, it was to be expected that a mighty ship like the Lusitania would remain above water long enough, even after the torpedoing, to permit the passengers to enter the ship's boats. Circumstances of a very peculiar kind, especially the presence on board of large quantities of highly explosive materials, defeated this expectation. In addition, it may be pointed out that if the Lusitania had been spared, thousands of cases of ammunition would have been sent to Germany's enemies and thereby thousands of German mothers and children, robbed of their supporters.

## THE ADAMSON ACT (1916)

Just as the Presidential campaign of 1916 was unfolding, the railroad unions had threatened a nationwide strike unless they were granted an eight-hour work day without reduction of wages. President Wilson supported the unions' demand, and appeared before Congress to ask for the enactment of the following law providing for the shortened work day. Charles Evans Hughes, the Republican Party candidate for the Presidency, quickly criticized the act and accused Wilson of being a captive of labor, but the Republicans soon backed off when they discovered that millions of average Americans wildly approved of the eight-hour day idea.

U. S. Statutes at Large, 64th Congress, 1st session, vol. XXXIX, Part 1 (Public Laws), Chap. 436, pp. 721-722.

An act to establish an eight-hour day for employees of carriers engaged in interstate and foreign commerce, and for other purposes.

BE it enacted, by the Senate and House of Representatives of the United States of America in Congress assembled, That beginning January first, nineteen hundred and seventeen, eight hours shall, in contracts for labor and service, be deemed a day's work and the measure or standard of a day's work for the purpose of reckoning the compensation for services of all employees who are now or may hereafter be employed by any common carrier by railroad, except railroads independently owned and operated not exceeding one hundred miles in length, electric street railroads, and electric interurban railroads, which is subject to the provisions of the Act of February, fourth, eighteen hundred and eighty seven, entitled "An Act to regulate commerce," as amended, and who are now or may hereafter be actually engaged in any capacity in the operation of trains used for the transportation of persons or property on railroads, . . . . from any State or Territory of the United States or the District of Columbia to any other State or Territory of the United States or the District of Columbia or from one place in a Territory to another place in the same Territory, or from any place in the United States to be adjacent foreign country, or from any place in the United States through a foreign country to any other place in the United States: Provided, That the above exceptions shall not apply to railroads though less than one hundred miles in length whose principal business is leasing or furnishing terminal or transfer facilities to other railroads, or are themselves engaged in transfers of freight between railroads or between railroads and industrial plants.

Sec. 2. That the President shall appoint a commission of three, which shall observe the operation and effects of the institution of the eight-hour standard workday as above defined . . . .

Sec. 3. That pending the report of the commission herein provided for and for a period of thirty days thereafter, the compensation of railway employees subject to this Act for a standard eight-hour workday shall not be reduced below the present standard day's wage.

## THE ZIMMERMANN NOTE (1917)

On February 24, 1917, the British government revealed to the United States the text of an intercepted German message. The U.S. Ambassador in London claimed that the British "lost no time in communicating it to me," but there is some evidence that the British first considered the advantages and disadvantages of giving the Americans the note (which, if published, would let the Germans know that their code had been broken). Dr. Artur Zimmermann, the German Foreign Minister, wrote the note to the German Ambassador in Mexico City. Upon reading this message, President Wilson immediately asked Congress for the authority to arm U.S. merchant ships.

---

U. S. Department of State, Papers Relating to the Foreign Relations of the United States, 1915, Supplement, The World War (Washington, D.C., 1928), pp. 147-148.

We intend to begin on the 1st of February unrestricted submarine warefare. We shall endeavor in spite of this to keep the United States of America neutral. In the event of this not succeeding, we make Mexico a proposal of alliance on the following basis: make war together, make peace together, generous financial support and an understanding on our part that Mexico is to reconquer the lost territory in Texas, New Mexico, and Arizona. The settlement in detail is left to you. You will inform the President of the above most secretly as soon as the outbreak of war with the United States of America is certain and add the suggestion that he should, on his own initiative, invite Japan to immediate adherence and at the same time mediate between Japan and ourselves. Please call the President's attention to the fact that the ruthless employment of our submarines now offers the prospect of compelling England in a few months to make peace. Signed, Zimmermann.

## THE SENATE ON THE VERSAILLES TREATY (1919)

Many senators did not share Wilson's optimistic outlook about the League of Nations. Because the charter (or "Covenant") which set up the League of Nations was embodied in the Versailles Treaty, these senators threatened to vote against the treaty unless Wilson agreed to certain changes and interpretations of the language in the treaty. Several senators offered their reservations about the treaty (and the League Covenant); three of the most influential were William Borah, Hiram Johnson, and Henry Cabot Lodge.

(a) Borah's Reservations

The United States assumes no obligation to perserve the territorial integrity or political independence of any other country or to interfere in controversies between nations--whether members of the league or not--under the provisions of Article X or to employ the military or naval forces of the United States under any article of the treaty for any purpose.

(b) Johnson's Reservations

[1.] When any member of the League has or possesses self-governing dominions or colonies or parts of empire, which are also members of the league, the United States shall have representatives in the council and assembly, and in any labor conference or organization under the league or treaty, numerically equal to the aggregate number of representatives of such member of the league and its self-governing dominions and colonies and parts of empire in such council and assembly of the league, and labor conference or organization under the league or treaty; and such representatives of the United States shall have the same powers and rights as the representatives of said member and its self-governing dominions or colonies or parts of empire;

---

U. S., Congress, Senate, Document 150, "Proposed Reservations to the Treaty of Peace with Germany," 60th Cong., 1st sess., November 6, 1919, pp. 35, 43-47, 49-50.

and upon all matters whatsoever, except where a party to a dispute, the United States shall have votes in the Council and assembly, and in any labor conference or organization under the league or treaty numerically equal to the aggregate vote to which any such member of the league and its self-governing dominions and colonies and parts of empire are entitled.

[2.] Whenever a case referred to the council or assembly involves a dispute between the United States and another member of the league whose self-governing dominions or colonies or parts of empire are also represented in the council or assembly, or between the United States and any dominion, colony, or part of any other member of the league, neither the disputant members nor any of their said dominions, colonies, or parts of empire shall have a vote upon any phase of the question.

[3.] Whenever the United States is a party to a dispute, which is referred to the council or assembly, and can not, because a party, vote upon such dispute, any other member of the council or assembly having self-governing dominions or colonies or parts of empire also members, upon such dispute to which the United States is a party or upon any phase of the questions, shall have and cast for itself and its self-governing dominions and colonies and parts of empires, all together, but one vote.

(c) Lodge's Reservations

1. The reservations and understandings adopted by the Senate are to be made a part and a condition of the resolution of ratification, which ratification is not to take effect or bind the United States until the said reservations and understandings adopted by the Senate have been accepted by an exchange of notes as a part and a condition of said resolution of ratification by at least three of the four Principal Allied and Associated Powers, to wit: Great Britain, France Italy, and Japan.

2. The United States so understands and construes Article 1 that in case of notice of withdrawal from the league of nations, as provided in said article, the United States shall be the sole judge as to whether all its international obligations and all its obligations under the said covenant have been fulfilled, and notice of withdrawal by the United States may be given by a concurrent resolution of the Congress of the United States.

3. The United States assumes no obligation to preserve the territorial integrity or political independence of any other country or to interfere in controversies between nations--whether members of the league or not--under the provisions of Article 10, or to employ the military or naval forces of the United States under any article of the treaty for any purpose, unless in any particular case the Congress, which, under the Constitution, has the sole power to declare war or authorize the employment of the military or naval forces of the United States, shall by act or joint resolution so provide.

4. No mandate shall be accepted by the United States under Article 22, Part 1, or any other provision of the treaty of peace with Germany, except by action of the Congress of the United States.

5. The United States reserves to itself exclusively the right to decide what questions are within its domestic jurisdiction and declares that all domestic and political questions relating wholly or in part to its internal affairs, including immigration, labor, coastwise traffic, the tariff, commerce, the suppression of traffic in women and children and in opium and other dangerous drugs, and all other domestic questions, are solely within the jurisdiction of the United States and are not under this treaty to be

submitted in any way either to arbitration or to the consideration of the council or of the assembly of the league of nations, or any agency thereof, or to the decision or recommendation of any other power.

6. The United States will not submit to arbitration or to inquiry by the assembly or by the council of the league of nations, provided for in said treaty of peace, any questions which in the judgment of the United States depend upon or relate to its long established policy commonly known as the Monroe doctrine; said doctrine is to be interpreted by the United States alone and is hereby declared to be wholly outside the jurisdiction of said league of nations and entirely unaffected by any provision contained in the said treaty of peace with Germany.

7. The United States withholds its assent to Articles 156, 157 and 158 and reserves full liberty of action with respect to any controversey which may arise under said articles between the Republic of China and the Empire of Japan.

8. The Congress of the United States will provide by law for the appointment of the representatives of the United States in the assembly and the council of the league of nations and may in its discretion provide for the participation of the United States in any commission, committee, tribunal, court, council or conference, or in the selection of any members thereof and for the appointment of members of said commissions, committees, tribunals, courts, councils or conferences, or any other representatives under the treaty of peace, or in carrying out its provisions, and until such participation and appointment have been so provided for and the powers and duties of such representatives have been defined by law, no person shall represent the United States under either said league of nations or the treaty of peace with Germany or be authorized to perform any act for or on behalf of the United States thereunder and no citizen of the United States shall be selected or appointed as a member of said commissions, committees, tribunals, courts, councils or conferences, except with the approval of the Senate of the United States.

9. The United States understands that the reparation commission will regulate or interfere with exports from the United States to Germany, or from Germany to the United States only when the United States by Act or Joint Resolution of Congress approves such regulation or interference.

10. The United States shall not be obligated to contribute to any expenses of the league of nations, or of the secretariat, or of any commission, or committee, or conference, or other agency, organized under the league of nations or under the treaty or for the purpose of carrying out the treaty provisions, unles and until an appropriation of funds available for such expenses shall have been made by the Congress of the United States.

11. If the United States shall at any time adopt any plan for the limitation of armaments proposed by the council of the league of nations under the provisions of Article 8, it reserves the right to increase such armaments without the consent of the council whenever the United States is threatened with invasion or engaged in war.

12. The United States reserves the right to permit, in its discretion, the nationals of a covenant-breaking State, as defined in Article 16 of the covenant of the league of nations, residing within the United States or in countries other than that violating said Article 16, to continue their commercial, financial and personal relations with the nationals of the United States.

13. Nothing in Articles 296, 297, or in any of the annexes thereto or in any other article, section or annex of the treaty of peace with Germany shall, as against citizens of the United States, be taken to mean any confirmation, ratification or approval of any act otherwise illegal or in contravention of the rights of citizens of the United States

14. The United States declines to accept, as trusteee or in her own right, any interest in or any responsibility for the government or disposition of the overseas possessions of Germany, her rights and titles to which Germany renounces to the Principal Allied and Associated Powers under Articles 119 to 127 inclusive.

15. The United States reserves to itself exclusively the right to decide what questions affect its honor or its vital interests and declares that such questions are not under this treaty to be submitted in any way either to arbitration or to the consideration of the council or of the assembly of the league of nations or any agency thereof or to the decision or recommendation of any other power.

## THE VERSAILLES TREATY (1919)

(a) The Covenant of the League of Nations and Article 10

> The first 26 articles of the Versailles Treaty comprised the Covenant of the League of Nations. Article 10 stirred great controversy in the United States because it seemed (under certain circumstances) to permit the League Council to call U.S. troops into combat, whereas our Constitution clearly stipulated that only Congress could declare war (and send U.S. troops into combat).

THE HIGH Contracting Parties,
In order to promote international co-operation and to achieve international peace and security
    by the acceptance of obligations not to resort to war,
    by the prescription of open, just and honourable relations between nations,
    by the firm establishment of the understandings of international law as the actual rule of conduct among Governments, and
    by the maintenance of justice and a scrupulous respect for all treaty obligations in the dealings of organized peoples with one another,
Agree to this Covenant of the League of Nations. . . .
    Article 10. The members of the League undertake to respect and preserve as against external aggression the territorial integrity and existing political independence of all Members of the League. In case of any such aggression or in case of any threat or danger of such aggression the Council shall advise upon the means by which this obligation shall be fulfilled.

---

U. S. Department of State, Papers Relating to the Foreign Relations of the United States: The Paris Peace Conference, 1919 (Washington, D.C., 1947), pp. 1-10, 413-425, 523-524.

(b) Article 231

> This is the famous (or notorious) "war guilt" clause. For Germans, this wording incorporated the additional insult of meaning moral guilt as well as political responsibility for the war (kriegschuldt).

The Allied and Associated Governments affirm and Germany **accepts the** responsibility of Germany and her Allies for causing all the loss **and damage** to which the Allied and Associated Governments and their nationals **have been** subjected as a consequence of the war imposed upon them by the **aggression of** Germany and her allies.

(c) Article 232

> This article is based on the preceding one. That is, with German responsibility for the war having been established, this section built on that premise as the rationale for imposing reparations upon Germany.

The Allied and Associated Governments recognize that the resources of Germany are not adequate, after taking into account permanent diminutions of such resources which will result from other provisions of the present Treaty, to make complete reparation for all such loss and damage.

The Allied and Associated Governments, however, require, and Germany undertakes, that she will make compensation for all damage done to the civilan population of the Allied and Associated Powers and to their property during the period of the belligerency of each as an Allied or Associated Power against Germany by such aggression by land, by sea and from the air, and in general all damage as defined in Annex I hereto.

(d) Article 246

> Note all the articles in the Versailles Treaty dealt with earth-shaking matters. For example, this article (and its accompanying note) carry an air of comic relief.

Within six months from the coming into force of the present Treaty, Germany will restore to His Majesty the King of the Hedjaz the original Koran of the Caliph Othman, which was removed from Medina by the Turkish authorities and is stated to have been presented to the ex-Emperor William II.

Within the same period Germany will hand over to His Britanic Majesty's Government the skull of the Sultan Mkwawa which was removed from the Protectorate of German East Africa and taken to Germany.

The delivery of the articles above referred to will be effected in such place and in such conditions as may be laid down by the Governments to which they are to be restored.

[Note: With respect to the Koran of the Caliph Othman, the Germany Peace Delegation wrote the president of the peace conference on January 21, 1921 as follows:

"The supposition that this Koran was presented to the ex-Emperor of Germany is erroneous. It was, moreover, never transferred to Germany nor into German hands."

Sultan Okwawa, or M'Kwawa, was chief of the Wahibis, German East Africa. This tribe under several sultans from 1870 to 1898 gathered to itself much native support and was continuously hostile to the Germans. M'Kwawa, the last of the warrior line, added a religious superstition to his prestige by preaching that he could not be captured and committed suicide when capture was inevitable. The British demand for the return of his skull could not be granted, according to the German report sent to the British Government for verification. One sergeant Merkl cut off M'Kwawa's head when he killed himself to escape capture by Captain von Prinz. Merkl preserved the skull in alcohol at the nearest German fort against the time when he could claim the reward of 6,000 rupees. The affidavits of Merkl, the widow of Captain von Prinz, and other witnesses stated that negro warriors broke into the fort and stole the alcohol and the sultan's head, leaving in place of the latter the freshly severed head of some other negro. The theft became known when the substitute head, without the alcohol, came to the olfactory attention of the German garrison. The Germans found that the theft had been committed by retainers of M'Kwawa, who had buried the head in this family vault, and decided not to prosecute the case further.]

## JOHN MAYNARD KEYNES ON THE ECONOMIC CONSEQUENCES OF THE TREATY OF VERSAILLES (1918)

The well-known British economist, John Maynard Keynes, was severely critical of the financial settlement of the main treaty ending the Great War. He warned that unfortunate consequences would result from the outrageous economic demands made on a defeated, humiliated Germany.

I believe that the campaign for securing out of Germany the general costs of the war was one of the most serious acts of political unwisdom for which our statesmen have ever been responsible. To what a different future Europe might have looked forward if either Mr. Lloyd George or Mr. Wilson had apprehended that the most serious of the problems which claimed their attention were not political or territorial but financial and economic, and that the perils of the future lay not in frontiers or sovereignties but in food, coal, and transport. Neither of them paid adequate attention to these problems at any stage of the Conference. But in any event the atmosphere for the wise and reasonable consideration of them was hopelessly befogged by the commitments of the British delegation on the question of Indemnities. The hopes to which the Prime Minister had given rise not only compelled him to advocate an unjust and unworkable economic basis to the Treaty with Germany, but set him at variance with the President, and on the other hand with competing interests to those of France and Belgium. The clearer it became that but little could be expected from Germany, the more necessary it was to exercise patriotic greed and "sacred egotism" and snatch the bone from the juster claims and greater need of France or the well-founded expectations of Belgium. Yet the financial problems which were about to exercise Europe could not be solved by greed. The possibility of their cure lay in magnanimity.

Europe, if she is to survive her troubles, will need so much magnanimity from America, that she must herself practise it. It is useless for the

John Maynard Keynes, The Economic Consequences of the Peace (London, 1919), pp. 134-136, 144-146, 209-210.

Allies, hot from stripping Germany and one another, to turn for help to the United States to put the States of Europe, including Germany, on to their feet again. If the General Election of December 1918 had been fought on lines of prudent generosity instead of imbecile greed, how much better the financial prospect of Europe might now be. I still believe that before the main Conference, or very early in its proceedings, the representatives of Great Britain should have entered deeply, with those of the United States, into the economic and financial situation as a whole, and that the former should have been authorised to make concrete proposals on the general lines (1) that all inter-allied indebtedness be canceled outright; (2) that the sum to be paid by Germany be fixed at Ł200 million; (3) that Great Britain renounce all claim to participation in this sum, and that any share to which she proves entitle be placed at the disposal of the Conference for the purpose of aiding the finances of the New States about to be established; (4) that in order to make some basis of credit immediately available an appropriate proportion of the German obligations representing the sum to be paid by her should be guaranteed by all parties to the Treaty; and (5) that the ex-enemy Powers should also be allowed, with a view to their economic restoration, to issue a moderate amount of bonds carrying a similar guarantee. Such proposals involved an appeal to the generosity of the United States. But that was inevitable; and, in view of her far less financial sacrifices, it was an appeal which could fairly have been made to her. Such proposals would have been practicable. There is nothing in them quixotic or Utopian. And they would have opened up for Europe some prospect of financial stability and reconstruction . . . .

What had really happened was a compromise between the Prime Minister's pledge to the British electorate to claim the entire costs of the war and the pledge to the contrary which the Allies had given to Germany at the Armistice. The Prime Minister could claim that although he had not secured the entire costs of the war, he had nevertheless secured an important contribution towards them, that he had always qualified his promises by the limiting condition of Germany's capacity to pay, and that the bill as now presented more than exhausted this capacity as estimated by the more sober authorities. The President, on the other hand, had secured a formula, which was not too obvious a breach of faith, and had avoided a quarrel with his Associates on an issue where the appeals to sentiment and passion would all have been against him, in the event of its being made a matter of open popular controversy. In view of the Prime Minister's election pledges, the President could hardly hope to get him to abandon them in their entirety without a struggle in public; and the cry of pensions would have had an overwhelming popular appeal in all countries. Once more the Prime Minister had shown himself a political tactician of a high order.

A further point of great difficulty may be readily perceived between the lines of the Treaty. It fixes no definite sum as representing Germany's liability. This feature has been the subject of very general criticism,—that it is equally inconvenient to Germany and to the Allies themselves that she should not know what she has to pay or they what they are to receive. The method, apparently contemplated by the Treaty, of arriving at the final result over a period of many months by an addition of hundreds of thousands of individual claims for damage to land, farm buildings, and chickens, is evidently impracticable; and the reasonable course would have been for both parties to compound for a round sum without examination of details. If this round sum had been named in the Treaty, the settlement would have been placed on a more business-like basis.

But this was impossible for two reasons. Two different kinds of false statements had been widely promulgated, one as to Germany's capacity to pay, the other as to the amount of the Allies' just claim in respect of the devastated areas. The fixing of either of these figures presented a dilemma. A figure for Germany's prospective capacity to pay, not too much in excess of the estimates of most candid and well-informed authorities, would have fallen hopelessly far short of popular expectations both in England and in France. On the other hand, a definitive figure for damage done which would not disastrously disappoint the expectations which had been raised in France and Belgium might have been incapable of substantiation under challenge, and open to damaging criticism on the part of the Germans, who were believed to have been prudent enough to accumulate considerable evidence as to the extent of their own misdoings.

By far the safest course for the politicians was therefore, to mention no figure at all . . . .

I cannot leave this subject as though its just treatment wholly depended either on our own pledges or on economic facts. The policy of reducing Germany to servitude for a generation, of degrading the lives of millions of human beings, and of depriving a whole nation of happiness should be abhorrent and detestable,--abhorrent and detestable, even if it were possible, even if it enriched ourselves, even if it did not sow the decay of the whole civilized life in Europe. Some preach it in the name of Justice. In the great events of man's history, in the unwinding of the complex fates of nations Justice is not so simple. And if it were, nations are not authorized, by religion or by natural morals, to visit on the children of their enemies the misdoings of parents or of rulers.


SCHENCK v. UNITED STATES (1919)
------

As a result of the Espionage and Sedition Acts passed during World War I, freedom of speech and of the press were curtailed in America. Schenck, the general secretary of the Socialist Party (which opposed the war) appealed his Espionage Act conviction for circulating anti-draft leaflets among the armed forces. Justice Oliver Wendell Holmes wrote the opinion of the Court on the question of the constitutionality of the Espionage Act, and the degree to which 1st amendment rights were guaranteed in wartime. The decision establishes the "clear and present danger" doctrine. Under the Espionage Act about 2,000 Americans were convicted for criticizing the war, the Administration, or the government in general. The Court also upheld the Sedition Act in Abrams v. United States, but Justice Holmes dissented in that important test of the clear and present danger doctrine.

---

Schenck v. United States, 249 U. S. 47 (1919).

The document in question upon its first printed side recited the 1st section of the 13th Amendment, said the idea embodied in it was violated by the Conscription Act and that a conscript is little better than a convict. In impassioned language it intimated that conscription was despotism in its worst form and a monstrous wrong against humanity, in the interest of Wall Street's chosen few. It said: "Do not submit to intimidation;" but in form at least confined itself to peaceful measures, such as a petition for the repeal of the act. The other and later printed side of the sheet was headed, "Assert Your Rights." It stated reasons for alleging that anyone violated the Constitution when he refused to recognize "your right to assert your opposition to the draft," and went on: "If you do not assert and support your rights, you are helping to deny or disparage rights which it is the solemn duty of all citizens and residents of the United States to retain." It described the arguments on the other side as coming from cunning politicians and a mercenary capitalist press, and even silent consent to the Conscription Law as helping to support an infamous conspiracy. It denied the power to send our citizens away to foreign shores to shoot up the people of other lands, and added that words could not express the condemnation such cold-blooded ruthlessness deserves, etc., etc., winding up, "You must do your share to maintain, support, and uphold the rights of the people of this country." Of course the document would not have been sent unless it had been intended to have some effect, and we do not see what effect it could be expected to have upon persons subject to the draft except to influence them to obstruct the carrying of it out. The defendants do not deny that the jury might find against them on this point.

But it is said, suppose that that was the tendency of this circular, it is protected by the 1st Amendment to the Constitution . . . . We admit that in many places and in ordinary times the defendants, in saying all that was said in the circular, would have been within their constitutional rights. But the character of every act depends upon the circumstances in which it is done. . . . The most stringent protection of free speech would not protect a man in falsely shouting fire in a theater, and causing a panic. It does not even protect a man from an injunction against uttering words that may have all the effect of force . . . . The question in every case in whether the words used are used in such circumstances and are of such a nature as to create a clear and present danger that they will bring about the substantive evils that Congress has a right to prevent. It is a question of proximity and degree. When a nation is at war many things that might be said in time of peace are such a hindrance to its effort that their utterance will not be endured so long as men fight and that no court could regard them as protected by any constitutional right. It seems to be admitted that if an actual obstruction of the recruiting service were proved, liability for words that produced that effect might be enforced. The Statute of 1917 in section 4, punishes conspiracies to obstruct as well as actual obstruction. If the act (speaking, or circulating a paper), its tendency and the intent with which it is done, are the same, we perceive no ground for saying that success alone warrants making the act a crime.

## WARREN G. HARDING ON HIS PRESIDENCY (1922)[1]

The American people in 1920 called Warren G. Harding to the presidency. One cannot imagine a greater contrast to Woodrow Wilson, in terms of philosophy and policy, personality and ability. Harding was a man ill-fit to be president, and he knew it. Here journalist William Allen White reports a conversation he once had with Jud Welliver, the president's secretary and White's friend.

"Lord, Lord, man! You can't know what the President is going through. You see he doesn't understand it; he just doesn't know a thousand things that he ought to know. And he realizes his ignorance, and he is afraid. He has no idea where to turn. Not long ago, when the first big tax bill came up, you remember there were two theories of taxation combating for the administration's support. He would listen for an hour to one side, become convinced; and then the other side would get him and overwhelm him with its contentions. Some good friend would walk into the White House all cocked and primed with facts and figures to support one side, and another man who he thought perhaps ought to know would reach him with a counter argument which would brush his friend's theory aside. I remember he came in here late one afternoon after a long conference, in which both sides appeared, talked at each other, wrangled over him. He was weary and confused and heartsick, for the man really wants to do the right and honest thing. But I tell you, he doesn't know. That afternoon he stood at my desk and looked at me for a moment and began talking out loud: "'Jud,' he cried, 'you have a college education, haven't you? I don't know what to do or where to turn in this taxation matter. Somewhere there must be a book that tells all about it, where I could go to straighten it out in my mind. But I don't know where the book is, and maybe I couldn't read it if I found it! And there must be a man in the country somewhere who could weigh both sides and know the truth. Probably he is in some college or other. But I don't know where to find him. I don't know who he is, and I don't know how to get him. My God, but this is a hell of a place for a man like me to be!'. . .

I never knew a man who was having such a hard time to find the truth. How Roosevelt used to click into truth with the snap of his teeth! How Wilson sensed it with some engine of erudition under the hood of his cranium! But this man paws for it, wrestles for it, cries for it, and has to take the luck of the road to get it."

## THE KU KLUX KLAN ON ITS BELIEFS (1924)[2]

After the retreat of the federal government and the Republican Party from the South at the end of Reconstruction, the Ku Klux Klan virtually disappeared.

---

[1] William Allen White, *The Autobiography of William Allen White* (New York, 1946), pp. 616-617.

[2] Knights of the Ku Klux Klan, *Klansman's Manual* (n. p., 1924), pp. 9-19.

> Its terriorism was no longer needed by those who favored white supremacy, for by the end of the century white supremacy was law. In 1915 the Klan reappeared, however, and it soon was affected by the organizational revolution that was transforming America. Recruitment efforts were directed from a national office whose treasury was soon fat. But marketing strategies were not the whole story, for the 1920s (during which the Klan had perhaps two million members) provided a very fertile ground for the growth of Klan doctrines. The Klan in the 20th century was no longer only anti-black, and no longer found only in the South. The following excerpts are from an official manual for Klansmen and their officers, the Klaliffs and Kleepers and Kligrapps and Cyclops.

Six outstanding features are particularized in describing the nature of this Order. Klansmen will do well to fix them in mind so that they will know the kind of an order they have joined.

1. <u>Patriotic.</u> One of the paramount purposes of this Order is to "Exemplify a pure patriotism toward our country. . . " And when [the Klansman] knelt at the "sacred Altar of the Klan," he was solemnly and symbolically dedicated "To the holy service of our country. . . . "

2. <u>Military.</u> This characteristic feature applies to its form of organization and its method of operations. It is so organized on a military plan that the whole power of the whole Order, or of any part of it, may be used in quick, united action for the execution of the purposes of the Order. . . .

3. <u>Benevolent.</u> This means that the movement is also committed to a program of sacrifical service for the benefit of others. The Klan motto (Not for self but for others) must be traslated into real, active, unselfish helpfulness. . . .

4. <u>Ritualistic.</u> In common with other Orders, the Knights of the Ku Klux Klan confers ritualistic degrees and obligations, and commits its grips, signs, words, and other secret work to those persons who so meet its requirements as to find membership in the Order. The ritualistic devices become the ceremonial ties that bind Klansmen to one another.

5. <u>Social.</u> The Knights of the Ku Klux Klan endeavors to unite in companionable relationship and congenial association those men who possess the essential qualifications for membership. It is so designed that kinship of race, belief, spirit, character, and purpose, will engender a real, vital, and enduring fellowship among Klansmen.

6. <u>Fraternal.</u> . . .
Klansmen have committed themselves to the practice of "Klannishness toward fellow-klansmen. . . ."

II.
OBJECTS AND PURPOSES. . .

I. Mobilization:

1. <u>This is its primary purpose:</u> "To unite white male persons, native born, Gentile citizens of the United States of America, who owe no allegiance of any nature or degree to any foreign government, nation, institition, sect, ruler, person, or people; whose morals are good; whose reputations and

vocations are respectable; whose habits are exemplary; who are of sound minds and eighteen years or more of age, under a common oath into a brotherhood of strict regulations. . . . "

IV. Beneficent:

This purpose is expressed in the words: "To exemplify a practical benevolence;" and "To relieve the injured and the oppressed; to succor the suffering and unfortunate, especially widows and orphans."

The supreme Pattern for all true Klansmen is their Criterion of Character, Jesus Christ, "who sent about doing good." The Knights of the Ku Klux Klan in making effective its beneficent purpose, will emphasize the need of helpful service to the needy, the weak, the afflicted and the oppressed. The movement accepts the full Christian program of unselfish helpfulness, and will seek to carry it on in the manner commanded by the one Master of Men, Christ Jesus.

V. Protective:

1. The Home. "To shield the sanctity of the home." The American home is fundamental to all that is best in life, in society, in church, and in the nation. . . .

2. Womanhood. The Knights of the Ku Klux Klan declares that it is committed to "the sacred duty of protecting womanhood;" and announces that one of its purposes is "to shield . . . . the chastity of womanhood . . . . "

The Knights of the Ku Klux Klan demands reverence for American womanhood; and insists that her person shall be respected as sacred, that her chastity be kept inviolate, and that she not be deprived of her right to the glory of an unstained body. . . .

The Knights of the Ku Klux Klan is solemnly committed to the defense and perpetuation of every American interest and institution, to the support of the American Government, to the preservation of all the rights, liberties, and privileges of the American people, . . .

VI. Racial:

"To maintain forever white supremacy." Or as the Declaration proclaims it, "To maintain forever the God-given supremacy of the white race. . ."

IX. Co-Operative: . . .

The Knights of the Ku Klux Klan is committed to the program of law-observance and law enforcement, and is pledged to "help, aid and assist the duly constituted officers of the Law in the proper performance of their legal duties."

The Knights of the Ku Klux Klan is sworn to the chivalric task of suppressing all menaces to the integrity of America and the rights, liberties, and privileges of the American people.

## WILLIAM ALLEN WHITE ON THE PHILOSOPHY OF CALVIN COOLIDGE (1925)

> President Ronald Reagan once said that the President he most admired was Calvin Coolidge, and in the following passage it is not difficult to perceive the similarities between the two administrations. In five short years Coolidge undid many of the accomplishments of Teddy Roosevelt, Woodrow Wilson, and the Progressives.

"The business of America," quoth Calvin Coolidge, addressing a group of American editors in January, 1925, "is business. . . ." Lincoln's whole life was devoted to showing that the business of America is freedom. Roosevelt's life was consecrated to the theory that the business of America is justice. Wilson's one life-long message to the world is, that the business of America is peace. . . . Coolidge exalts the ideals of the peddler, the horse trader, the captain of industry. He believes that in some occult way, out of their activities will be secreted through the distribution of goods under the beneficence of business ethics and business methods, such justice as mankind needs to grease the wheel of progress . . . .

After his election in 1924, President Coolidge felt definitely the mandate to reconstruct American government along the lines of his own deep conviction that the business of America is business. Thus one by one the various commissions of government, the Interstate Commerce Commission, the Federal Trade Commission, the Tariff Commission, accepted the dictum of the President that the business of America is business. To protect business, to promote business, to provide for more and better business is the chief aim of every governmental agency in Washington which the President controls. And he is engaging in all this activity for business not stealthily, not with a Puritan sense of sin, but with a high pride, a glowing zeal in his work. . . . He has the fanatic's faith in prosperity as the savior of mankind . . . .

Coolidge thinks concretely. He takes no chances. His feet are on the ground of a beaten path. He knows his way. He has his faith; he lives up to it. And it has been justified by popular acclaim. He is obeying a mandate.

Those who held opposing views to the President, who held that justice rather than business is our reason for being a country, were appalled . . . . The Sherman Act came and its interpretation by the Supreme Court in the Standard Oil cases in 1911. For a decade and a half America, under the Supreme Court decision of 1911, seemed to have concluded that restraint of trade, if handled in behalf of the public successfully, should be surrounded by governmental vigilance which would in itself affect a partial correction. This public vigilance, which was a part of our anti-trust policy, would naturally find governmental agencies in a continuous and intimate society of restraint which promises a means of permanent remedy. Roosevelt accented publicity as a remedy of restraint. . . . The commission made economic reports showing trust tendencies and practices. The (Federal Trade) commission issued legal orders subject to court review forbidding specified acts of unfair competition. Under Wilson and Harding the commission, because of its personnel, was bold in cleaving to the hard letter of the law which put stress upon publicity of procedure. Coolidge changed the personnel. He put in men of his way of thinking. Cases which formerly had to be held and

---

William Allen White, Calvin Coolidge: The Man Who is President (New York, 1925), pp. 218, 221-227.

settled in the open could, under the new procedure, be settled in conferences that were not public. Publicity withdrew as an agency in the restraint of trade. Naturally trade was happy. Business put a handkerchief over the vigilant eye that was watching it, the eye of publicity. Then the great national resolution began to wane; the resolution to get at the heart of the perplexing thing which seems at times to lead democracy toward justice and at other times seems to leave democracy only a choice between socialism and plutocracy, each equally obnoxious. But President Coolidge, with all the sincerity of his faith, in business as a civilizing agent among men, feels deeply that this purpose to control business in the interests of justice which the people once had has been revoked by the Coolidge mandate from the people to safeguard prosperity.

The President's faith in the Divine ordination of wealth to rule the world and promote civilized progress is evidenced in his opposition to the inheritance tax. He seems to feel rather deeply that interference with the accumulation of fortunes, however great, is a wicked perversion of natural law. For the doctrinaire cult which holds that great fortunes should be disbursed at death, first, to equalize opportunity in a new generation; second, to produce necessary revenue; and third, to eliminate the danger to organized society from vast sums snowballing the wealth of the community in a few hands, Calvin Coolidge has expressed a rather definite scorn. In his speech to the editors in December, 1924, in which he said "the business of America is business," he further declared that he had no faith in Goldsmith's couplet:

"Ill fares the land to hastening ills a prey,
Where wealth accumulates and men decay."

He just does not believe that men decay where wealth accumulates and he said so, contending that the benefits that come from great fortunes through their charitable benevolences offset any evils which might possibly be imagined. His speeches clearly show a deep conviction that in the accumulation of past industry which we call capital lies the intelligent ruling forces of a forward-moving civilization . . . .

When the oil scandal touched his administration, he let two members in his Cabinet resign after long weeks of cold, inexorable inaction in their behalf which became finally translated in their hearts into orders of dismissals. But if we are forced to conclude that political corruption irks rather than arouses him, we must remember that he is a man of small emotional content. He boils at an extremely high temperature. And being congealed, naturally he moves slowly but rather surely to chase the thieves from the sanctuary. He never, however, mistakes the mendacity of the thieves which to him is casual, accidental and sporadic with the business of the holy temple, the accumulation of wealth and its sacred preservation in the hands that hold it. He is more than property-minded. In his creed it would seem that few human rights may not be resolved into property rights. To him how mad must appear the whole era behind him, when men sought to regulate capital, to restrict the activities of capital; when men questioned the wisdom of benevolent plutocracy; the era of reform and reconstruction which closed with the Treaty of Versailles. The leaders of that era made quick exit. Bryan, Roosevelt, Wilson, La Follette passed with their times.

## H. L. MENCKEN COMMENTS ON CALVIN COOLIDGE (1933)[1]

H. L. Mencken, editor of the <u>American Mercury</u>, was a pundit whose commentaries on American life and politics were never bland and never polite. A critic of provincialism and small-mindedness, Mencken was often far from fair himself, but many of his portraits of people and mores were as incisive as they were vicious.

His record as President, in fact, is almost a blank. No one remembers anything that he did or anything that he said. His chief feat during five years and seven months in office was to sleep more than any other President-- to sleep more and to say less. Wrapped in a magnificent silence, his feet upon his desk, he drowsed away the lazy days. He was no fiddler like Nero; he simply yawned and stretched. And while he yawned and stretched the United States went slam-bang down the hill--and he lived just long enough to see it fetch up with a horrible bump at the bottom.

It was this snoozing, I suspect, that was at the bottom of such moderate popularity as he enjoyed. . . . The itch to run things did not afflict him; he was content to let them run themselves. Nor did he yearn to teach, for he was plainly convinced that there was nothing worth teaching. . . . The people generally believed that simple peace was all that was needed to cure the bruises and blisters of war time, and simple peace was what Dr. Coolidge gave them. He never made inflammatory speeches. He engaged in no public combats with other statesmen. He had no ideas for the overhauling of the government. He read neither the <u>Nation</u> nor the <u>New Republic</u>, and even in the New York <u>Times</u> he apparently read only the weather report. Wall Street got no lecturing from him. . . . The President's chosen associates were prosperous storekeepers, professional politicans, and the proprietors of fifth-rate newspapers. When his mind slid downhill toward the fine arts, he sent for a couple of movie actors.

## THE SCOPES TRIAL (1925)[2]

The decade of the 1920s saw repeated clashes between fundamentalist, traditional, small-town values and the modernism that heralded the new twentieth century. Such clashes could become quite bitter, as is seen here, in the notorious Scopes Trial. John Thomas Scopes was a high school biology teacher who violated the Tennessee statute that opens this excerpt from the trial. The

---

[1] Malcolm Moos, ed., <u>H. L. Mencken: A Carnvial of Buncombe</u> (Baltimore, 1956), pp. 135-136.

[2] <u>The World's Most Famous Court Trial: State of Tennessee v. John Thomas Scopes</u> (New York, 1971), pp. 200, 203, 211, 285, 290-91, 294, 299, 301.

judge, whose courtroom was decorated with a large sign that advised "Read Your Bible," and who allowed blatantly prejudicial prayers to open the day in court, ruled that scientific testimony on the theories of Darwin was inadmissible, while defense attorney Clarence Darrow of the American Civil Liberties Union was reduced to questioning William Jennings Bryan, a prosecuting attorney in this case, as an "expert witness" on the Bible.

[Judge Raulston] The first section of the statute involved in this case reads as follows: "Be it enacted by the general assembly of the state of Tennessee, that it shall be unlawful for any teacher in any of the universities, normals and all other public schools of the state which are supported in whole or in part by the public school funds of the state, to teach any theory that denies the story of divine creation as taught in the Bible, and to teach instead that man has descended from a lower order of animals.". . .

In the final analysis this court, after a most earnest and careful consideration, has reached the conclusions that under the provisions of the act involved in this case, it is made unlawful thereby to teach in the public schools of the state of Tennessee the theory that man descended from a lower order of animals. If the court is correct in this, then the evidence of experts would shed no light on the issues.

Therefore, the court is content to sustain the motion of the attorney-general to exclude the expert testimony. . . .
SEVENTH DAY OF DAYTON EVOLUTION TRIAL--MONDAY, JULY 20, 1925. . .
Prayer by Rev. Standefer:

Almighty God, our Father in Heaven, we thank Thee for all the kindly influences Thou hast surrounded our lives with. Thou hast been constantly seeking to invite us to contemplate higher and better and richer creations of Thine, and sometimes we have been stupid enough to match our human minds with revelations of the infinite and eternal. May we, as a nation, have Thy guiding and directing presence with us in all ultimate things, and wilt Thou this morning be the directing presence that supplements human limitations and enables each individual in his respective position to meet the full requirements of 'this position. Do Thou grant to all of us Thy presence and Thy direction in all things, we ask for Christ sake. Amen. . . .

Q[Darrow]--But when you read that Jonah swallowed the whale--or that the whale swallowed Jonah--excuse me please--how do you literally interpret that?

A[Bryan]--When I read that a big fish swallowed Jonah--it does not say whale.

Q--Doesn't it? Are you sure?

A--That is my recollection of it. A big fish, and I believe it, and I believe in a God who can make a whale and can make a man and make both do what He pleases. . . .

Q--Now, you say, the big fish swallowed Jonah, and he there remained how long--three days--and then he spewed him upon the land. You believ that the big fish was made to swallow Jonah?

A--I am not prepared to say that; the Bible merely says it was done.

Q--You don't know whether it was the ordinary run of fish, or made for that purpose?

A--You may guess; you evolutionists guess. . . .

Mr. Darrow—You do know that there are thousands of people who profess to be Christians who believe the earth is much more ancient and that the human race is much more ancient?

A—I think there may be.

Q—And you never have investigated to find out how long man has been on the earth?

A—I have never found it necessary. . .

Q—Have you ever read anything about the origins of religions?

A—Not a great deal.

Q—You have never examined any other religion?

A—Yes, sir.

Q—And you don't know whether any other religion ever gave a similar account of the destruction of the earth by the flood? . . .

A—The Christian religion has satisfied me, and I have never felt it necessary to look up some competing religions. . .

Q—You don't care how old the earth is, how old man is and how long the animals have been here?

A—I am not so much interested in that.

Q—You have never made any investigation to find out?

A—No, sir, I have never. . . .

Gen. Stewart—I want to interpose another objection. What is the purpose of this examination?

Mr. Bryan—The purpose is to cast ridicule on everybody who believes in the Bible, and I am perfectly willing that the world shall know that these gentlemen have no other purpose than ridiculing every Christian who believes in the Bible.

Mr. Darrow—We have the purpose of preventing bigots and ignoramuses from controlling the education of the United States and you know it, and that is all. . .

Mr. Bryan—. . . I am simply trying to protect the word of God against the greatest atheist or agnostic in the United States. (Prolonged applause.). . . I think it would be just as easy for the kind of God we believe in to make the earth in six days as in six years or in 6,000,000 years or in 600,000,00 years. I do not think it important whether we believe one or the other.

Q—Do you think those were literal days?

A—My impression is they were periods, but I would not attempt to argue as against anybody who wanted to believe in literal days.

Q—Have you any idea of the length of the periods?

A—No; I don't.

Q—Do you think the sun was made on the fourth day?

A—Yes.

Q—And they had evening and morning without the sun?

A—I am simply saying it is a period.

Q—They had evening and morning for four periods without the sun, do you think?

A—I believe in creation as there told, and if I am not able to explain it I will aceept it. Then you can explain it to suit yourself.

## BRUCE BARTON ON JESUS, THE FOUNDER OF MODERN BUSINESS (1925)

Son of a minister and founder of a successful advertising firm, Bruce Barton wrote a book that seems to offer evidence that business was indeed America's religion in the 1920s. Convinced that Jesus was not meek or weak, lowly or humorless, and that he was not a failure but an organization man, Barton proclaimed that Jesus embodied all the traits of a modern businessman. The book became a best-seller and was translated into several languages. In 1956 Barton published a revised version of the book in which many of the more blatant and crass comparisons of Christianity to business for profit were softened.

Years went by and the boy grew up and became a business man.

He began to wonder about Jesus.

He said to himself: "Only strong magnetic men inspire great enthusiasm and build great organizations. Yet Jesus built the greatest organization of all. It is extraordinary."

The more sermons the man heard and the more books he read the more mystified he became.

One day he decided to wipe his mind clean of books and sermons.

He said, "I will read what the men who knew Jesus personally said about him. I will read about him as though he were a new historical character, about whom I had never heard anything at all."

The man was amazed.

A physical weakling! Where did they get that idea? Jesus pushed a plane and swung an adze; he was a successful carpenter. He slept outdoors and spent his days walking around his favorite lake. His muscles were so strong that when he drove the money-changers out, nobody dared to oppose him!

A kill-joy! He was the most popular dinner guest in Jerusalem! The criticism which proper people made was that he spent too much time with publicans and sinners (very good fellows, on the whole, the man thought) and enjoyed society too much. They called him a "wine bibber and a gluttonous man."

A failure! He picked up twelve men from the botton ranks of business and forged them into an organization that conquered the world.

When the man had finished his reading he exclaimed, "This is a man nobody knows.

"Some day," said he, "some one will write a book about Jesus. Every business man will read it and send it to his partners and his salesmen. For it will tell the story of the founder of modern business. . . ."

I am not a doctor, or lawyer or critic but an advertising man. As a profession advertising is young; as a force it is as old as the world. The first four words ever uttered, "Let there be light," constitute its charter. . . .

I propose in this chapter to speak of the advertisements of Jesus which have survived for twenty centuries and are still the most potent influence in the world.

---

Bruce Barton, The Man and the Book Nobody Knows (Indianapolis, 1925), pp. xi-xxiii, 124-126, 159-167.

Let us begin by asking why he was so successful in mastering public attention and why in contrast, his churches are less so? The answer is twofold. In the first place he recognized the basic principle that all good advertising is news. He was never trite or commonplace; he had no routine. . . .

When Jesus was twelve years old his father and mother took him to the Feast at Jerusalem. . . .

In such a mass of folk it was not surprising that a boy of twelve should be lost. When Mary and Joseph missed him on the homeward trip, they took it calmly and began a search among the relatives.

The inquiry produced no result. Some remembered having seen him in the Temple, but no one had seen him since. Mary grew frightened: where could he be? . . . Nervously she and Joseph hurried back over the hot roads, through the suburbs, up through the narrow city streets, up to the courts of the Temple itself.

And there he was. . . .

"Son, why hast thou thus dealt with us?" she demanded. "Behold thy father and I have sought thee sorrowing. . . ."

He spoke to her now with deference, as always, but in words that did not dispel but rather added to her uncertainty.

"How is it that ye sought me?" he asked. "Wist ye not that I must be about my father's business?"

His father's business, indeed, as if that wasn't exactly where they wanted him to be. His father owned a prosperous carpenter shop in Nazareth, and that was the place for the boy, as he very well knew. . . .

He did not say, "Wist ye not that I must practise preaching?" or "Wist ye not that I must get ready to meet the arguments of men like these?" The language was quite different, and well worth remembering. "Wist ye not that I must be about my father's business?" he said. He thought of his life as business. What did he mean by business? To what extent are the principles by which he conducted his business applicable to ours? And if he were among us again, in our highly competitive world, would his business philosophy work?

On one occasion, you recall, he stated his recipe for success. It was on the afternoon when James and John came to ask him what promotion they might expect. . . .

"Master," they said, "we want to ask what plans you have in mind for us. You're going to need big men around you when you establish your kingdom; our ambition is to sit on either side of you, one on your right hand and the other on your left. . . ."

Jesus answered with a sentence which sounds poetically absurd.

"Whosoever will be great among you, shall be your minister," he said, "and whosoever of you will be the chiefest, shall be servant of all."

A fine piece of rhetoric, now isn't it? Be a good servant and you will be great; be the best possible servant and you will occupy the highest possible place. Nice idealistic talk but utterly impractical; nothing to take seriously in a common sense world. That is just what men thought for some hundreds of years; and then, quite suddenly, Business woke up to a great discovery proclaimed in every sales convention as something distinctly modern and up to date. It is emblazoned in the advertising pages of every magazine.

Look through those pages.

Here is the advertisement of an automobile company, one of the greatest in the world. And why is it greatest? On what does it base its claim to leadership? On its huge factories and financial strength? They are never mentioned. On its army of workmen or its high salaried executives? You might read its advertisements for years without suspecting that it had either. No. "We are great because of our service," the advertisements cry. "We will crawl under your car oftener and get our backs dirtier than any of our competitors. Drive up to our service stations and ask for anything at all--it will be granted cheerfully. We serve; therefore we grow. . . ."

They call it the "spirit of modern business"; they suppose, most of them, that it is something very new. But Jesus preached it more than nineteen hundred years ago. . . .

"If you're forever thinking about saving your life," Jesus said, "you'll lose it; but the man who loses his life shall find it."

Because he said it and he was a religious teacher, because it's printed in the Bible, the world has dismissed it as high minded ethics but not hard headed sense. But look again! . . . [they] buried themselves in their great undertaking, literally lost their lives in it[.] And when they found their lives again, they were all of them bigger and richer than they had ever supposed they could be.

## KELLOGG-BRIAND PACT (1928)

This treaty emerged partly as a result of French efforts after World War I to obtain American guarantees in case Germany should once again threaten the security of France. The French Foreign Minister, Aristide Briand, approached the State Department with the suggestion that France and the United States enter into a treaty renouncing war in favor of arbitration of their differences. The American Secretary of State, Frank B. Kellogg, suspiciously viewed the idea as a possible French scheme to entrap the United States in some form of binding commitment. Kellogg deflected the French offer by proposing a general international treaty which declared war illegal. Over sixty nations signed this "Treaty for the Renunication of War as an Instrument of National Policy."

Article 1. The High Contracting Parties solemnly declare in the names of their respective peoples that they condemn recourse to war for the solution of international controversies, and renounce it as an instrument of national policy in their relations with one another.

Article 2. The High Contracting Parties agree that the settlement or solution of all disputes or conflicts of whatever nature or of whatever origin they may be, which may arise among them, shall never be sought except by pacific means. . . .

---

U. S. Department of State, Papers Relating to the Foreign Relations of the United States, 1928 (Washington, D.C., 1942), I, 153-157.

# HERBERT HOOVER ON RUGGED INDIVIDUALISM (1928)

> This speech, delivered by Hoover in New York during the 1928 presidential campaign, displays a view of the expansion of governmental functions that is both naive and doctrinaire, finding its roots in 18th and 19th-century (but not 20th-century) liberalism. Hoover's unyielding insistence that any departure from free-wheeling, unregulated capitalism would entail an end to democracy made it impossible for him to deal imaginatively or effectively with the Great Depression, which followed close on the heels of the election.

During the war we necessarily turned to the government to solve every difficult economic problem. The government having absorbed every energy of our people for war, there was no other solution. For the preservation of the state the Federal Government became a centralized despotism which undertook unprecedented responsibilities, assumed autocratic powers, and took over the business of citizens. To a large degree we regimented our whole people temporarily into a socialistic state. However justified in time of war, if continued in peacetime it would destroy not only our American system but with it our progress and freedom as well.

When the war closed, the most vital of all issues both in our own country and throughout the world was whether governments should continue their wartime ownership and operation of many instrumentalities of production and distribution. We were challenged with a peace-time choice between the American system of rugged individualism and a European philosophy of diametrically opposed doctrines--doctrines of paternalism and state socialism. The acceptance of these ideas would have meant the destruction of self-government through centralization of government. It would have meant the undermining of the individual initiative and enterprise through which our people have grown to unparalleled greatness. . . .

When the Republican Party came into full power it went at once resolutely back to our fundamental conception of the state and the rights and responsibilities of the individual. Thereby it restored confidence and hope in the American people, it freed and stimulated enterprise, it restored the government to its position as an umpire instead of a player in the economic game. For these reasons the American people have gone forward in progress while the rest of the world has halted, and some countries have even gone backwards. If anyone will study the causes of retarded recuperation in Europe, he will find much of it due to stifling of private initiative on one hand, and overloading of the government with business on the other.

There has been revived in this campaign, however, a series of proposals which, if adopted, would be a long step toward the abandonment of our American system and a surrender to the destructive operation of governmental conduct of commercial business. Because the country is faced with difficulty and doubt over certain national problems--that is, prohibition, farm relief, and electrical power--our opponents propose that we must thrust government a long way into the businesses which give rise to these problems. In effect, they

---

Herbert Hoover, The New Day: Campaign Speeches of Herbert Hoover, 1928 (Stanford, 1928), pp. 153-157, 162-165, 168, 175.

abandon the tenets of their own party and turn to state socialism as a solution for the difficulties presented by all three. It is proposed that we shall change from prohibition to the state purchase and sale of liquor. If their agricultural relief program means anything, it means that the government shall directly or indirectly buy and sell and fix prices of agricultural products. And we are to go into the hydro-electric power business. In other words, we are confronted with a huge program of government in business.

There is, therefore, submitted to the American people a question of fundamental principle. That is: shall we depart from the principles of our American political and economic system, upon which we have advanced beyond all the rest of the world, in order to adopt methods based on principles destructive of its very foundations? And I wish to emphasize the seriousness of these proposals. I wish to make my position clear; for this goes to the very roots of American life and progress.

I should like to state to you the effect that this projection of government in business would have upon our system of self-government and our economic system. That effect would reach to the daily life of every man and woman. It would impair the very basis of liberty and freedom not only for those left outside the fold of expanded bureaucracy but for those embraced within it.

Let us first see the effect upon self-government. When the Federal Government undertakes to go into commercial business it must at once set up the organization and administration of that business, and it immediately finds itself in a labyrinth, every alley of which leads to the destruction of self-government.

Commercial business requires a concentration of responsibility. Self-government requires decentralization and many checks and balances to safeguard liberty. Our Government to succeed in business would need become in effect a despotism. There at once begins the destruction of self-government. . . .

It is a false liberalism that interprets itself into the government operation of commercial business. Every step of bureaucratizing of the business of our country poisons the very roots of liberalism--that is, political equality, free speech, free assembly, free press, and equality of opportunity. It is the road not to more liberty, but to less liberty. Liberalism should be found not striving to spread bureaucracy but striving to set bounds to it. True liberalism seeks all legitimate freedom first in the confident belief that without such freedom the pursuit of all other blessings and benefits is vain. That belief is the foundation of all American progress, political as well as economic.

Liberalism is a force truly of the spirit, a force proceeding from the deep realization that economic freedom cannot be sacrificed if political freedom is to be preserved. Even if governmental conduct of business could give us more efficiency instead of less efficiency, the fundamental objection to it would remain unaltered and unabated. It would destroy political equality. It would increase rather than decrease abuse and corruption. It would stifle initiative and invention. It would undermine the development of leadership. It would cramp and cripple the mental and spiritual energies of our people. It would extinguish equality and opportunity. It would dry up the spirit of liberty and progress. For these reasons primarily it must be resisted. For a hundred and fifty years liberalism has found its true spirit in the American system, not in the European systems. . . .

[I do not] wish to be misinterpreted as believing that the United States is free-for-all and devil-take-the-hindmost. The every essence of equality of opportunity and of American individualism is that there shall be no domination by any group or combination in this republic, whether it be business or political. On the contrary, it demands economic justice as well as political and social justice. It is no system of laissez faire.

I feel deeply on this subject because during the war I had some practical experience with governmental operation and control. I have witnessed not only at home but abroad the many failures of government in business. I have seen its tyrannies, its injustices, its destructions of self-government, its undermining of the very instincts which carry our people forward to progress. I have witnessed the lack of advance, the lowered standards of living, the depressed spirits of people working under such a system. . . .

Our people have the right to know whether we can continue to solve our great problems without abandonment of our American system. . . .

By adherence to the principles of decentralized self-government, ordered liberty, equal opportunity, and freedom to the individual, our American experiment in human welfare has yielded a degree of well-being unparalleled in all the world. It has come nearer to the abolition of poverty, to the abolition of fear of want, than humanity has ever reached before. Progress of the past seven years is the proof of it. . . .

I have endeavored to present to you that the greatness of America has grown out of a political and social system and a method of control of economic forces distinctly its own--our American system--which has carried this great experiment in human welfare farther than ever before in all history. We are nearer today to the ideal of the abolition of poverty and fear from the lives of men and women than ever before in any land. And I again repeat that the departure from our American system by injecting principles destructive to it which our opponents propose, will jeopardize the very liberty and freedom of our people, and will destroy equality of opportunity not alone to ourselves but to our children.

## HOOVER ON THE G.O.P. RECORD AND THE DANGERS OF THE DEMOCRATIC PARTY (1932)

On the eve of the 1932 election, President Herbert Hoover elaborated on the differences between the two major parties. Hoover spoke in St. Paul, Minnesota on November 5, 1932.

I would recall to you the unprecedented measures which we have introduced by which we have brought the full reserve powers of the Federal Government to save community values and protect every family and fireside so far as it was humanly possible from deterioration. . . .

1. The first of our measures, which subsequently proved of great emergency service, was the revision of the tariff. By this act we gave protection to our agriculture, from a world demoralization which would have

Herbert Hoover, *Public Papers of the Presidents of the United States: Herbert Hoover, 1932-1933* (Washington, D.C., 1977), pp. 746-768.

been far worse than anything we have suffered and we prevented unemployment to millions of workmen.

2. We have secured extension of authority to the Tariff Commission by which the adjustments can be made to correct inequities in the tariff, and to make changes to meet economic tides, thereby avoiding the national disturbance of general revision of the tariff with all its greed and log rolling. That authority becomes a vital importance today in the face of depreciated currencies abroad.

3. At the outset of the depression we brought about an understanding between employers and employees that wages should be maintained. They were maintained until the cost of living had decreased and the profits had practically vanished. They are now the highest real wages in the world.

With the concurrent agreement of labor leaders at that time to minimize strikes, we have had a degree of social stability hitherto unknown in the history of any depression in our country. I cannot pay too high a tribute to the leaders of labor, leaders of industry and the population in general, for their intelligent self-control and their devotion to the cause of order in time of stress.

Last night one of the eminent orators of the Democratic Party began his speech in New York by accusing the Republican Party of waging a campaign of fear, declaring that the success of the Republican Party at the polls next Tuesday might be followed by mob disturbances to public order. How does the gentleman explain the last three years of unparalleled social calm? Does he mean to charge that this magnificent body of self disciplined citizens is suddenly overnight to become a mob? Or does he mean to imply that his party is the party of the mob? In either event does he mean that we must accept the threat of mob rule in the United States as a guide to our conduct on election day?

4. An agreement to a spread of work where employers were compelled to reduce production was brought about in order that none might be deprived of all their living and all might participate in the existing jobs and thus give real aid to millions of families.

5. We have mobilized throughout the country private charity and local and state support for the care of distress under which our women and men have given such devoted service that the health of our country has actually improved.

6. By the expansion of state, municipal, and private construction work as an aid to employment, and by the development of an enlarged program of Federal construction which has been maintained at the rate of $600,000,000 a year throughout the depression, we have given support to hundreds of thousands of families.

7. By the negotiation of the German moratorium and the standstill agreements upon external debts of that country we saved their people from a collapse that would have set a prairie afire and possibly have involved all civilization itself.

8. We created the National Credit Association by cooperation of the bankers of the country, with a capital of $500,000,000 which prevented the failure of a thousand banks with all the tragedies to their depositors and borrowers.

9. By drastic reduction in the ordinary operating expenses of the Federal Government, together with the increasing of the revenues in the year 1932, we contributed to balancing the Federal Budget, and thus held impregnable the credit of the United States.

10. We created the Reconstruction Finance Corporation originally, with $2,000,000,000 of resources, in order that, having maintained national credit, we should thrust the full resources of public credit behind private credit of the country and thus reestablish and maintain private enterprise in an unassailable position that with this backing of the Federal credit, acting through existing institutions, we might protect depositors in savings banks, insurance policy holders, lenders and borrowers in building and loan associations; through banking institutions expand the funds available for loans to merchants, manufacturers, farmers, and marketing associations; that we should protect the railways from receiverships in order that in turn railway securities in the great fiduciary institutions such as insurance companies and savings banks might be protected and a score of other services performed.

11. In addition to strengthening the capital of the Federal Land Banks by $125,000,000, we have, through the Reconstruction Corporation, made large loans to mortgage associations for the same purpose, and lately we have organized all lending agencies into cooperative action to give the farmer who wants to make a fight for his home a chance to hold it from foreclosure.

12. We extended authorities under the Federal Reserve Act to protect beyond all question the gold standard of the United States and at the same time expand the credit in counter action to the strangulation due to hoarding and foreign withdrawals of gold.

13. We created the Home Loan Discount Banks with direct and indirect resources of several hundred millions, also acting through existing institutions in such fashion as to mobilize the resoureces of building and loan associations and saving banks and other institutions, furnishing to them cheaper and longer term capital, to give to them the ability to save homes from foreclosure, to furnish credit to create new homes, and expand employment.

14. We secured further authorites to the Reconstruction Corporation to assist in the earlier liquidation of deposits in closed banks in order that we might relieve distress to millions of depositors. Through Democratic opposition we failed to secure authority from Congress to carry this on a scale the country so sorely needs.

15. We secured increased authorities to the Reconstruction Corporation to loan up to $300,000,000 to the states whose resources had been exhausted, to enable them to extend full relief to distress and to prevent any hunger and cold in the United States.

16. We increased the resources to the Reconstruction Corporation by a further $1,500,000,000 for the undertaking of great public works which otherwise would have to await finance, due to the stringency of credit. These works are of a character which by their own earnings will enable disposal of the repayment of these loans without charge upon the taxpayer.

17. We have erected a new system of agricultural credit banks with indirect resources of $300,000,000 to reinforce the work of the intermediate credit banks in the financing of production and livestock loans to farmers.

18. We have extended the authority to the Reconstruction Corporation to make loans for financing the normal movement of agricultural commodities to markets both at home and abroad.

19. We have systematically mobilized banking and industry and business with the cooperation of labor and agricultural leaders to attack the depression on every front. They have sought out and given assurance of credits to business and industry where employment would be increased and have cooperated in relief of agricultural mortgage pressures.

20. We have developed, together with European nations, a world-wide economic conference with view to relieving pressure upon us from foreign countries, to increase their stability, to deal with silver, and to prevent recurrence of these calamities for the future.

21. We have given American leadership in development of drastic reductions of armament in order to reduce our own expenditures by $200,000,000 a year and to increase the financial stability of foreign nations and to relieve the world of fear and political friction. . . .

I may mention that in employment over a million men have now returned to work in these four months. This is the estimate of our Government departments. The estimate of our employers place the number at a million and a half. Certainly we are now gaining a half million a month.

Production of boots and shoes amounted to 34,000,000 pairs in October, the highest output for any month in the year and higher than the same month of the previous year.

Hoarded currency continues to return; imports of gold withdrawn by frightened European holders have continued to increase; deposits of banks continue to show steady expansion. In four months they have increased by nearly a billion dollars. This is money being put to work and an evidence of renewed confidence.

A further indication of the upward movement of industry lies in the increased demand for electrical power, which has increased by over 8 per cent in the last four months. Every business index shows some progress somewhere in the Nation. . . .

And now in contrast with this construction program of the Republican Party I wish to develop for you the Democratic program to meet this depression as far as we have been able to find any definition to it. . . .

1. They passed the Collier Bill, providing for destruction of the Tariff Commission by reducing it again to a mere statistical body controlled by the Congress. Had they succeeded, the relief which you so sorely require from competition from countries of depreciated curriencies would now be impossible.

2. They attempted to instruct me by legislation to call an international conference through which the aid of foreign nations was requested to lower American tariffs, by which the independence of the United States in control of its domestic policies was to be placed in the hands of an international body.

3. They passed an act instructing me to negotiate reciprocal tariffs, the result of which could only be to deprive some locality of its tariff protection for the benefit of another, and by which the only possible agreements would involve the reduction of farm tariffs in order to build up markets for other goods.

4. They passed an omnibus pension bill with unworthy payments as an indication of their economical temper.

5. They passed an inadequate, patchwork revenue bill, the injustices of which to different industries and groups must yet be remedied.

6. They passed Indian claims bills to reopen settlements 75 years ago in order to favor certain localities at the expense of the public Treasury.

7. They passed a bill instructing the Federal Reserve System and the Treasury to fix prices at averages prevailing during the years 1921 to 1929 by constantly shifting the volume of currency and credit and thus creation of every uncertainty to business and industry by a rubber dollar. This bill was stopped, but it has not been removed from their political calendar.

8. They defeated a large part of the national economy measure proposed by the Administration, by reduction of ordinary expeditures from $250,000,000 to less than $50,000,000, a part of which we subsequently rescued in the Senate.

9. They passed the Garner-Rainey pork barrel bill increasing expenditures by $1,200,000,000 for unnecessary, non-productive public works, purely for the benefit of favored localities. We stopped this bill, but it is still on their political calendar.

10. They passed the cash prepayment of the bonus calling for immediate expenditure of $2,300,000,000 and for actual increase in liabilities of the Federal Government over the original act over $1,300,000,000. We stopped this bill but it is still on their political calendar.

11. They passed the provision for the issuance of over $2,200,000,000 of greenback currency, a reversion to vicious practices already demonstrated in the last hundred years as the most destructive to labor, agriculture, and business. We stopped this bill and even as late as last night the Democratic candidate failed to frankly disavow it.

12. They passed the Rainey Bill providing for direct personal banking for any conceivable purpose on every conceivable security to everyone who wants money, and thus the most destructive entry of the Government into private business in a fashion that violates every principle of our Nation. I vetoed this bill--but Mr. Garner still advocates it and it has not been removed from their political promises.

13. They injected an expenditure of $322,000,000 for entirely unnecessary purposes in time of great emergency. They complain daily that we do not spend it fast enough.

14. The Congress passed proper authority to the Executive for reorganization and elimination of useless Government commissions and bureaus, but by refusing my recommendations for immediate action they destroyed its usefulness for a long time to come and probably destroyed its consummation.

15. The Democratic candidate eloquently urges the balancing of the Budget, but nowhere disavows these gigantic raids on the Treasury, under which a budget cannot be balanced.

Thus far is the program of the Democratic House under the leadership of Mr. Garner whose policies the Democratic Party ratified by nominating him Vice President.

16. The Democratic candidate adds to this program the proposal to plant a billion trees and thereby immediately employ a million men, but the Secretary of Agriculture has shown that the trees available to plant will give them a total less than three days' work.

17. The candidate promises to relieve agriculture with a 6-point program which amounts to envisaging to distressed farmers a great structure of agricultural relief, but he has refused to submit it to debate. He disclosed no details of the plan except six methods by which he can escape from the promise.

18. The candidate has promised the immediate inauguration of a program of self-liquidating public works, such as utilization of our water resources, flood control and land reclamation, to provide "employment for all surplus labor at all times." It would exceed in cost $9,000,000,000 a year. The works are unavailable, the cost would destroy the credit of the Government, deprive vast numbers of the men now working of their jobs and thus destroy the remedy itself. This fantasy is a cruel promise to these suffering men and women that they will be given jobs by the Government which no government could fulfill.

19. The Democratic Party makes its contribution to the emergency by proposing to reduce the tariff to a "competitive tariff for revenue." Their candidate states that he supports this promise 100 per cent. A competitive tariff today would be ruinous to American agriculture and industry.

These are the only reliefs to this emergency that I can find in the whole Democratic program. They are mostly destructive. The Nation would collapse under them.


TESTIMONY BEFORE CONGRESS ON THE DEPRESSION (1932)

In 1932, an election year, America was in the depths of the Great Depression. Had Roosevelt not been elected, would the United States have edged closer to revolution? It is impossible to say, but what is certain is that the suffering of the American people was profound and widespread. Hours upon hours of evidence of this suffering were offered in testimony before a committee of the House of Representatives in February, 1932. One witness was Oscar Ameringer, an Oklahoma newspaper editor whose travels through 20 states and whose close knowledge of the condition of miners made him a valuable witness.

I have not come here to stir you in a recital of the necessity for relief for our suffering fellow citizens. However, unless something is done for them and done soon, you will have a revolution on hand. And when that revolution comes it will not come from Moscow, it will not be made by the poor communists whom our police are heading up regularly and efficiently. When the revolution comes it will bear the label "Laid in the U.S.A." and its chief promoters will be the people of American stock. . . .

Some time ago a cowman came into my office in Oklahoma City. He was one of these double-fisted gentlemen, with the gallon hat and all. He said, "You do not know me from Adam's ox." I said, "No; I do not believe I know you." He said, "But I know you and I used to hear you make speeches, and I came to tell you that I used to think you were a darned fool, but now I am the fool." I asked, "What has happened?" He said, "I came to this country without a cent, but, knowing my onions, and by tending strictly to business, I finally accumulated two sections of land and a fine herd of white-faced Hereford cattle. I was independent." I remarked that anybody could do that if he worked hard and did not gamble and used good management. He said, "After the war cattle began to drop, and I was feeding them corn, and by the time I got them to Chicago the price of cattle, considering the price of corn I had fed them, was not enough to even pay my anything."

Continuing, he said, "I mortgaged my two sections of land, and to-day I am cleaned out; by God, I am not going to stand for it." I asked him what he was going to do about it, and he said, "We have got to have a revolution here like they had in Russia and clean them up." I finally asked him, "Who is

---

Unemployment in the United States, Hearings Before A Subcommittee of the Committee on Labor, House of Representatives, 72nd Cong., 1 sess., 1932, pp. 99-101.

going to make the revolution?" He said, "I just want to tell you that I am going to be one of them, and I am going to do my share in it." I asked what his share was and he said, "I will capture a certain fort I know I can get in with 20 of my boys," meaning his cowboys, "because I know the inside and outside of it, and I [will] capture that with my men." I rejoined, "Then what?" He said, "We will have 400 machine guns; so many batteries of artillery, tractors, and munitions and rifles; and everything else needed to supply a pretty good army." Then I asked, "What then?" He said, "If there are enough fellows with guts in this country to do like us, we will march eastward and we will cut the East off. We will cut the East off from the West. We have got the granaries; we have the hogs, the cattle, the corn, and East has nothing but mortgages on our places. We will show them what we can do."

That man may be very foolish, and I think he is, but he is in dead earnest, he is a hard-shelled Baptist and a hard shelled Democrat, not a Socialist or a Communist, but just a plain American cattleman whose ancestors went from Carolina to Tennessee, then to Arkansas, and then to Oklahoma. I have heard much of this talk from serious-minded prosperous men of other days.

As you know, talk is always a mental preparation for action. Nothing is done until people talk and talk and talk it, and they finally get the notion that they will do it.

I do not say we are going to have a revolution on hand within the next year or two, perhaps never. I hope we may not have such; but the danger is here. That is the feeling of our people--as reflected in the letters I have read. I have met these people virtually every day all over the country. There is a feeling among the masses generally that something is radically wrong. They are despairing of political action. They say the only thing you do in Washington is to take money from the pockets of the poor and put it into the pockets of the rich. They say that this Government is a conspiracy against the common people to enrich the already rich. I hear such remarks every day.

I never pass a hitch hiker without inviting him in and talking to him. Bankers even are talking about that. They are talking in irrational tones. You have more Bolshevism among the bankers to-day than the hod carriers, I think. It is a terrible situation, and I think something should be done and done immediately.


FRANKLIN D. ROOSEVELT ON PROGRESSIVE GOVERNMENT (1932)

In this campaign speech, Franklin Roosevelt presented a realistic view of the nation's past and future that was quite different from the naive, simplistic views of Herbert Hoover and the Republican Party. F.D.R. argued

---

Samuel I. Rosenman, comp., The Public Papers and Addresses of Franklin D. Roosevelt (New York, 1938), I, 746-756.

persuasively that it was time for a new kind of governmental policy, one designed to meet the huge problems of mid-Twentieth-Century America. These words are extremely significant since they give an early indication of the momentous changes that Roosevelt would initiate as President. Actually the speech was not an accurate expression of F.D.R.'s ideas at that time, but those of two of his close advisors, Rexford Tugwell and Adolf Berle, members of F.D.R.'s "Brains Trust."

So began, in American political life, the new day, the day of the individual against the system, the day in which individualism was made the great watchword of American life. The happiest of economic conditions made that day long and splendid. On the Western frontier, land was substantially free. No one, who did not shirk the task of earning a living, was entirely without opportunity to do so. Depressions could, and did, come and go; but they could not alter the fundamental fact that most of the people lived partly by selling their labor and partly by extracting their livelihood from the soil, so that starvation and dislocation were practically impossible. At the very worst there was always the possibility of climbing into a covered wagon and moving west where the untilled prairies afforded a haven for men to whom the East did not provide a place. So great were our natural resources that we could offer this relief not only to our own people, but to the distressed of all the world; we could invite immigration from Europe, and welcome it with open arms. Traditionally, when a depression came a new section of land was opened in the West; and even our temporary misfortune served our manifest destiny.

It was in the middle of the nineteenth century that a new force was released and a new dream created. The force was what is called the industrial revolution, the advance of steam and machinery and the rise of the forerunners of the modern industrial plant. The dream was the dream of an economic machine, able to raise the standard of living for everyone; to bring luxury within the reach of the humblest; the annihilate distance by steam power and later by electricity, and to release everyone from the drudgery of the heaviest manual toil. It was to be expected that this would necessarily affect Government. Heretofore, Government had merely been called upon to produce conditions within which people could live happily, labor peacefully, and rest secure. Now it was called upon to aid in the consummation of this new dream. There was, however, a shadow over the dream. To be made real, it required use of the talents of men of tremendous will and tremendous ambition, since by no other force could the problems of financing and engineering and new developments be brought to a consummation.

So manifest were the advantages of the machine age, however, that the United States fearlessly, cheerfully, and I think, rightly, accepted the bitter with the sweet. It was thought that no price was too high to pay for the advantages which we could draw from a finished industrial system. The history of the last half century is accordingly in large measure a history of a group of financial Titans, whose methods were not scrutinized with too much care, and who were honored in proportion as they produced the results, irrespective of the means they used. The financiers who pushed the railroads to the Pacific were always ruthless, often wasteful, and frequently corrupt; but they did build railroads, and we have them today. It has been estimated that the American investor paid for the American railway system more than three times over in the process; but despite this fact the net advantage was to the United States. As long as we had free land; as long as population was growing by leaps and bounds; as long as our industrial plants were insufficient to supply our own needs, society chose to give the ambitious man free play and unlimited reward provided only that he produced the economic plant so much desired.

During this period of expansion, there was equal opportunity for all and the business of Government was not to interfere but to assist in the development of industry. This was done at the request of business men themselves. The tariff was originally imposed for the purpose of "fostering our infant industry," a phrase I think the older among you will remember as a political issue not so long ago. The railroads were subsidized, sometimes by grants of money, oftener by grants of land; some of the most valuable oil lands in the United States were granted to assist the financing of the railroad which pushed through the Southwest. A nascent merchant marine was assisted by grants of money, or by mail subsides, so that our steam shipping might ply the seven seas. Some of my friends tell me that they do not want the Goverment in business. With this I agree; but I wonder whether they realize the implications of the past. For while it has been American doctrine that the Government must not go into business in competition with private enterprises, still it has been traditional, particularly in Republican administrations, for business urgently to ask the Government to put at private disposal all kinds of Government assistance. The same man who tells you that he does not want to see the Government interfere in business—and he means it, and has plenty of good reasons for saying so—is the first to go to Washington and ask the Government for a prohibitory tariff on his product. When things get just bad enough, as they did two years ago, he will go with equal speed to the United States Government and ask for a loan; and the Reconstruction Finance Corporation is the outcome of it. Each group has sought protection from the Government for its own special interests, without realizing that the function of Government must be to favor no small group at the expense of its duty to protect the rights of personal freedom and of private property of all its citizens.

In retrospect we can now see that the turn of the tide came with the turn of the century. We were reaching our last frontier; there was no more free land and our industrial combinations had become great uncontrolled and irresponsible units of power within the State. Clear-sighted men saw with fear the danger that opportunity would no longer be equal; that the growing corporation, like the fedual baron of old, might threaten the economic freedom of individuals to earn a living. In that hour, our antitrust laws were born. The cry was raised against the great corporations. Theodore Roosevelt, the first great Republican Progessive, fought a Presidential campaign on the issue of "trust busting" and talked freely about malefactors of great wealth. If the Government had a policy it was rather to turn the clock back, to destroy the large combinations and to return to the time when every man owned his individual small business. This was impossible; Theodore Roosevelt, abandoning the idea of "trust busting," was forced to work out a difference between "good" trusts and "bad" trusts. The Supreme Court set forth the famous "rule of reason" by which it seems to have meant that a concentration of industrial power was permissible if the the method by which it got its power, and the use it made of that power, was reasonable

Woodrow Wilson, elected in 1912, saw the situation more clearly. Where Jefferson had feared the encroachment of political power on the lives of individuals, Wilson knew that the new power was financial. He saw, in the highly centralized economic system, the despot of the twentieth century, on whom great masses of individuals relied for their safety and their livelihood, and whose irresponsibility and greed (if they were not controlled) would reduce them to starvation and penury. The concentration of financial power had not proceeded so far in 1912 as it has today; but it had grown far enough for Mr. Wilson to realize fully its implications . . . .

A glance at the situation today only too clearly indicates that equality of opportunity as we have known it no longer exists. Our industrial plant is built; the problem just now is whether under existing conditions it is not overbuilt. Our last frontier has long since been reached, and there is practically no more free land. More than half of our people do not live on the farms or on lands and cannot derive a living by cultivating their own property. There is no safety valve in the form of a Western prairie to which those thrown out of work by the Eastern economic machines can go for a new start. We are not able to invite the immigration from Europe to share our endless plenty. We are now providing a drab living for our own people.

Our system of constantly rising tariffs has at last reacted against us to the point of closing our Canadian frontier on the north, our European markets on the east, many of our Latin-American markets to the south, and a goodly proportion of our Pacific markets on the west, through the retaliatory tariffs of those countries. It has forced many of our great industrial institutions which exported their surplus production to such countries, to establish plants in such countries, within the tariff walls. This has resulted in the reduction of the operation of their American plants and opportunity for employment.

Just as freedom to farm has ceased, so also the opportunity in business has narrowed. It still is true that men can start small enterprises, trusting to native shrewdness and ability to keep abreast of competitors; but area after area has been preempted altogether by the great corporations, and even in the fields which still have no great concerns, the small man starts under a handicap. The unfeeling statistics of the past three decades show that the independent business man is running a losing race. Perhaps he is forced to the wall; perhaps he cannot command credit; perhaps he is "squeezed out," in Mr. Wilson's words, by highly organized corporate competitors, as your corner grocery man can tell you. Recently a careful study was made of the concentration of business in the United States. It showed that our economic life was dominated by some six hundred odd corporations who controlled two-thirds of American industry. Ten million small business men divided the other third. More striking still, it appeared that if the process of concentration goes on at the same rate, at the end of another century we shall have all American industry controlled by a dozen corporations, and run by perhaps a hundred men. Put plainly, we are steering a steady course toward economic oligarchy, if we are not there already.

Clearly, all this calls for a re-appraisal of values. A mere builder of more industrial plants, a creator of more railroad systems, an organizer of more corporations, is as likely to be a danger as a help. The day of the great promoter or the financial Titan, to whom we granted anything if only he would build, or develop, is over. Our task now is not discovery or exploitation of natural resources, or necessarily producing more goods. It is the soberer, less dramatic business of administrating resources and plants already in hand, of seeking of reestablish foreign markets for our surplus production, of meeting the problem of underconsumption, of adjusting production to consumption, of distributing wealth and products more equitably, of adapting existing economic organizations to the service of the people. The day of enlightened administration has come.

Just as in older times the central Government was first a haven of refuge, and then a threat, so now in a closer economic system the central and ambitious financial unit is no longer a servant of national desire, but a danger. I would draw the parallel one step further. We did not think because national Government had become a threat in the 18th century that therefore we should abandon the principle of national Government. Nor today should we abandon the principle of strong economic units called corporations, merely because their power is susceptible of easy abuse. In other times we dealt with the problem of an unduly ambitious central Government by modifying it gradually into a constitutional democratic Government. So today we are modifying and controlling our economic units.

As I see it, the task of Government in its relation to business is to assist the development of an economic declaration of rights, an economic constitutional order. This is the common task of statesman and business man. It is the minimum requirement of a more permanently safe order of thing. . . .

Every man has a right to life; and this means that he has also a right to make a comfortable living. He may by sloth or crime decline to exercise that right; but it may not be denied him. We have no actual famine or dearth; our industrial and agricultural mechanism can produce enough and to spare. Our Government formal and informal, political and economic, owes to everyone an avenue to possess himself of a portion of that plenty sufficient for his needs, through his own work.

Every man has a right to his own property; which means a right to be assured, to the fullest extent attainable, in the safety of his savings. By no other means can men carry the burdens of those parts of life which, in the nature of things, afford no chance of labor; childhood, sickness, old age. In all thought of property, this right is paramount; all other property rights must yield to it. If, in accord with this principle, we must restrict the operations of the speculator, the mainpulator, even the financier, I believe we must accept the restriction as needful, not to hamper individualism but to protect it . . . .

The Government should assume the function of economic regulation only as a last resort, to be tried only when private initiative, inspired by high responsibility, with such assistance and balance as Government can give, has finally failed. As yet there has been no final failure, because there has been no attempt; and I decline to assume that this Nation is unable to meet the situation.

The final term of the high contract was for liberty and the pursuit of happiness. We have learned a great deal of both in the past century. We know that individual liberty and individual happiness mean nothing unless both are ordered in the sense that one man's meat is not another man's poison. We know that the old "rights of personal competency", the right to read, to think, to speak, to choose and live a mode of life, must be respected at all hazards. We know that libery to do anything which deprives others of those elemental rights is outside the protection of any compact; and that Government in this regard is the maintenance of a balance, within which every individual may have a place if he will take it; in which every individual may find safety if he wishes it; in which every individual may attain such power as his ability permits, consistent with his assuming the accompanying responsibility . . . .

Faith in America, faith in our tradition of personal responsibility, faith in our institutions, faith in ourselves demands that we recognize the new terms of the old social contact. We shall fulfill them, as we fulfilled the obligation of the apparent Utopia which Jefferson imagined for us in 1776, and which Jefferson, Roosevelt and Wilson sought to bring to realization. We must do so, lest a rising tide of misery, engendered by our common failure, engulf us all. But failure is not an American habit; and in the strength of great hope we must all shoulder our common load.

### FRANKLIN D. ROOSEVELT'S FIRST INAUGURAL ADDRESS (1933)

Seldom in American history has the nation awaited an inaugural address so eagerly as this one. With unemployment at a staggering level, the banking establishment on the verge of total collapse, and hope in the future all but vanished for millions of our people, Roosevelt's first order of business was to reinstill faith in the system and ourselves. In this masterly speech F.D.R. attempted to calm a people's fears and assure them that with his strong leadership good times would return eventually.

I am certain that my fellow Americans expect that on my induction into the Presidency I will address them with a candor and a decision which the present situation of our Nation impels. This is preeminently the time to speak the truth, the whole truth, frankly and boldly. Nor need we shrink from honestly facing conditions in our country today. This great Nation will endure as it has endured, will revive and will prosper. So, first of all, let me assert my firm belief that the only thing we have to fear is fear itself--nameless, unreasoning, unjustified terror which paralyzes needed efforts to convert retreat into advance. In every dark hour of our national life a leadership of frankness and vigor has met with that understanding and support of the people themselves which is essential to victory. I am convinced that you will again give that support to leadership in these critical days.

In such a spirit on my part and on yours we face our common difficulties. They concern, thank God, only material things. Values have shrunken to fantastic levels; taxes have risen; our ability to pay has fallen; government of all kinds is faced by serious curtailment of income; the means of exchange are frozen in the currents of trade; the withered leaves of industrial enterprise lie on every side; farmers find no markets for their produce; the savings of many years in thousands of families are gone.

More important, a host of unemployed citizens face the grim problem of existence, and an equally great number toil with little return. Only a foolish optimist can deny the dark realities of the moment.

Yet our distress comes from no failure of substance. We are stricken by no plague of locusts. Compared with the perils which our forefathers conquered because they believed and were not afraid, we have still much to be thankful for. Nature still offers her bounty and human efforts have multiplied it. Plenty is at our doorstep, but a generous use of it languishes in the very sight of the supply. Primarily this is because the rulers of the exchange of mankind's goods have failed through their own stubbornness and their own incompetence, have admitted their failure, and have abdicated. Practices of the unscrupulous money changers stand indicted in the court of public opinion, rejected by the hearts and minds of men.

Samuel I. Rosenman, comp., The Public Papers and Addresses of Franklin D. Roosevelt (New York, 1938), II, 11-16.

True they have tried, but their efforts have been case in the pattern of an outworn tradition. Faced by failure of credit they have proposed only the lending of more money. Stripped of the lure of profit by which to induce our people to follow their false leadership, they have resorted to exhortations, pleading tearfully for restored confidence. They know only the rules of a generation of self-seekers. They have no vision, and when there is no vision the people perish.

The money changers have fled from their high seats in the temple of our civilization. We may now restore that temple to the ancient truths. The measure of the restoration lies in the extent to which we apply social values more noble than mere monetary profit.

Happiness lies not in the mere possession of money; it lies in the joy of achievement, in the thrill of creative effort. The joy and moral stimulation of work no longer must be forgotten in the mad chase of evanescent profits. These dark days will be worth all they cost us if they teach us that our true destiny is not to be ministered unto but to minister to ourselves and to our fellow men.

Recognition of the falsity of material wealth as the standard of success goes hand in hand with the abandonment of the false belief that public office and high political position are to be valued only by the standards of pride of place and personal profit; and there must be an end to a conduct in banking and in business which too often has given to a sacred trust the likeness of callous and selfish wrongdoing. Small wonder that confidence languishes, for it thrives only on honesty, on honor, on the sacredness of obligations, on faithful protection, on unselfish performance; without them it cannot live.

Restoration calls, however, not for changes in ethics alone. This Nation asks for action, and action now.

Our greatest primary task is to put people to work. This is no unsolvable problem if we face it wisely and courageously. It can be accomplished in part by direct recruiting by the Government itself, treating the task as we would treat the emergency of a war, but at the same time, through this employment, accomplishing greatly needed projects to stimulate and recognize the use of our natural resources.

Hand in hand with this we must frankly recognize the overbalance of population in our industrial centers and, by engaging on a national scale in the redistribution, endeavor to provide a better use of the land for those best fitted for the land. The task can be helped by definite efforts to raise the values of agricultural products and with this the power to purchase the output of our cities. It can be helped by preventing realistically the tragedy of the growing loss through foreclosure of our small homes and our farms. It can be helped by insistence that the Federal, State, and local governments act forthwith on the demand that their cost be drastically reduced. It can be helped by the unifying of relief activities which today are often scattered, uneconomical, and unequal. It can be helped by national planning for and supervision of all forms of transportation and of communications and other utilities which have a definitely public character. There are many ways in which it can be helped, but it can never be helped merely by talking about it. We must act and act quickly.

Finally, in our progress toward a resumption of work we require two safequards against a return of the evils of the older order: there must be a strict supervision of all banking and credits and investments, so that there will be an end to speculation with other people's money, and there must be provision for an adequate but sound currency.

These are the lines of attack. I shall presently urge upon a new Congress, in special session, detailed measures for their fulfillment, and I shall seek the immediate assistance of the several States.

Through this program of action we address ourselves to putting our own national house in order and making income balance outgo. Our international trade relations, though vastly important, are in point of time and necessity secondary to the establishment of a sound national economy. I favor as a practical policy the putting of first things first. I shall spare no effort to restore world trade by international economic readjustment, but the emergency at home cannot wait on that accomplishment.

The basic thought that guides these specific means of national recovery is not narrowly nationalistic. It is the insistence, as a first consideration, upon the interdependence of the various elements in and parts of the United States--a recognition of the old and permanently important manifestation of the American spirit of the pioneer. It is the way to recovery. It is the immediate way. It is the strongest assurance that the recovery will endure.

In the field of world policy I would dedicate this Nation to the policy of the good neighbor--the neighbor who resolutely respects himself and, because he does so, respects the rights of others--the neighbor who respects his obligations and respects the sanctity of his agreements in and with a world of neighbors.

If I read the temper of our people correctly, we now realize as we have never before our interdependence on each other; that we cannot merely take but we must give as well; that it we are to go forward, we must move as a trained and loyal army willing to sacrifice for the good of a common discipline, because without such discipline no progress is made, no leadership becomes effective. We are, I know, ready and willing to submit our lives and property to such discipline, because it makes possible a leadership which aims at a larger good. This I propose to offer, pledging that the larger purposes will bind upon us all as a sacred obligation with a unity of duty hitherto evoked only in time of armed strife.

With this pledge taken, I assume unhesitatingly the leadership of this great army of our people dedicated to a disciplined attack upon our common problems.

Action in this image and to this end is feasible under the form of government which we have inherited from our ancestors. Our Constitution is so simple and practical that it is possible always to meet extraordinary needs by changes in emphasis and arrangement without loss of essential form. That is why our constitutional system has proved itself the most superbly enduring political mechanism the modern world has produced. It has met every stress of vast expansion of territory, of foreign wars, of bitter internal strife, or world relations.

It is to be hoped that the normal balance of Executive and legislative authority may be wholly adequate to meet the unprecedented task before us. But it may be that an unprecedented demand and need for undelayed action may call for temporary departure from that normal balance of public procedure.

I am prepared under my constitutional duty to recommend the measures that a stricken Nation in the midst of a stricken world may require. These measures, or such other measures as the Congress may build out of its experience and wisdom, I shall seek, within my constitutional authority, to bring to speedy adoption.

But in the event that the Congress shall fail to take one of these two courses, and in the event that the national emergency is still critical, I shall not evade the clear course of duty that will then confront me.

I shall ask the Congress for the one remaining instrument to meet the crisis--broad Executive power to wage a war against the emergency, as great as the power that would be given me if we were in fact invaded by a foreign foe.

For the trust reposed in me I will return the courage and the devotion that befit the time. I can do no less.

We face the arduous days that lie before us in the warm courage of national unity; with the clear consciousnes of seeking old and precious moral values; with the clean satisfaction that comes from the stern performance of duty by old and young alike. We aim at the assurance of a rounded and permanent national life.

We do not distrust the future of essential democracy. The people of the United States have not failed. In their need they have registered a mandate that they want direct, vigorous action. They have asked for discipline and direction under leadership. They have made me the present instrument of their wishes. In the spirit of the gift I take it.

In this dedication of a Nation we humbly ask the blessing of God. May He protect each and every one of us. May He guide me in the days to come.

ELEANOR ROOSEVELT ON HER HUSBAND'S PERSONALITY (1949)

People who called on F.D.R. usually found an amiable host who seemed to respond agreeably to whatever was said. These visitors often found, however, that they had not convinced the President at all, and critics sometimes charged Roosevelt with being deliberately deceitful, whether for the sake of expediency or political advantage. Eleanor Roosevelt addresses these charges in this passage from her memoirs.

The few books that have already been written about Franklin show quite plainly that everyone writes from his own point of view, and that a man like my husband, who was particularly susceptible to people, took color from whomever he was with, giving to each one something different of himself. Because he disliked being disagreeable, he made an effort to give each person who came in contact with him the feeling that he understood what his particular interest was. . . .

Often people have told me that they were misled by Franklin. Even when they have not said it in so many words, I have sometimes felt that he left them, after an interview, with the idea that he was in entire agreement with them. I would know quite well, however, that he was not and that they would be very much surprised when later his actions were in complete contradiction to what they thought his attitude would be.

---

Eleanor Roosevelt, <u>This I Remember</u> (New York, 1949), p. 2.

This misunderstanding not only arose from his dislike of being disagreeable, but from the interest that he always had in somebody else's point of view and his willingness to listen to it. If he thought it was well expressed and clear, he nodded his head and frequently said, "I see," or something of the sort. This did not mean that he was convinced of the truth of the arguments, or even that he entirely understood them, but only that he appreciated the way in which they were presented.

## FRANKLIN D. ROOSEVELT'S "FOUR FREEDOMS" SPEECH (1941)

In his annual message to Congress President Roosevelt provided an excellent statement of the principles for which the American nation was prepared to fight in the approaching war.

TO THE CONGRESS OF THE UNITED STATES:

I address you, the Members of the Seventy-seventh Congress, at a moment unprecedented in the history of the Union. I use the word "unprecedented," because at no previous time has American security been as seriously threatened from without as it is today . . . .

It is true that prior to 1914 the United States often had been disturbed by events in other Continents. We had even engaged in two wars with European nations and in a number of undeclared wars in the West Indies, in the Mediterranean and in the Pacific for the maintenance of American rights and for the principles of peaceful commerce. But in no case, had a serious threat been raised against our national safety or our continued independence.

What I seek to convey is the historic truth that the United States as a nation has at all times maintained clear, definite opposition to any attempt to lock us in behind an ancient Chinese wall while the procession of civilization went past. Today, thinking of our children and their children, we oppose enforced isolation for ourselves or for any part of the Americas. . . . '

Even when the World War broke out in 1914, it seemed to contain only small threat of danger to our own American future. But, as time went on, the American people began to visualize what the downfall of democratic nations might mean to our own democracy.

We need not over emphasize imperfections in the Peace of Versailles. We need not harp on failure of the democracies to deal with problems of world reconstruction. We should remember that the Peace of 1919 was far less unjust than the kind of "pacification" which began even before Munich, and which is being carried on under the new order of tyranny that seeks to spread over every continent today. The American people have unalterably set their faces against that tyranny.

Every realist knows that the democratic way of life is at this moment being directly assailed in every part of the world--assailed either by arms, or by secret spreading of poisonous propaganda by those who seek to destroy unity and promote discord in nations still at peace. . . .

---

U. S. Congress, 77th Cong., 1st sess., January 6, 1941, <u>Congressional Record</u>, LXXXVII, 44-47.

Therefore, as your President, performing my constitutional duty to "give the Congress information of the state of the Union," I find it, unhappily, necessary to report that the future and the safety of our country and of our democracy are overwhelmingly involved in events far beyond our borders. . . .

In times like these it is immature--and incidentally, untrue--for anybody to brag that an unprepared America, single-handed, and with one hand tied behind its back, can hold off the whole world.

No realistic American can expect from a dictator's peace international generosity, or return of true independence, or world disarmament, or freedom of expression, or freedom of religion--or even good business.

Such a peace would bring no security for us or for our neighbors. "Those, who would give up essential liberty to purchase a little temporary safety, deserve neither liberty nor safety."

As a nation, we may take pride in the fact that we are soft-hearted; but we cannot afford to be soft-headed.

We must always be wary of those who with sounding brass and a tinkling cymbal preach the "ism" of appeasement.

We must especially beware of that small group of selfish men who would clip the wings of the American eagle in order to feather their own nests.

I have recently pointed out how quickly the tempo of modern warfare could bring into our very midst the physical attack which we must expect if the dictator nations win this war. . . .

As long as the aggressor nations maintain the offensive, they--not we--will choose the time and the place and the method of their attack.

That is why the future of all American Republics is today in serious danger.

That is why this Annual Message to the Congress is unique in our history.

That is why every member of the Executive Branch of the Government and every member of the Congress face great responsibility and great accountability.

The need of the moment is that our actions and our policy should be devoted primarily--almost exclusively--to meeting this foreign peril. For all our domestic problems are now a part of the great emergency.

Just as our national policy in internal affairs has been based upon a decent respect for the rights and dignity of all our fellow men within our gates, so our national policy in foreign affairs has been based on a decent respect for the rights and dignity of all nations, large and small. And the justice of morality must and will win in the end.

Our national policy is this.

First, by an impressive expression of the public will and without regard to partisanship, we are committed to all-inclusive national defense.

Second, by an impressive expression of the public will and without regard to partisanship, we are committed to full support of all those resolute peoples, everywhere, who are resisting aggression and are thereby keeping war away from our Hemisphere. By this support, we express our determination that the democratic cause shall prevail; and we strengthen the defense and security of our own nation.

Third, by an impressive expression of the public will and without regard to partisanship, we are committed to the proposition that principles of morality and considerations for our own security will never permit us to acquiesce in a peace dictated by aggressors and sponsored by appeasers. We know that enduring peace cannot be bought at the cost of other people's freedom. . . .

I also ask this Congress for authority and for funds sufficient to manufacture additional munitions and war supplies of many kinds, to be turned over to those nations which are now in actual war with aggressor nations.

Our most useful and immediate role is to act as an arsenal for them as well as for ourselves. They do not need man power, but they do need billions of dollars worth of the weapons of defense . . . .

A free nation has the right to expect full cooperation from all groups. A free nation has the right to look to the leaders of business, of labor, and of agriculture to take the lead in stimulating effort, not among other groups but within their own groups.

The best way of dealing with the few slackers or trouble makers in our midst is, first, to shame them by patriotic example, and, if that fails, to use the sovereignty of Government to save Government. . . .

Certainly this is no time for any of us to stop thinking about the social and economic problems which are the root cause of the social revolution which is today a supreme factor in the world.

For there is nothing mysterious about the foundations of a healthy and strong democracy. The basic things expected by our people of their political and economic systems are simple. They are:

Equality of opportunity for youth and for others.
Jobs for those who can work.
Security for those who need it.
The ending of special privilege for the few.
The preservation of civil liberties for all.
The enjoyment of the fruits of scientific progress in a wider and constantly rising standard of living.

These are the simple, basic things that must never be lost sight of in the turmoil and unbelievable complexity of our modern world. The inner and abiding strength of our economic and political systems is dependent upon the degree to which they fulfill these expectations. . . .

In the future days, which we seek to make secure, we look forward to a world founded upon four essential human freedoms.

The first is freedom of speech and expression--everywhere in the world.

The second is freedom of every person to worship God in his own way--everywhere in the world.

The third is freedom from want--which, translated into world
terms, means economic understandings which will secure to every nation a healthy peacetime life for its inhabitants--everywhere in the world.

The fourth is freedom from fear--which, translated into world terms, means a world-wide reduction of armaments to such a point and in such a thorough fashion that no nation will be in a position to commit an act of physical aggression against any neighbor--anywhere in the world.

That is no vision of a distant millennium. It is a definite basis for a kind of world attainable in our own time and generation. That kind of world is the very antithesis of the so-called new order of tyranny which the dictators seek to create with the crash of a bomb.

To that new order we oppose the greater conception--the moral order. A good society is able to face schemes of world domination and foreign revolutions alike without fear.

Since the beginning of our American history we have been engaged in change--in a perpetual peaceful revolution--a revolution which goes on steadily, quietly adjusting itself to changing conditions--without the concentration camp or the quick-lime in the ditch. The world order which we seek is the cooperation of free countries, working together in a friendly, civilized society.

This nation has placed its destiny in the hands and heads and hearts of its millions of free men and women; and its faith in freedom under the guidance of God. Freedom means the supremacy of human rights everywhere. Our support goes to those who struggle to gain those rights or keep them. Our strength is in our unity of purpose.

To that high concept there can be no end save victory.

## THE LEND-LEASE ACT (1941)

With the British facing bankruptcy and desperately struggling to resist Nazi aggression, Roosevelt submitted to Congress a proposal to lend or lease equipment and supplies to the British. The national debate over lend-lease (H.R. 1776) was ferocious. The President sought support for the bill by using the analogy of a prudent man lending his garden hose to a neighbor whose house was on fire. Senator Burton K. Wheeler, who believed that passage of the bill would eventually mean U.S. entry into the war, complained bitterly about "The New Deal's Triple-A foreign policy [which] will plow under every fourth American boy." Lend-lease passed through Congress by comfortable margins and became law in March 1941. Later, the benefits of lend-lease were extended to other Allies, most notably the Soviet Union and China. Although the United States presented no bills after the war for repayment of lend-lease goods, the precise totals were carefully recorded.

[T]his Act may be cited as "An Act to Promote the Defense of the United States".
   Sec. 2.  As used in this Act--
   (a)  The term "defense article" means--
        (1)  Any weapon, munition, aircraft, vessel, or boat;
        (2)  Any machinery, facility, tool, material, or supply necessary for the manufacture, production, processing, repair, servicing, or operation of any article described in this subsection;
        (3)  Any component material or part of or equipment for any article described in this subsection;
        (4)  Any agricultural, industrial or other commodity or article for defense. . . .

---

U. S. Department of State, Peace and War, 1931-1941 (Washington, D.C., 1943), pp. 627-630.

Sec. 3. (a) Notwithstanding the provisions of any other law, the President may, from to time, when he deems it in the interest of national defense, authorize the Secretary of War, the Secretary of the Navy, or the head of any other department or agency of the Government--

    (1) To manufacture in arsenals, factories, and shipyards under their jurisdiction, or otherwise procure, to the extent to which funds are made available therefor, or contracts are authorized from time to time by the Congress, or both, any defense article for the government of any country whose defense the President deems vital to the defense of the United States.

    (2) To sell, transfer title to, exchange, lease, lend, or otherwise dispose of, to any such government any defense article, but no defense article not manufactured or procured under paragraph (1) shall in any way be disposed of under this paragraph, except after consultation with the Chief of Staff of the Army or the Chief of Naval operations of the Navy, or both. The value of defense articles disposed of in any way under authority of this paragraph, and procured from funds heretofore appropriated, shall not exceed $1,300,000,000. The value of such defense articles shall be determined by the head of the department or agency concerned or such other department, agency or officer as shall be designated in the manner provided in the rules and regulations issued hereunder. Defense articles procured from funds hereafter appropriated to any department or agency of the Government, other than from funds authorized to be appropriated under this Act, shall not be disposed of in any way under authority of this paragraph except to the extent hereafter authorized by the Congress in the Acts appropriating such funds or otherwise.

    (3) To test, inspect, prove, repair, outfit, recondition, or otherwise to place in good working order, to the extent to which funds are made available therefor, or contracts are authorized from time to time by the Congress, or both, any defense article for any such government, or to procure any or all such services by private contract.

    (4) To communicate to any such government any defense information, pertaining to any defense article furnished to such government under paragraph (2) of this subsection.

    (5) To release for export any defense article disposed of in any way under this subsection to any such government.

(b) The terms and conditions upon which any such foreign government receives any aid authorized under subsection (a) shall be those which the President deems satisfactory, and the benefit to the United States may be payment or repayment in kind or property, or any other direct or indirect benefit which the President deems satisfactory. . . .

(d) Nothing in this Act shall be construed to authorize or to permit the authorization of convoying vessels by naval vessels of the United States.

(e) Nothing in this Act shall be construed to authorize or to permit the authorization of the entry of any American vessel into a combat area in violation of section 3 of the Neutrality Act of 1939.

Sec. 4. All contracts or agreements made for the disposition of any defense article or defense information pursuant to section 3 shall contain a clause by which the foreign government undertakes that it will not, without the consent of the President, transfer title to or possession of such defense article or defense information by gift, sale, or otherwise, or permit its use by anyone not an officer, employee, or agent of such foreign government. . . .

Sec. 9. The President may, from time to time, promulgate such rules and regulations as may be necessary and proper to carry out any of the provisions of this Act; and he may exercise any power or authority conferred on him by this Act through such department, agency, or officer as he shall direct.

## CHARLES LINDBERGH ON AMERICA AND WORLD WAR II (1941)

It is testament to the depth and strength of interwar isolationism that a lively argument in favor of non-intervention could be sustained as late as 1941, after the fall of France to Nazi tyranny and onset of the Battle of Britain. The "America First" movement and its spokesman, aviator-hero Charles Lindbergh, argued that America had no need to fear the Nazis, who could not be defeated in the air by the Americans in any case. (Lindbergh had visited Hitler and his air force three years earlier, and had been warmly received.) This is from Lindbergh's speech at a mass meeting in New York in April, 1941, shortly before Hitler invaded Russia. Ten thousand people, some of them standing outside the meeting hall, heard Lindbergh argue against falling victim to Britain's desperate plan to draw America into the "fiasco" of the war.

When England asks us to enter this war, she is considering her own future, and that of her empire. In making our reply, I believe we should consider the future of the United States and that of the Western Hemisphere.

. . . I have been forced to the conclusion that we cannot win this war for England, regardless of how much assistance we send. . . .

We have weakened ourselves for many months, and still worse, we have divided our own people, by this dabbling in Europe's wars. While we should have been concentrating on American defense we have been forced to argue over foreign quarrels. We must turn our eyes and our faith back to our own country before it is too late. And when we do this, a different vista opens before us. Practically every difficulty we would face in invading Europe becomes an asset to us in defending America. Our enemy, and not we, would then have the problem of transporting millions of troops across the ocean and landing them on a hostile shore. They, and not we, would have to furnish the convoys to transport guns and trucks and munitions and fuel across three thousand miles of water. Our battleships and [our] submarines would then be fighting close to their home bases. We would then do the bombing from the air and the

---

Quoted in The New York Times, April 24, 1941.

torpedoing at sea. And if any part of an enemy convoy should ever pass our navy and our air force, they would still be faced with the guns of our coast artillery and behind them the divisions of our Army.

The United States is better situated from a military standpoint than any other nation in the world. Even in our present condition of unpreparedness no foreign power is in a position to invade us today. If we concentrate on our own defenses and build the strength that this nation should maintain, no foreign army will ever attempt to land on American shores.

War is not inevitable for this country. Such a claim is defeatism in the true sense. No one can make us fight abroad unless we ourselves are willing to do so. No one will attempt to fight us here if we arm ourselves as a great nation should be armed. Over a hundred million people in this nation are opposed to entering the war. If the principles of democracy mean anything at all, that is reason enough for us to stay out. If we are forced into a war against the wishes of an overwhelming majority of our people, we will have proved democracy such a failure at home that there will be little use fighting for it abroad.

The time has come when those of us who believe in an independent American destiny must band together and organize for strength. We have been led toward war by a minority of our people. This minority has power. It has influence. It has a loud voice. But it does not represent the American people. During the last several years I have traveled over this country from one end to the other. I have talked to many hundreds of men and women, and I have letters from tens of thousands more, who feel the same way as you and I.

## THE ATLANTIC CHARTER (1941)

In August 1941, President Franklin D. Roosevelt met with Prime Minister Winston S. Churchill at Placentia Bay. The two leaders, each anxious to talk with the other, set forth their hopes for the future. Although the United States was not yet officially involved in the war, this document later served as a statement of the common war aims of the world's two leading democracies.

Joint declaration of the President of the United States of America and the Prime Minister, Mr. Churchill, representing His Majesty's Government in the United Kingdom, being met together, deem it right to make known certain common principles in the national policies of their respective countries on which they base their hopes for a better future for the world.

First, their countries seek no aggrandizement, territorial or other;

Second, they desire to see no territorial changes that do not accord with the freely expressed wishes of the peoples concerned;

Third, they respect the right of all peoples to choose the form of government under which they will live; and they wish to see sovereign rights and self government restored to those who have been forcibly deprived of them;

---

U. S. Department of State, The Foreign Relations of the United States, 1941 (Washington, D.C., 1958), I, 367-369.

Fourth, they will endeavor, with due respect for their existing obligations, to further the enjoyment by all States, great or small, victor or vanquished, of access, on equal terms, to the trade and to the raw materials of the world which are needed for their economic prosperity;

Fifth, they desire to bring about the fullest collaboration between all nations in the economic field with the object of securing, for all, improved labor standards, economic advancement and social security;

Sixth, after the final destruction of the Nazi tyranny, they hope to see established a peace which will afford to all nations the means of dwelling in safety within their own boundaries, and which will afford assurance that all the men in all the lands may live out their lives in freedom from fear and want;

Seventh, such a peace should enable all men to traverse the high seas and oceans without hindrance;

Eighth, they believe that all of the nations of the world, for realistic as well as spiritual reasons[,] must come to the abandonment of the use of force. Since no future peace can be maintained if land, sea or air armaments continue to be employed by nations which threaten, or may threaten, aggression outside of their frontiers, they believe, pending the establishment of a wider and permanent system of general security, that the disarmament of such nations is essential. They will likewise aid and encourage all other practicable measures which will lighten for peace-loving peoples the crushing burden of armaments.

## ROOSEVELT ON RACIAL MIXING

The war against Japan provided an opportunity for Americans (and other Westerners) to vent racist attitudes, which were commonly held among white peoples. This remarkable letter indicated some of the directions Roosevelt's racism had taken him during the war. Sir Ronald I. Campbell served as a counselor at the British Embassy in Washington; Sir Alexander Cadogan was the Permanent Under Secretary of State for Foreign Affairs. Dr. Ales Hrdlicka was curator of the Division of Physical Anthropology at the Smithsonian Institute.

6 August, 1942

Dear Cadogan,

Amongst many other thoughts thrown out by the President, when I saw him on August 2, was the following:

---

PREM 4/42/9, Public Record Office, London, England.

He had set one Professor [Ales] Hrdlicka of the Smithsonian Institute, to work on a private study of the effect of racial crossing. A preliminary report had been given him, with all of which he by no means agreed. But it seemed to him that if we got the Japanese driven back within their islands, racial crossing might have interesting effects, particularly in the Far East. For instance Dutch-Javanese crossings were good, and Javanese-Chinese. Chinese-Malayan was a bad mixture. Hrdlicka said that the Japanese-European cross was bad and the Chinese-European equally so. It was here he disagreed with the Professor. Experience, the President said, had shown that unlike the Japanese-European mixture, which was, he agreed, thoroughly bad, Chinese-European was not at all bad.

The President had asked the Professor why the Japanese were as bad as they were, and had followed up by asking about the Hairy Ainus. The Professor had said the skulls of these people were some 2,000 years less developed than ours (this sounds very little doesn't it?). The President asked whether this might account for the nefariousness of the Japanese and had been told it might, as they might well be the basic stock of the Japanese.

As far as I could make it out, the line of the President's thought is that an Indo-Asian or Eurasion or (better) Eurindasian race, could be developed which would be good and produce a good civilisation and Far East "order", to the exclusion of the Japanese, languishing in Coventry within their original islands.

                Yours ever,
                (Sgd.) R.I. Campbell.


## THE FULBRIGHT AND CONNALLY RESOLUTIONS (1943)

In 1943, each house of Congress passed a resolution which signalled the end of U. S. isolationism and noninterventionism. Congress had declared America ready to accept international responsibilities.

(a) The Fulbright Resolution (September 21, 1943)[1]

Resolved by the House of Representatives (the Senate concurring), That the Congress hereby expresses itself as favoring the creation of appropriate international machinery with power adequate to establish and to maintain a just and lasting peace, among the nations of the world, and as favoring participation by the United States therein through its constitutional processes.

(b) The Connally Resolution (November 5, 1943)[2]

Resolved, That the war against all our enemies be waged until complete victory is achieved.

---

[1] U. S. Congress, House, 78th Cong., 1st sess., September 21, 1943, Congressional Record, LXXXIX, 7729.

[2] U. S. Congress, Senate, 78th Cong., 1st sess., November 5, 1943, Congressional Record, LXXXIX, 9222.

That the United States cooperate with its comrades-in-arms in securing a just and honorable peace.

That the United States, acting through its consitutional processes, join with free and sovereign nations in the establishment and maintenance of international authority with power to prevent aggression and to preserve the peace of the world.

That the Senate recognizes the necessity of there being established at the earliest practicable date a general international organization, based on the principle of the sovereign equality of all peace-loving states, and open to membership by all such states, large and small, for the maintenance of international peace and security.

That, pursuant to the Constitution of the United States, any treaty made to effect the purposes of this resolution, on behalf of the Government of the United States with any other nation or any association of nations, shall be made only by and with the advice and consent of the Senate of the United States, provided two-thirds of the Senators present concur.

## GENERAL PATTON ON MALINGERERS (1943)

In August 1943, Lieutenant General George Patton was involved in two controversial--and highly publicized--incidents. Patton sent this letter of explanation and apology to Secretary of War Henry L. Stimson.

Owing to the many years during which you have shown exceptional kindness and consideration for me, I believe that in justice to both of us you should have an exact statement of the incident for which I am being criticized; of the causes leading up to them; and of my subsequent actions.

I believe that in war the good of the individual must be subordinated to the good of the army.

I love and admire good soldiers and brave men. I hate and despise slackers and cowards.

I am quite tender-hearted and emotional in my dealings with wounded men.

Like all commanders I am constantly faced with the problem of malingering. If it is not checked it spreads like a prairie fire.

On August 8, 1943 I inspected some 50 freshly wounded men who had gallantly and unflinchingly done their duty, and who, in spite of their wounds, were cheerful and uncomplaining. The last man I came to was a forlorn individual sitting on a box, apparently waiting to have a wound dressed. I asked him whre he had been hit. He replied that he had not been hit but that he, "Just could not take it," and so had come to the hospital.

---

Patton to Stimson, November 27, 1943, Box 143, file 12, Papers of Henry L. Stimson, Sterling Library, Yale University, New Haven, Connecticut.

The contrast between this man and the others I had just been talking to so moved me that I slapped him across the face with the gloves I was carrying in my hand, shook him, and called him a coward, and told him to get back to his outfit and try to be a man.

When I left I told the officer who was with me that I hoped I had made a man of him, and that if so, I had saved an immortal soul.

The other practically identical incident occurred on August 10, 1943.

I had just talked to over a hundred wounded, the last of whom had lost his right arm and was joking about it when I came on a second man who also told men, "He could not take it." I simply shook him, cussed him out, and told the hospital to return him to his outfit.

There is no possible doubt that my methods were too forthright and very ill-chosen. They will not be repeated, even though my own experience and that of others has indicated that under similar conditions, a slap in the face and a little rough talk is all that is needed to restore composure to hysterical and nervously upset people.

My greatest fault was my failure to appreciate the fact that men who have temporarily or permanently lost their nerve are physically sick at the time.

The thought that hurts me most is that through my acts I have given the impression of undue severity to soldiers. No one has visited more wounded or worked harder and longer to insure the health and comfort of our soldiers.

On those occasions when I have reprimanded men I have done so to correct breaches or discipline which, were they committed in battle, would probably result in the death or wounding of the individual. It is my firm belief that officers who permit breaches of discipline are potential murderers.

Further, it is a well-known fact that for every soldier I have gotten after, there are hundreds whom I have stopped to compliment.

General Eisenhower wrote me a forceful personal letter very rightly calling my attention to the bad effects may action had on public opinion and directing me to make certain amends.

These amends were as follows: I apologized to the two men. I called in the medical personnel who witnessed the incidents, explained to them the reasons for my action, and my regret for the same. I made a speech to each of the divisions telling the men what they were fighting for, and emphasizing how proud I was of them. I ended by saying that if any of them felt I had been too severe I apologized, but for every man I had corrected for this own good, I had complimented a thousand.

Any other prejudicial statements concerning me as an officer or soldier are not true.

## KOREMATSU V. UNITED STATES (1944)

The equal protection clause of the 14th Amendment did little to protect the civil rights of blacks in the first half of the Twentieth Century, and it did nothing to prevent the Supreme Court from endorsing the internment

---

Korematsu v. United States, 323 U. S. 214 (1944).

of Japanese-Americans on the West Coast during World War II, based on the assumption that an entire race was "suspect" as a threat to national security. Since it proved impossible to discover who of Japanese ancestry was loyal and who was disloyal, the military resorted to the exclusion of <u>all</u> people of this racial group from certain west coast areas. The majority on the Court upheld a conviction for violating a military order to this effect. Justice Black delivered the court's opinion. He likened this case to an earlier one, in which a curfew for Japanese-Americans was upheld.

[E]xclusion of those of Japanese origin was deemed necessary because of the presence of an unascertained number of disloyal members of the group, most of whom we have no doubt were loyal to this country. It was because we could not reject the finding of the military authorities that it was impossible to bring about an immediate segregation of the disloyal from the loyal that we sustained the validity of the curfew order as applying to the whole group. In the instant case, temporary exclusion of the entire group was rested by the military on the same ground. . . . That there were members of the group who retained loyalties to Japan has been confirmed by investigations made subsequent to the exclusion. Approximately five thousand American citizens of Japanese ancestry refused to swear unqualified allegiance to the United States and to renounce allegiance to the Japanese Emperor, and several thousand evacuees requested repatriation to Japan. . . .

[W]e are not unmindful of the hardships imposed by it upon a large group of American citizens. . . . But hardships are part of war, and war is an aggregation of hardships. . . . Compulsory exclusion of large groups of citizens from their homes, except under circumstances of direst emergency and peril, is inconsistent with our basic governmental institutions. But when under conditions of modern warfare our shores are threatened by hostile forces, the power to protect must be commensurate with the threatened danger. . . .

Korematsu was not excluded from the Military Area because of hostility to him or his race. He <u>was</u> excluded because we are at war with the Japanese Empire, because the properly constituted military authorities feared an invasion of our West Coast and felt constrained to take proper security measures, because they decided that the military urgency of the situation demanded that all citizens of Japanese ancestry be segregated from the West Coast temporarily, and finally, because Congress, reposing its confidence in this time of war in our military leaders—as inevitably it must—determined that they should have the power to do just this. There was evidence of disloyalty on the part of some, the military authorities considered that the need for action was great, and time was short. We cannot—by availing ourselves of the calm perspective of hindsight—now say that at that time these actions were unjustified. . . .

Mr. Justice MURPHY, dissenting.

This exclusion of "all persons of Japanese ancestry, both alien and non-alien," from the Pacific Coast area on a plea of military necessity in the absence of martial law ought not to be approved. Such exclusion goes over "the very brink of constitutional power" and falls into the ugly abyss of racism.

In dealing with matters relating to the prosecution and progress of a war, we must accord great respect and consideration to the judgments of the military authorities who are on the scene and who have full knowledge of the military facts. The scope of their discretion must, as a matter of necessity and common sense, be wide. . . .

At the same time, however, it is essential that there be definite limits to military discretion, especially where martial law has not been declared. Individuals must not be left impoverished of their constitutional rights on a plea of military necessity that has neither substance nor support. Thus, like other claims conflicting with the asserted constitutional rights of the individual, the military claim must subject itself to the judicial process of having its reasonableness determined and its conflicts with other interests reconciled. . . .

The judicial test of whether the Government, on a plea of military necessity, can validly deprive an individual of any of his constitutional rights is whether the deprivation is reasonably related to a public danger that is so "immediate, imminent, and impending" as not to admit of delay and not to permit the intervention of ordinary constitutional processes to alleviate the danger. . . . Being an obvious racial discrimination, the order deprives all those within its scope of the equal protection of the laws as guaranteed by the Fifth Amendment. It further deprives these individuals of their constitutional rights to live and work where they will, to establish a home where they choose and to move about freely. In excommunicating them without benefit of hearings, this order also deprives them of all their constitutional rights to procedural due process. Yet no reasonable relation to an "immediate, imminent, and impending" public danger is evident to support this racial restriction which is one of the most sweeping and complete deprivations of constitutional rights in the history of this nation in the absence of martial law.

It must be conceded that the military and naval situation in the spring of 1942 was such as to generate a very real fear of invasion of the Pacific Coast, accompanied by fears of sabotage and espionage in that area. The military command was therefore justified in adopting all reasonable means necessary to combat these dangers. . . . [I]t is necessary only that the action have some reasonable relation to the removal of the dangers of invasion, sabotage and espionage. But the exclusion, either temporarily or permanently, of all persons with Japanese blood in their veins has no such reasonable relation. And that relation is lacking because the exclusion order necessarily must rely for its reasonableness upon the assumption that <u>all</u> persons of Japanese ancestry may have a dangerous tendency to commit sabotage and espionage and to aid our Japanese enemy in other ways. It is difficult to believe that reason, logic or experience could be marshalled in support of such an assumption. . . .

[T]o infer that examples of individual disloyalty prove group disloyalty and justify discriminatory action against the entire group is to deny that under our system of law individual guilt is the sole basis for deprivation of rights. Moreover, this inference, which is at the very heart of the evacuation orders, has been used in support of the abhorrent and despicable treatment of minority groups by the dictatorial tyrannies which this nation is now pledged to destroy. To give constitutional sanction to that inference in this case, however well-intentioned may have been the military command on the Pacific Coast, is to adopt one of the cruelest of the rationales used by our enemies to destroy the dignity of the individual and to encourage and open the door to discriminatory actions against other minority groups in the passions of tomorrow. . . .

Moreover, there was no adequate proof that the Federal Bureau of Investigation and the military and naval intelligence services did not have the espionage and sabotage situation well in hand during this long period. Nor is there any denial of the fact that not one person of Japanese ancestry was accused or convicted of espionage or sabotage after Pearl Harbor while they were still free, a fact which is some evidence of the loyalty of the vast majority of these individuals and of the effectiveness of the established methods of combatting these evils. . . .

I dissent, therefore, from this legalization of racism.

## THE (YALTA) CRIMEA CONFERENCE (1945)

In February 1945, the Big Three leaders--Roosevelt, Churchill, and Stalin--met at the summer palace of a former czar on the Crimean peninsula in the Black Sea. With the impending victory over Nazi Germany, the three leaders turned more of their attention to the shape of the postwar world. The decisions reached at the Yalta Conference remain controversial even today.

(a) Communique Issued at the End of the Conference [February 11, 1945]

The following statement is made by the Prime Minister of Great Britain, the President of the United States of America, and the Chairman of the Council of Peoples' Commissars of the Union of Soviet Socialist Republics on the results of the Crimean Conference:
[I. The Defeat of Germany] We have considered and determined the military plans of the three allied powers for the final defeat of the common enemy. . . . The timing, scope and coordination of new and even more powerful blows to be launched by our armies and air forces into the heart of Germany from the East, West, North and South have been fully agreed and planned in detail.

Our combined military plans will be made known only as we execute them, but we believe that the very close working partnership among the three staffs attained at this Conference will result in shortening the war. Meetings of the three staffs will be continued in the future whenever the need arises.

Nazi Germany is doomed. The German people will only make the cost of their defeat heavier to themselves by attempting to continue a hopeless resistance.
[II. The Occupation and Control of Germany] We have agreed on common policies and plans for enforcing the unconditional surrender terms which we shall

---

U. S. Department of State, Foreign Relations of the United States: The Conferences at Malta and Yalta, 1945 (Washington, D.C., 1955), pp. 968-984.

impose together on Nazi Germany after German armed resistance has been finally crushed. These terms will not be made known until the final defeat of Germany has been accomplished. Under the agreed plan, the forces of the Three Powers will each occupy a separate zone of Germany. Coordinated administration and control has been provided for under the plan through a central Control Commission consisting of the Supreme Commanders of the Three Powers with headquarters in Berlin. It has been agreed that France should be invited by the Three Powers, if she should so desire, to take over a zone of occupation, and to participate as a fourth member of the Control Commission. The limits of the French zone will be agreed by the four governments concerned through their representatives on the European Advisory Commission.

It is our inflexible purpose to destroy German militarism and Nazism and to ensure that Germany will never again be able to disturb the peace of the world. We are determined to disarm and disband all German armed forces; break up for all time the German General Staff that has repeatedly contrived the resurgence of German militarism; remove or destroy all German military equipment; eliminate or control all German industry that could be used for military production; bring all war criminals to just and swift punishment and exact reparation in kind for the destruction wrought by the Germans; wipe out the Nazi party, Nazi laws, organizations and institutions, remove all Nazi and militarist influences from public office and from the cultural and economic life of the German people; and take in harmony such other measures in Germany as may be necessary to the future peace and safety of the world. It is not our purpose to destroy the people of Germany, but only when Nazism and Militarism have been extirpated will there be hope for a decent life for Germans, and a place for them in the comity of nations.

[III. Reparation by Germany] We have considered the question of the damage caused by Germany to the Allied Nations in this war and recognized it as just that Germany be obliged to make compensation for this damage in kind to the greatest extent possible. A Commission for the Compensation of Damage will be established. . . .

[IV. United Nations Conference] We are resolved upon the earliest possible establishment with our allies of a general international organization to maintain peace and security. We believe that this is essential, both to prevent aggression and to remove the political, economic and social causes of war through the close and continuing collaboration of all peace-loving peoples.

The foundations were laid at Dumbarton Oaks. On the important question of voting procedure, however, agreement was not there reached. The present conference has been able to resolve this difficulty.

We have agreed that a Conference of United Nations should be called to meet at San Francisco in the United States on April 25th, 1945, to prepare the charter of such an organization, along the lines proposed in the informal conversations at Dumbarton Oaks.

The Government of China and the Provisional Government of France will be immediately consulted and invited to sponsor invitations to the Conference jointly with the Governments of the United States, Great Britain and the Union of Soviet Socialist Republics. As soon as the consultation with China and France has been completed, the text of the proposals on voting procedure will be made public.

[V. Declaration on Liberated Europe] We have drawn up and subscribed to a Declaration on liberated Europe. This Declaration provides for concerting the policies of the three Powers and for joint action by them in meeting the political and economic problems of liberated Europe in accordance with democratic principles. The text of the Declaration is as follows:

The Premier of the Union of Soviet Socialist Republics, the Prime Minister of the United Kingdom, and the President of the United States of America have consulted with each other in the common interests of the peoples of their countries and those of liberated Europe. They jointly declare their mutual agreement to concert during the temporary period of instability in liberated Europe the policies of their three governments in assisting the peoples liberated from the domination of Nazi Germany and the peoples of the former Axis satellite states of Europe to solve by democratic means their pressing political and economic problems.

The establishment of order in Europe and the rebuilding of national economic life must be achieved by processes which will enable the liberated peoples to destroy the last vestiges of Nazism and Fascism and to creat[e] democratic institutions of their own choice. This is a principle of the Atlantic Charter--the right of all peoples to choose the form of government under which they will live--the restoration of sovereign rights and self-government to those peoples who have been forcibly deprived of them by the aggressor nations.

To foster the conditions in which the liberated peoples may exercise these rights, the three governments will jointly assist the people in any European liberated state or former Axis satellite state in Europe where in their judgment conditions require (a) to establish conditions of internal peace; (b) to carry out emergency measures for the relief of distressed people; (c) to form interim governmental authorities broadly representative of all democratic elements in the population and pledged to the earliest possible establishment through free elections of governments responsive to the will of the people; and (d) to facilitate where necessary the holding of such elections.

The three governments will consult the other United Nations and provisional authorities or other governments in Europe when matters of direct interest to them are under consideration.

When, in the opinion of the three governments, conditions in any European liberated state or any former Axis satellite state in Europe make such action necessary, they will immediately consult together on the neasures necessary to discharge the joint responsibilities set forth in this declaration.

By this declaration we reaffirm our faith in the principles of the Atlantic Charter, our pledge in the Declaration by the United Nations, and our determination to build in cooperation with other peace-loving nations a world order under law, dedicated to peace, security, freedom and the general well-being of all mankind. . . .

[VI. Poland] We came to the Crimea Conference resolved to settle our differences about Poland. We discussed fully all aspects of the question. We reaffirm our common desire to see established a strong, free, independent and democratic Poland. As a result of our discussions we have agreed on the conditions in which a new Polish Provisional Government of National Unity may be formed in such a manner as to command recognition by the three major powers.

The agreement reached is as follows:

A new situation has been created in Poland as a result of her complete liberation by the Red Army. This calls for the establishment of a Polish Provisional Government which can be more broadly based than was possible before the recent liberation of western Poland. The Provisional Government which is now functioning in Poland should therefore be reorganized on a broader democratic basis with the inclusion of democratic leaders from Poland itself and from Poles abroad. This new Government should then be called the Polish Provisional Government of National Unity.

[IX Unity for Peace As For War] Our meeting here in the Crimea has reaffirmed our common determination to maintain and strengthen in the peace to come that unity of purpose and of action which has made victory possible and certain for the United Nations in this war. We believe that this is a sacred obligation which our Governments owe to our peoples and to all the peoples of the world.

Only with continuing and growing co-operation and understanding among our three countries and among all the peace-loving nations can the highest aspiration of humanity be realized--a secure and lasting peace which will, in the words of the Atlantic Charter, "afford assurance that all the men in all the lands may live out their lives in freedom from fear and want".

Victory in this war and establishment of the proposed international organization will provide the greatest opportunity in all history to create in the years to come the essential conditions of such a peace.

(b) Agreement Regarding Entry of the Soviet Union Into the War Against Japan [February 11, 1945]

The leaders of the three Great Powers--the Soviet Union, the United States of America and Great Britain--have agreed that in two or three months after Germany has surrendered and the war in Europe has terminated the Soviet Union shall enter into the war against Japan on the side of the Allies on condition that:

  1. The status quo in Outer-Mongolia (The Mongolian People's Republic) shall be preserved;
  2. The former rights of Russia violated by the treacherous attack of Japan in 1904 shall be restored, viz:
  (a) the southern part of Sakhalin as well as all the islands adjacent to it shall be returned to the Soviet Union,
  (b) the commercial port of Dairen shall be internationalized, the preeminent interests of the Soviet Union in this port being safeguarded and the lease of Port Arthur as a naval base of the USSR restored,
  (c) the Chinese-Eastern Railroad and the South-Manchurian Railroad which provides an outlet to Dairen shall be jointly operated by the establishment of a joint Soviet-Chinese Company it being understood that the preeminent interests of the Soviet Union shall be safeguarded and that China shall retain full sovereignty in Manchuria;
  3. The Kuril islands shall be handed over to the Soviet Union.

It is understood, that the agreement concerning Outer-Mongolia and the ports and railroads referred to above will require concurrence of Generalissimo Chiang Kai-Shek. The President will take measures in order to obtain this concurrence on advice from Marshal Stalin.

The Heads of the three Great Powers have agreed that these claims of the Soviet Union shall be unquestionably fulfilled after Japan has been defeated.

For its part the Soviet Union expresses its readiness to conclude with the National Government of China a pact of friendship and alliance between the USSR and China in order to render assistance to China with its armed forces for the purpose of liberating China from the Japanese yoke.

# THE DECISION TO USE THE ATOMIC BOMB (1945)

The decision to use the atomic bomb remains one of the most controversial issues in American history. As the following selection of documents indicates, this debate embraces several different perspectives.

(a) "Proclamation Calling for the Surrender of Japan" (United States, China, and United Kingdom at Potsdam), July 26, 1945[1]

The result of the futile and senseless German resistance to the might of the aroused free peoples of the world stands forth in awful clarity as an example to the people of Japan. The might that now converges on Japan is immeasurably greater than that which, when applied to the resisting Nazis, necessarily laid waste to the lands, the industry and the method of life of the whole German people. The full application of our military power, backed by our resolve, <u>will</u> mean the inevitable and complete destruction of the Japanese armed forces and just as inevitably the utter devastation of the Japanese homeland. . . .

We call upon the Government of Japan to proclaim now the unconditional surrender of all the Japanese armed forces, and to provide proper and adequate assurances of their good faith in such action. The alternative for Japan is prompt and utter destruction.

(b) Truman's Address to the Nation (August 9, 1945)[2]

The world will note that the first atomic bomb was dropped on Hiroshima, a military base. That was because we wished in this first attack to avoid in so far as possible, the killing of civilians. But that attack is only a warning of things to come. If Japan does not surrender, bombs will have to be dropped on war industries and, unfortunately, thousands of civilian lives will be lost. I urge Japanese civilians to leave industrial cities immediately, and save themselves from destruction.

I realize the tragic significance of the atomic bomb.

Its production and its use were not lightly undertaken by this Government. But we knew that our enemies were on the search for it. We know now how close they were to finding it. And we knew the disaster which would come to this nation, to all peaceful nations, to all civilization, if they had found it first.

That is why we felt compelled to undertake the long and uncertain and costly labor of discovery and production.

We won the race of discovery against the Germans.

Having found the bomb we have used it. We have used it against those who attacked us without warning at Pearl Harbor, against those who have starved and beaten and executed American prisoners of war, against those who have abandoned all pretense of obeying international laws of warfare. We have used it in order to shorten the agony of war, in order to save the lives of thousands and thousands of young Americans.

We shall continue to use it until we completely destroy Japan's power to make war. Only a Japanese surrender will stop us.

---

[1] U. S. Department of State, <u>Foreign Relations of the United States, The Conference of Berlin, 1945</u> (Washington, D.C., 1960), II, 1474-1476.

[2] U. S. Department of State, <u>Bulletin</u> (August 12, 1945), XIII, 212-13.

The atomic bomb is too dangerous to be loose in a lawless world. That is why Great Britain, Canada, and the United States, who have the secret of its production, do not intend to reveal that secret until means have been found to control the bomb so as to protect ourselves and the rest of the world from the danger of total destruction.

(c) Lord Mountbatten (Supreme Allied Commander, South East Asia) to Douglas MacArthur (August 16, 1945)[1]

I am sure that your views coincide with mine, namely that it will be the greatest mistake to be soft with the Japanese. The fact that you have been prevented from inflicting the crushing victory with OLYMPIC and CORONET [invasion of Japan] would undoubtedly have produced and that I have been prevented from carrying our ZIPPER and MAILFIST [Malaya-Singapore-NEI] will, I fear, enable the Japanese leaders to delude their people into thinking they were defeated only by the scientists and not in battle, unless we can so humble them that the completeness of the defeat is brought home to them.

Normally I am not a vindictive person, but I cannot help feeling that unless we really are tough with all the Japanese leaders they will be able to build themselves up eventually for another war. . . .

Although everyone must be delighted at the early termination of the war, nevertheless, I cannot refrain from expressing my feelings to you on realizing that the tremendous operations that you were to command will not now take place.

(d) Committee on Social and Political Implications, "Report to the Secretary of War" (June 1945)[2]

The development of nuclear power not only constitutes an important addition to the technological and military power of the United States, but also creates grave political and economic problems for the future of this country.

Nuclear bombs cannot possibly remain a "secret weapon" at the exclusive disposal of this country for more than a few years. The scientific facts on which their construction is based are well known to scientists of other countries. Unless an effective international control of nuclear explosives is instituted, a race for nuclear armaments is certain to ensue following the first revelation of our possession of nuclear weapons to the world. Within ten years other countries may have nuclear bombs, each of which, weighing less than a ton, could destroy an urban area of more than ten square miles. In the war to which such an armaments race is likely to lead, the United States, with its agglomeration of population and industry in comparatively few metropolitan districts, will be at a disadvantage compared to nations whose population and industry are scattered over large areas.

We believe that these considerations make the use of nuclear bombs for an early unannounced attack against Japan inadvisable. If the United States were to be the first to release this new means of indiscriminate destruction

---

[1] Major General Sir Ronald C. Penney Papers, file 5/11, University of London, King's College, London, Liddell Hart Centre for Military Archives, London.

[2] Reprinted by permission of The Bulletin of the Atomic Scientists, a magazine of science and world affairs. Copyright (c) 1946 by the Educational Foundation for Nuclear Science, Chicago, IL 60637.

upon mankind, she would sacrifice public support throughout the world, precipitate the race for armaments, and prejudice the possibility of reaching an international agreement on the future control of such weapons.

Much more favorable conditions for the eventual achievement of such an agreement could be created if nuclear bombs were first revealed to the world by a demonstration in an appropriately selected uninhabited area.

In case chances for the establishment of an effective international control of nuclear weapons should have to be considered slight at the present time, then not only the use of these weapons against Japan, but even their early demonstration, may be contrary to the interests of this country. A postponement of such a demonstration will have in this case the advantage of delaying the beginning of the nuclear armaments race as long as possible.

If the government should decide in favor of an early demonstration of nuclear weapons, it will then have the possibility of taking into account the public opinion of this country and of the other nations before deciding whether these weapons should be used against Japan. In this way, other nations may assume a share of responsibility for such a fateful decision.

(e) Editoral, "America's Atomic Atrocity" (August 29, 1945)

Something like a moral earthquake has followed the dropping of atomic bombs on two Japanese cities. Its continued tremors throughout the world have diverted attention even from the military victory itself. . . . It is our belief that the use made of the atomic bomb has placed our nation in an indefensible moral position.

We do not propose to debate the issue of military necessity, though the facts are clearly on one side of this issue. The atomic bomb was used at a time when Japan's navy was sunk, her airforce virtually destroyed, her homeland surrounded, her supplies cut off, and our forces poised for the final stroke. Recognition of her imminent defeat could be read between the lines of every Japanese communique. Neither do we intend to challenge Mr. Churchill's highly speculative assertion that the use of the bomb saved the lives of more than one million American and 250,000 British soldiers. We believe, however, that these lives could have been saved had our government followed a different course, more honorable and more humane. Our leaders seem not to have weighed the moral considerations involved. No sooner was the bomb ready than it was rushed to the front and dropped on two helpless cities, destroying more lives than the United States has lost in the entire war.

Perhaps it was inevitable that the bomb would ultimately be employed to bring Japan to the point of surrender. . . . But there was no military advantage in hurling the bomb upon Japan without warning. The least we might have done was to announce to our foe that we possessed the atomic bomb; that its destructive power was beyond anything known in warfare; and that its terrible effectiveness had been experimentally demonstrated in this country. We could thus have warned Japan of what was in store for her unless she surrendered immediately. If she doubted the good faith of our representations, it would have been a simple matter to select a demonstration target in the enemy's own country at a place where the loss of human life would be a minimum.

If, despite such warning, Japan had still held out, we would have been in a far less questionable position had we then dropped the bombs on Hiroshima and Nagasaki. At least our record of deliberation and ample warning would have been clear. Instead, with brutal disregard of any principle of humanity we "demonstrated" the bomb on two great cities, utterly extinguishing them.

Christian Century (August 29, 1945), LXII, 974-76.

This course has placed the United States in a bad light throughout the world. What the use of poison gas did to the reputation of Germany in World War I, the use of the atomic bomb has done for the reputation of the United States in World War II. Our future security is menaced by our own act, and our influence for justice and humanity in international affairs has been sadly crippled. . . .

The future is further complicated by the fact that the Christian church, which holds in its hands the only power of radical reconciliation, has also suffered a heavy blow. The atomic bomb can fairly be said to have struck Christianity itself. Only Christianity has the required resources for the problem of reconciliation at the deep spiritual level where it must finally be resolved. The Christian people of this country have been looking forward to the revival of their mission in Japan on an unprecedented scale, and on a broader and more cooperative basis than in the past. The same bomb that estinguished Hiroshima and Nagasaki struck this missionary enterprise. It will take endless explaining to the Japanese to dissociate Christianity, the Christian church and the Christian mission from the act of the American government in unleashing the atomic bomb. This act which has put the United States on the moral defensive has also put the Christian church on the defensive throughout the world and especially in Japan. . . .

With the ending of the war the time has now come for the Christian Church in this country to gather the fruit of its dissociation from the conflict. In no previous war has the church so boldly and generally seized the opportunity to be the church, and not a trailer behind the war chariot of the state. The widespread adoption of the concept that the church was not at war, and the almost universal conformity of its utterances and practice to this concept, should now come to fruition in the opening of the channels of ecumenical fellowship with the churches in all enemy countries, and particularly in Japan. But a church which condemns war and will not be a party to it, has a peculiar resonsibility to condemn those acts of war which trespass the limits beyond which the Christian conscience, though distressed by all the frightful dilemmas in which it is placed by war itself, will not knowingly go.

(f) The Secretary of War Explains the Decision to Use the Atomic Bomb (1947)

The policy adopted and steadily pursued by President Roosevelt and his advisers was a simple one. It was to spare no effort in securing the earliest possible successful development of an atomic weapon. The reasons for this policy were equally simple. The original experimental achievement of atomic fission had occurred in Germany in 1938, and it was known that the Germans had continued their experiments. In 1941 and 1942 they were believed to be ahead of us, and it was vital that they should not be the first to bring atomic weapons into the field of battle. Furthermore, if we should be the first to develop the weapon, we should have a great new instrument for shortening the war and minimizing destruction. At no time, from 1941 to 1945, did I ever hear it suggested by the President, or by any other responsible member of the government, that atomic energy should not be used in the war. All of us of course understood the terrible responsibility involved in our attempt to

---

Approximately 800 words abridged from "The Decision to Use the Atomic Bomb" as it appeared in Harper's Magazine, later incorporated in chapter "The Atomic Bomb and the Surrender of Japan" from On Active Service in Peace and War by Henry L. Stimson and McGeorge Bundy, (c) 1947 by Henry L. Stimson. Reprinted by permission of Harper & Row, Publishers, Inc.

unlock the doors to such a devastating weapon; President Roosevelt particularly spoke to me many times of his own awareness of the catastrophic potentialities of our work. But we were at war, and the work must be done. I therefore emphasize that it was our common objective, throughout the war, to be the first to produce an atomic weapon and use it. The possible atomic weapon was considered to be a new and tremendously powerful explosive, as legitimate as any other of the deadly explosive weapons of modern war. . . .

By the nature of atomic chain reactions, it was impossible to state with certainty that we had succeeded until a bomb had actually exploded in a full-scale experiment; nevertheless it was considered exceedingly probable that we should by midsummer [1945] have successfully detonated the first atomic bomb. . . .

On June 1, after its discussions with the Scientific Panel, the Interim Committee unanimously adopted the following recommendations:

(1) The bomb should be used against Japan as soon as possible.

(2) It should be used on a dual target--that is, a military installation or war plant surrounded by or adjacent to houses and other buildings most susceptible to damage, and

(3) It should be used without prior warning [of the nature of the weapon]. . . .

In reaching these conclusions the Interim Committee carefully considered such alternatives as a detailed advance warning or a demonstration in some uninhabited area. Both of these suggestions were discarded as impractical. They were not regarded as likely to be effective in compelling a surrender of Japan, and both of them involved serious risks. Even the New Mexico test would not give final proof that any given bomb was certain to explode when dropped from an airplane. Quite apart from the generally unfamiliar nature of atomic explosives, there was the whole problem of exploding a bomb at a predetermined height in the air by a complicated mechanism which could not be tested in the static test of New Mexico. Nothing would have been more damaging to our effort to obtain surrender than a warning or a demonstration followed by a dud--and this was a real possibility. Furthermore, we had no bombs to waste. It was vital that a sufficient effect be quickly obtained with the few we had. . . .

Hiroshima was bombed on August 6, and Nagasaki on August 9. These two cities were active working parts of the Japanese war effort. One was an army center; the other was naval and industrial. Hiroshima was the headquarters of the Japanese Army defending southern Japan and was a major military storage and assembly point. Nagasaki was a major seaport and it contained several large industrial plants of great wartime importance. . . .

I have tried to give an accurate account of my own personal observations of the circumstances which led up to the use of the atomic bomb and the reasons which underlay our use of it. To me they have always seemed compelling and clear, and I cannot see how any person vested with such responsbilities as mine could have taken any other course or given any other advice to his chiefs. . . .

My chief purpose was to end the war in victory with the least possible cost in the lives of the men in the armies which I had helped to raise. In the light of the alternatives which, on a fair estimate, were open to us I believe that no man, in our position and subject to our responsibilities, holding in his hands a weapon of such possibilities for accomplishing this purpose and saving those lives, could have failed to use it and afterwards looked his countrymen in the face.

(g) An Eyewitness Account: Fr. John A. Siemes, S.J. (1945)

August 6th began in a bright, clear, summer morning. About seven o'clock, there was an air raid alarm which we had heard almost every day and a few planes appeared over the city. No one paid any attention and at about eight o'clock, the all-clear was sounded. . . .

Suddenly--the time is approximately 8:14--the whole valley is filled by a garish light which resembles the magnesium light used in photography, and I am conscious of a wave of heat. I jump to the window to find out the cause of this remarkable phenomenon, but I see nothing more than that brillant yellow light. As I make for the door, it doesn't occur to me that the light might have something to do with enemy planes. On the way from the window, I hear a moderately loud explosion which seems to come from a distance and, at the same time, the windows are broken in with a loud crash. There has been an interval of perhaps ten seconds since the flash of light. I am sprayed by fragments of glass. The entire window frame has been forced into the room. I realize now that a bomb has burst and I am under the impression that it exploded directly over our house or in the immediate vicinity. . . .

Perhaps a half-hour after the explosion, a procession of people begins to stream up the valley from the city [2 kms away]. The crowd thickens continuously. A few come up the road to our house. We give them first aid and bring them into the chapel, which we have in the meantime cleaned and cleared of wreckage, and put them to rest on the straw mats which constitute the floor of Japanese houses. A few display horrible wounds of the extremities and back. The small quantity of fat which we possessed during this time of war was soon used up in the care of the burns. . . .

More and more of the injured come to us. The least injured drag the more seriously wounded. There are wounded soldiers, and mothers carrying burned children in their arms. From the houses of the farmers in the valley comes word: "Our houses are full of wounded and dying. Can you help, at least by taking the worst cases?" The wounded come from the sections at the edge of the city. They saw the bright light, their houses collapsed and buried the inmates in their rooms. Those that were in the open suffered instantaneous burns, particularly on the lightly clothed or unclothed parts of the body. Numerous fires sprang up which soon consumed the entire district. . . .

The magnitude of the disaster that befell Hiroshima on August 6th was only slowly pieced together in my mind. I lived through the catastrophe and saw it only in flashes, which only gradually were merged to give me a total picture. What actually happened simultaneously in the city as a whole is as follows: As a result of the explosion of the bomb at 8:15, almost the entire city was destroyed at a single blow. Only small outlying districts in the southern and eastern parts of the town escaped complete destruction. The bomb exploded over the center of the city. As a result of the blast, the small Japanese houses in a diameter of five kilometers, which compressed 99% of the city, collapsed or were blown up. Those who were in the houses were buried in the ruins. Those who were in the open sustained burns resulting from contact with the substance or rays emitted by the bomb. Where the substance struck in quantity, fires sprang up. These spread rapidly.

The heat which rose from the center created a whirlwind which was effective in spreading fire throughout the whole city. Those who had been caught beneath the ruins and who could not be freed rapidly, and those who had

---

U. S. Air force, Historical Records Center, Maxwell AFB, Alabama, 137.717-92A.

been caught by the flames, became casualties. As much as six kilometers from the center of the explosion, all houses were damaged and many collapsed and caught fire. Even fifteen kilometers away, windows were broken. . . .

How many people were a sacrifice to this bomb? Those who had lived through the catastrophe placed the number of dead at at least 100,000. Hiroshima had a population of 400,000. . . .

Thousands of wounded who died later could doubtless have been rescued had they received proper treatment and care, but rescue work in a catastrophe of this magnitude had not been envisioned; since the whole city had been knocked out at a blow, everything which had been prepared for emergency work was lost, and no preparation had been made for rescue work in the outlying districts. Many of the wounded also died because they had been weakened by under-nourishment and consequently lacked in strength to recover. Those who had their normal strength and who received good care slowly healed the burns which had been occasioned by the bomb. There were also cases, however, whose prognosis seemed good who died suddenly. There were also some who had only small external wounds who died within a week or later, after an inflammation of the pharynx and oral cavity had taken place. We thought at first that this was the result of inhalation of the substance of the bomb. Later, a commission established the thesis that gamma rays had been given out at the time of the explosion, following which the internal organs had been injured in a manner resembling that consequent upon Roentgen irradiation. This produces a diminution in the number of the white corpuscles. . . .

None of us in those days heard a single outburst against the Americans on the part of the Japanese, nor was there any evidence of a vengeful spirit. . . . After the victories at the beginning of the war, the enemy was rather looked down upon, but when allied offensive gathered momentum and especially after the advent of the majestic B-29's, the technical skill of America became an object of wonder and admiration.


WINSTON CHURCHILL ON THE IRON CURTAIN IN EUROPE (1946)

Few speeches captured the spirit of the close of the Allied wartime coalition and the onset of the Cold War more effectively than did the famous Churchill speech at Fulton, Missouri. The ex-Prime Minister commanded global respect for his wartime leadership--and his oratorical skills. At Fulton (and with President Truman in the audience) Churchill warned of the growing menace from the Soviet Union. His use of the term "the iron curtain" became fixed in the English language to describe the divisive conditions in Europe.

---

Randolph Churchill, ed., The Sinews of Peace, (Boston, 1949), pp. 93-105. First published in the United States in 1949. Reprinted by permission of Houghton Mifflin Company.

The United States stands at this time at the pinnacle of world power. It is a solemn moment for the American Democracy. For with primacy in power is also joined an awe-inspiring accountability to the future. If you look around you, you must feel not only the sense of duty done but also you must feel anxiety lest you fall below the level of achievement. Opportunity is here now, clear and shining for both our countries. To reject it or ignore it or fritter it away wil bring upon us all the the long reproaches of the after-time. It is necessary that constancy of mind, persistency of purpose, and the grand simplicity of decision shall guide and rule the conduct of the English-speaking peoples in peace as they did in war. We must, and I believe we shall, prove ourselves equal to this severe requirement. . . .

. . . .A world organisation has already been erected for the prime purpose of preventing war. UNO, the successor of the League of Nations, with the decisive addition of the United States and all that that means, is already at work. We must make sure that its work is fruitful, that it is a reality and not a sham, that it is a force for action, and not merely a frothing of words, that it is a true temple of peace in which the shields of many nations can some day be hung up and not merely a cockpit in a Tower of Babel. Before we cast away the solid assurances of national armaments for self-preservation we must be certain that our temple is built, not upon shifting sands or quagmires, but upon the rock. Anyone can see with his eyes open that our path will be difficult and also long, but if we persevere together as we did in the two world wars—though not, alas, in the interval between them—I cannot doubt that we shall achieve our common purpose in the end. . . .

. . . .Neither the sure prevention of war, nor the continuous rise of world organisation will be gained without what I have called the fraternal association of the English-speaking peoples. This means a special relationship between the British Commonwealth and Empire and the United States. This is no time for generalities, and I will venture to be precise. Fraternal association requires not only the growing friendship and mutual understanding between our two vast but kindred systems of society, but the continuance of the intimate relationship between our military advisers, leading to common study of potential dangers, the similarity of weapons and manuals of instructions, and to the interchange of officers and cadets at technical colleges. It should carry with it the continuance of the present facilities for mutual security by the joint use of all Naval and Air Force bases in the possession of either country all over the world. . . .

There is however an important question we must ask ourselves. Would a special relationship between the United States and the British Commonwealth be inconsistent with our over-riding loyalties to the World Organisation? I reply that, on the contrary, it is probably the only means by which that organisation will achieve its full stature and strength. There are already the special United States relations with Canada which I have just mentioned, and there are the special relations between the United States and the South American Republics. We British have our twenty years Treaty of Collaboration and Mutual Assistance with Soviet Russia. I agree with Mr. Bevin, the Foreign Secretary of Great Britain, that it might well be a fifty years Treaty so far as we are concerned. We aim at nothing but mutual assistance and collaboration. The British have an alliance with Portugal unbroken since 1384, and which produced fruitful results at critical moments in the late war. None of these clash with the general interest of a world agreement, or a world organisation; on the contrary they help it. "In my father's house are many mansions." Special associations between members of the United Nations which have no aggressive point against any other country, which harbour no design incompatible with the Charter of the United Nations, far from being harmful, are beneficial and, as I believe, indispensable. . . .

A shadow has fallen upon the scenes so lately lighted by the Allied victory. Nobody knows what Soviet Russia and its Communist international organisation intends to do in the immediate future, or what are the limits, if any, to their expansive and proselytising tendencies. I have a strong admiration and regard for the valiant Russian people and for my wartime comrade, Marshal Stalin. There is deep sympathy and goodwill in Britain--and I doubt not here also--towards the peoples of all the Russias and a resolve to persevere through many differences and rebuffs in establishing lasting friendships. We understand the Russian need to be secure on her western frontiers by the removal of all possibility of German aggression. We welcome Russia to her rightful place among the leading nations of the world. We welcome her flag upon the seas. Above all, we welcome constant, frequent and growing contacts between the Russian people and our own people on both sides of the Atlantic. It is my duty however, for I am sure you would wish me to state the facts as I see them to you, to place before you certain facts about the present position in Europe.

From Stettin in the Baltic to Trieste in the Adriatic, an iron curtan has descended across the Continent. Behind that line lie all the capitals of the ancient states of Central and Eastern Europe. Warsaw, Berlin, Prague, Vienna, Budapest, Belgrade, Bucharest and Sofia, all these famous cities and the populations around them lie in what I must call the Soviet sphere, and all are subject in one form or another, not only to Soviet influence but to a very high and, in many cases, increasing measure of control from Moscow. Athens alone--Greece with its immortal glories--is free to decide its future at an election under British, American and French observation. The Russian-dominated Polish Government has been encouraged to make enormous and wrongful inroads upon Germany, and mass expulsions of millions of Germans on a scale grievous and undreamed-of are now taking place. The Communist parties, which were very small in all these Eastern States of Europe, have been raised to pre-eminence and power far beyond their numbers and are seeking everywhere to obtain totalitarian control. Police governments are prevailing in nearly every case, and so far, except in Czechoslovakia, there is no true democracy.

Turkey and Persia are both profoundly alarmed and disturbed at the claims which are being made upon them and at the pressure being exerted by the Moscow Government. An attempt is being made by the Russians in Berlin to build up a quasi-Communist party in their zone of Occupied Germany by showing special favours to groups of left-wing German leaders. At the end of the fighting last June, the American and British Armies withdrew westwards, in accordance with an earlier agreement, to a depth at some points of 150 miles upon a front of nearly four hundred miles, in order to allow our Russian allies to occupy this vast expanse of territory which the Western Democracies had conquered.

If now the Soviet Government tries, by separate action, to build up a pro-Communist Germany in their areas, this will cause new serious difficulties in the British and American zones, and will give the defeated Germans the power of putting themselves up to auction between the Soviets and the Western Democracies. Whatever conclusions may be drawn from these facts--and facts they are--this is certainly not the Liberated Europe we fought to build up. Nor is it one which contains the essentials of permanent peace.

The safety of the world requires a new unity in Europe, from which no nation should be permanently outcast. It is from the quarrels of the strong parent races in Europe that the world wars we have witnessed, or which occurred in former times, have sprung. . . .

Surely we should work with conscious purpose for a grand pacification of Europe, within the structure of the United Nations and in accordance with its Charter. That I feel is an open cause of policy of very great importance.

In front of the iron curtain which lies across Europe are other causes for anxiety. In Italy the Communist Party is seriously hampered by having to support the Communist-trained Marshal Tito's claims to former Italian territory at the head of the Adriatic. Nevertheless the future of Italy hangs in the balance. Again one cannot imagine a regenerated Europe without a strong France. All my public life I have worked for a strong France and I never lost faith in her destiny, even in the darkest hours. I will not lose faith now. However, in a great number of countries, far from the Russian frontiers and throughout the world, Communist fifth columns are established and work in complete unity and absolute obedience to the directions they receive from the Communist centre. Except in the British Commonwealth and in the United States where Communism is in its infancy, the Communist parties or fifth columns constitute a growing challenge and peril to Christian civilisation. These are sombre facts for anyone to have to recite on the morrow of a victory gained by so much splendid comradeship in arms and in the cause of freedom and democracy; but we should be most unwise not to face them squarely while time remains. . . .

From what I have seen of our Russian friends and Allies during the war, I am convinced that there is nothing they admire so much as strength, and there is nothing for which they have less respect than for weakness, especially military weakness. For that reason the old doctrine of a balance of power is unsound. We cannot afford, if we can help it, to work on narrow margins, offering temptations to a trial of strength. If the Western Democracies stand together in strict adherence to the principles of the United Nations Charter, their influence for furthering those principles will be immense and no one is likely to molest them. If however they become divided or falter in their duty and if these all-important years are allowed to slip away then indeed catastrophe may overwhelm us all.

Last time I saw it all coming and cried aloud to my own fellow-countrymen and to the world, but no one paid any attention. Up till the year 1933 or even 1935, Germay might have been saved from the awful fate which has overtaken her and we might all have been spared the miseries Hitler let loose upon mankind. There never was a war in all history easier to prevent by timely action than the one which has just desolated such great areas of the globe. It could have been prevented in my belief without the firing of a single shot, and Germany might be powerful, prosperous and honoured to-day; but no one would listen and one by one we were all sucked into the awful whirlpool. We surely must not let that happen again. This can only be achieved by reaching now, in 1946, a good understanding on all points with Russia under the general authority of the United Nations Organisation and by the maintenance of that good understanding through many peaceful years, by the world instrument, supported by the whole strength of the English-speaking world and all its connections. There is the solution which I respectfully offer to you in this Address to which I have given the title "The Sinews of Peace".

# GEORGE KENNAN ON CONTAINING THE SOVIET UNION (1947)

George F. Kennan, a foreign service officer and trained expert in Soviet affairs, introduced the concept of the containment of communism to President Truman and the foreign policy-making community in an article written under the pseudonym "Mr. X." What the article meant, and what action should be taken on the basis of the article's content, depended almost entirely on the predilections of the reader. Much controversy has raged over the article, and indeed over the Cold War whose policies were at least partially the result of "containment" thinking. This article is a seminal one for developing U.S. perceptions of the Soviet Union, and those perceptions have to a great degree governed the course of U.S. foreign policy from 1947 to the present day.

The political personality of Soviet power as we know it today is the product of ideology and circumstances: ideology inherited by the present Soviet leaders from the movement in which they had their political origin, and circumstances of the power which they now have exercised for nearly three decades in Russia. There can be few tasks of psychological analysis more difficult than to try to trace the interaction of these two forces and the relative role of each in the determination of official Soviet conduct. . . .

The circumstances of the immediate post-Revolution period--the existence in Russia of civil war and foreign intervention, together with the obvious fact that the Communists represented only a tiny minority of the Russian people--made the establishment of dictatorial power a necessity . . . . Now the outstanding circumstance concerning the Soviet regime is that down to the present day this process of political consolidation has never been completed and the men in the Kremlin have continued to be predominantly absorbed with the struggle to secure and make absolute the power which they seized in November 1917. They have endeavored to secure it primarily against forces at home, within Soviet society itself. But they have also endeavored to secure it against the outside world. For ideology, as we have seen, taught them that the outside world was hostile and that it was their duty eventually to overthrow the political forces beyond their borders.

. . . . [S]ince capitalism supposedly no longer existed in Russia and since it could not be admitted that there could be serious or widespread opposition to the Kremlin springing spontaneously from the liberated masses under its authority, it became necessary to justify the retention of the dictatorship by stressing the menace of capitalism abroad . . . .

Now the maintenance of this pattern of Soviet power, namely, the pursuit of unlimited authority domestically, accompanied by the cultivation of the semi-myth of implacable foreign hostility, has gone far to shape the actual machinery of Soviet power as we know it today. . . . The security of Soviet power came to rest on the iron discipline of the Party, on the severity and ubiquity of the secret police, and on the uncompromising economic monopolism of the state. . . . Today the major part of the structure of Soviet power is

---

"X" [George Kennan], "The Sources of Soviet Conduct," Foreign Affairs, XXV (July, 1947), 566-582. Excerpted by permission of Foreign Affairs, July, 1947. Copyright 1947 by the Council on Foreign Relations, Inc.

committed to the perfection of the dictatorship and to the maintenance of the concept of Russia as in a state of siege, with the enemy lowering beyond the walls. . . .

Of the original ideology, nothing has been officially junked. Belief is maintained in the basic badness of capitalism, in the inevitability of its destruction, in the obligation of the proletariat to assist in that destruction and to take power into its own hands. But stress has come to be laid primarily on those concepts which relate most specifically to the Soviet regime itself: to its position as the sole truly Socialist regime in a dark and misguided world, and to the relationships of power within it.

The first of these concepts is that of the innate antagonism between capitalism and Socialism. . . . It has profound implications for Russia's conduct as a member of international society. It means that there can never be on Moscow's side any sincere assumption of a community of aims between the Soviet Union and powers which are regarded as capitalist. It must invariably be assumed in Moscow that the aims of the capitalist world are antagonistic to the Soviet regime, and therefore to the interests of the peoples it controls. If the Soviet government occasionally sets its signature to documents which would indicate the contrary, this is to be regarded as a tactical maneuver permissible in dealing with the enemy (who is without honor) and should be taken in the spirit of <u>caveat emptor</u>. Basically, the antagonism remains. It is postulated. And from it flow many of the phenomena which we find disturbing in the Kremlin's conduct of foreign policy: the secretiveness, the lack of frankness, the duplicity, the war suspiciousness, and the basic unfriendliness of purpose. . . .

This means that we are going to continue for a long time to find the Russians difficult to deal with. It does not mean that they should be considered as embarked upon a do-or-die program to overthrow our society by a given date. The theory of the inevitability of the eventual fall of capitalism has the fortunate connotation that there is no hurry about it. . . .Meanwhile, what is vital is that the "Socialist fatherland"--. . . should be cherished and defended. . . .

Once a given party line has been laid down on a given issue of current policy, the whole Soviet governmental machine, including the mechanism of diplomacy, moves inexorably along the prescribed path, like a persistent toy automobile wound up and headed in a given direction, stopping only when it meets with some unanswerable force. The individuals who are the components of this machine are unamenable to argument or reason which comes to them from outside sources. . . .

But we have seen that the Kremlin is under no ideological compulsion to accomplish its purposes in a hurry. Like the Church, it is dealing in ideological concepts which are of long-term validity, and it can afford to be patient. . . . Thus the Kremlin has no compunction about retreating in the face of superior force. And being under the compulsion of no timetable, it does not get panicky under the necessity for such retreat. Its political action is a fluid stream which moves constantly, wherever it is permitted to move, toward a given goal. Its main concern is to make sure that it has filled every nook and cranny available to it in the basin of world power. But if it finds unassailable barriers in its path, it accepts these philosophically and accommodates itself to them. The main thing is that there should always be pressure, unceasing constant pressure, toward the desired goal. . . .

These considerations make Soviet diplomacy at once easier and more difficult to deal with than the diplomacy of individual aggressive leaders like Napoleon and Hitler. On the one hand it is more sensitive to contrary force, more ready to yield on individual sectors of the diplomatic front when that force is felt to be too strong, and thus more rational in the logic and rhetoric of power. On the other hand it cannot be easily defeated or discouraged by a single victory on the part of its opponents. And the patient persistence by which it is animated means that it can be effectively countered not by sporadic acts which represent the momentary whims of democratic opinion but only by intelligent long-range policies on the part of Russia's adversaries—policies no less steady in their purpose, and no less variegated and resourceful in their application, than those of the Soviet Union itself.

In these circumstances it is clear that the main element of any United States policy toward the Soviet Union must be that of a long-term, patient but firm and vigilant containment of Russian expansive tendencies. It is important to note, however, that such a policy has nothing to do with outward histrionics: with threats or blustering or superfluous gestures of outward "toughness." . . . they are highly conscious that loss of temper and of self-control is never a source of strength in political affairs. They are quick to exploit such evidences of weakness. For these reasons, it is a <u>sine qua non</u> of successful dealing with Russia that the foreign government in question should remain at all times cool and collected and that its demands on Russian policy should be put forward in such a manner as to leave the way open for a compliance not too detrimental to Russian prestige.

In the light of the above, it will be clearly seen that the Soviet pressure against the free institutions of the western world is something that can be contained by the adroit and vigilant application of counter-force at a series of constantly shifting geographical and political points, corresponding to the shifts and manoeuvres of Soviet policy, but which cannot be charmed or talked out of existence. . . .

[Kennan goes on to predict the decline of the Soviet dictatorship, if only the West is firm and vigilant.]

It is clear that the United States cannot expect in the foreseeable future to enjoy political intimacy with the Soviet regime. It must continue to regard the Soviet Union as a rival, not a partner, in the political arena. It must continue to expect that Soviet policies will reflect no abstract love of peace and stability, no real faith in the possibility of a permanent happy coexistence of the Socialist and capitalistic worlds, but rather a cautious, persistent pressure toward the disruption and weakening of all rival influence and rival power. . . .

It would be an exaggeration to say that American behavior unassisted and alone could exercise a power of life and death over the Communist movement and bring about the early fall of Soviet power in Russia. But the United States has it in its power to increase enormously the strains under which Soviet policy must operate, to force upon the Kremlin a far greater degree of moderation and circumspection than it has had to observe in recent years, and in this way to promote tendencies which must eventually find their outlet in either the breakup or the gradual mellowing of Soviet power. . . .

Surely, there was never a fairer test of national quality than this. In the light of these circumstances, the thoughtful observer of Russian-American relations will find no cause for complaint in the Kremlin's challenge to American society. He will rather experience a certain gratitude to a Providence which, by providing the American people with this implacable challenge, has made their entire security as a nation dependent on their pulling themselves together and accepting the responsibilities of moral and political leadership that history plainly intended them to bear.

## THE TRUMAN DOCTRINE (1947)

> Faced with the aggression and subversion of the Soviet Union following the end of World War II, President Harry Truman had decided that the United States must accept its responsibilities as the most powerful democracy in the world. Truman's policy for the United States to underwrite at great expense the defense of any free state against totalitarian regimes was quite different from our irresponsible withdrawal from world affairs after World War I under the Republican administrations of the Twenties.

The gravity of the situation which confronts the world today necessitates my appearance before a joint session of the Congress.

The foreign policy and the national security of this country are involved.

One aspect of the present situation, which I wish to present to you at this time for your consideration and decision, concerns Greece and Turkey.

The United States has received from the Greek Government an urgent appeal for financial and economic assistance. Preliminary reports from the American Economic Mission now in Greece and reports from the American Ambassador in Greece corroborate the statement of the Greek Government that assistance is imperative if Greece is to survive as a free nation.

I do not believe that the American people and the Congress wish to turn a deaf ear to the appeal of the Greek Government . . . .

The very existence of the Greek state is today threatened by the terrorist activities of several thousand armed men, led by Communists, who defy the government's authority at a number of points, particularly along the northern boundaries. A Commission appointed by the United Nations Security Council is at present investigating disturbed conditions in northern Greece and alleged border violations along the frontiers between Greece on the one hand and Albania, Bulgaria, and Yugoslavia on the other.

Meanwhile, the Greek Government is unable to cope with the situation. The Greek Army is small and poorly equipped. It needs supplies and equipment if it is to restore the authority to the government throughout Greek territory.

Greece must have assistance if it is to become a self-supporting and self-respecting democracy.

The United States must supply this assistance. We have already extended to Greece certain types of relief and economic aid but these are inadequate. . . .

---

Harry S. Truman, Public Papers of the Presidents of the United States: Harry S. Truman, 1947 (Washington, 1963), pp. 176-180.

Greece's neighbor, Turkey, also deserves our attention. . . .

As in the case of Greece, if Turkey is to have the assistance it needs, the United States must supply it. We are the only country able to provide that help.

I am fully aware of the broad implications involved if the United States extends assistance to Greece and Turkey, and I shall discuss these implications with you at this time.

One of the primary objectives of the foreign policy of the United States is the creation of conditions in which we and other nations will be able to work out a way of life free from coercion. This was a fundamental issue in the war with Germany and Japan. Our victory was won over countries which sought to impose their will, and their way of life, upon other nations.

To ensure the peaceful development of nations, free from coercion, the United States has taken a leading part in establishing the United Nations. The United Nations is designed to make possible lasting freedom and independence for all its members. We shall not realize our objectives, however, unless we are willing to help free peoples to maintain their free institutions and their national integrity against aggressive movements that seek to impose on them totalitarian regimes. This is no more than a frank recognition that totalitarian regimes imposed on free peoples, by direct or indirect aggression, undermine the foundations of international peace and hence the security of the United States.

The peoples of a number of countries of the world have recently had totalitarian regimes forced upon them against their will. The Government of the United States has made frequent protests against coercion and intimidation, in violation of the Yalta Agreement, in Poland, Rumania, and Bulgaria. I must also state that in a number of other countries there have been similar developments. . . .

I believe that it must be the policy of the United States to support free peoples who are resisting attempted subjugation by armed minorities or by outside pressures.

I believe that we must assist free peoples to work out their own destinies in their own way.

I believe that our help should be primarily through economic and financial aid which is essential to economic stability and orderly political processes.

The world is not static, and the status quo is not sacred. But we cannot allow changes in the status quo in violation of the Charter of the United Nations by such methods as coercion, or by such subterfuges as political infiltration. In helping free and independent nations to maintain their freedom, the United States will be giving effect to the principles of the Charter of the United Nations.

It is necessary only to glance at a map to realize that the survival and integrity of the Greek nation are of grave importance in a much wider situation. If Greece should fall under the control of an armed minority, the effect upon its neighbor, Turkey, would be immediate and serious. Confusion and disorder might well spread throughout the entire Middle East.

Moreover, the disappearance of Greece as an independent state would have a profound effect upon those countries in Europe whose peoples are struggling against great difficulties to maintain their freedoms and their independence while they repair the damages of war.

It would be an unspeakable tragedy if these countries, which have struggled so long against overwhelming odds, should lose that victory for which they sacrificed so much. Collapse of free institutions and loss of independence would be disastrous not only for them but for the world. Discouragement and possibly failure would quickly be the lot of neighboring peoples striving to maintain their freedom and independence.

Should we fail to aid Greece and Turkey in this fateful hour, the effect will be far reaching to the West as well as to the East.

We must take immediate and resolute action

I therefore ask the Congress to provide authority for assistance to Greece and Turkey in the amount of $400,000,000 for the period ending June 30, 1948 . . . .

In addition to funds, I ask the Congress to authorize the detail of American civilian and military personnel to Greece and Turkey, at the request of those countries, to assist in the tasks of reconstruction and for the purpose of supervising the use of such financial and material assistance as may be furnished. I recommend that authority also be provided for the instruction and training of selected Greek and Turkish personnel.

Finally, I ask that the Congress provide authority which will permit the speediest and most effective use, in terms of needed commodities, supplies, and equipment, of such funds as may be authorized . . . .

The seeds of totalitarian regimes are nurtured by misery and want. They spread and grow in the evil soil of poverty and strife. They reach their full growth when the hope of a people for a better life has died.

We must keep that hope alive.

The free peoples of the world look to us for support in maintaining their freedoms.

If we falter in our leadership, we may endanger the peace of the world--and we shall surely endanger the welfare of this Nation.

Great responsibilities have been placed upon us by the swift movement of events.

I am confident that the Congress will face these responsibilities squarely.

## NSC 68 (1950)

In April 1950 the National Security Council approved a policy paper (later endorsed by President Truman) which established general guidelines for dealing with monolithic communism. A few months later, the North Korean invasion of South Korea seemed to justify the conclusions in NSC 68--and helped the Truman Administration "sell" to the American people the sharp increases in defense spending secretly called for in NSC 68.

In the light of present and prospective Soviet atomic capabilities, the action which can be taken under present programs and plans. . . becomes dangerously inadequate, in both timing and scope, to accomplish the rapid progress toward the attainment of the United States political, economic, and military objectives which is now imperative.

---

U. S. Department of State, <u>Foreign Relations of the United States, 1950</u> (Washington, D.C., 1977), I, 290-292.

A continuation of present trends would result in a serious decline in the strength of the free world relative to the Soviet Union and its satellites. This unfavorable trend arises from the inadequacy of current programs and plans rather than from any error in our objectives and aims. These trends lead in the direction of isolation, not by deliberate decision but by lack of the necessary basis for a vigorous initiative in the conflict with the Soviet Union.

Our position as the center of power in the free world places a heavy responsibility upon the United States for leadership. We must organize and enlist the energies and resources of the free world in a positive program for peace which will frustrate the Kremlin design for world domination by creating a situation in the free world to which the Kremlin will be compelled to adjust. Without such a cooperative effort, led by the United States, we will have to make gradual withdrawals under pressure until we discover one day that we have sacrificed positions of vital interest.

It is imperative that this trend be reversed by a much more rapid and concerted build-up of the actual strength of both the United States and the other nations of the free world. The analysis shows that this will be costly and will involve significant domestic financial and economic adjustments.

The execution of such a build-up, however, requires that the United States have an affirmative program beyond the solely defensive one of countering the threat posed by the Soviet Union. This program must light the path to peace and order among nations in a system based on freedom and justice, as contemplated in the Charter of the United Nations. Further, it must envisage the political and economic measures with which and the military shield behind which the free world can work to frustrate the Kremlin design by the strategy of the cold war; for every consideration of devotion to our fundamental values and to our national security demands that we achieve our objectives by the strategy of the cold war, building up our military strength in order that it may not have to be used. The only sure victory lies in the frustration of the Kremlin design by the steady development of the moral and material strength of the free world and its projection into the Soviet world in such a way as to bring about an internal change in the Soviet system. Such a positive program—harmonious with our fundamental national purpose and our objectives—is necessary if we are to regain and retain the initiative and to win and hold the necessary popular support and cooperation in the United States and the rest of the free world.

This program should include a plan for negotiation with the Soviet Union, developed and agreed with our allies and which is consonant with our objectives. . . . The present world situation, however, is one which militates against successful negotiations with the Kremlin—for the terms of agreements on important pending issues would reflect present realities and would therefore be unacceptable, if not disastrous, to the United States and the rest of the free world. After a decision and a start on building up the strength of the free world has been made, it might then be desirable for the United States to take an initiative in seeking negotiations in the hope that it might facilitate the process of accommodation by the Kremlin to the new situation. Failing that, the unwillingness of the Kremlin to accept equitable terms or its bad faith in observing them would assist in consolidating popular opinion in the free world in support of the measures necessary to sustain the build-up. . . .

The whole success of the proposed program hangs ultimately on recognition by this Government, the American people, and all free peoples, that the cold war is in fact a real war in which the survival of the free world is at stake. Essential prerequisites to success are consultations with Congressional leaders designed to make the program the object of non-partisan legislative support, and a presentation to the public of a full explanation of the facts and implications of the present international situation. The prosecution of the program will require of us all the ingenuity, sacrifice, and unity demanded by the vital importance of the issue and the tenacity to persevere until our national objectives have been attained.

## TRUMAN VETOES THE McCARRAN ACT (1950)

In 1950 Congress took a step beyond the 1940 Smith Act by passing the Internal Security Act, known as the McCarran Act. Although it did not directly outlaw the Communist Party, it required the party to publish its records. It further denied federal defense-related employment or passports to Communists, and it established a Subversive Activities Control Board. This Board of five men was to rule on whether an organization was communist-related, whatever the organization's own claims. To put the law into effect Congress had to override the veto of President Truman, who explains here his opposition to the bill. Truman felt that the McCarran Act was both useless and dangerous.

To the House of Representatives:

I return herewith, without my approval, H.R. 9490, the proposed "Internal Security Act of 1950". . . .

The ostensible purpose . . . . is to prevent persons who would be dangerous to our national security from entering the country or becoming citizens. In fact, present law already achieves that objective.

What these provisions would actually do is to prevent us from admitting to our country, or to citizenship, many people who could make real contributions to our national strength. The bill would deprive our Government and our intelligence agencies of the valuable services of aliens in security operations. It would require us to exclude and to deport the citizens of some friendly non-communist countries. Furthermore, it would actually make it easier for subversive aliens to become United States citizens. Only the Communist movement would gain from such actions . . . .

In brief, when all the provisions of H.R. 9490 are considered together, it is evident that the great bulk of them are not directed toward the real and present dangers that exist from communism. Instead of striking blows at communism, they would strike blows at our own liberties and at our position in the forefront of those working for freedom in the world . . . .

The idea of requiring communist organizations to divulge information about themselves is a simple and attractive one. But it is about as practical as requiring thieves to register with the sheriff. Obviously, no such organization as the Communist Party is likely to register voluntarily . . . .

Harry S. Truman, *Public Papers of the Presidents of the United States: Harry S. Truman, 1950* (Washington, 1965), pp. 645, 647-650, 653.

Unfortunately, these provisions are not merely ineffective and unworkable. They represent a clear and present danger to our institutions.

In so far as the bill would require registration by the Communist Party itself, it does not endanger our traditional liberties. However, the application of the registration requirements to so-called communist-front organizations can be the greatest danger to freedom of speech, press and assembly, since the Alien and Sedition Laws of 1798. This danger arises out of the criteria or standards to be applied in determining whether an organization is a communist-front organization.

There would be no serious problem if the bill required proof that an organization was controlled and financed by the Communist Party before it could be classified as a communist front organization. However, recognizing the difficulty of proving those matters, the bill would permit such a determination to be based solely upon "the extent to which the positions taken or advanced by it from time to time on matters of policy do not deviate from those" of the communist movement.

This provision could easily be used to classify as a communist-front organization any organization which is advocating a single policy or objective which is also being urged by the Communist Party or by a communist foreign government . . . . Thus, an organization which advocates low-cost housing for sincere humanitarian reasons might be classified as a communist-front organization because the Communists regularly exploit slum conditions as one of their fifth-column techniques.

It is not enough to say that this probably would not be done. The mere fact that it could be done shows clearly how the bill would open a Pandora's box of opportunities for official condemnation of organizations and individuals for perfectly honest opinions which happen to be stated also by communists.

The basic error of these sections is that they move in the direction of suppressing opinion and belief. This would be a very dangerous course to take, not because we have any sympathy for Communist opinions, but because any governmental stifling of the free expression of opinion is a long step toward totalitarianism.

There is no more fundamental axiom of American freedom than the familiar statement: In a free country, we punish men for the crimes they commit but never for the opinions they have. And the reason this is so fundamental to freedom is not, as many suppose, that it protects the few unorthodox from suppression by the majority. To permit freedom of expression is primarily for the benefit of the majority, because it protects criticism, and criticism leads to progress.

We can and we will prevent espionage, sabotage, or other actions endangering our national security. But we would betray our finest traditions if we attempted, as this bill would attempt, to curb the simple expression of opinion. This we should never do, no matter how distasteful the opinion may be to the vast majority of our people. The course proposed by this bill would delight the communists, for it would make a mockery of the Bill of Rights and of our claims to stand for freedom in the world.

And what kind of effect would these provisions have on the normal expression of political views? Obviously, if this law were on the statute books, the part of prudence would be to avoid saying anything that might be construed by someone as not deviating sufficiently from the current communist propaganda line. And since no one could be sure in advance what views were safe to express, the inevitable tendency would be to express no views on controversial subjects.

The result could only be to reduce the vigor and strength of our political life--an outcome that the communists would happily welcome, but that freemen should abhor.

We need not fear the expression of ideas--we do need to fear their suppression.

Our position in the vanguard of freedom rests largely on our demonstration that the free expression of opinion, coupled with government by popular consent, leads to national strength and human advancement. Let us not, in cowering and foolish fear, throw away the ideals which are the fundamental basis of our free society . . . .

I do not undertake lightly the responsibility of differing with the majority in both Houses of Congress who have voted for this bill. We are all Americans; we all wish to safeguard and preserve our constitutional liberties against internal and external enemies. But I cannot approve this legislation, which instead of accomplishing its avowed purpose would actually interfere with our liberties and help the communist against whom the bill was aimed.

This is a time when we must marshal all our resources and all the moral strength of our free system in self-defense against the threat of communist aggression. We will fail in this, and we will destroy all that we seek to preserve, if we sacrifice the liberties of our citizens in a misguided attempt to achieve national security.

## JOSEPH McCARTHY ON TREASON (1951)

Shortly after the Second World War, another "Red Scare" gripped American society. Congressman Richard M. Nixon earned national prominence during the investigation of Alger Hiss--a State Department official who was accused of being a communist. Another member of Congress, Senator Joseph McCarthy of Wisconsin, also created quite a stir with his sensational charges about "traitors high in this Government."

Mr. McCARTHY. I may say that I certainly want to compliment the Senator from Nebraska [Mr. Wherry] for having recognized in Dean Acheson, long before some of the rest of us, the dangerous man that he is. I shall forever be ashamed of the fact that I voted for the confirmation of Dean Acheson. . . .

In searching for the answer to why there are traitors high in this Government, it must be remembered that communism has already the equivalent of three Communist military divisions in this country. The authority for this statement is none other than our Director of the Federal Bureau of Investigation, J. Edgar Hoover. He estimates the number of Communists in this country to be around 55,000. Those are the Communists carried by the FBI in its files as members of the Communist Party--in other words, the equivalent of three military divisions. Every one of the 55,000 has taken an oath of

---

U. S. Congress, Senate, 82nd Cong., 1st sess., March 14, 1951, <u>Congressional Record</u>, XCVII, 2389-2390.

loyalty to Stalin which is an oath of disloyalty to the United States. Each one of those 55,000 works for the same things that the head of the Chinese Communist Party, the head of the Russian Army, and the men of the Kremlin are working for.

That the members of those three divisions would aim for the highest places in this Government is not the exception, but the rule. It follows as the night follows the day that high Government positions are their most logical targets. Some of them succeeded as we well know, in arriving at the very highest level of Government. This is attested to by the convictions of the Hisses, the Remingtons, and the Marzanis.

Most of the 55,000 Communists remain unnamed and unknown to the American people. Once they are known, once they are publicly labeled as the traitors they are, they cannot then do too much damage any longer. However, one does not need to know the name and card number of a Communist to know of his presence. . . .

Likewise, when one sees the phony planning—and I use these words advisedly, Mr. President—for phony resistance to communism in both Europe and Asia, he does not need to have the names of the Communist planners in order to know that they are there. One knows that traitors are at work. One sees the political fingerprints of the Communists on every document drafted. One can see the footprints of Communist betrayals down every path they travel.

As I named those who left a trail of Communist fingerprints, Communist footprints, and Communist calling cards wherever they went, I was accused of smearing innocent people because I could not swear that I saw them attend Communist meetings or that I had attended such meetings with them. That is the hue and cry that the three divisions and their camp followers always raise when they are in danger of being exposed. Remember when J. Edgar Hoover says that there are 55,000 actual active members of the Communist Party in this country, he is not indulging in any speculation or guess work. And remember, too, that for each of the sworn party members of the three Communist Divisions, there are at least 10 camp followers with varying degrees of loyalty to the party. Those camp followers in the press, radio, and motion pictures have done deadly damage to this Nation in aiding the conspiracy of the three active Communist divisions at work in America.

As we know, while some of our very able Senators and Congressmen were attempting to focus attention upon our disastrous foreign policy, I was attempting to focus attention upon the individuals in the three Communist divisions who were responsible for this foreign policy—on their motives, their activities, and their backgrounds—with the hope that in this way their treachery could be unmistakably spotlighted and a halt called to their evil machinations. . . .

There is nothing secret about the final aim of international communism, namely, the conquest of the world. There is nothing secret about their intermediate aims. There is nothing secret about the preliminary steps which they contemplate as a prelude to the conquest of America.

# MARGARET CHASE SMITH ON McCARTHYISM (1950)

> Those Americans, whether in public or private walks of life, who would denounce the works of Joseph McCarthy were few and far between. Polls showed a high degree of public support for McCarthy (at least up until the televised army hearings in 1954), but even for those who disapproved of the vitriolic Senator from Wisconsin and his witch-hunt, silence was the safest course. Margaret Chase Smith, Senator from Maine, was one of the courageous few who spoke out.

I think that it is high time for the United States Senate and its Members to do some real soul searching and to weigh our consciences as to the manner in which we are performing our duty to the people of America and the manner in which we are using or abusing our individual powers and privileges.

I think it is high time that we remembered that we have sworn to uphold and defend the Constitution. I think it is high time that we remembered that the Constitution, as amended, speaks not only of the freedom of speech but also of trial by jury instead of trial by accusation.

Whether it be a criminal prosecution in court or a character prosecution in the Senate, there is little practical distinction when the life of a person has been ruined.

Those of us who shout the loudest about Americanism in making character assassinations are all too frequently those who, by our own words and acts, ignore some of the basic principles of Americanism -

The right to criticize.
The right to hold unpopular beliefs.
The right to protest.
The right of independent thought.

The exercise of these rights should not cost one single American citizen his reputation or his right to a livelihood, nor should he be in danger of losing his reputation or livelihood merely because he happens to know some one who holds unpopular beliefs. Who of us does not? Otherwise none of us could call our souls our own. Otherwise thought control would have set in.

The American people are sick and tired of being afraid to speak their minds lest they be politically smeared as Communists or Fascists by their opponents. Freedom of speech is not what it used to be in America. It has been so abused by some that it is not exercised by others.

The American people are sick and tired of seeing innocent people smeared and guilty people whitewashed. But there have been enough proved cases, such as the Amerasia case, the Hiss case, the Coplon case, the Gold case, to cause Nation-wide distrust and strong suspicion that there may be something to the unproved, sensational accusations. . . .

Today our country is being psychologically divided by the confusion and the suspicions that are bred in the United States Senate to spread like cancerous tentacles of "know nothing, suspect everything" attitudes . . . .

As a United States Senator, I am not proud of the way in which the Senate has been made a publicity platform for irresponsible sensationalism. I

---

United States, Congress, 81st Cong., 2nd sess., June 1, 1950, <u>Congressional Record</u>, XCVI, 7894-7895.

am not proud of the reckless abandon in which unproved charges have been hurled from this side of the aisle. I am not proud of the obviously staged, undignified countercharges which have been attempted in retaliation from the other side of the aisle.

I do not like the way the Senate has been made a rendezvous for vilification, for selfish political gain at the sacrifice of individual reputations and national unity. I am not proud of the way we smear outsiders from the floor of the Senate and hide behind the cloak of congressional immunity, and still place ourselves beyond criticism on the floor of the Senate.

As an American, I am shocked at the way Republicans and Democrats alike are playing directly into the Communist design of "confuse, divide, and conquer." As an American, I do not want a Democratic administration white wash or cover up any more than I want a Republican smear or witch hunt.

As an American, I condemn a Republician Fascist just as much as I condemn a Democratic Communist. I condemn a Democratic Fascist just as much as I condemn a Republican Communist. They are equally dangerous to you and me and to our country. As an American, I want to see our Nation recapture the strength and unity it once had when we fought the enemy instead of ourselves.


## TRUMAN AND MacARTHUR ON THE KOREAN WAR (1951)

The Korean War led to bitter feeling between General MacArthur and President Truman. They disagreed on the fundamental strategy of how to deal with North Korea and Communist China.

(a) MacArthur's Letter to Congressman Joseph W. Martin (March 20, 1951)

My views and recommendations with respect to the situation created by Red China's entry into war against us in Korea have been submitted to Washington in most complete detail. Generally these views are well known and clearly understood, as they follow the conventional pattern of meeting force with maximum counter-force as we have never failed to do in the past. Your view with respect to the utilization of the Chinese forces on Formosa is in conflict with neither logic nor this tradition.

It seems strangely difficult for some to realize that here in Asia is where the Communist consipirators have elected to make their play for global conquest, and that we have joined the issue thus raised on the battlefield; that here we fight Europe's war with arms while the diplomats there still fight it with words; that if we lose the war to Communism in Asia the fall of Europe is inevitable, win it and Europe most probably would avoid war and yet preserve freedom. As you point out, we must win. There is no substitute for victory.

---

Record Group 9, Special Folder: "Truman-MacArthur Controversy," and Record Group 25, box 2, Douglas MacArthur Papers, MacArthur Memorial, Norfolk, Virginia.

(b)  Truman's Statement on Firing MacArthur (April 11, 1951)

With deep regret, I have concluded that General of the Army Douglas MacArthur is unable to give his wholehearted support to the policies of the United States Government and of the United Nations in matters pertaining to his official duties. In view of the specific responsibilities imposed upon me by the Constitution of the United States and the added responsibility which has been entrusted to me by the United Nations, I have decided that I must make a change of command in the Far East. . . .

Full and vigorous debate on matters of national policy is a vital element in the constitutional system of our free Democracy. It is fundamental, however, that military commanders must be governed by the policies and directives issued to them in the manner provided by our laws and Constitution. In time of crisis, this consideration is particularly compelling.

(c)  MacArthur's Speech to Congress (April 19, 1951)

While I was not consulted prior to the President's decision to intervene in support of the Republic of Korea, that decision from a military standpoint, proved a sound one as we hurled back the invader and decimated his forces. Our victory was complete and our objectives within reach when Red China intervened with numerically superior ground forces.

This created a new war and an entirely new situation--a situation not contemplated when our forces were committed against the North Korean invaders--a situation which called for new decisions in the diplomatic sphere to permit the realistic adjustment of military strategy. Such decisions have not been forthcoming.

While no man in his right mind would advocate sending our ground forces into continental China, and such as never given a thought, the new situation did urgently demand a drastic revision of strategic planning if our political aim was to defeat this new enemy as we had defeated the old.

Apart from the military need, as I saw it, to neutralize the sanctuary protection given the enemy north of the Yalu, I felt that military necessity in the conduct of the war made mandatory.

(1)  The intensification of our economic blockade against China;
(2)  The imposition of a naval blockade against the China coast;
(3)  Removal of restrictions on air reconnaissance of China's coastal areas and of Manchuria;
(4)  Removal of restrictions on the forces of the Republic of China on Formosa, with logistical support to contribute to their effective operations against the common enemy.

For entertaining these views, all professionally designed to support our forces committed to Korea and bring hostilities to an end with the least possible delay and at a saving of countless American and Allied lives, I have been severely criticized in lay circles, principally abroad, despite my understanding that from a military standpoint the above views have been fully shared in the past by practically every military leader concerned with the Korean campaign, including our own Joint Chiefs of Staff. . . .

We could hold in Korea by constant maneuver and at an approximate area where our supply line advantages were in balance with the supply line disadvantages of the enemy, but we could hope at best for only an indecisive campaign with its terrible and constant attrition upon our forces if the enemy utilized his full military potential. I have constantly called for the new political decisions essential to a solution. Efforts have been made to distort my position. It has been said in effect that I am a warmonger.

Nothing could be further from the truth. I know war as few other men now living know it, and nothing to me is more revolting. I have long advocated its complete abolition, as its very destructiveness on both friend and foe has rendered it useless as a means of settling international disputes. . . .

But once war is forced upon us, there is no other alternative than to apply every available means to bring it to a swift end. War's very object is victory--not prolonged indecision. In war there can be no substitute for victory.

There are some who for varying reasons would appease Red China. They are blind to history's clear lesson, for history teaches with unmistakable emphasis that appeasement but begets new and bloodier war. It points to no single instance where the end has justified that means--where appeasement has led to more than a sham peace. Like blackmail, it lays the basis for new and successively greater demands until, as in blackmail, violence becomes the only other alternative. Why, my soldiers asked of me, surrender military advantages to an enemy in the field? I could not answer. Some may say to avoid spread of conflict into an all-out war with China; others, to avoid Soviet intervention. Neither explanation seems valid. For China is already engaging with the maximum power it can commit, and the Soviet will not necessarily mesh its actions with our moves. Like a cobra, any new enemy will more likely strike whenever it feels that the relativity in military or other potential is in its favor on a world-wide basis.

The tragedy of Korea is further heightened by the fact that its military action is confined to its territorial limits. It condemns that nation, which it is our purpose to save, to suffer the devastating impact of full naval and air bombardment while the enemy's sanctuaries are fully protected from such attack and devastation.

## BROWN v. BOARD OF EDUCATION OF TOPEKA (1954)

Despite the assurances of the post-Civil War amendments that blacks were citizens entitled to the equal protection of the laws (14th Amendment), and that blacks could vote (15th Amendment), "Jim Crow" legislation in the South in the late 19th century established a rigid system of racial segregation and disfranchised black voters. In 1896 the Supreme Court, in Plessy v. Ferguson, held that such "separate but equal" legislation did not violate the 14th Amendment, and that there was no legal remedy for social inequality. In the case cited here, the Court reconsiders the Plessy decision, and in doing so, takes an activist position, recognizing its own part in creating a system of social inequality and injustice in the first place. The Court also weighs, as

---

Brown v. Board of Education of Topeka, 347 U.S. 483 (1954).

it was unwilling to do in 1896, sociological and psychological as well as legal evidence in arriving at its decision. Chief Justice Warren delivers the opinion of the Court.

In approaching this problem, we cannot turn the clock back to 1868 when the [14th] Amendment was adopted, or even to 1896 when Plessy v. Ferguson was written. We must consider public education in the light of its full development and its present place in American life throughout the Nation. Only in this way can it be determined if segregation in public schools deprives these plaintiffs of the equal protection of the laws.

Today, education is perhaps the most important function of state and local governments. Compulsory school attendance laws and the great expenditures for education both demonstrate our recognition of the importance of education to our democratic society. It is required in the performance of our most basic public responsibilities, even service in the armed forces. It is the very foundation of good citizenship. Today it is a principal instrument in awakening the child to cultural values, in preparing him for later professional training, and in helping him to adjust normally to his environment. In these days, it is doubtful that any child may reasonably be expected to succeed in life if he is denied the opportunity of an education. Such an opportunity, where the state has undertaken to provide it, is a right which must be made available to all on equal terms.

We come then to the question presented: Does segregation of children in public schools solely on the basis of race, even though the physical facilities and other "tangible" factors may be equal, deprive the children of the minority group of equal educational opportunities? We believe that it does . . . .

Such considerations apply with added force to children in grade and high schools. To separate them from others of similar age and qualifications solely because of their race generates a feeling of inferiority as to their status in the community that may affect their hearts and minds in a way unlikely ever to be undone. The effect of this separation on their educational opportunities was well stated by a finding in the Kansas case by a court which nevertheless felt compelled to rule against the Negro plaintiffs:

"Segregation of white and colored children in public schools has a detrimental effect upon the colored children. The impact is greater when it has the sanction of the law; for the policy of separating the races is usually interpreted as denoting the inferiority of the Negro group. A sense of inferiority affects the motivation of a child to learn. Segregation with the sanction of law, therefore, has a tendency to [retard] the educational and mental development of Negro children and to deprive them of some of the benefits they would receive in a racial[ly] integrated school system."

Whatever may have been the extent of psychological knowledge at the time of Plessy v. Ferguson, this finding is amply supported by modern authority.

We conclude that in the field of public education the doctrine of "separate but equal" has no place. Separate educational facilities are inherently unequal. Therefore, we hold that the plaintiffs and others similarly situated for whom the actions have been brought are, by reason of the segregation complained of, deprived of the equal protection of the laws guaranteed by the Fourteenth Amendment.

## THE "SOUTHERN MANIFESTO" (1956)

Although advocates of civil rights for blacks hailed the Brown decision as a long-overdue remedy to an evil of long standing, the Court had many loud critics and the decision met with "massive resistance." One hundred and one members of Congress signed the following Manifesto, while elsewhere enraged citizens denounced the activism of the Court and sought Chief Justice Warren's impeachment. Especially interesting is the way in which the signatories of the Southern Manifesto define their constitutional position, how they view their Jim Crow laws, how they characterize the Supreme Court, and what consequences they predict.

We regard the decision of the Supreme Court in the school cases as a clear abuse of judicial power. It climaxes a trend in the Federal judiciary undertaking to legislate, in derogation of the authority of Congress, and to encroach upon the reserved rights of the States and the people.

The original Constitution does not mention education. Neither does the 14th amendment nor any other amendment. The debates preceding the submission of the 14th amendment clearly show that there was no intent that it should affect the systems of education maintained by the States. . . .

In the case of Plessy v. Ferguson, in 1896, the Supreme Court expressly declared that under the 14th Amendment no person was denied any of his rights if the States provided separate but equal public facilities. This decision has been followed in many other cases. It is notable that the Supreme Court, speaking through Chief Justice Taft, a former President of the United States, unanimously declared, in 1927, in Lum v. Rice that the "separate but equal" principle is "within the discretion of the State in regulating its public schools and does not conflict with the 14th Amendment."

This interpretation, restated time and again, became a part of the life of the people of many of the States and confirmed their habits, customs, traditions and way of life. It is founded on elemental humanity and commonsense, for parents should not be deprived by Government of the right to direct the lives and education of their own children.

Though there has been no constitutional amendment or act of Congress changing this established legal principle almost a century old, the Supreme Court of the United States, with no legal basis for such action, undertook to exercise their naked judicial power and substituted their personal political and social ideas for the established law of the land.

This unwarranted exercise of power by the court, contrary to the Constitution, is creating chaos and confusion in the States principally affected. It is destroying the amicable relations between the white and Negro races that have been created through 90 years of patient effort by the good people of both races. It has planted hatred and suspicion where there has been heretofore friendship and understanding.

Without regard to the consent of the governed, outside agitators are threatening immediate and revolutionary changes in our public-school systems.

---

United States, Congress, 84th Cong., 2nd sess., March 12, 1956, Congressional Record, CII, 4515-4516.

If done, this is certain to destroy the system of public-education in some of the States.

With the gravest concern for the explosive and dangerous conditions created by this decision and inflamed by outside meddlers:

We reaffirm our reliance on the Constitution as the fundamental law of the land.

We decry the Supreme Court's encroachments on rights reserved to the States and to the people, contrary to established law and to the Constitution.

We commend the motives of those States which have declared the intention to resist forced integration by any lawful means.

We appeal to the States and people who are not directly affected by these decisions to consider the constitutional principles involved against the time when they, too, on issues vital to them, may be the victims of judicial encroachment.

Even though we constitute a minority in the present Congress, we have full faith that a majority of the American people believe in the dual system of government which has enabled us to achieve our greatness and will in time demand that the reserved rights of the State and of the people be made secure against judicial usurpation.

We pledge ourselves to use all lawful means to bring about a reversal of this decision which is contrary to the Constitution, and to prevent the use of force in its implementation.

In this trying period, as we all seek to right this wrong, we appeal to our people not to be provoked by the agitators and troublemakers invading our States and to scrupulously refrain from disorder and lawless acts.


EISENHOWER ON THE MILITARY - INDUSTRIAL COMPLEX (1961)

A beloved general who served as President during the Cold War and the Korean conflict, Dwight D. Eisenhower might have been expected to sound a call to arms in his final address to the American people. He did, indeed, see communism as a persistent threat to freedom and democracy. Yet, Eisenhower issued some somber warnings regarding possible solutions to that threat. Even today his observations on American power remain relevant.

We now stand ten years past the midpoint of a century that has witnessed four major wars among great nations. Three of these involved our own country. Despite these holocausts America is today the strongest, the most influential and most productive nation in the world. Understandably proud of this pre-eminence, we yet realize that America's leadership and prestige depend, not merely upon our unmatched material progress, riches and military strength, but on how we use our power in the interests of world peace and human betterment.

Throughout America's adventure in free government, our basic purposes have been to keep the peace; to foster progress in human achievement, and to

---

Dwight D. Eisenhower, Public Papers of the Presidents of the United States: Dwight D. Eisenhower, 1960-1961 (Washington, D.C., 1961), pp. 1035-1040.

enhance liberty, dignity, and integrity among people and among nations. To strive for less would be unworthy of a free and religious people. Any failure traceable to arrogance, or our lack of comprehension or readiness to sacrifice would inflict upon us grievous hurt both at home and abroad.

Progress toward these noble goals is persistently threatened by the conflict now engulfing the world. It commands our whole attention, absorbs our very beings. We face a hostile ideology--global in scope, atheistic in character, ruthless in purpose, and isidious in method. Unhappily the danger it poses promises to be of indefinite duration. To meet it successfully, there is called for, not so much the emotional and transitory sacrifices of crisis, but rather those which enable us to carry forward steadily, surely, and without complaint the burdens of a prolonged and complex struggle--with liberty the stake. Only thus shall we remain, despite every provocation, on our charted course toward permanent peace and human betterment.

Crises there will continue to be. In meeting them, whether foreign or domestic, great or small, there is a recurring temptation to feel that some spectacular and costly action could become the miraculous solution to all current difficulties. A huge increase in newer elements of our defense; development of unrealistic programs to cure every ill in agriculture; a dramatic expansion in basic and applied research--these and many other possibilities, each possibly promising in itself, may be suggested as the only way to the road we wish to travel.

But each proposal must be weighed in the light of a broader consideration: the need to maintain balance in and among national programs-- balance between the private and the public economy, balance between cost and hoped for advantage--balance between the clearly necessary and the comfortably desirable; balance between our essential requirements as a nation and the duties imposed by the nation upon the individual; balance between actions of the moment and the national welfare of the future. Good judgment seeks balance and progress; lack of it eventually finds imbalance and frustration.

The record of many decades stands as proof that our people and their government have, in the main, understood these truths and have responded to them well, in the face of stress and threat. But threats, new in kind or degree, constantly arise. I mention two only.

A vital element in keeping the peace is our military establishment. Our arms must be mighty, ready for instant action, so that no potential aggressor may be tempted to risk his own destruction.

Our military organization today bears little relation to that known by any of my predecessors in peacetime, or indeed by the fighting men of World War II or Korea.

Until the latest of our world conflicts, the United States had no armaments industry. American makers of plowshares could, with time and as required, make swords as well. But now we can no longer risk emergency improvisation of national defense; we have been compelled to create a permanent armaments industry of vast proportions. Added to this, three and a half million men and women are directly engaged in the defense establishment. We annually spend on military security more than the net income of all United States corporations.

This conjunction of an immense military establishment and a large arms industry is new in the American experience. The total influence--economic, political, even spiritual--is felt in every city, every State house, every office of the Federal government. We recognize the imperative need for this development. Yet we must not fail to comprehend its grave implications. Our toil, resources and livelihood are all involved; so is the very structure of our society.

In the councils of government, we must guard against the acquisition of unwarranted influence, whether sought or unsought, by the military-industrial complex. The potential for the disastrous rise of misplaced power exists and will persist.

We must never let the weight of this combination endanger our liberties or democratic processes. We should take nothing for granted. Only an alert and knowledgeable citizenry can compel the proper meshing of the huge industrial and military machinery of defense with our peaceful methods and goals, so that security and liberty may prosper together.

Akin to, and largely responsible for the sweeping changes in our industrial-military posture, has been the technological revolution during recent decades.

In this revolution, research has become central; it also becomes more formalized, complex, and costly. A steadily increasing share is conducted for, by, or at the direction of, the Federal government. . . .

The prospect of domination of the nation's scholars by Federal employment, project allocations, and the power of money is ever present--and is gravely to be regarded.

Yet, in holding scientific research and discovery in respect, as we should, we must also be alert to the equal and opposite danger that public policy could itself become the captive of a scientific-technological elite.

It is the task of statesmanship to mold, to balance, and to integrate these and other forces, new and old, within the principles of our democratic system--ever aiming toward the supreme goals of our free society.

Another factor in maintaining balance involves the element of time. As we peer into society's future, we--you and I, and our government--must avoid the impulse to live only for today, plundering, for our own ease and convenience, the precious resources of tomorrow. We cannot mortgage the material assets of our grandchildren without risking the loss also of their political and spiritual heritage. We want democracy to survive for all generations to come, not to become the insolvent phantom of tomorrow.

Down the long lane of the history yet to be written America knows that this world of ours, ever growing smaller, must avoid becoming a community of dreadful fear and hate, and be, instead, a proud confederation of mutual trust and respect.

Such a confederation must be one of equals. The weakest must come to the conference table with the same confidence as do we, protected as we are by our moral, economic, and military strength. That table, though scarred by many past frustrations, cannot be abandoned for the certain agony of the battlefield.

Disarmament, with mutual honor and confidence, is a continuing imperative. Together we must learn how to compose differences, not with arms, but with intellect and decent purpose. Because this need is so sharp and apparent I confess that I lay down my official responsibilities in this field with a definite sense of disappointment. As one who has witnessed the horror and the lingering sadness of war--as one who knows that another war could utterly destroy this civilization which has been so slowly and painfully built over thousands of years--I wish I could say tonight that a lasting peace is in sight.

Happily, I can say that war has been avoided. Steady progress toward our ultimate goal has been made. But, so much remains to be done. As a private citizen, I shall never cease to do what little I can to help the world advance along that road.


## JOHN F. KENNEDY'S INAUGURAL ADDRESS (1961)

John Kennedy had won the election of 1960 with 50.1% of the popular vote to become the youngest man ever elected to the Presidency. In his inaugural speech Kennedy set the tone of challenge and duty and excitement that was the hallmark of his tragically short-lived administration.

We observe today not a victory of party but a celebration of freedom--symbolizing an end as well as a beginning--signifying renewal as well as change. For I have sworn before you and Almighty God the same solemn oath our forebears prescribed nearly a century and three quarters ago.
The world is very different now. For man holds in his mortal hands the power to abolish all forms of human poverty and all forms of human life. And yet the same revolutionary beliefs for which our forebears fought are still at issue around the globe--the belief that the rights of man come not from the generosity of the state but from the hand of God.
We dare not forget today that we are the heirs of that first revolution. Let the word go forth from this time and place, to friend and foe alike, that the torch has been passed to a new generation of Americans--born in this century, tempered by war, disciplined by a hard and bitter peace, proud of our ancient heritage--and unwilling to witness or permit the slow undoing of those human rights to which this nation has always been committed, and to which we are committed today at home and around the world.
Let every nation know, whether it wishes us well or ill, that we shall pay any price, bear any burden, meet any hardship, support any friend, oppose any foe to assure the survival and the success of liberty.
This much we pledge--and more.
To those old allies whose cultural and spiritual origins we share, we pledge the loyalty of faithful friends. United, there is little we cannot do in a host of cooperative ventures. Divided, there is little we can do--for we dare not meet a powerful challenge at odds and split asunder.
To those new states whom we welcome to the ranks of the free, we pledge our word that one form of colonial control shall not have passed away merely to be replaced by a far more iron tyranny. We shall not always expect to find them suporting our view. But we shall always hope to find them strongly supporting their own freedom--and to remember that, in the past, those who foolishly sought power by riding the back of the tiger ended up inside.
To those peoples in the huts and villages of half the globe struggling to break the bonds of mass misery, we pledge our best efforts to help them help themselves, for whatever period is required--not because the communists may be doing it, not because we seek their votes, but because it is right. If a free society cannot help the many who are poor, it cannot save the few who are rich.

John F. Kennedy, *Public Papers of the Presidents of the United States: John F. Kennedy, 1961* (Washington, D.C., 1962), pp. 1-3.

To our sister republics south of our border, we offer a special pledge--to convert our goods words into good deeds--in a new alliance for progress--to assist free men and free governments in casting off the chains of poverty. But this peaceful revolution of hope cannot become the prey of hostile powers. Let all our neighbors know that we shall join with them to oppose aggression or subversion anywhere in the Americas. And let every other power know that this Hemisphere intends to remain the master of its own house.

To that world assembly of sovereign states, the United Nations, our last best hope in an age where the instruments of war have far outpaced the instruments of peace, we renew our pledge of support--to prevent it from becoming merely a forum for invective--to strengthen its shield of the new and the weak--and to enlarge the area in which its writ may run.

Finally, to those nations who would make themselves our adversary, we offer not a pledge but a request: that both sides begin anew the quest for peace, before the dark powers of destruction unleashed by science engulf all humanity in planned or accidental self-destruction.

We dare not tempt them with weakness. For only when our arms are sufficient, beyond doubt can we be certain beyond doubt that they will never be employed.

But neither can two great and powerful groups of nations take comfort from our present course--both sides overburdened by the cost of modern weapons, both rightly alarmed by the steady spread of the deadly atom, yet both racing to alter that uncertain balance of terror that stays the hand of mankind's final war.

So let us begin anew--remembering on both sides that civility is not a sign of weakness, and sincerity is always subject to proof. Let us never negotiate out of fear. But let us never fear to negotiate.

Let both sides explore what problems unite us instead of belaboring those problems which divide us.

Let both sides, for the first time, formulate serious and precise proposals for the inspection and control of arms--and bring the absolute power to destroy other nations under the absolute control of all nations.

Let both sides seek to invoke the wonders of science instead of its terrors. Together let us explore the stars, conquer the deserts, eradicate disease, tap the ocean depths and encourage the arts and commerce.

Let both sides unite to heed in all corners of the earth the command of Isaish--to "undo. the heavy burdens. . . (and) let the oppressed go free."

And if a beach-head of cooperation may push back the jungle of suspicion, let both sides join in creating a new endeavor, not a new balance of power, but a new world of law, where the strong are just and the weak secure and the peace preserved.

All this will not be finished in the first one hundred days. Nor will it be finished in the first one thousand days, nor in the life of this Administration, nor even perhaps in our lifetime on this planet. But let us begin.

In your hands, my fellow citizens, more than mine, will rest the final success or failure of our course. Since this country was founded, each generation of Americans has been summoned to give testimony to its national loyalty. The graves of young Americans who answered the call to service surround the globe.

Now the trumpet summons us again—not as a call to bear arms, though arms we need—not as a call to battle, though embattled we are—but a call to bear the burden of a long twilight struggle, year in and year out, "rejoicing in hope, patient in tribulation"—a struggle against the common enemies of man: tyranny, poverty, disease and war itself.

Can we forge against these enemies a grand and global alliance, North and South, East and West, that can assure a more fruitful life for all mankind? Will you join in that historic effort?

In the long history of the world, only a few generations have been granted the role of defending freedom in its hour of maximum danger. I do not shrink from this responsibility—I welcome it. I do not believe that any of us would exchange places with any other people or any other generation. The energy, the faith, the devotion which we bring to this endeavor will light our country and all who serve it—and the glow from that fire can truly light the world.

And so, my fellow Americans: ask not what your country can do for you—ask what you can do for your country.

My fellow citizens of the world: ask not what America will do for you, but what together we can do for the freedom of man.

Finally, whether you are citizens of America or citizens of the world, ask of us here the same high standards of strength and sacrifice which we ask of you. With a good conscience our only sure reward, with history the final judge of our deeds, let us go forth to lead the land we love, asking His blessing and His help, but knowing that here on earth God's work must truly be our own.

## THE PORT HURON STATEMENT (1962)

In 1962, a group of student activists from the University of Michigan organized a conference of the Students for a Democratic Society (SDS) at Port Huron. At that conference, participants endorsed this statement of principles, which was drafted principally by Tom Hayden. It is a curious mixture of traditional calls for reform of existing institutions and recommendations for radical structural changes in America in an effort to build a more responsive, democratic society.

We are people of this generation, bred in at least modest comfort, housed now in universities, looking uncomfortably to the world we inherit.

When we were kids the United States was the wealthiest and strongest country in the world; the only one with the atom bomb, the least scarred by modern war, an initiator of the United Nations that we thought would distribute Western influence throughout the world. Freedom and equality for each individual, government of, by, and for the people—these American values we found good, principles by which we could live as men. Many of us began maturing in complacency.

As we grew, however, our comfort was penetrated by events too troubling to dismiss. First, the permeating and victimizing fact of human degradation, symbolized by the Southern struggle against racial bigotry, compelled most of

---

Excerpts reprinted with the permission of Tom Hayden.

us from silence to activism. Second, the enclosing fact of the Cold War, symbolized by the presence of the Bomb, brought awareness that we ourselves, and our friends, and millions of abstract "others" we knew more directly because of our common peril, might die at any time. . . .

Our work is guided by the sense that we may be the last generation in the experiment with living. But we are a minority--the vast majority of our people regard the temporary equilibriums of our society and world as eternally-functional parts. . . .The search for truly democratic alternatives to the present, and a commitment to social experimentation with them, is a worthy and fulfilling human enterprise, one which moves us and, we hope, others today. . . .

If student movements for change are still rareties on the campus scene, what is commonplace there? The real campus, the familiar campus, is a place of private people, engaged in their notorious "inner emigration." It is a place of commitment to business-as-usual, getting ahead, playing it cool, It is a place of mass affirmation of the Twist, but mass reluctance toward the controversial public stance. Rules are accepted as "inevitable," bureaucracy as "just circumstances," irrelevance as "scholarship," selflessness as "martyrdom," politics as "just another way to make people, and an unprofitable one, too."

Tragically, the university could serve as a significant source of social criticism and an initiator of new modes and molders of attitudes. But the actual intellectual effect of the college experience is hardly distinguishable from that of any other communications channel--say, a television set--passing on the stock truths of the day. Students leave college somewhat more "tolerant" than when they arrived, but basically unchallenged in their values and political orientations. With administrators ordering the institution, and faculty the curriculum, the student learns by his isolation to accept elite rule within the university, which prepares him to accept later forms of minority control. The real function of the educational system--as opposed to its more rhetorical function of "searching for truth"--is to impart the key information and styles that will help the student get by, modestly but comfortably, in the big society beyond.

Look beyond the campus, to America itself. That student life is more intellectual, and perhaps more comfortable, does not obscure the fact that the fundamental qualities of life on the campus reflect the habits of society of large. The fraternity president is seen at the junior manager levels; the sorority queen has gone to Grosse Pointe; the serious poet burns for a place, any place, to work; the once-serious and never-serious poets work at the advertising agencies. The desperation of people threatened by forces about which they know little and of which they can say less; the cheerful emptiness of people "giving up" all hope of changing things; the faceless ones polled by Gallup who listed "international affairs" fourteenth on their list of "problems" but who also expected thermonuclear war in the next few years; in these and other forms, Americans are in withdrawal from public life, from any collective effort at directing their own affairs.

Some regard these national doldrums as a sign of healthy approval of the established order--but is it approval by consent or manipulated acquiescence? . . .

There are no convincing apologies for the contemporary malaise. While the world tumbles toward final war, while men in other nations are trying desperately to alter events, while the very future qua future is uncertain--

America is without community, impulse, without the inner momentum necessary for an age when societies cannot successfully perpetuate themselves by their military weapons, when democracy must be viable because of the quality of life, not its quantity of rockets.

The apathy here is, first <u>subjective</u>--the felt powerlessness of ordinary people, the resignation before the enormity of events. But subjective apathy is encouraged by the <u>objective</u> American situation--the actual structural separation of people from power, from relevant knowledge, from pinnacles of decision-making. Just as the university influences the student way of life, so do major social institutions create the circumstances in which the isolated citizen will try hopelessly to understand his world and himself. . . .

The American political system is not the democratic model of which its glorifiers speak. In actuality it frustrates democracy by confusing the individual citizen, paralyzing policy discussion, and consolidating the irresponsible power of military and business interests.

A crucial feature of the political apparatus in America is that greater differences are harbored within each major party than the differences existing between them. Instead of two parties presenting distinctive and significant differences of approach, what dominates the system is a natural interlocking of Democrats from Southern states with the more conservative elements of the Republican party. This arrangement of forces is blessed by the seniority system of Congress which guarantees congressional committee domination by conservatives--ten of 17 committees in the Senate and 13 of 21 in the House of Representatives are chaired currently by Dixiecrats.

The party overlap, however, is not the only structural antagonist of democracy in politics. First, the localized nature of the party system does not encourage discussion of national and international issues: . . .Second, whole constituencies are divested of the full political power they might have: . . .Third, the focus of political attention is significantly distorted by the enormous lobby force, composed predominantly of business interests, . . ."[A]nticommunism" becomes an umbrella by which to protest liberalism, internationalism, welfareism, the active civil rights and labor movements. It is to the disgrace of the United States that such a movement should become a prominent kind of public participation in the modern world--but, ironically, it is somewhat to the interests of the United States that such a movement should be a public constituency pointed toward realignment of the political parties, demanding a conservative Republic Party in the South and an exclusion of the "leftist" elements of the national GOP.

American captialism today advertises itself as the Welfare State. Many of us comfortably expect pensions, medical care, unemployment compensation, and other social services in our lifetimes. . . . But in spite of the benign yet obscuring effects of the New Deal reforms and the reassuring phrases of government economists and politicians, the paradoxes and myths of the economy are sufficient to irritate our complacency and reveal to us some essential causes of the American malaise.

We live amidst a national celebration of economic prosperity while poverty and deprivation remain an unbreakable way of life for millions in the "affluent society," including many of our own generation. We hear glib references to the "welfare state," "free enterprise," and "shareholder's democracy" while military defense is the main item of "public" spending and obvious oligopoly and other forms of minority rule defy real individual initiative or popular control. Work, too, is often unfulfilling and victimizing, accepted as a channel to status or plenty, if not a way to pay the bills, rarely as a means of understanding and controlling self and events.

In work and leisure the individual is regulated as part of the system, a consuming unit, bombarded by hard-sell, soft-sell, lies and semi-true appeals to his basest drives. . . .

The most spectacular and important creation of the authoritarian and oligopolistic structure of economic decision-making in America is the institution called "the military-industrial complex" by former President Eisenhower--the powerful congruence of interest and structure among military and business elites which affects so much of our development and destiny. Not only is ours the first generation to live with the possibility of world-wide cataclysm--it is the first to experience the actual social preparation for cataclysm, the general militarization of American society. . . .

Without new vision, the failure to achieve our potentialities will spell the inability of our society to endure in a world of obvious, crying needs and rapid change. . . .

1. America must abolish its political party stalemate. . . .

2. Mechanisms of voluntary association must be created through which political information can be imparted and political participation encouraged. . . .

3. Institutions and practices which stifle dissent should be abolished, and the promotion of peaceful dissent should be actively promoted. . . .

4. Corporations must be made publicly responsible. . . .

5. The allocation of resources must be based on social needs. A truly "public sector" must be established, and its nature debated and planned. . . .

6. America should concentrate on its genuine social priorities: abolish squalor, terminate neglect, and establish an environment for people to live in with dignity and creativeness.

A. A program against poverty must be just as sweeping as the nature of poverty itself. It must not be just palliative, but directed to the abolition of the structural circumstances of poverty. . . .

B. A full-scale public initiative for civil rights should be undertaken despite the clamor among conservatives (and liberals) about gradualism, property rights, and law and order. The executive and legislative branches of the Federal government should work by enforcement and enactment against any form of exploitation of minority groups. . . .

C. The promise and problems of long-range Federal economic development should be studied more constructively. . . .

D. We must meet the growing complex of "city" problems; over 90 percent of Americans will live in urban areas within two decades. Juvenile delinquency, untended mental illness, crime increase, slums, urban tenantry and non-rent controlled housing, the isolation of the individual in the city--all are problems of the city and are major symptoms of the present system of economic priorities and lack of public planning. . . .

E. Mental health institutions are in dire need; . . .

F. Our prisons are too often the enforcers of misery. . . .

G. Education is too vital a public problem to be completely entrusted to the province of the various states and local units. . . .

H. America should eliminate agricultural policies based on scarcity and pent-up surplus. . . .

I. Science should be employed to constructively transform the conditions of life throughout the United States and the world.

# MARTIN LUTHER KING, JR.: "I HAVE A DREAM" SPEECH (1963)

On August 28, 1963, Washington, D.C. witnessed the largest mass demonstration in the capital's history. The peaceful march moved from the Washington monument to the Lincoln Memorial, where in the shadow of the "Great Emancipator" black civil rights leaders addressed the multitude. The Rev. Dr. Martin Luther King, Jr., whose stature as a religious and political leader of blacks calling for the fulfillment of the American promise of freedom and justice was in full flower, spoke to an enthusiastic audience.

I am happy to join with you today in what will go down in history as the greatest demonstration for freedom in the history of our nation.

Five score years ago, a great American, in whose symbolic shadow we stand, signed the Emancipation Proclamation. This momentous decree came as a great beacon light of hope to millions of Negro salves who had been seared in the flames of withering injustice. It came as a joyous daybreak to end the long night of captivity.

But one hundred years later, the Negro is still not free; one hundred years later, the life of the Negro is still sadly crippled by the mancles of segregation and the chains of discrimination; one hundred years later, the Negro lives on a lonely island of poverty in the midst of a vast ocean of material prosperity; one hundred years later, the Negro still languishes in the corners of American society and finds himself an exile in his own land.

So we've come here today to dramatize a shameful condition. In a sense we've come to our nation's capital to cash a check. When the architects of our republic wrote the magnificent words of the Constitution and the Declaration of Independence, they were signing a promissory note to which every American was to fall heir. This note was a promise that all men, yes, black men as well as white men, would be guaranteed the unalienable rights of life, liberty, and the pursuit of happiness.

It is obvious today that America has defaulted on this promissory note in so far as her citizens of color are concerned. Instead of honoring this sacred obligation, America has given the Negro people a bad check; a check which has come back marked "insufficient funds." But we refuse to believe that the bank of justice is bankrupt. We refuse to believe that there are insufficient funds in the great vaults of opportunity of this nation. And so we've come to cash this check, a check that will give us upon demand the riches of freedom and the security of justice.

We have also come to this hallowed spot to remind America of the fierce urgency of now. This is no time to engage in the luxury of cooling off or to take the tranquilizing drug of gradualism. Now is the time to make real the promises of democracy; now is the time to rise from the dark and desolate valley of segregation to the sunlit path of racial justice; now is the time to

---

Dr. Martin Luther King, Jr., "I Have A Dream," August 28, 1963, Martin Luther King, Jr., Library, Atlanta, Georgia.

lift our nation from the quicksands of racial injustice to the solid rock of brotherhood; now is the time to make justice a reality for all God's children. It would be fatal for the nation to overlook the urgency of the moment. This sweltering summer of the Negro's legitimate discontent will not pass until there is an invigorating autumn of freedom and equality.

Nineteen Sixty-Three is not an end, but a beginning. And those who hope that the Negro needed to blow off steam and will now be content, will have a rude awakening if the nation returns to business as usual. There will be neither rest nor tranquillity in America until the Negro is granted his citizenship rights. The whirlwinds of revolt will continue to shake the foundations of our nation until the bright day of justice emerges.

But there is something that I must say to my people, who stand on the warm threshold which leads into the palace of justice. In the process of gaining our rightful place, we must not be guilty of wrongful deeds. Let us not seek to satisfy our thirst for freedom by drinking from the cup of bitterness and hatred. We must forever conduct our struggle on the high plane of dignity and discipline. We must not allow our creative protest to degenerate into physical violence. Again and again we must rise to the majestic heights of meeting physical force with soul force; and the marvelous new militancy, which has engulfed the Negro community, must not lead us to a distrust of all white people. For many of our white brothers, as evidenced by their presence here today, have come to realize that their destiny is tied up with our destiny. And they have come to realize that their freedom is inextricably bound to our freedom. We cannot walk alone. And as we walk, we must make the pledge that we shall march ahead. We cannot turn back.

There are those who are asking the devoteees of Civil Rights, "When will you be satisfied?" We can never be satisfied as long as the Negro is the victim of the unspeakable horrors of police brutality; we can never be satisfied as long as our bodies, heavy with the fatigue of travel, cannot gain lodging in the motels of the highways and the hotels of the cities; we cannot be satisfied as long as the Negro's basic mobility is from a smaller ghetto to a larger one; we can never be satisfied as long our children are stripped of their selfhood and robbed of their dignity by signs stating "For Whites Only"; we cannot be satisfied as long as the Negro in Mississippi cannot vote and a Negro in New York believes he has nothing for which to vote. No! No, we are not satisfied, and we will not be satisfied until "justice rolls down like waters and righteousness like a mighty stream."

I am not unmindful that some of you have come here out of great trials and tribulations. Some of you have come fresh from narrow jail cells. Some of you have come from areas where your quest for freedom left you battered by the storms of persecution and staggered by the winds of police brutality. You have been the veterans of creative suffering. Continue to work with the faith that unearned suffering is redemptive. Go back to Mississippi. Go back to Alabama. Go back to South Carolina. Go back to Georgia. Go back to Louisiana. Go back to the slums and ghettos of our Northern cities, knowing that somehow this situation can and will be changed. Let us not wallow in the valley of despair.

I say to you today, my friends, so even though we face the difficulties of today and tomorrow, I still have a dream. It is a dream deeply rooted in the American dream. I have a dream that one day this nation will rise up and live out the true meaning of its creed, "We hold these truths to be self-evident, that all men are created equal." I have a dream that one day on the red hills of Georgia, sons of former slaves and the sons of former slave owners will be able to sit down together at the table of brotherhood. I have a dream that one day even the state of Mississippi, a state sweltering with the heat of injustice, sweltering with the heat of oppression, will be transformed into an oasis of freedom and justice. I have a dream that my four little children will one day live in a nation where they will not be judged by the color of their skin, but by the content of their character.

I have a dream today!

I have a dream that one day down in Alabama with its vicious racists, with its Governor having his lips dripping with the words of interposition and nullification--one day right there in Alabama, little black boys and black girls will be able to join hands with little white boys and white girls as sisters and brothers.

I have a dream today!

I have a dream that one day "every valley shall be exalted and every hill and mountain shall be made low. The rough places will be made plain and the crooked places will be made straight, and the glory of the Lord shall be revealed, and all flesh shall see it together."

This is our hope. This is the faith that I go back to the South with. With this faith we will be able to hew out of the mountain of despair, a stone of hope. With this faith we will be able to transform the jangling discords of our nation into a beautiful symphony of brotherhood. With this faith we will be able to work together, to pray together, to struggle together, to go to jail together, to stand up for freedom together, knowing that we will be free one day. And this will be the day. This will be the day when all of God's children will be able to sing with new meaning, "My country 'tis of thee, sweet land of liberty, of thee I sing. Land where my fathers died, land of the pilgrim's pride, from every mountain side, let freedom ring." And if America is to be a great nation this must become true.

So let freedom ring from the prodigious hilltops of New Hampshire; let freedom ring from the mighty mountains of New York; let freedom ring from the heightening Alleghenies of Pennsylvania; let freedom ring from the snow-capped Rockies of Colorado; let freedom ring from the curvaceous slopes of California. But not only that. Let freedom ring from Stone Mountain of Georgia; let freedom ring from Lookout Mountain of Tennessee; let freedom ring from every hill and mole hill of Mississippi. From every mountainside, let freedom ring.

And when this happens, and when we allow freedom to ring, when we let it ring from every village and every hamlet, from every state and every city, we will be able to speed up that day when all of God's children, black men and white men, Jews and gentiles, Protestants and Catholics, will be able to join hands and sing in the words of the old Negro spiritual: "Free at last. Free at last. Thank God Almighty, we are free at last."


## STOKELY CARMICHAEL ON BLACK POWER (1966)

Leader of SNCC, the Student Nonviolent Coordinating Committee, Stokely Carmichael spoke for the frustration of blacks whose faith in the white-dominated political and economic systems in America had faded. Justice,

---

Stokely Carmichael, "What We Want," New York Review of Books, VII, (September 22, 1966), 5-8.

Carmichael felt, could not be won by polite requests that whites confer equality on them, or that blacks be allowed in white schools and neighborhoods. Carmichael's more far-reaching and disturbing demands are defined here, as he answers the fears of conservatives that blacks are just out to "get whitey," and the queries of well-meaning liberals who asked blacks what they really wanted. This radicalization of the civil rights movement in the turbulent 1960s is evidence of the violence and depth of black suffering and resentment after centuries of repression.

An organization which claims to speak for the needs of a community--as does the Student Nonviolent Coordinating Committee--must speak in the tone of that community, not as somebody else's buffer zone. This is the significance of black power as a slogan. For once, black people are going to use the words they want to use--not just the words whites want to hear. And they will do this no matter how often the press tries to stop the use of the slogan by equating it with racism or separatism. . . .
We should begin with the basic fact that black Americans have two problems: they are poor and they are black. All other problems arise from this two-sided reality: lack of education, the so-called apathy of black men. . . .
We had to work for power, because this country does not function by morality, love, and nonviolence, but by power. Thus we determined to win political power, with the idea of moving on from there into activity that would have economic effects. . . .
The right to vote had to be won, and SNCC workers devoted their energies to this from 1961 to 1965. . . .
All of the efforts were attempts to win black power. Then, in Alabama, the opportunity came to see how blacks could be organized on an independent party basis. An unusual Alabama law provides that any group of citizens can nominate candidates for county office and, if they win 20 per cent of the vote, may be recognized as a county political party. The same then applies on a state level. SNCC went to organize in several counties such as Lowndes, where black people--who form 80 per cent of the population and have an average annual income of $943--felt they could accomplish nothing within the framework of the Alabama Democratic Party because of its racism and because the qualifying fee for this year's elections was raised from $50 to $500 in order to prevent most Negroes from becoming candidates. On May 3, five new county "freedom organizations" convened and nominated candidates for the offices of sheriff, tax assessor, members of the school boards. These men and women are up for election in November--if they live until then. Their ballot symbol is the black panther: a bold, beautiful animal, representing the strength and dignity of black demands today. A man needs a black panther on his side when he and his family must endure--as hundreds of Alabamians have endured--loss of job, eviction, starvation, and sometimes death, for political activity. He may also need a gun and SNCC reaffirms the right of black men everywhere to defend themselves when threatened or attacked. As for initiating the use of violence, we hope that such programs as ours will make that unnecessary; but it is not for us to tell black communities whether they can or cannot use any particular form of action to resolve their problems. Responsibility for the use of violence by black men, whether in self defense or initiated by them, lies with the white community. . . .

The colonies of the United States--and this includes the black ghettoes within its borders, north and south--must be liberated. For a century, this nation has been like an octopus of exploitation, its tentacles stretching from Mississippi and Harlem to South America, the Middle East, southern Africa, and Vietnam; the form of exploitation varies from area to area but the essential result has been the same--a powerful few have been maintained and enriched at the expense of the poor and voiceless colored masses. This pattern must be broken. . . . For racism to die, a totally different America must be born. . . .

Integration today means the man who "makes it," leaving his black brothers behind in the ghetto as fast as his new sports car will take him. It has no relevance to the Harlem wino or to the cottonpicker making three dollars a day. As a lady I know in Alabama once said, "the food that Ralph Bunche eats doesn't fill my stomach."

Integration, moreover, speaks to the problem of blackness in a despicable way. As a goal, it has been based on complete acceptance of the fact that in order to have a decent house or education, blacks must move into a white neighborhood or send their children to a white school. This reinforces, among both black and white, the idea that "white" is automatically better and "black" is by defnition inferior. This is why integration is a subterfuge for the maintenance of white supremacy. . . .

We will not be told whom we should choose as allies. We will not be isolated from any group or nation except by our own choice. We cannot have the oppressors telling the oppressed how to rid themselves of the oppressor.

Black people do not want to "take over" this country. They don't want to "get whitey"; they just want to get him off their backs, as the saying goes. . . .

But our vision is not merely of a society in which all black men have enough to buy the good things of life. When we urge that black money go into black pockets, we mean the communal pocket. We want to see money go back into the community and used to benefit it. . . .

The society we seek to build among black people, then, is not a capitalist one. It is a society in which the spirit of community and humanistic love prevail.

## LYNDON JOHNSON'S WAR ON POVERTY (1964)

Forgotten amongst the materialism and prosperity and productivity of the 1950s was the existence of what Michael Harrington called the "Other America"--the poor. A government report in 1964 said that 1/5 of all American families struggled to survive with an income of under $3,000 a year. Despite the New Deal and President Eisenhower's promise that the federal government would intervene to prevent a recurrence of suffering like that

---

Lyndon B. Johnson, Public Papers of the Presidents of the United States: Lyndon B. Johnson, 1963-1964 (Washington, D.C., 1965), Book 1, 375-377.

which occurred during the Depression, this poverty persisted. President Kennedy had moved in the direction of relief, but it was President Johnson who called for all-out "war on poverty." If Johnson promised too much (as is often charged), those promises were not empty. Such programs as food stamps, the Job Corps, Medicare, and others provided untold relief to millions until severely curtailed or totally abolished by the administration of Ronald Reagan.

There are millions of Americans--one fifth of our people--who have not shared in the abundance which was been granted to most of us, and on whom the gates of opportunity have been closed.

What does this poverty mean to those who endure it?

It means a daily struggle to secure the necessities for even a meager existence. It means that the abundance, the comforts, the opportunities they see all around them are beyond their grasp.

Worst of all, it means hopelessness for the young.

The young man or woman who grows up without a decent education, in a broken home, in a hostile and squalid environment, in ill health or in the face of racial injustice--that young man or woman is often trapped in a life of poverty.

He does not have the skills demanded by a complex society. He does not know how to acquire those skills. He faces a mounting sense of despair which drains initiative and ambition and energy . . . .

The war on poverty is not a struggle simply to support people, to make them dependent on the generosity of others.

It is a struggle to give people a chance.

It is an effort to allow them to develop and use their capacities, as we have been allowed to develop and use ours, so that they can share, as others share, in the promise of this nation.

We do this, first of all, because it is right that we should.

From the establishment of public education and land grant colleges through agricultural extension and encouragement to industry, we have pursued the goal of a nation with full and increasing opportunities for all its citizens.

The war on poverty is a further step in that pursuit.

We do it also because helping some will increase the prosperity of all.

Our fight against poverty will be an investment in the most valuable of our resources--the skills and strength of our people.

And in the future, as in the past, this investment will return its cost many fold to our entire economy.

If we can raise the annual earnings of 10 million among the poor by only $1,000 we will have added 14 billion dollars a year to our national output. In addition we can make important reductions in public assistance payments which now cost us 4 billion dollars a year, and in the large costs of fighting crime and delinquency, disease and hunger.

This is only part of the story.

Our history has proved that each time we broaden the base of abundance, giving more people the chance to produce and consume, we create new industry, higher production, increased earnings and better income for all.

Giving new opportunity to those who have little will enrich the lives of all the rest.

Because it is right, because it is wise, and because, for the first time in our history, it is possible to conquer poverty, I submit, for the consideration of the Congress and the country, the Economic Opportunity Act of 1964.

The Act does not merely expand old programs or improve what is already being done.

It charts a new course.

It strikes at the causes, not just the consequences of poverty.

It can be a milestone in our one-hundred eighty year search for a better life for our people.

## LYNDON B. JOHNSON ON THE VOTING RIGHTS ACT (1965)

In response to bloody repression in Selma, Alabama, and the murder of the Reverend James Reeb, President Johnson delivered the most emotional speech of his career, calling for voting rights legislation to be enacted immediately by Congress. The subsequent passage of the monumental act was one of Johnson's greatest achievements.

I speak tonight for the dignity of man and the destiny of democracy.

I urge every member of both parties, Americans of all religions and of all colors, from every section of this country, to join me in that cause.

At times history and fate meet at a single time in a single place to shape a turning point in man's unending search for freedom. So it was at Lexington and Concord. So it was a century ago at Appomattox. So it was last week in Selma, Alabama.

There, long-suffering men and women peacefully protested the denial of their rights as Americans. Many were brutally assaulted . . . .

There is no Negro problem. There is no Southern problem. There is no Northern problem. There is only an American problem. And we are met here tonight as Americans--not as Democrats or Republicans--we are met here as Americans to solve that problem.

This was the first nation in the history of the world to be founded with a purpose. The great phrases of that purpose still sound in every American heart, North and South: "All men are created equal"--"government by consent of the governed"--give me liberty or give me death." . . . .

Those words are a promise to every citizen that he shall share in the dignity of man. This dignity cannot be found in a man's possessions; it cannot be found in his power, or in his position. It really rests on his right to be treated as a man equal in opportunity to all others. It says that he shall share in freedom, he shall choose his leaders, educate his children, and provide for his family according to his ability and his merits as a human being . . . .

---

Lyndon B. Johnson, <u>Public Papers of the Presidents of the United States: Lyndon B. Johnson, 1965</u> (Washington, D.C., 1966), Book 1, 281-284.

Many of the issues of civil rights are very complex and most difficult. But about this there can and should be no argument. Every American citizen must have an equal right to vote. There is no reason which can excuse the denial of that right. There is no duty which weighs more heavily on us than the duty we have to insure that right.

Yet the harsh fact is that in many places in this country men and women are kept from voting simply because they are Negroes . . . .

Experience has clearly shown that the existing process of law cannot overcome systematic and ingenious discrimination. No law that we now have on the books--and I have helped to put three of them there--can insure the right to vote when local officials are determined to deny it.

In such a case our duty must be clear to all of us. The Constitution says that no person shall be kept from voting because of his race or his color. We have all sworn an oath before God to support and to defend that Constitution. We must now act in obedience to that oath.

Wednesday I will send to Congress a law designed to eliminate illegal barriers to the right to vote . . . .

To those who seek to avoid action by their National Government in their own communities; who want to and who seek to maintain purely local control over elections, the answer is simple:

Open your polling places to all your people.

Allow men and women to register and vote whatever the color of their skin.

Extend the rights of citizenship to every citizen of this land.

There is no constitutional issue here. The command of the Constitution is plain.

There is no moral issue. It is wrong--deadly wrong--to deny any of your fellow Americans the right to vote in this country.

There is no issue of States Rights or national rights. There is only the struggle for human rights.

I have not the slightest doubt what will be your answer . . . .

But even if we pass this bill, the battle will not be over. What happened in Selma is part of a far larger movement which reaches into every section and State of America. It is the effort of American Negroes to secure for themselves the full blessings of American life.

Their cause must be our cause too. Because it is not just Negroes, but really it is all of us, who must overcome the crippling legacy of bigotry and injustice.

And we shall overcome . . . .

This great, rich, restless country can offer opportunity and education and hope to all: black and white, North and South, sharecropper and city dweller. These are the enemies: poverty, ignorance, disease. They are the enemies and not our fellow man, not our neighbor. And these enemies too, poverty, disease, and ignorance, we shall overcome.

## THE KERNER COMMISSION REPORT ON CIVIL DISTURBANCES (1968)

The U.S. Kerner Commission, appointed by President Johnson, published a voluminous study of the riots that spread from Newark, New Jersey in 1967 to other large cities. The Commission did a thorough job of fact-finding, carefully describing the usually fairly trivial specific events that triggered the violence and chronicling the course of events. The Report then inquired into the root causes of the riots, and offered observations on what public policy options existed, rejecting calls by conservatives for a "get-tough" policy of beefing up police forces and imposing stricter penalties on those who threatened public order.

II. Choices for the Future

The complexity of American society offers many choices for the future of relations between central cities and suburbs and patterns of white and Negro settlement in metropolitan areas. For practical purposes, however, we see two fundamental questions:
1. Should future Negro population growth be concentrated in central cities, as in the past 20 years, and should Negro and white populations become even more residentially segregated?
2. Should society provide greatly increased special assistance to Negroes and other relatively disadvantaged population groups?

For purposes of analysis, the Commission has defined three basic choices for the future embodying specific answers to these questions.

The Present Policies Choice

Under this course, the nation would maintain approximately the share of resources now being allocated to programs of assistance for the poor, unemployed, and disadvantaged. These programs are likely to grow, given continuing economic growth and rising federal revenues, but they will not grow fast enough to stop, let alone reverse, the already deteriorating quality of life in central-city ghettos.

This choice carries the highest ultimate price, as we will point out.

The Enrichment Choice

Under this course, the nation would seek to offset the effects of continued Negro segregation and deprivation in large city ghettos. The Enrichment Choice would aim at creating dramatic improvements in the quality of life in disadvantaged central-city neighborhoods--both white and Negro. It would require marked increases in federal spending for education, housing, employment, job training, and social services.

The Enrichment Choice would seek to lift poor Negroes and whites above poverty status and thereby give them the capacity to enter the mainstream of American life. But it would not, at least for many years, appreciably affect either the increasing concentration of Negroes in the ghetto or racial segregation in residential areas outside the ghetto.

The Integration Choice

This choice would be aimed at reversing the movement of the country toward two societies, separate and unequal.

---

Report of the National Advisory Commission on Civil Disorders (New York, 1968), pp. 395-407.

The Integration Choice--like the Enrichment Choice--would call for large-scale improvement in the quality of ghetto life. But it would also involve both creating strong incentives for Negro movement out of central-city ghettos and enlarging freedom of choice concerning housing, employment, and schools.

The result would fall considerably short of full integration. The experience of other ethnic groups indicates that some Negro households would be scattered in largely white residential areas. Others--probably a larger number--would voluntarily cluster together in largely Negro neighborhoods. The Integration Choice would thus produce both integration and segregation. But the segregation would be voluntary.

Articulating these three choices plainly oversimplifies the possibilities open to the country. We believe, however, that they encompass the basic issues--issues which the American public must face if it is serious in its concern not only about civil disorder, but the future of our democratic society . . . .

IV. The Enrichment Choice

The Present Policies Choice plainly would involve continuation of efforts like Model Cities, manpower programs, and the War on Poverty. These are in fact enrichment programs, designed to improve the quality of life in the ghetto.

Because of their limited scope and funds, however, they constitute only very modest steps toward enrichment--and would continue to do so even if these programs were somewhat enlarged or supplemented.

The premise of the Enrichment Choice is performance. To adopt this choice would require a substantially greater share of national resources--sufficient to make a dramatic, visible impact on life in the urban Negro ghetto.

The Effect of Enrichment on Civil Disorders

Effective enrichment policies probably would have three immediate effects on civil disorders.

First, announcement of specific large-scale programs and the demonstration of a strong intent to carry them out might persuade ghetto residents that genuine remedies for their problems were forthcoming, thereby allaying tensions.

Second, such announcements would strongly stimulate the aspirations and hopes of members of these communities--possibly well beyond the capabilities of society to deliver and to do so promptly. This might increase frustration and discontent, to some extent cancelling the first effect.

Third, if there could be immediate action on meaningful job training and the creation of productive jobs for large numbers of unemployed young people, they would become much less likely to engage in civil disorders.

Such action is difficult now, when there are about 583,000 young Negro men aged 16 to 24 in central cities--of whom 131,000 or 22.5 percent, are unemployed and probably two or three times as many are underemployed. It will not become easier in the future. By 1975, this age group will have grown to nearly 700,000 . . . .

Consequently, there is no certainty that the Enrichment Choice would do much more in the near future to diminish violent incidents in central cities than would the Present Policies Choice. However, if enrichment programs can succeed in meeting the needs of residents of disadvantaged areas for jobs, education, housing, and city services, then over the years this choice is almost certain to reduce both the level and frequency of urban disorder. . . .

Separate But Equal Societies?

The Enrichment Choice by no means seeks to perpetuate racial segregation. In the end, however, its premise is that disadvantaged Negroes can achieve equality of opportunity with whites while continuing in conditions of nearly complete separation.

This premise has been vigorously advocated by black power proponents. While most Negroes originally desired racial integration, many are losing hope of ever achieving it because of seemingly implacable white resistance. Yet they cannot bring themselves to accept the conclusion that most of the millions of Negroes who are forced to live racially segregated lives must therefore be condemned to inferior lives—to inferior educations, or inferior housing, or inferior status.

Rather, they reason, there must be some way to make the quality of life in the ghetto areas just as good. And if equality cannot be achieved through integration then it is not surprising that some Black Power advocates are denouncing integration and claiming that, given the hypocrisy and racism that pervade white society, life in a black society is, in fact, morally superior. This argument is understandable, but there is a great deal of evidence that it is false.

The economy of the United States and particularly the sources of employment are preponderantly white. In this circumstance, a policy of separate but equal employment could only relegate Negroes permanently to inferior incomes and economic status.

In the end, whatever its benefits, the Enrichment Choice might well invite a prospect similar to that of the Present Policies Choice: separate white and black societies . . . .

V. The Integration Choice

The third and last course open to the nation combines enrichment with programs designed to encourage integration of substantial numbers of Negroes into the society outside the ghetto.

Enrichment must be an important adjunct to any integration course. No matter how ambitious or energetic such a program may be, few Negroes now living in central-city ghettos would be quickly integrated. In the meantime, significant improvement in their present environment is essential.

The enrichment aspect of this third choice should, however, be recognized as interim action, during which time expanded and new programs can work to improve education and earning power. The length of the interim period surely would vary. For some it may be long. But in any event, what should be clearly recognized is that enrichment is only a means toward the goal; it is not the goal.

The goal must be achieving freedom for every citizen to live and work according to his capacities and desires, not his color.

We believe there are four important reasons why American society must give this course the most serious consideration. First, future jobs are being created primarily in the suburbs, but the chronically unemployed population is increasingly concentrated in the ghetto. This separation will make it more and more difficult for Negroes to achieve anything like full employment in decent jobs. But if, over time, these residents began to find housing outside central cities, they would be exposed to more knowledge of job opportunities. They would have to make much shorter trips to reach jobs. They would have a far better chance of securing employment on a self-sustaining basis.

Second, in the judgment of this Commission, racial and social-class integration is the most effective way of improving the education of ghetto children.

Third, developing an adequate housing supply for low-income and middle-income families and true freedom of choice of housing for Negroes of all income levels will require substantial out-movement. We do not believe that such an out-movement will occur spontaneously merely as a result of increasing prosperity among Negroes in central cities. A national fair housing law is essential to begin such movement. In many suburban areas, a program combining positive incentives with the building of new housing will be necessary to carry it out.

Fourth, and by far the most important, integration is the only course which explicitly seeks to achieve a single nation rather than accepting the present movement toward a dual society. This choice would enable us at least to begin reversing the profoundly divisive trend already so evident in our metropolitan areas--before it becomes irreversible.

## THE EQUAL RIGHTS AMENDMENT (1972)

Despite the great promise of civil and political rights offered by the 14th and 15th amendments, women did not win equality in the 19th century. The women's rights movement of the late 19th and early 20th centuries narrowed its focus from the broad concerns voiced in the Declaration of Sentiments at Seneca Falls to the one issue the movement felt was the key to unlocking all other doors: the vote. But the 19th amendment, ratified in time for women to vote in the 1920 presidential election, did not automatically transform America into a nation that practiced equality of the sexes, as some suffragists had hoped. The campaign for a broad view of equality gathered steam in the 1960s, and was conducted on a variety of fronts--the courtroom, the workplace, and even the home. And once again, a group of Americans who felt they had been denied fulfillment of America's basic promises of equality and justice sought constitutional remedy: an equal rights amendment. Such amendments had been proposed in every session of Congress since 1923, but in 1972 the following amendment was approved and sent to the states for ratification. In 1979 Congress extended the deadline for ratification to 1982. Born of the liberal aspirations and devotion to legal equality and civil rights of the 1960s and early seventies, the ERA succumbed to intensive opposition from groups such as the ultraconservative John Birch Society and well-financed lobbyists, the most famous of whom was Phyllis Schlafly. The amendment failed to be ratified by the requisite number of states to become America's 27th Amendment in the more conservative 1980s. Its wording may be compared with that of the 15th and 19th Amendments.

---

H. R. J. Res. 208, 92d Cong., 1st sess., 86 Stat, 1523 (1971).

Sec. 1.  Equality of rights under the law shall not be denied or abridged by the United States or by any State on account of sex.
Sec. 2.  The Congress shall have the power to enforce, by appropriate legislation, the provisions of this article.
Sec. 3.  This amendment shall take effect two years after the date of ratification.

## ORIGINS OF AMERICAN INVOLVEMENT IN INDOCHINA (1950)[1]

The invasion of South Korea by North Korean forces in June, 1950, set in motion a new determination in Washington to resist the perceived international communist conspiracy directed from Moscow. Although President Truman, in a speech on June 27, dealt primarily with the crisis in Korea, he also addressed communist threats to Formosa (Taiwan) and French Indochina.

 The attack upon Korea makes it plain beyond all doubt that communism has passed beyond the use of subversion to conquer independent nations and will now use armed invasion and war. It has defied the orders of the Security Council of the United Nations issued to preserve international peace and security . . . .
 Accordingly I have ordered the 7th Fleet to prevent any attack on Formosa . . . .
 I have similarly directed acceleration in the furnishing of military assistance to the forces of France and the Associated States in Indochina and the dispatch of a military mission to provide close working relations with those forces.
 I know that all members of the United Nations will consider carefully the consequences of this latest aggression in Korea in defiance of the Charter of the United Nations. A return to the rule of force in international affairs would have far-reaching effects. The United States will continue to uphold the rule of law.

## GULF OF TONKIN RESOLUTION (1964)[2]

Cn August 2, 1964, three North Vietnamese torpedo boats attacked the American destroyer Maddox, in international waters. The Johnson administration chose to ignore the incident but did dispatch another

---

[1] Harry S. Truman, Public Papers of the Presidents of the United States: Harry S. Truman, 1950 (Washington, D.C., 1965), p. 492.

[2] Public Law 88-408, U. S. Statutes at Large, 88th Cong., 2nd sess., LXXVIII (1964), p. 384.

destroyer, C. Turner Joy, to join the Maddox. During the night of August 4, the two destroyers reported that they were being attacked. Subsequent investigations, which took note of unusual weather conditions and confused radar procedures, have since called into question whether or not an attack actually occurred that night. In any event, leaders in Washington, including Secretary of Defense Robert S. MacNamara, believed that an attack was taking place, and they acted accordingly. Early on August 5, U. S. planes--with the approval of the National Security Council and the President--struck North Vietnam in retaliation. Moreover, President Johnson asked Congress for a statement of support. Congress then adopted the so-called Gulf of Tonkin Resolution on August 7.

Whereas naval units of the Communist regime in Vietnam, in violation of the principles of the Charter of the United Nations and of international law, have deliberately and repeatedly attacked United States naval vessels lawfully present in international waters, and have thereby created a serious threat to international peace; and

Whereas these attacks are part of a deliberate and systematic campaign of aggression that the Communist regime in North Vietnam has been waging against its neighbors and the nations joined with them in the collective defense of their freedom; and

Whereas the United States is assisting the peoples of southeast Asia to protect their freedom and has no territorial, military or political ambitions in that area, but desires only that these peoples should be left in peace to work out their own destinies in their own way: Now, therefore, be it

Resolved by the Senate and House of Representatives of the United States of America in Congress assembled, That the Congress approves and supports the determination of the President, as Commander in Chief, to take all necessary measures to repel any armed attack against the forces of the United States and to prevent further aggression.

Sec. 2. The United States regards as vital to its national interest and to world peace the maintenance of international peace and security in southeast Asia. Consonant with the Constitution of the United States and the Charter of the United Nations and in accordance with its obligations under the Southeast Asia Collective Defense Treaty, the United States is, therefore, prepared, as the President determines, to take all necessary steps, including the use of armed force, to assist any member or protocol state of the Southeast Asia Collective Defense Treaty requesting assistance in defense of its freedom.

Sec. 3. This resolution shall expire when the President shall determine that the peace and security of the area is reasonably assured by international conditions created by action of the United Nations or otherwise, except that it may be terminated earlier by concurrent resolution of the Congress.

## PRESIDENT JOHNSON ON U.S. INVOLVEMENT IN VIETNAM (1965)

Even before the massive American buildup in Southeast Asia, President Johnson sought to prepare a convincing case which would justify U.S. involvement in the war. His speech at The Johns Hopkins University, entitled "Peace Without Conquest," on April 7, 1965 furnished an important part of the framework for Johnson's rationale.

Tonight Americans and Asians are dying for a world where each people may choose its own path to change.

This is the principle for which our ancestors fought in the valleys of Pennsylvania. It is the principle for which our sons fight tonight in the jungles of Viet-Nam.

Viet-Nam is far away from this quiet campus. We have no territory there, nor do we seek any. The war is dirty and brutal and difficult. And some 400 young men, born into an America that is bursting with opportunity and promise, have ended their lives on Viet-Nam's steaming soil.

Why must we take this painful road?

Why must this Nation hazard its ease, and its interest, and its power for the sake of a people so far away?

We fight because we must fight if we are to live in a world where every country can shape its own destiny. And only in such a world will our own freedom be finally secure. . . .

The world as it is in Asia is not a serene or peaceful place.

The first reality is that North Viet-Nam has attacked the independent nation of South Viet-Nam. Its object is total conquest.

Of course, some of the people of South Viet-Nam are participating in attack on their own government. But trained men and supplies, orders and arms, flow in a constant stream from north to south.

This support is the heartbeat of the war. . . .

The confused nature of this conflict cannot mask the fact that it is the new face of an old enemy.

Over this war--and all Asia--is another reality: the deepening shadow of Communist China. The rulers in Hanoi are urged on by Peking. This is a regime which has destroyed freedom in Tibet, which has attacked India, and has been condemned by the United Nations for aggression in Korea. It is a nation which is helping the forces of violence in almost every continent. The contest in Viet-Nam is part of a wider pattern of aggressive purposes.

Why are these realities our concern? Why are we in South Viet-Nam?

<u>We are there because we have a promise to keep.</u> Since 1954 every American President has offered support to the people of South Viet-Nam. We have helped to build, and we have helped to defend. Thus, over many years, we have made a national pledge to help South Viet-Nam defend its independence. And I intend to keep that promise.

To dishonor that pledge, to abandon this small and brave nation to its enemies, and to the terror that must follow, would be an unforgivable wrong.

<u>We are also there to strengthen world order.</u> Around the globe, from Berlin to Thailand, are people whose well-being rests, in part, on the belief

---

Lyndon B. Johnson, <u>Public Papers of the Presidents of the United States: Lyndon B. Johnson, 1965</u> ( Washington, D.C., 1966), I, 394-399.

that they can count on us if they are attacked. To leave Viet-Nam to its fate would shake the confidence of all these people in the value of an American commitment and in the value of America's word. The result would be increased unrest and instability, and even wider war.

<u>We are also there because there are great stakes in the balance</u>. Let no one think for a moment that retreat from Viet-Nam would bring an end to conflict. The battle would be renewed in one country and then another. The central lesson of our time is that the appetite of aggression is never satisfied. To withdraw from one battlefield means only to prepare for the next. We must say in southeast Asia--as we did in Europe--in the words of the Bible: "Hitherto shalt thou come, but no further."

There are those who say that all our effort there will be futile--that China's power is such that it is bound to dominate all southeast Asia. But there is no end to that argument until all of the nations of Asia are swallowed up.

There are those who wonder why we have a responsibility there. Well, we have it there for the same reason that we have a responsibility for the defense of Europe. World War II was fought in both Europe and Asia, and when it ended we found ourselves with continued responsibility for the defense of freedom.

Our objective is the independence of South Viet-Nam, and its freedom from attack. We want nothing for ourselves--only that the people of South Viet-Nam be allowed to guide their own country in their own way.

We will do everything necessary to reach that objective. And we will do only what is absolutely necessary.

In recent months attacks on South Viet-Nam were stepped up. Thus, it became necessary for us to increase our response and to make attacks by air. This is not a change of purpose. It is a change in what we believe that purpose requires.

We do this in order to slow down aggression.

We do this to increase the confidence of the brave people of South Viet-Nam who have bravely borne this brutal battle for so many years with so many casualties.

And we do this to convince the leaders of North Viet-Nam--and all who seek to share their conquest--of a very simple fact:

We will not be defeated.

We will not grow tired.

We will not withdraw, either openly or under the cloak of a meaningless agreement.

We know that air attacks alone will not accomplish all of these purposes. But it is our best and prayerful judgment that they are a necessary part of the surest road to peace.

We hope that peace will come swiftly. But that is in the hands of others besides ourselves. And we must be prepared for a long continued conflict. It will require patience as well as bravery, the will to endure as well as the will to resist.

I wish it were possible to convince others with words of what we now find it necessary to say with guns and planes: Armed hostility is futile. Our resources are equal to any challenge. Because we fight for values and we fight for principles, rather than territory or colonies, our patience and our determination are unending.

Once this is clear, than it should also be clear that the only path for reasonable men is the path of peaceful settlement.

Such peace demands an independent South Viet-Nam--securely guaranteed and able to shape its own relationships to all others--free from outside interference--tied to no alliance--a military base for no other country.

These are the essentials of any final settlement.

We will never be second in the search for such a peaceful settlement in Viet-Nam. . . .

We have stated this position over and over again, fifty times and more, to friend and foe alike. And we remain ready, with this purpose, for unconditional discussions.

And until that bright and necessary day of peace we will try to keep conflict from spreading. We have no desire to see thousands die in battle-- Asians or Americans. We have no desire to devastate that which the people of North Viet-Nam have built with toil and sacrifice. We will use our power with restraint and with all the wisdom that we can command.

But we will use it.

This war, like most wars, is filled with terrible irony. For what do the people of North Viet-Nam want? They want what their neighbors also desire: food for their hunger; health for their bodies; a chance to learn; progress for their country; and an end to the bondage of material misery. And they would find all these things far more readily in peaceful association with others than in the endless course of battle. . . .

The first step is for the countries of southeast Asia to associate themselves in a greatly expanded cooperative effort for development. We would hope that North Viet-Nam would take its place in the common effort just as soon as peaceful cooperation is possible.

The United Nations is already actively engaged in development in this area. As far back as 1961 I conferred with our authorities in Viet-Nam in connection with their work there. And I would hope tonight that the Secretary General of the United Nations could use the prestige of his great office, and his deep knowledge of Asia, to initiate, as soon as possible, with the countries of that area, a plan for cooperation in increased development.

For our part I will ask the Congress to join in a billion dollar American investment in this effort as soon as it is underway.

And I would hope that all other industrialized countries, including the Soviet Union, will join in this effort to replace despair with hope, and terror with progress.

The task is nothing less than to enrich the hopes and the existence of more than a hundred million people. And there is much to be done.

**The va**st Mekong River can provide food and water and power on a scale to dwarf even our own TVA.

The wonders of modern medicine can be spread through villages where thousands die every year from lack of care.

Schools can be established to train people in the skills that are needed to manage the process of development.

And these objectives, and more, are within the reach of a cooperative and determined effort.

I also intend to expand and speed up a program to make available our farm surpluses to assist in feeding and clothing the needy in Asia. We should not allow people to go hungry and wear rags while our own warehouses overflow with an abundance of wheat and corn, rice and cotton. . . .

This will be a disorderly planet for a long time. In Asia, as elsewhere, the forces of the modern world are shaking old ways and uprooting ancient civilizations. There will be turbulence and struggle and even violence. Great social change--as we see in our own country now--does not always comes without conflict.

We must also expect that nations will on occasion be in dispute with us. It may be because we are rich, or powerful; or because we have made some mistakes; or because they honestly fear our intentions. However, no nation need ever fear that we desire their land, or to impose our will, or to dictate their institutions.

But we will always oppose the effort of one nation to conquer another nation.

We will do this because our own security is at stake. . . .

We often say how impressive power is. But I do not find it impressive at all. The guns and the bombs, the rockets and the warships, are all symbols of human failure. They are necessary symbols. They protect what we cherish. But they are witness to human folly.

A dam built across a great river is impressive.

In the countryside where I was born, and where I live, I have seen the night illuminated, and the kitchens warmed, and the homes heated, where once the cheerless night and the ceaseless cold held sway. And all this happened because electricity came to our area along the humming wires of the REA. Electrification of the countryside--yes, that, too, is impressive.

A rich harvest in a hungry land is impressive.

The sight of healthy children in a classroom is impressive.

These--not mighty arms--are the achievements which the American Nation believes to be impressive.

And, if we are steadfast, the time may come when all other nations will also find it so.

Every night before I turn out the lights to sleep I ask myself this question: Have I done everything that I can do to unite this country? Have I done everything I can to help unite the world, to try to bring peace and hope to all the peoples of the world? Have I done enough?

Ask yourselves that question in your homes--and in this hall tonight. Have we, each of us, all done all we could? Have we done enough?

We may well be living in the time foretold many years ago when it was said: "I call heaven and earth to record this day against you, that I have set before you life and death, blessing and cursing: therefore choose life, that both thou and they seed may live."

This generation of the world must choose: destroy or build, kill or aid, hate or understand.

We can do all these things on a scale never dreamed of before.

<u>Well, we will choose life</u>. In so doing we will prevail over the enemies within man, and over the natural enemies of all mankind.

## ROBERT F. KENNEDY ON THE VIETNAM WAR (1968)

*During the early stages of America's active involvement in Vietnam, Robert F. Kennedy supported the Johnson administration. As the war dragged on, however, and with the spectacular events of Tet 1968, Senator Kennedy publicly dissented from President Johnson's policies. Shortly after the Tet Offensive began, Kennedy made the following speech. He would soon declare himself a candidate for president.*

The events of the last few weeks have demonstrated anew the truth of Lord Halifax's dictum that although hope "is very good company by the way . . . (it) is generally a wrong guide."

Our enemy, savagely striking at will across all of South Vietnam, has finally shattered the mask of official illusion with which we have concealed our true circumstances, even from ourselves. But a short time ago we were serene in our reports and predictions of progress. . . .

Those dreams are gone. The Vietcong will probably withdraw from the cities, as they were forced to withdraw from the American Embassy. Thousands of them will be dead. But they will, nevertheless, have demonstrated that no part or person of South Vietnam is secure from their attacks: neither district capitals nor American bases, neither the peasant in his rice paddy nor the commanding general of our own great forces. . . .

For the sake of those young Americans who are fighting today, if for no other reason, the time has come to take a new look at the war in Vietnam; not by cursing the past but by using it to illuminate the future. And the first and necessary step is to face the facts. It is to seek out the austere and painful reality of Vietnam, freed from wishful thinking, false hopes and sentimental dreams. It is to rid ourselves of the "good company" of those illusions which have lured us into the deepening swamp of Vietnam. "If you would guide by the light of reason," said Holmes, "you must let your mind be bold." We will find no guide to the future in Vietnam unless we are bold enough to confront the grim anguish, the reality, of that battlefield which was once a nation called South Vietnam, stripped of deceptive illusions. It is time for the truth.

We must, first of all, rid ourselves of the illusion that the events of the past two weeks represent some sort of victory. That is not so.

It is said the Vietcong will not be able to hold the cities. This is probably true. But they have demonstrated despite all our reports of progress, of government strength and enemy weakness, that half a million American soldiers with 700,000 Vietnamese allies, with total command of the air, total command of the sea, backed by huge resources and the most modern weapons, are unable to secure even a single city from the attacks of an enemy whose total strength is about 250,000. . . .

We are told that the enemy suffered terrible losses; and there is no doubt he did. They cannot, however, be as devastating as the figures appear. The Secretary of Defense has told us that "during all of 1967 the Communists lost about 165,000 effectives," yet enemy main force strength "has been maintained at a relatively constant level of about 110,000-115,000 during the past year." Thus it would seem that no matter how many Vietcong and North

---

U. S. Congress, Senate, 90th Cong., 2nd sess., February 8, 1968, <u>Congressional Record</u>, CXIV, 2671-2672.

Vietnamese we claim to kill, through some miraculous effort of will, enemy strength remains the same. Now our intelligence chief tells us that of 60,000 men thrown into the attacks on the cities, 20,000 have been killed. If only two men have been seriously wounded for everyone dead--a very conservative estimate--the entire enemy force has been put out of action. Who, then, is doing the fighting?

Again it is claimed that the Communists expected a large-scale popular uprising which did not occur. How ironic it is that we should claim a victory because a people whom we have given sixteen thousand lives, billions of dollars and almost a decade to defend, did not rise in arms against us. . . .

For years we have been told that the measure of our success and progress in Vietnam was increasing security and control for the population. Now we have seen that none of the population is secure and no area is under sure control. Four years ago when we only had about 30,000 troops in Vietnam, the Vietcong were unable to amount the assaults on cities they have now conducted against our enormous forces. At one time a suggestion that we protect enclaves was derided. Now there are no protected enclaves.

This has not happened because our men are not brave or effective, because they are. It is because we have misconceived the nature of the war: it is because we have sought to resolve by military might a conflict whose issue depends upon the will and conviction of the South Vietnamese people. It is like sending a lion to halt an epidemic of jungle rot.

This misconception rests on a second illusion--the illusion that we can win a war which the South Vietnamese cannot win for themselves.

Two Presidents and countless officials have told us for seven years that although we can help the South Vietnamese, it is their war and they must win it; as Secretary of Defense McNamara told us last month, "We cannot provide the South Vietnamese with the will to survive as an independent nation . . . or with the ability and self-discipline a people must have to govern themselves. These qualities and attributes are essential contributions to the struggle only the South Vietnamese can supply". Yet this wise and certain counsel has gradually become an empty slogan, as mounting frustration has led us to transform the war into an American military effort. . . .

Perhaps, we could live with corruption and inefficiency by themselves. However the consequence is not simply the loss of money or popular confidence; it is the loss of American lives. For government corruption is the source of the enemy's strength. It is, more than anything else, the reason why the greatest power on earth cannot defeat a tiny and primitive foe.

You cannot expect people to risk their lives and endure hardship unless they have a stake in their own society. They must have a clear sense of identification with their own government, a belief they are participating in a cause worth fighting for. Political and economic reform are not simply idealistic slogans or noble goals to be postponed until the fighting is over. They are the principal weapons of battle. People will not fight to line the pockets of generals or swell the bank accounts of the wealthy. They are far more likely to close their eyes and shut their doors in the face of their government--even as they did last week. . . .

The third illusion is that the unswerving pursuit of military victory, whatever its cost, is in the interest of either ourselves or the people of Vietnam. For the people of Vietnam, the last three years have meant little but horror. Their tiny land has been devastated by a weight of bombs and shells greater than Nazi Germany knew in the Second World War. We have dropped twelve tons of bombs for every square mile in North and South Vietnam. Whole provinces have been substantially destroyed. More than two million

South Vietnamese are now homeless refugees. Imagine the impact in our own country if an equivalent number--over 25 million Americans--were wandering homeless or interned in refugee camps, and millions more refugees were being created as New York and Chicago, Washington and Boston, were being destroyed by a war raging in their streets. Whatever the outcome of these battles, it is the people we seek to defend who are the greatest losers. . . .

The fourth illusion is that the American national interest is identical with--or should be subordinated to--the selfish interest of an incompetent military regime. We are told, of course, that the battle for South Vietnam is in reality a struggle for 250 million Asians--the beginning of a Great Society for all of Asia. But this is pretension. We can and should offer reasonable assistance to Asia; but we cannot build a Great Society there if we cannot build one in our own country. We cannot speak extravagantly of a struggle for 250 million Asians, when a struggle for 15 million in one Asian country so strains our forces, that another Asian country, a fourth-rate power which we have already once defeated in battle, dares to seize an American ship and hold and humiliate her crew. . . .

There is an American interest in South Vietnam. We have an interest in maintaining the strength of our commitments--and surely we have demonstrated that. With all the lives and resources we have poured into Vietnam, is there anyone to argue that a government with any support from its people, with any competence to rule, with any determination to defend itself, would not long ago have been victorious over any insurgent movement, however assisted from outside its borders?

And we have another, more immediate interest: to protect the lives of our gallant young men, and to conserve American resourcs. But we do not have an interest in the survival of a privileged class, growing ever more wealthy from the corruption of war, which after all our sacrifices on their behalf, can ask why Vietnamese boys should die for Americans.

The fifth illusion is that this war can be settled in our own way and in our own time on our own terms. Such a settlement is the privilege of the triumphant; or those who crush their enemies in battle or wear away their will to fight.

We have not done this, nor is there any prospect we will achieve such a victory. . . .

Unable to defeat our enemy or break his will--at least without a huge, long, and ever more costly effort--we must actively seek a peaceful settlement. We can no longer harden our terms everywhere Hanoi indicates it may be prepared to negotiate; and we must be willing to foresee a settlement which will give the Vietcong a chance to participate in the political life of the country. Not because we want them to, but because that is the only way in which this struggle can be settled. No one knows if negotiations will bring a peaceful settlement, but we do know there will be no peaceful settlement without negotiations. Nor can we have these negotiations just on our own terms. We may have to make concessions and take risks, and surely we will have to negotiate directly with the NLF as well as Hanoi. Surely it is only another illusion that still denies this basic necessity. What we must not do is confuse the prestige staked on a particular policy with the interest of the United States; nor should we be unwilling to take risks for peace when we are willing to risk so many lives in war. . . .

These are some of the illusions which must be discarded if the events of last week are to prove not simply a tragedy, but a lesson: a lesson which carries with it some basic truths.

First, that a total military victory is not within sight or around the corner; that, in fact, it is probably beyond our grasp; and that the effort to win such a victory will only result in the further slaughter of thousands of innocent and helpless people--a slaughter which will forever rest on our national conscience.

Second, that the pursuit of such a victory is not necessary to our national interest and is even damaging that interest.

Third, that the progress we have claimed toward increasing our control over the country and the security of the population is largely illusory.

Fourth, that the central battle in this war cannot be measured by body counts or bomb damage, but by the extent to which the people of South Vietnam act on a sense of common purpose and hope with those that govern them.

Fifth, that the current regime in Saigon is unwilling or incapable of being an effective ally in the war against the Communists.

Sixth, that a political compromise is not just the best path to peace, but the only path, and we must show as much willingness to risk some of our prestige for peace as to risk the lives of young men in war.

Seventh, that the escalation policy in Vietnam, far from strengthening and consolidating international resistance to aggression, is injuring our country through the world, reducing the faith of other peoples in our wisdom and purpose and weakening the world's resolve to stand together for freedom and peace.

Eighth, that the best way to save our most precious stake in Vietnam-- the lives of our soldiers--is to stop the enlargement of the war, and that the best way to end casualties is to end the war.

Ninth, that our nation must be told the truth about this war, in all its terrible reality, both because it is right--and because only in this way can any administration rally the public confidence and unity for the shadowed days which lie ahead.

No war has ever demanded more bravery from our people and our government--not just bravery under fire or the bravery to make sacrifices--but the bravery to discard the comfort of illusion--to do away with false hopes and alluring promises. Reality is grim and painful. But it is only a remote echo of the anguish toward which a policy founded on illusion is surely taking us. This is a great nation and a strong people. All who seek to comfort rather than speak plainly, reassure rather than instruct, promise satisfaction rather than reveal frustration--they deny that greatness and drain that strength. For today as it was in the beginning, it is the truth that makes us free.


SENATOR GEORGE McGOVERN ON THE VIETNAM WAR (1969)

No figure was more prominent in the anti-war movement than Senator George McGovern. He consistently called for U.S. disengagement from Vietnam as a course of action that best served American interests.

---

U. S. Congress, Senate, 91st Cong., 1st sess., October 27, 1969, Congressional Record, CXV, 31513-31514.

We meet today for the purpose of putting an end to the most tragic mistake in our national history--the cruel and futile war in Vietnam. We meet today to call our government away from folly into the paths that lead to peace.

This is a day both of regret and affirmation. This is a day not of name calling or violence or destruction. This is a day that calls not for the politics of revenge; but the politics of reconciliation--both at home and abroad.

We seek not to break the President, but to lift the terrible burden of war from his shoulders and from the American people. To do that we must accelerate the agonizingly slow pace of withdrawal from this hopeless conflict. That withdrawal will not be entirely free from pain and embarrassment, but it will be no easier a year from now or two years or five years after more thousands have died and our own society has been further eroded. The President has described Vietnam as our finest hour; it is not, it is our worst hour. The most urgent and responsible act of American citizenship in 1969 is to bring all possible pressure to bear on the Administration to order our troops out of Vietnam <u>now</u>. We are here to assert the claims of life over the further claims of death. . . .

Vietnam has taught us that we are capable of wandering away from the great traditions of our nation. But we have also demonstrated that we cannot surrender the ideals of Jefferson and Lincoln and the great moral principles of our society without setting in motion the forces of dissent and redemption.

So perhaps out of the blood-soaked jungles of Southeast Asia will come the humility and the national wisdom that will lead us into the light of a new day. This is the faith that brings us together this moratorium day--a day of conscience and commitment.

The President has said that his concern at this point is not how we got into Vietnam, but how we bring the war to an honorable conclusion. To me the most honorable way to end the war is to relax our embrace of General Thieu and begin the systematic withdrawal of our troops. . . . We must learn that it is madness--not security--to devote 70% of our controllable federal budget to armaments and only 11% to the quality of life. It is not national defense to spend $25 billion for a worthless Anti-ballistic missile defense and then render 15 million Americans defenseless by malnutrition. We must stop permitting the economy of death to starve the economy of life. We must stop trying to be the policeman of a revolutionary world!. . .

Our plea today is that our government get out of this war that breeds violence both at home and abroad. The Thieu-Ky regime is not worth the 40,000 young Americans who have died. It is not worth the 8,000 who have died in 1969. It is not worth the scores who will die this week. It is not worth one additional young life. Let's stop saving face and begin saving lives. Let us stop killing Asians and begin the healing of our own land . . . .

## WASHINGTON ON COMMUNIST VIOLATIONS OF THE 1973 TREATY (1975)

With the renewed communist military offensive in the south directed from Hanoi, Washington delivered this diplomatic protest. President Nixon had resigned in the aftermath of the Watergate disclosures, and neither President Gerald Ford nor Congress was in the

U. S. Department of State, <u>Bulletin</u>, LXXII (February 3, 1975, 144-45.

mood to fulfill the secret pledges.

When the Agreement was concluded nearly two years ago, our hope was that it would provide a framework under which the Vietnamese people could make their own political choices and resolve their own problems in an atmosphere of peace. Unfortunately this hope, which was clearly shared by the Republic of Viet-Nam and the South Vietnamese people, has been frustrated by the persistent refusal of the Democratic Republic of Viet-Nam to abide by the Agreement's most fundamental provisions. Specifically, in flagrant violation of the Agreement, the North Vietnamese and "Provisional Revolutionary Government" authorities have:

--built up the North Vietnamese mainforce army in the South through the illegal infiltration of over 160,000 troops;

--tripled the strength of their armor in the South by sending in over 400 new vehicles, as well as greatly increased their artillery and anti-aircraft weaponry;

--improved their military logistics system running through Laos, Cambodia and the Demilitarized Zone as well as within South Viet-Nam, and expanded their armament stockpiles;

--refused to deploy the teams which under the Agreement were to oversee the cease-fire;

--refused to pay their prescribed share of the expenses of the International Commission of Control and Supervision;

--failed to honor their commitment to cooperate in resolving the status of American and other personnel missing in action, even breaking off all discussions on this matter by refusing for the past seven months to meet with U.S. and Republic of Viet-Nam representatives in the Four-Party Joint Military Team;

--broken off all negotiations with the Republic of Viet-Nam including the political negotiations in Paris and the Two Party Joint Military Commission talks in Saigon, answering the Republic of Viet-Nam's repeated calls for unconditional resumption of the negotiations with demands for the overthrow of the government as a pre-condition for any renewed talks; and

--gradually increased their military pressure, over-running several areas, including 11 district towns, which were clearly and unequivocally held by the Republic of Viet-Nam at the time of the cease-fire. Their latest and most serious escalation of the fighting began in early December with offensives in the southern half of South Viet-Nam which have brought the level of casualties and destruction back up to what it was before the agreement. These attacks, which included for the first time since the massive North Vietnamese 1972 offensive the over-running of a province capital (Song Be in Phuoc Long Province)--appear to reflect a decision by Hanoi to seek once again to impose a military solution in Viet-Nam.

## NIXON ON U.S. PROMISES TO PROTECT THE REPUBLIC OF SOUTH VIETNAM (1972-73)

During the course of the negotiations leading to the 1973 treaty, President Thieu worried that the United States, in its eagerness to disengage from the war,

---

The texts of both letters were printed in New York Times, May 1, 1975.

might agree to terms which were unacceptable to his government. In fact, Thieu successfully resisted U. S. pressure to accept a proposed treaty just prior to the 1972 American presidential election because he felt the proposed agreement gave the communists too strong a position in South Vietnam. President Nixon, for his part, sought not only to allay anxieties in Saigon but also to ensure final approval of the proposed treaty. These secret Nixon letters were made public by a bitter President Thieu in 1975 during the final days before the communist victory.

a. Letter to Thieu, November 14, 1972

I understand from your letter and from General [Alexander] Haig's personal report that your principal remaining concern with respect to the draft agreement is the status of North Vietnamese forces now in South Vietnam. As General Haig explained to you, it is our intention to deal with this problem first by seeking to insert a reference to respect for the demilitarized zone in the proposed agreement and, second, by proposing a clause which provides for the reduction and demobilization of forces on both sides in South Vietnam on a one-to-one basis and to have demobilized personnel return to their homes. . . .

But far more important than what we say in the agreement on this issue is what we do in the event the enemy renews its aggression. You have my absolute assurance that if Hanoi fails to abide by the terms of this agreement it is my intention to take swift and severe retaliatory action. . . .

If, on the other hand, we are unable to agree on the course that I have outlined, it is difficult for me to see how we will be able to continue our common effort towards securing a just and honorable peace. As General Haig told you I would with great reluctance be forced to consider other alternatives. For this reason, it is essential that we have your agreement as we proceed into our next meeting with Hanoi's negotiators. . . .

Above all we must bear in mind what will really maintain the agreement. It is not any particular clause in the agreement but our joint willingness to maintain its clauses. I repeat my personal assurances to you that the United States will react very strongly and rapidly to any violation of the agreement. But in order to do this effectively it is essential that I have public support and that your government does not emerge as the obstacle to a peace which American public opinion now universally desires. It is for this reason that I am pressing for the acceptance of an agreement which I am convinced is honorable and fair and which can be made essentially secure by our joint determination.

b. Letter to Thieu, January 5, 1973

Accordingly, if the North Vietnamese meet our concerns. . . we will proceed to conclude the settlement. The gravest consequence would then ensue if your government chose to reject the agreement and split off from the United States. . . .

I can only repeat what I have so often said: The best guarantee for the survival of South Vietnam is the unity of our two countries which would be gravely jeopardized if you persist in your present course. The actions of our Congress since its return have clearly borne out the many warnings we have made.

Should you decide, as I trust you will, to go with us, you have my assurance of continued assistance in the post-settlement period and that we will respond with full force should the settlement be violated by North Vietnam. So once more I conclude with an appeal to you to close ranks with us.

## NIXON ON CHINA (1971-1972)

President Richard M. Nixon initiated a bold new move in recent American foreign policy when he arranged for closer ties between the United States and the People's Republic of China in 1971 - 1972. Early in his career, Nixon had made his political reputation as a staunch opponent of communism. It has been suggested that perhaps only someone with anti-communist credentials like his could make such a move politically and minimize the domestic repercussions, especially from American conservatives.

(a) Presidential Statement, July 15, 1971[1]

Premier Chou En-lai and Dr. Henry Kissinger, President Nixon's Assistant for National Security Affairs, held talks in Peking from July 9 to 11, 1971. Knowing of President Nixon's expressed desire to visit the People's Republic of China, Premier Chou En-lai on behalf of the Government of the People's Republic of China has extended an invitation to President Nixon to visit China at an appropriate date before May 1972.

President Nixon has accepted the invitation with pleasure.

The meeting between the leaders of China and the United States is to seek the normalization of relations between the two countries and also to exchange views on questions of concern to the two sides.

(b) Nixon's Report on His Journey to Peking (1972)[2]

My trip to the People's Republic of China from February 21 to February 28, 1972 was the watershed in reestablishing Sino-American relations. . . .

Seldom have the leaders of two major countries met with such an opportunity to create a totally new relationship. It had taken two and a half years to cross the gulf of isolation and reach the summit. At the same time, the very factors which had made this journey so complicated offered unusual opportunities. The absence of communication, while making initial contact complex to arrange, also gave us a clean slate to write upon. Factors such as geography and China's recent concentration on internal matters meant that we had few bilateral matters of contention, though we lined up often on different sides of third country or multilateral problems.

---

[1] Richard M. Nixon, Public Papers of the Presidents of the United States: Richard Nixon, 1972 (Washington, D.C., 1974), p. 212.

[2] Richard M. Nixon, Public Papers of the Presidents of the United States: Richard Nixon, 1973 (Washington, D.C., 1975), pp. 358-365.

Accordingly, the agenda for our discussions could be general and our dialogue philosophical to a much greater extent than is normally possible between nations. Indeed, it was this context and these prospects that, in our view, called for a summit meeting. With the Soviet Union a meeting at the highest levels was required to give impetus to, and conclude, a broad range of concrete negotiations. With the People's Republic of China, on the other hand, such a meeting was needed to set an entirely new course. Only through direct discussions at the highest levels could we decisively bridge the gulf that had divided us, conduct discussions on a strategic plane, and launch a new process with authority.

The primary objective, then, of my talks with the Chinese leaders was not the reaching of concrete agreements but a sharing of fundamental perspectives on the world. First, we had to establish a joint perception of the shape of our future relationship and its place in the international order. We needed a mutual assessment of what was involved in the new process we were undertaking and of one another's reliability in carrying the process forward. If we could attain this type of mutual comprehension, agreements could and would flow naturally. . . .

Accordingly, in the communique we agreed that despite differences in social systems and foreign policies, countries should conduct their relations on the basis of respect for sovereignty and territorial integrity, non-aggression against other states, non-interference in the internal affairs of others, equality and mutual benefit, and peaceful coexistence. International disputes should be settled on this basis without the use or threat of force. We and the People's Republic of China agreed to apply these principles to our mutual relations.

With these international principles in mind we stated that:

--progress toward the normalization of relations between China and the United States is in the interests of all countries;

--both wish to reduce the danger of international military conflict;

--neither should seek hegemony in the Asia-Pacific region and each is opposed to efforts by any other country or group of countries to establish such hegemony; and

--neither is prepared to negotiate on behalf of any third party or to enter into agreements or understandings with the other directed at other states.

Both sides are of the view that it would be against the interests of the peoples of the world for any major country to collude with another against other countries, or for major countries to divide up the world into spheres of interest.

These principles were of major significance. They demonstrated that despite our clear disagreements and our long separation we shared some fundamental attitudes toward international relations. They provided both a framework for our future relations and a yardstick by which to measure each other's performance.

With respect to the relationship of Taiwan to the mainland, the United States reaffirmed its interest in a peaceful solution of this question by the Chinese themselves. We based this view on the fact that all Chinese on either side of the Taiwan Strait maintain that there is but one China and that Taiwan is a part of China.

The communique then laid down the foundations for tangible improvements in our relations. These would allow us to move from the elimination of mistrust and the establishment of broad understandings to more concrete accomplishments:

--We agreed to facilitate bilateral exchanges in order to broaden the understanding between our peoples. Specific areas mentioned were science, technology, culture, sports, and journalism.
--We undertook to facilitate the progressive growth of trade between our countries. Both sides viewed economic relations based on equality and mutual benefit as being in the interests of our peoples.
--We decided to maintain contact through various channels, including sending a senior U.S. representative to Peking periodically to exchange views directly. This reflected a mutual desire to expand our communications.
--We also subsequently established a formal channel through our two embassies in Paris. This would institutionalize our contacts and facilitate exchanges, trade, and travel.

## WATERGATE, IMPEACHMENT PROCEEDINGS, AND THE RESIGNATION OF A PRESIDENT (1972-1974)

The burglarizing of the Democratic Party Headquarters in the Watergate Complex in Washington, D.C., during the campaign of 1972 had led to the arrest and conviction of men who were subsequently linked to the White House staff. Due to the dogged efforts of two reporters from the Washington Post, an honest Federal judge, and a Senate select committee, the government of Richard Nixon had been proven conclusively to be the most seriously corrupt administration in the history of the American Republic. The House of Representatives was preparing to impeach the President when he suddenly resigned.

(a) Resolution of the Committee on the Judiciary of the House of Representatives

Resolved, 'That Richard M. Nixon, President of the United States, is impeached for high crimes and midemeanors, and that the following articles of impeachment be exhibited to the Senate . . . .

[Article I] In his conduct of the office of President, Richard M. Nixon, in violation of his constitutional oath faithfully to execute the office of President and to the best of his ability, preserve, protect and defend the Constitution of the United States, and in violation of his constitutional duty to take care that the laws be faithfully executed, has prevented, obstructed, and impeded the administration of justice, in that:

Impeachment Inquiry Hearings Before the Committee on the Judiciary, House of Representatives, 93rd Congress, 2nd sess., Book III, pp. 2255-2256

On June 17, 1972, and prior thereto, agents of the committee for the Re-election of the President committed illegal entry of the headquarters of the Democratic National Committee in Washington, D.C., for the purpose of securing political intelligence. Subsequent thereto, Richard M. Nixon, using the powers of his high office, has made it his continuing policy to act, and in furtherance of that policy, did act, directly and personally and through his close subordinates and agents to delay, impede, and obstruct the investigation of such illegal entry; to cover up and conceal the identity of those responsible; and, to cover up and to conceal the existence and scope of related unlawful covert activities.

The means used to implement this policy have included one or more of the following or others:

(1) Making false or misleading statements to lawfully authorized investigative officers and employees of the Government of the United States or in duly instituted judicial proceedings.
(2) Approving, condoning, acquiescing in, and counseling witnesses to give false or misleading statements to investigative officers or false or misleading testimony in duly instituted judical and congressional proceedings.
(3) Interferring with the conduct of investigations by the Department of Justice, the Federal Bureau of Investigation, and the Watergate Special Prosecution Force.
(4) Approving and concealing the payment of money for the purpose of obtaining the silence of participants in the illegal entry into the headquarters of the Democratic National Committee and other illegal activities.
(5) Endeavoring to misuse the Central Intelligence Agency.
(6) Suppressing, withholding, and concealing relevant and material evidence.
(7) Endeavoring to cause prospective defendants, and persons duly tried and convicted, to expect favored treatment in return for their silence or false testimony.
(8) Disseminating information received from officers of the U.S. Department of Justice to subjects of investigations for the purpose of aiding and assisting their avoidance of criminal liability.
(9) Making false or misleading public statements in his capacity as President for the purpose of deceiving the people of the United States into believing that a thorough and complete investigation had been conducted into allegations of misconduct at the White House and the Committee for the Re-election of the President and that there was no involvement of personnel from the White House or the Committee to Re-elect the President in such misconduct.

All of this has been carried on by Richard M. Nixon in a manner contrary to his trust as President, to the manifest injury of the confidence of the Nation and to the great prejudice of the cause of law and justice, and to the subversion of constitutional government.

Wherefore, Richard M. Nixon by such conduct, warrants impeachment and trial, and removal from office.

(b) President Nixon Announces His Resignation (8 August 1974)

This is the 37th time I have spoken to you from this office, where so many decisions have been made that shaped the history of this Nation. Each time I have done so to discuss with you some matter that I believe affected the national interest.

---

Richard M. Nixon, <u>Public Papers of the Presidents of the United States: Richard Nixon, 1974</u> (Washington, D.C., 1974), p. 626-629.

In all the decisions I have made in my public life, I have always tried to do what was best for the Nation. Throughout the long and difficult period of Watergate, I have felt it was my duty to persevere, to make every possible effort to complete the term of office to which you elected me.

In the past few days, however, it has become evident to me, that I no longer have a strong enough political base in the Congress to justify continuing that effort. As long as there was such a base, I felt strongly that it was necessary to see the constitutional process through to its conclusion, that to do otherwise would be unfaithful to the spirit of that deliberately difficult process and a dangerously destabilizing precedent for the future.

But with the disappearance of that base, I now believe that the constitutional purpose has been served, and there is no longer a need for the process to be prolonged.

I would have preferred to carry through to the finish, whatever the personal agony it would have involved, and my family unanimously urged me to do so. But the interest of the Nation must always come before any personal considerations.

From the discussions I have had with Congressional and other leaders, I have concluded that because of the Watergate matter, I might not have the support of the Congress that I would consider necessary to back the very difficult decisions and carry out the duties of this office in the way the interests of the Nation would require . . . .

Therefore, I shall resign the Presidency effective at noon tomorrow. Vice President Ford will be sworn in as President at that hour in this office.

As I recall the high hopes for America with which we began this second term, I feel a great sadness that I will not be here in this office working on your behalf to achieve those hopes in the next $2\frac{1}{2}$ years. But in turning over direction of the Government to Vice President Ford, I know, as I told the Nation when I nominated him for that office 10 months ago, that the leadership of America will be in good hands . . . .

By taking this action, I hope that I will have hastened the start of that process of healing which is so desperately needed in America.

I regret deeply any injuries that may have been done in the course of the events that led to this decision. I would say only that if some of my judgments were wrong--and some were wrong--they were made in what I believed at the time to be the best interest of the Nation.

To those who have stood with me during these past difficult months--to my family, my friends, to many others who joined in supporting my cause because they believed it was right--I will be eternally grateful for your support.

And to those who have not felt able to give me your support, let me say I leave with no bitterness toward those who have opposed me, because all of us, in the final analysis, have been concerned with the good of the country, however our judgments might differ.

So, let us all now join together in affirming that common commitment and in helping our new President succeed for the benefit of all Americans . . . .

For more than a quarter of a century in public life, I have shared in the turbulent history of this era. I have fought for what I believed in. I have tried, to the best of my ability, to discharge those duties and meet those responsibilities that were entrusted to me.

Sometimes I have succeeded and sometimes I have failed, but always I have taken heart from what Theodore Roosevelt once said about the man in the arena, "whose face is marred by dust and sweat and blood, who strives valiantly, who errs and comes short again and again because there is not effort without error and shortcoming, but who does actually strive to do the deed, who knows the great enthusiasms, the great devotions, who spends himself in a worthy cause, who at the best knows in the end the triumphs of high achievements and who at the worst, if he fails, at least fails while daring greatly."

I pledge to you tonight that as long as I have a breath of life in my body, I shall continue in that spirit. I shall continue to work for the great causes to which I have been dedicated throughout my years as a Congressman, A Senator, Vice President, and President, the cause of peace, not just for America but among all nations--prosperity, justice, and opportunity for all of our people.

There is is one cause above all to which I have been devoted and to which I shall always be devoted for as long as I live.

When I first took the oath of office as President 5½ years ago, I made this sacred commitment: to "consecrate my office, my energies, and all the wisdom I can summon to the cause of peace among nations."

I have done my very best in all the days since to be true to that pledge. As a result of these efforts, I am confident that the world is a safer place today, not only for the people of America but for the people of all nations, and that all of our children have a better chance than before of living in peace rather than dying in war.

This, more than anything, is what I hoped to achieve when I sought the Presidency. This, more than anything, is what I hope will be my legacy to you, to our country, as I leave the Presidency.


## JIMMY CARTER ON HUMAN RIGHTS (1977)

A key ingredient of Jimmy Carter's approach to foreign policy was his emphasis on human rights. Carter insisted that America's friends, as well as foes, uphold certain standards of conduct. In May 1977, Carter set human rights within the broad framework of his foreign policy. It proved to be a controversial policy for Carter--both inside and outside the United States.

I want to speak to you today about the strands that connect our actions overseas with our essential character as a nation. I believe we can have a foreign policy that is democratic, that is based on fundamental values, and that uses power and influence, which we have, for humane purposes. We can also have a foreign policy that the American people both support and, for a change, know about and understand.

I have a quiet confidence in our own political system. Because we know that democracy works, we can reject the arguments of those rulers who deny human rights to their people. . . .

---

Jimmy Carter, <u>Public Papers of the Presidents of the United States: Jimmy Carter, 1977</u> (Washington, D.C., 1977), pp. 954-961.

For too many years, we've been willing to adopt the flawed and erroneous principles and tactics of our adversaries, sometimes abandoning our own values for theirs. We've fought fire with fire, never thinking that fire is better quenched with water. This approach failed, with Vietnam the best example of its intellectual and moral poverty. But through failure we have now found our way back to our own principles and values, and we have regained our lost confidence.

By the measure of history, our Nation's 200 years are very brief, and our rise to world eminence is briefer still. It dates from 1945, when Europe and the old international order lay in ruins. Before then, America was largely on the periphery of world affairs. But since then, we have inescapably been at the center of world affairs.

Our policy during this period was guided by two principles: a belief that Sovet expansion was almost inevitable but that it must be contained, and the corresponding belief in the importance of an almost exclusive alliance among non-Communist nations on both sides of the Atlantic. That system could not last forever unchanged. Historical trends have weakened its foundation. The unifying threat of conflict with the Soviet Union has become less intensive, even though the competition has become more extensive. . . .

It is a new world, but America should not fear it. It is a new world, and we should help to shape it. It is a new world that calls for a new American foreign policy--a policy based on constant decency in its values and on optimism in our historical vision. . . .

We cannot make this kind of policy by manipulation. Our policy must be open; it must be candid; it must be one of constructive global involvement, resting on five cardinal principles. . . .

First, we have reaffirmed America's commitment to human rights as a fundamental tenet of our foreign policy. In ancestry, religion, color, place of origin, and cultural background, we Americans are as diverse a nation as the world has even [sic] seen. No common mystique of blood or soil unites us. What draws us together, perhaps more than anything else, is a belief in human freedom. We want the world to know that our Nation stands for more than financial prosperity.

This does not mean that we can conduct our foreign policy by rigid moral maxims. We live in a world that is imperfect and which will always be complex and confused.

I understand fully the limits of moral suasion. We have no illusion that changes will come easily or soon. But I also believe that it is a mistake to undervalue the power of words and of the ideas that words embody. In our own history, that power has ranged from Thomas Paine's "Common Sense" to Martin Luther King, Jr.'s "I Have a Dream."

In the life of the human spirit, words _are_ action, much more so than many of us may realize who live in countries where freedom of expression is taken for granted. The leaders of totalitarian nations understand this very well. The proof is that words are precisely the action for which dissidents in those countries are being persecuted.

Nonetheless, we can already see dramatic, worldwide advances in the protection of the individual from the arbitrary power of the state. For us to ignore this trend would be to lose influence and moral authority in the world. To lead it will be to regain the moral stature that we once had.

The great democracies are not free because we are strong and prosperous. I believe we are strong and influential and prosperous because we are free.

Throughout the world today, in free nations and in totalitarian countries as well, there is a preoccupation with the subject of human freedom, human rights. And I believe it is incumbent on us in this country to keep that discussion, that debate, that contention alive. No other country is as well-qualified as we to set an example. We have our own shortcomings and faults, and we should strive constantly and with courage to make sure that we are legitimately proud of what we have.

Second, we've moved deliberately to reinforce the bonds among our democracies. In our recent meetings in London, we agreed to widen our economic cooperation, to promote free trade, to strengthen the world's monetary system, to seek ways of avoiding nuclear proliferation. We prepared constructive proposals for the forthcoming meetings on North-South problems of poverty, development, and global well-being. And we agreed on joint efforts to reinforce and to modernize our common defense. . . .

Third, we've moved to engage the Soviet Union in a joint effort to halt the strategic arms race. This race is not only dangerous, it's morally deplorable. We must put an end to it. . . .

Now, I believe in détente with the Soviet Union. To me it means progress toward peace. But the effects of détente should not be limited to our own two countries alone. We hope to persuade the Soviet Union that one country cannot impose its system of society upon another, either through direct military intervention or through the use of a client state's military force, as was the case with Cuban intervention in Angola.

Cooperation also implies obligation. We hope that the Soviet Union will join with us and other nations in playing a larger role in aiding the developing world, for common aid efforts will help us build a bridge of mutual confidence in one another.

Fourth, we are taking deliberate steps to improve the chances of lasting peace in the Middle East. Through wide-ranging consultation with leaders of the countries involved--Israel, Syria, Jordan, and Egypt--we have found some areas of agreement and some movement toward consensus. The negotiations must continue. . . .

And fifth, we are attempting, even at the risk of some friction with our friends, to reduce the danger of nuclear proliferation and the worldwide spread of conventional weapons. . . .

But all of this that I've described is just the beginning. It's a beginning aimed towards a clear goal: to create a wider framework of international cooperation suited to the new and rapidly changing historical circumstances. . . .

Let me conclude by summarizing: Our policy is based on an historical vision of America's role. Our policy is derived from a larger view of global change. Our policy is rooted in our moral values, which never change. Our policy is reinforced by our material wealth and by our military power. Our policy is designed to serve mankind. And it is a policy that I hope will make you proud to be Americans.

## JIMMY CARTER ON THE CRISIS OF THE AMERICAN SPIRIT (1979)

> More than half-way through his presidency, Jimmy Carter saw fit to address the nation about the deep wounds American society had suffered since 1960. Whatever his intention, his words did not soothe the American people. Ironically, a few months later, the seizure of over 450 U.S. hostages in Iran would further dampen the American spirit--and contribute heavily to Carter's electoral defeat in 1980.

During the past 3 years I've spoken to you on many occasions about national concerns, the energy crisis, reorganizing the Government, our Nation's economy, and issues of war and especially peace. But over those years the subjects of the speeches, the talks, and the press conferences have become increasingly narrow, focused more and more on what the isolated world of Washington thinks is important. Gradually, you've heard more and more about what the Government thinks or what the Government should be doing and less and less about our Nation's hopes, our dreams, and our vision of the future. . . .

I began to ask myself the same question that I now know has been troubling many of you. Why have we not been able to get together as a nation to resolve our serious energy problem?

It's clear that the true problems of our Nation are much deeper--deeper than gasoline lines or energy shortages, deeper even than inflation or recession. And I realize more than ever that as President I need your help. So, I decided to reach out and listen to the voices of America.

I invited to Camp David people from almost every segment of our society--business and labor, teachers and preachers, Governors, mayors, and private citizens. And then I left Camp David to listen to other Americans, men and women like you. It has been an extraordinary 10 days, and I want to share with you what I've heard.

These 10 days confirmed my belief in the decency and the strength and the wisdom of the American people, but it also bore out some of my longstanding concerns about our Nation's underlying problems.

I know, of course, being President, that government actions and legislation can be very important. That's why I've worked hard to put my campaign promises into law--and I have to admit, with just mixed success. But after listening to the American people I have been reminded again that all the legislation in the world cannot fix what's wrong with America. So I want to speak to you first tonight about a subject even more serious than energy or inflation. I want to talk to you right now about a fundamental threat to American democracy.

I do not mean our political and civil liberties. They will endure. And I do not refer to the outward strength of America, a nation that is at peace tonight everywhere in the world, with unmatched economic power and military might.

The threat is nearly invisible in ordinary ways. It is a crisis of confidence. It is a crisis that strikes at the very heart and soul and spirit of our national will. We can see this crisis in the growing doubt about the meaning of our own lives and in the loss of a unity of purpose for our Nation.

Jimmy Carter, <u>Public</u> <u>Papers</u> of <u>the</u> <u>Presidents</u> of <u>the</u> <u>United</u> <u>States</u>: <u>Jimmy</u> <u>Carter</u>, <u>1979</u> (Washington, D.C., 1980), II, 1235-1241.

The erosion of our confidence in the future is threatening to destroy the social and the political fabric of America.

The confidence that we have always had as a people is not simply some romantic dream or a proverb in a dusty book that we read just on the Fourth of July. It is the idea which founded our Nation and has guided our development as a people. Confidence in the future has supported everything else--public institutions and private enterprise, our own families, and the very Constitution of the United States. Confidence has defined our course and has served as a link between generations. We've always believed in something called progress. We've always had a faith that the days of our children would be better than our own.

Our people are losing that faith, not only in government itself but in the ability as citizens to serve as the ultimate rulers and shapers of our democracy. As a people we know our past and we are proud of it. Our progress has been part of the living history of America, even the world. We always believed that we were part of a great movement of humanity itself called democracy, involved in the search for freedom, and that belief has always strengthened us in our purpose. But just as we are losing our confidence in the future, we are also beginning to close the door on our past.

In a nation that was proud of hard work, strong families, close-knit communities, and our faith in God, too many of us now tend to worship self-indulgence and consumption. Human identity is no longer defined by what one does, but by what one owns. But we've discovered that owning things and consuming things does not satisfy our longing for meaning. We've learned that piling up material goods cannot fill the emptiness of lives which have no confidence or purpose.

The symptoms of this crisis of the American spirit are all around us. For the first time in the history of our country a majority in the history of our country a majority of our people believe that the next 5 years will be worse than the past 5 years. Two-thirds of our people do not even vote. The productivity of American workers is actually dropping, and the willingness of Americans to save for the future has fallen below that of all other people in the Western world.

As you know, there is a growing disrespect for government and for churches and for schools, the news media, and other institutions. This is not a message of happiness or reassurance, but it is the truth and it is a warning.

These changes did not happen overnight. They've come upon us gradually over the last generation, years that were filled with shocks and tragedy.

We were sure that ours was a nation of the ballot, not the bullet, until the murders of John Kennedy and Robert Kennedy and Martin Luther King, Jr. We were taught that our armies were always invincible and our causes were always just, only to suffer the agony of Vietnam. We respected the Presidency as a place of honor until the shock of Watergate.

We remember when the phrase "sound as a dollar" was an expression of absolute dependability, until 10 years of inflation began to shrink our dollar and our savings. We believed that our Nation's resources were limitless until 1973, when we had to face a growing dependence on foreign oil.

These wounds are still very deep. They have never been healed.

Looking for a way out of this crisis, our people have turned to the Federal Government and found it isolated from the mainstream of our Nation's life. Washington, D.C., has become an island. The gap between our citizens and our Government has never been so wide. The people are looking for honest answers, not easy answers; clear leadership, not false claims and evasiveness and politics as usual.

What you see too often in Washington and elsewhere around the country is a system of government that seems incapable of action. You see a Congress twisted and pulled in every direction by hundreds of well-financed and powerful special interests. You see every extreme position defended to the last vote, almost to the last breath by one unyielding group or another. You often see a balanced and a fair approach that demands sacrifice, a little sacrifice from everyone, abandoned like an orphan without support and without friends.

Often you see paralysis and stagnation and drift. You don't like it, and neither do I. What can we do?

First of all, we must face the truth, and then we can change our course. We simply must have faith in each other, faith in our ability to govern ourselves, and faith in the future of this Nation. Restoring that faith and that confidence to America is now the most important task we face. It is a true challenge of this generation of Americans. . . .

We know the strength of America. We are strong. We can regain our unity. We can regain our confidence. We are the heirs of generations who survived the threats much more powerful and awesome than those that challenge us now. Our fathers and mothers were strong men and women who shaped a new society during the Great Depression, who fought world wars, and who carved out a new charter of peace for the world.

We ourselves are the same Americans who just 10 years ago put a man on the Moon. We are the generation that dedicated our society to the pursuit of human rights and equality. And we are the generation that will win the war on the energy problem and in that process rebuild the unity and confidence of America.

We are at a turning point in our history. There are two paths to choose. One is a path I've warned about tonight, a path that leads to fragmentation and self-interest. Down that road lies a mistaken idea of freedom, the right to grasp for ourselves some advantage over others. That path would be one of constant conflict between narrow interests ending in chaos and immobility. It is a certain route to failure.

All the traditions of our past, all the lessons of our heritage, all the promises of our future point to another path, the path of common purpose and the restoration of American values. That path leads to true freedom for our Nation and ourselves. We can take the first steps down that path as we begin to solve our energy problem.

Energy will be the immediate test of our ability to unite this Nation, and it can also be the standard around which we rally. On the battlefield of energy we can win for our Nation a new confidence, and we can seize control again of our common destiny. . . .

Little by little we can and we must rebuild our confidence. We can spend until we empty our treasuries, and we may summon all the wonders of science. But we can succeed only if we tap our greatest resources--America's people, America's values, and America's confidence.

I have seen the strength of America in the unexhaustible resources of our people. In the days to come, let us renew that strength in the struggle for an energy-secure nation.

In closing, let me say this: I will do my best, but I will not do it alone. Let your voice be heard. Whenever you have a chance, say something good about our country. With God's help and for the sake of our Nation, it is time for us to join hands in America. Let us commit ourselves together to a rebirth of the American spirit. Working together with our common faith we cannot fail.

## RONALD REAGAN ON HIS CONSERVATIVE MANDATE (1981-1985)

One of the chief reasons for first the election in 1980 and then the sweeping re-election in 1984 of Ronald Reagan was his persistent emphasis on the plight of the national economy. Reagan stressed two themes in particular: runaway inflation and skyrocketing deficits. During his first term, Reagan and his administration managed to bring inflation under control (some would say through methods that wrought a fearful toll in human suffering). Reduction of the national deficit, however, eluded the Reagan administration through both terms. In fact, the budget imbalance grew even worse. Reagan, in his First Inaugural Address, bemoaned the national deficit of almost $80 billion; yet, during his second term, the debt exceeded $200 billion. "Reaganomics" was a term which included a number of different approaches to American economic problems.

(a) First Inaugural Address (January 20, 1981)

The business of our nation goes forward. These United States are confronted with an economic affliction of great proportions. We suffer from the longest and one of the worst sustained inflations in our national history. It distorts our economic decisions, penalizes thrift, and crushes the struggling young and the fixed-income elderly alike. It threatens to shatter the lives of millions of our people.

Idle industries have cast workers into unemployment, human misery, and personal indignity. Those who do work are denied a fair return for their labor by a tax system which penalizes successful achievement and keeps us from maintaining full productivity.

But great as our tax burden is, it has not kept pace with public spending. For decades we have piled deficit upon deficit, mortgaging our future and our children's future for the temporary convenience of the present. To continue this long trend is to guarantee tremendous social, cultural, political, and economic upheavals.

You and I, as individuals, can, by borrowing, live beyond our means, but for only a limited period of time. Why, then, should we think that collectively, as a nation, we're not bound by that same limitation? We must act today in order to preserve tomorrow. And let there be no misunderstanding: We are going to begin to act, beginning today.

The economic ills we suffer have come upon us over several decades. They will not go away in days, weeks, or months, but they will go away. They will go away because we as Americans have the capacity now, as we've had in the past, to do whatever needs to be done to preserve this last and greatest bastion of freedom.

Ronald Reagan, _Public Papers of the Presidents of the United States: Ronald Reagan, 1981_ (Washington, D.C., 1982), pp. 1-4.

In this present crisis, government is not the solution to our problem; government is the problem. From time to time we've been tempted to believe that society has become too complex to be managed by self-rule, that government by an elite group is superior to government for, by, and of the people. Well, if no one among us is capable of governing himself, then who among us has the capacity to govern someone else? All of us together, in and out of government, must bear the burden. The solutions we seek must be equitable, with no one group singled out to pay a higher price. . . .

So, as we begin, let us take inventory. We are a nation that has a government--not the other way around. And this makes us special among the nations of the Earth. Our government has no power except that granted it by the people. It is time to check and reverse the growth of government, which shows signs of having grown beyond the consent of the governed.

It is my intention to curb the size and influence of the Federal establishment and to demand recognition of the distinction between the powers granted to the Federal Government and those reserved to the States or to the people. All of us need to be reminded that the Federal Government did not create the States; the States created the Federal Government.

Now, so there will be no misunderstanding, it's not my intention to do away with government. It is rather to make it work--work with us, not over us; to stand by our side, not ride on our back. Government can and must provide opportunity, not smother it; foster productivity, not stifle it.

If we look to the answer as to why for so many years we achieved so much, prospered as no other people on Earth, it was because here in this land we unleashed the energy and individual genius of man to a greater extent than has ever been done before. Freedom and the dignity of the individual have been more available and assured here than in any other place on Earth. The price for this freedom at times has been high, but we have never been unwilling to pay that price.

It is no coincidence that our present troubles parallel and are proportionate to the intervention and intrusion in our lives that result from unnecessary and excessive growth of government. It is time for us to realize that we're too great a nation to limit ourselves to small dreams. We're not, as some would have us believe, doomed to an inevitable decline. I do not believe in a fate that will fall on us no matter what we do. I do believe in a fate that will fall on us if we do nothing. So, with all the creative energy at our command, let us begin an era of national renewal. Let us renew our determination, our courage, and our strength. And let us renew our faith and our hope.

We have every right to dream heroic dreams. Those who say that we're in a time when there are not heroes, they just don't know where to look. You can see heroes every day going in and out of factory gates. Others, a handful in number, produce enough food to feed all of us and then the world beyond. You meet heroes across a counter, and they're on both sides of that counter. There are entrepreneurs with faith in themselves and faith in an idea who create new jobs, new wealth and opportunity. They're individuals and families whose taxes support the government and whose voluntary gifts support church, charity, culture, art, and education. Their patriotism is quiet, but deep. Their values sustain our national life.

(b) Second Inaugural Address (January 21, 1985)

At the heart of our efforts is one idea vindicated by 25 straight months of economic growth: Freedom and incentives unleash the drive and entrepreneurial genius that are the core of human progress. We have begun to increase the rewards for work, savings and investment, reduce the increase in the cost and size of government and its interference in people's lives. . . .

The time has come for a new American Emancipation, a great national drive to tear down economic barriers and liberate the spirit of enterprise in the most distressed areas of our country. . . . We have come to a turning point, a moment for hard decisions. I have asked the Cabinet and my staff a question and now I put the same question to all of you. If not us, who? And if not now, when? It must be done by all of us, going forward with a program aimed at reaching a balanced budget. We can then begin reducing the national debt.

The Washington Post, January 22, 1985.